SALONS, HISTORY, AND THE CREATION OF SEVENTEENTH-CENTURY FRANCE

Women and Gender in the Early Modern World

Series Editors: Allyson Poska and Abby Zanger

In the past decade, the study of women and gender has offered some of the most vital and innovative challenges to scholarship on the early modern period. Ashgate's new series of interdisciplinary and compararitive studies, 'Woman and Gender in the Early Modern World', takes up this challenge, reaching beyond geographical limitations to explore the experiences of early modern women and the nature of gender in Europe, the Americas, Asia, and Africa. Submissions of single-author studies and edited collections will be considered.

Titles in this series include:

Publishing Women's Life Stories in France, 1647–1720
From Voice to Print
Elizabeth C. Goldsmith

Women and the Book Trade in Sixteenth-Century France
Susan Broomhall

The Power and Patronage of Marguerite de Navarre
Barbara Stephenson

Women's Letters Across Europe, 1400–1700
Form and Persuasion
Edited by Jane Couchman and Ann Crabb

Women in the Seventeenth-Century Quaker Community
A Literary Study of Political Identities, 1650–1700
Catie Gill

Women, Space and Utopia 1600–1800
Nicole Pohl

Salons, History, and the Creation of Seventeenth-Century France

Mastering Memory

FAITH E. BEASLEY
Dartmouth College, USA

ASHGATE

Published by
Ashgate Publishing Limited
Gower House
Croft Road
Aldershot
Hampshire GU11 3HR
England

Ashgate Publishing Company
Suite 420
101 Cherry Street
Burlington, VT 05401-4405
USA

Ashgate website: http://www.ashgate.com

British Library Cataloguing in Publication Data
Beasley, Faith Evelyn
    Salons, history, and the creation of seventeenth–century France : mastering memory
    1. Women intellectuals – France – History – 17th century 2. France – Intellectual life –
    17th century 3. France – Social life and customs – 17th century
    I. Title
    944'.033

Library of Congress Cataloging-in-Publication Data
Beasley, Faith Evelyn.
  Salons, history, and the creation of seventeenth–century France : mastering memory /
Faith E. Beasley.
        p. cm. – (Women and gender in the early modern world)
    Includes bibliographical references and index.
    ISBN 0-7546-5354-4 (alk. paper)
  1. France–Intellectual life–17th century. 2. France–Social life and customs–17th century.
  3. Women intellectuals–France–History–17th century. I. Title. II. Series.

DC121.7.B43 2006
944'.033–dc22
                                                                                    2005011865
ISBN-10: 0 7546 5354 4

Printed and bound in Great Britain by MPG Books Ltd, Bodmin, Cornwall

For Janice Simon Candela
who first nourished and encouraged my fascination with France,
dear friend and mentor, whose wonderful spirit and love of people
and life are inspirational

Contents

A Note on Translations

All translations are my own unless otherwise indicated. I have been purposefully literal in an effort to come as close to the French terms as possible. I have also modernized the French throughout. Due to space constraints, I was able to include the original French only from works that would be difficult for the reader to have access to or find. Thus the majority of quotations from French sources published after the mid-nineteenth century are cited in English only.

Acknowledgments

This project has been a part of my life for many years, and has thus been shaped by myriad intellectual encounters and life experiences. I wish to express my profound gratitude to the many people whom I am privileged to call my colleagues and friends. This book would not exist without their invaluable support, insight, and knowledge so generously offered over the years. In particular, I wish to thank Katherine Ann Jensen and Allison Stedman for their careful readings of the manuscript in its final stages and for their insightful comments. Kate, my constant intellectual interlocutor, has been an essential source of support. Allison's passion for the subject was especially welcome and needed. I am very grateful to Harriet Stone for her wisdom and her intellectual inspiration. Without her unfailing support and calming presence this book would simply not exist. I have been very fortunate to have Lawrence Kritzman as my colleague at Dartmouth where I can call on him constantly, and often do, to discuss, critique, and question. I am inspired by his passion for literature and teaching. A number of seventeenth-century specialists generously shared their knowledge of the field and have been wonderful friends as well as colleagues, especially Richard Goodkin, Michèle Longino, Kathleen Wine, Louise Horowitz, and Danielle Haas-Dubosc. I wish to thank Nancy K. Miller for her wonderful work that always inspires me. I am very grateful to have her and Sandy Petrey as friends. Henriette Goldwyn and Allison Stedman welcomed me to their institutions to present portions of the book. John Rassias has been a pillar of support. He was always there to push me to finish and made me feel as though I had something worth saying. Other colleagues at Dartmouth have sustained me through this project, most notably Andrea Tarnowski, Mary Jean Green, Roxana Verona, and Marianne Hirsch. Keith Walker's enthusiasm was especially valuable during the last stages as he kept pressing me for the final product. Elizabeth MacArthur read earlier versions of chapter two. Her insightful comments led to important revisions.

I would like to thank my students past and present for their enthusiastic support over the years, in particular Angelina Stelmach and Melinda Waterhouse. Olga Milgrom was a superb research assistant during one summer. Patricia FitzGerald's expert help in preparing the manuscript was invaluable and saved me innumerable hours of computer frustration. I sincerely thank my editor, Erika Gaffney, and Allyson Poska and Abby Zanger, the series editors, for believing in this work and helping it to see the light of day. I appreciate the insightful comments of the anonymous reader for Ashgate. Those suggestions significantly improved the manuscript.

I wish to thank my family, especially my mother, Joann Weis, my stepfather Al Weis, and my father William D. Beasley for their patient understanding and constant support and encouragement. My wonderful grandfather, Marshall F. Rush, and my dearest friend, my grandmother Henrietta Marie Beasley, were by my side until very recently and were my strongest supporters. Their love of knowledge, well into their 90s, was and continues to be a source of inspiration for me. I am very blessed to have Janice and Vincent Candela as friends. Finally, I wish to express my profound gratitude to my daughter Anjali Marie, my son Christopher Suri, and to my wonderful husband Anant for showing me how incredibly wonderful life can be.

Portions of articles that previously appeared are now incorporated in revised form in Chapters 1 and 2. I am grateful to the editors and publishers for permission to use them; "Marguerite Buffet and la sagesse mondaine" in *Actes de Virginia*, edited by John Lyons, Tubingen, Gunter Narr: Biblio 17, 2003; "Elèves et collaborateurs: Les Lecteurs mondains de Mme de Villedieu" in *Madame de Villedieu*, edited by Edwige Keller, Lyon: Presses Universitaires de Lyon, 2004; "Apprentices and Collaborators: Villedieu's Worldly Readers," *A Labor of Love: Critical Reflections on the Writing of Mme de Villedieu*, ed. Roxanne Lalande, Fairleigh Dickinson University Press, 2000; "The Voices of Shadows: Lafayette's *Zayde*" in *Going Public: Women and Publishing in Early Modern France*, eds. Elizabeth Goldsmith and Dena Goodman, Cornell University Press, 1995; "Un Mariage Critique: *Zayde* et *De L'Origine des Romans*," *XVIIième Siècle*, octobre-décembre 1993, no. 181, no. 4, pp. 687–704; "Le Plaisir du public: querelles critiques et littéraires," in *Ordre et contestation au temps des classiques*, Paris: Biblio 17, 1992; "Anne-Thérèse de Lambert and the Politics of Taste," *Papers on French Seventeenth-Century Literature*, Vol. XIX, no. 37, 1992, 337–44. The Dartmouth Faculty Research Committee provided financial support necessary for preparation of the manuscript.

Introduction

In 1981, when Marguerite Yourcenar was admitted as the first woman to the French Academy, she faced a challenge that none of her male predecessors of the previous three hundred and fifty years had had to confront: how to compose an acceptance speech that would acknowledge the monumental departure from historical precedent that her election constituted. Yourcenar chose to evoke all her female counterparts who had not been so legitimized, surrounding herself as she was received into the bastion most identified with "Frenchness" with the "shadows" (*ombres*) of the female contributors to French culture:

> You have welcomed me, this me, uncertain and vacillating ... Here it is such as it is, accompanied by an invisible group of women who maybe should have received this honor much earlier, to the point that I'm tempted to step aside to let their shadows (*ombres*) pass.[1]

After acknowledging these historical shadows, Yourcenar offers, in what seems almost an about-face, an explanation for women's exclusion. The literary history she constructs justifies their erasure from official cultural memory by asserting that it was women's choice never to receive official recognition:

> The women of the Old Regime, queens of the salons, and earlier, of *ruelles*, didn't dream of crossing your threshhold and maybe they thought they would demean, if they did so, their feminine sovereignty. They inspired writers, ruled over them sometimes and frequently succeeded in getting one of their protégés into your company ... they cared very little about being candidates themselves.[2]

According to Yourcenar's explanation, which confirms the role attributed to women in traditional depictions of French literary culture, women were content to remain on the sidelines. They had their own space, the salons, through which they exercised their own forms of power, their "feminine sovereignty." This sphere intersected little with the officially recognized literary sphere, the one to which the French Academy belonged, the one sanctioned and supported by the state, the one that in fact determined the official shape of French cultural identity. In control of their own literary territory, women felt neither the need nor the desire to become part of the only institution in France that has historically been recognized as the legitimate authority of literature and language, both intrinsic qualities of France's sense of nationhood.

In his welcoming speech that same day, Jean d'Ormesson, secretary of the Academy, felt a similar need to acknowledge the gender of this new member, but then, like Yourcenar, he quickly sought to reaffirm the standard literary history according to which the Academy never consciously took gender into account. Women simply were not part of the official literary sphere.[3] How, then, does d'Ormesson explain the decision to include Yourcenar? Above all he stresses that, just as the Academy never consciously excluded women, so in the present case they have not actively sought to include a woman. The Academy was not changing with the times, redefining itself in light of the forces of feminism. Yourcenar just happened to be a woman. In both these speeches, French literary history remains intact and unquestioned.

Or does it? While seeming to legitimate the exclusion of women from this institution of French cultural identity, Yourcenar's carefully crafted speech contains too many "maybes," too many "shadows" to allow one to be totally convinced that the Academy's exclusion of one sex for three hundred and fifty years was comprehensible and totally justifiable, and that official French culture was naturally male. These "maybes" point to a possible alternative history. In this history, Yourcenar reinscribes the shadows and the arena associated with their influence, the salon, onto the literary landscape. Like the shadows that populated it, the salon has been essentially eliminated from France's memory of its literary past by critics and historians over the years. Certainly the cultural memory of the general public would not associate seventeenth-century salons with the production of the nation's canon of classical literature, and even scholars would find it difficult to name more than one or two salon figures, much less elaborate on if or how they influenced the literary field. In subtly drawing a parallel between the arenas of the salon and the Academy, Yourcenar invites a re-examination of this sphere of female influence and its relationship to mainstream French literary culture and history.

The salons, particularly those of seventeenth-century France, and their central figures are a rich terrain for the study of the fabrication of France's cultural memory.[4] Yourcenar's identification of salons as powerful spheres of influence, albeit separate from mainstream literary culture, contrasts with the image that has been passed down to posterity of this uniquely French institution. Today seventeenth-century salons are synonymous with *précieuse* (precious) a term that is itself conflated not with culture but with ridicule due largely to Molière's satirical portraits of the women who frequented the salon milieu. Molière has not only entered the canon of French literature, he has been embraced as a comedic cultural historian of his era. His portraits are thus often seen as historical truth, rather than as constructs, or representations of the past.

Even when descriptions of the seventeenth-century milieu are not colored by Magdelon, Cathos, and Trissotin's ridiculous antics, the original seventeenth-century manifestation of this institution is rarely, if ever, portrayed in a serious light, much less identified with serious literary production. Historians have frequently limited the influence of this worldly milieu to the development of social skills, eliminating any reference to the relationship between the salons and the literary field. Especially in the minds of the general public, salons are often viewed merely as "a school for civility" in which the female members who created and defined them are arbiters of social graces.[5] They are not seen as places where writing is fostered or even seriously critiqued, but where manners are formed. A frequently cited French historian of the salons, Roger Picard, offers the following assessment of women's position in the salons they founded and dominated:

> Very few learned women had renowned salons. Experience proves that it is not at all necessary for an intelligent woman to be able to direct the erudite and literary conversation in her salon, that she know more than her guests about the subjects they tackle. Her relative ignorance will save her from any pretention of governing her friends. Having a lot to learn, she will know how to listen better, and nothing is more flattering for those who are speaking.[6]

Women take on the passive role of the hostess who listens. Picard goes on to succinctly state the relationship between the salons and French character:

> Salon life, especially that of literary salons, is a purely French phenomenon due, probably, to the spirit of sociability and the love of conversation that appear to be typical characteristics of [French] national character.[7]

Absent from Picard's explanation is any reference to the literary nature of the salons, this despite the fact that he points to "literary salons" as offering a way of life that reflects the nation's character. *Sociabilité* and conversation supercede literary activity as the principal salon traits.[8]

In his recent history of France, Marc Ferro identifies the salons as typically French, but changes their history and eliminates them from the seventeenth century:

> One of the most original forms of sociability in France ... was the appearance of salons at the end of the seventeenth century and, a century or so later, their continuation by the circle ... Women disappeared from both.

> The salons constitute a kind of small private court initiated by aristocrats, usually created by women who gather the intellectual elite around them. The ideal of the "honest man" (*l'honnête homme*) was forged there ... but the salons blossomed little as long as the tyranny of fashion reigned at the court of Versailles. It is in the eighteenth century that, according to tradition, the salons spread the ideas of the Enlightenment.[9]

Again, despite the presence of an "intellectual elite," there is no sense of any effect on one of the primary products of the seventeenth century, the literary canon.

Even scholars who grant the salons some influence on literature usually assert that the specifically French institution of the salon exerted no influence on "great writers," thus ensuring that those writers of France's classical past, revered as the models of its literary canon, remain pure and unscathed by association with such a female-dominated institution.[10] Louis Gillet, for example, states categorically that "salons lose all significance during the great period of Louis XIV's reign."[11] This insistence on the salon's lack of power and influence, particularly during "the great reign of Louis XIV" like Yourcenar's "maybes," invites speculation. Are such rigorous denials simply accurate descriptions of the classical literary field? Or do they indicate a concerted effort to create a particular representation of this literary field, one that other perspectives on history and literature would perhaps not support? What has motivated the creation of these representations of the salons and women's participation in the cultural sphere of France's classical age? Are such representations simply a continuation of the age-old "querelle des femmes?"[12] Or is there something about the salons and their female participants that does not fit with the image that France has developed of its classical heritage?

If one returns to the voices, silenced as well as canonical, of seventeenth-century France, there is a clear disjuncture between the way many contemporaries viewed the worldly milieu of the salons and the image constructed by posterity over the succeeding centuries. The first half of this study reveals that admirers as well as critics of the *ruelles* specifically acknowledged the effect this worldly culture had on the literary field. In particular, women were seen as possessing an innate ability to judge the quality of artistic productions. In addition to their critical acumen, many salonnières were writers themselves and as such exerted another equally important force on the domain of literature. Yet despite contemporaries' recognition of the strong tie between the *ruelles* and literary production and critique, historically there as been an effort to shape the image of the salons, specifically those of the seventeenth century, in order to place women in "acceptable" roles especially with respect to literary culture. The second half of *Mastering Memory* explores the processes of historiography and the forces behind the erasure of the link between seventeenth-century literary culture and the worldly milieu of the salons.

In this study I focus exclusively on the seventeenth-century salon for a number of reasons. First, the *ruelles* and the roles of the women who founded them traditionally seen as beginning with the marquise de Rambouillet in the 1620s differ greatly from those of their followers. The seventeenth century witnessed a highly-developed relationship between these worldly gatherings and literary production, with many of the participants, especially female ones, composing letters, memoirs, and novels, to cite only the most popular genres of the *ruelles*. Instead of primarily occupying the role of hostess, which became the dominant female role in the eighteenth-century salons, the seventeenth-century salonnière set the agenda for *ruelle* gatherings and played a much more active role than that ascribed to her eighteenth-century counterpart. The eighteenth-century salon, with its decreased emphasis on literary production and a different role for women, becomes the model salon in the French imaginary, whereas its predecessor is either transformed to resemble its later counterpart, or eliminated from the historical record. One of the essential keys accounting for the revisionist history associated with the seventeenth-century salon movement is the role the seventeenth century, particularly its literary culture, plays in France's national memory and identity. The era that witnessed the birth of the French Academy, the reign of Louis XIV, one of Europe's most powerful monarchs, the expansion of France's political domination to such far reaches as southern India, and the influence of cultural luminaries such as Racine, Corneille, Descartes, Boileau, and Molière, to name only a few, is also the period that saw the birth of a seventeenth-century definition of what French culture was, and the exemplary nature of this culture and the society that produced it.[13] Moreover, depictions of French cultural superiority in the succeeding centuries continued to grant a large place to the seventeenth century, and constructed this period to reflect a particular vision of France. Given the importance of the seventeenth century to France's cultural heritage, and by extension to its concept of "Frenchness," defining who and what influenced and created this period, particularly its literary field, took on, and indeed still possesses, important political and cultural dimensions. The present study of the representation of the salons reveals some of the stakes involved in the construction of France's cultural image, and illuminates the processes involved in its creation.

* * * * *

The past decade has witnessed a flurry of questioning of France's national identity. *Mastering Memory* is inspired by this interrogation of what distinguishes France during this period of Europeanization and globalization. Of the many diverse qualities that constitute *francité*, or Frenchness, the country's relationship to its rich past is arguably at the center. In *Parlez-moi de la France*, Michel Winock succinctly states the symbiotic relationship between France, its sense of identity, and this rich past: "France is not a geographical place, it is a history." [14] André Burguière expands upon this French passion for its past and its relationship to collective identity. Citing the case of immigrants to France, Burguière remarks that the principal path to integration into French nationhood has been to learn French culture, and, in his words, "in this cultural immersion, history plays a primordial role: to be French is to first know the history of France." [15] While other nations may also exhibit an attachment to the past, for the French, history is more than a shared past: it is a national passion. Burguière goes on to explain that it is the "the all-consuming nature of this presence [of history] and the almost religious fervor that the French profess to it" that identifies the relationship between history and national identity as a specifically French phenomenon. [16] In the same volume, Philippe Joutard entitles his contribution "A French Passion: History" and meticulously delineates how this passionate national memory was constituted over time. In Joutard's words, the French "search for their identity in their history" and this past is at the core of France's collective sense of nation today. [17]

France's rich *patrimoine* (patrimony) is often identified as one of the key characteristics of this complex country. The notion of *patrimoine* offers interesting insights into France's collective psyche and its foundation in history. As the editors of a special edition of *Historia* devoted to "the masterpieces of the patrimony" highlight in its opening pages, "the patrimony is a very French invention." [18] The editors cite a definition of the concept offered by Frederick Gersal in *Les richesses de notre patrimoine*: "from the Latin *patrimoniu*, which signifies the father's legacy, the patrimony—evoking possessions, treasures from the past and the genetic richness of each human being—has become a heading under which many objects and monuments are classified." [19] In this same issue, Michel Mohrt of the French Academy offers his vision of this *patrimoine* and stresses the obligation of the state to protect and defend it: "The patrimony belongs to everyone. A homeland, according to the etymology of the word, is the father's house. One cannot accept to see it devastated." [20] He goes on to incite each individual to assume his/her responsibility towards this cultural heritage: "But the living, as Auguste Comte says, are ruled by the dead. They have received a patrimony from them that they are obliged to preserve and maintain."[21] This special issue illustrates particularly well the unique relationship France maintains with its past. As the editors point out, other countries such as Germany, Italy, and England have a very different sense of *patrimoine*, if they have one at all.[22] In those cases there is not one *patrimoine* defended and defined by a government in concert with its people. This notion is thus an integral part of France's official, state-sanctioned national identity. Turning the pages of this inventory of the *patrimoine*, one cannot help but recognize the deep imprint of the seventeenth century on its construction. The castles and palaces of Bussy-Rabutin, Grignan, Versailles, St. Fargeau, and Vaux-le-Vicomte, the figures associated with these places, and even the furniture that decorated this world are all highlighted as particularly stunning and representative examples of the *patrimoine*. It is intriguing to get a sense of what France is trying to conserve of its past, for many of the same processes involved in choosing these concrete representations of French national identity govern what the collective memory chooses to highlight through history and literary texts.

A fascinating exhibition at the Library of Congress in 1995 provocatively entitled "Creating French Culture: Treasures from the Bibliothèque Nationale de France," also illustrates the preponderant role attributed to the seventeenth century in the development of France's sense of official national culture.[23] To turn the pages of this depiction of French culture is to get a sense of what at least some would consider to be the essence of Frenchness. The manuscript pages, maps, paintings, newspapers, and other artistic treasures all attest to France's deep nurturing and appreciation of its past and its culture, especially its print culture. Indeed, culture is identified with France in a way that can be rivaled by few other Western countries. But what exactly is this culture that the exhibit seeks to embody and transmit? It is clear from the choices of artifacts that this is designed to be an exhibit that corresponds to the accepted, traditional view of the highlights of French culture and history as expressed in print. In the Foreword to the massive catalog of the exhibit, James Billington, the Librarian of Congress, explains the principles guiding the selection of the objects representative of the creation of official French culture, a selection process governed by the French end of the collaboration. The manuscripts, illuminations, paintings, and other artifacts all illustrate a theme that is particularly French in nature: the relationship between culture and power and the intimate rapport between the development of the French state and cultural production. Billington is aware that his American public may find the concept of the state using culture, especially literary culture, not only to sustain itself but as an actual instrument of power foreign and unintelligible, and seeks to explain this historical trait that distinguishes France from the United States.

> The marriage of culture and power is difficult for Americans to understand, born as we are under written documents that set free, that set bounds upon central authority, that are sceptical and separatist with respect to power, that use a language-English-voracious in its inclusion and adaptation of other modes of speech. It is difficult to imagine an English monarch saying "L'Etat, c'est moi," or an English Academy (much less an American) trying to purify the language. To follow the essays and study the objects in this catalogue is to realize that the French tradition is different.[24]

Culture, especially its written manifestations, is allied with power throughout the twelve centuries comprising the exhibit. Monarchs, powerful church figures, as well as secular luminaries all recognized and drew upon the power of word and image, influencing their creation but also, and more frequently, harnassing their power for their own purposes. Not surprising, of the four hundred and fifty-nine pages detailing this relationship between power and print culture, spanning twelve centuries of French history, almost a full quarter (one hundred and two) are devoted to one century, the seventeenth, and of the two hundred and seven elements chosen from the library's vast reserves for the exhibit, almost one-fourth date from the seventeenth century. This is especially remarkable given the vast scope of the exhibit. The first inclusion is a manuscript from the Carolingian period (eighth–ninth century AD) from the monastery of Corbie and the last is Leopold Dedar Senghor's "Elegie pour Martin Luther King", composed in 1976 and published in 1979. Thus one century out of thirteen accounts for nearly one quarter of the treasures chosen to illustrate French literary culture. *Le grand siècle* is peopled beginning to end by legendary figures, such as Richelieu, Colbert, and Louis XIV, who recognized the power inherent in cultural productions, sought to draw upon this influence in their creation of the French state, and developed a state-sponsored ideological machine. And the emergence of the French state coincides with what has been crowned as the highpoint of French artistic and literary achievement, embodied by Versailles and the classical canon of French literature.

Of particular importance for our discussion of the salons, the women who frequented them, and their collective impact on the literary arena in seventeenth-century France is the inclusion in the exhibition of two items that derive directly from the milieu of the *ruelles*: the "Guirlande de Julie," a collection of poems composed for Julie d'Angennes, the daughter of the marquise de Rambouillet, and Madeleine de Scudéry's "Carte de Tendre." Equally significant is the fact that, while manuscript pages or other works associated with Corneille, Molière, La Fontaine, Perrault and Pascal are considered worthy of inclusion, there is not one page of actual text from a seventeenth-century woman's work.[25] Both the "Guirlande de Julie" and the "Carte de Tendre," although meriting inclusion in this exhibit as representative treasures of French literary culture, also point to how women's participation in the creation of that culture has been transcribed into memory. Both artifacts are acknowledged as products of the collective literary creation associated with the salon movement. The "Guirlande" is a collection of creative and original verses composed by male salon habitués to honor Julie. As such the collection reflects a traditional relationship between male poet and female muse. As a product of the worldly salon milieu, the "Guirlande" offers an equally traditional image of the salon and its relationship to literary creation and culture. These poems have not entered literary history as examples of "le Grand Siècle's" extraordinary merit. While some of the names of the contributors have survived into posterity, overall the "Guirlande" is simply an example of the fun pastime of an aristocratic community whose members liked to dabble in literature. "La Carte de Tendre" plays a similar role in controlling the influence of the salon on the creation of France's literary capital. This "map of the heart" was composed by Madeleine de Scudéry and her salon. While a few scholars have attempted to analyze it seriously, for most, and certainly for the French public in general, the "carte" remains an example of the frivolous games that dominated seventeenth-century salon life.[26] Together the "Guirlande" and the "Carte" create a historical image of a separate salon society that, while indicative of the century's growing refinement, also present the salon world as separate from mainstream culture, especially literary culture, and not at all on a par with, or even intersecting with, France's great canonical literary works of the same period produced by the "real" authors of the seventeenth century, the Corneilles, Racines, Molières, Descartes, and Boileaus, whose names one would not traditionally associate with the world that produced "La Guirlande de Julie" and the "Carte de Tendre." Considered through the lense of this expression of France's rich literary history, women did not participate actively in the literary realm of seventeenth-century except to inspire poetry, as in the "Guirlande," or to imagine supposed games such as the "Carte de Tendre."

This choice of how to represent salon culture "Grand Siècle" reflects a process of "re-membering" France's literary history by rewriting the past and reconstituting the membership of those who occupied the literary arena that came to be designated as France's classical canon. From the late eighteenth century until very recently, the principal veins of scholarship, both historical and literary, have worked to suppress the influence women exerted upon the literary field, as writers and as powerful agents, especially through the salons. The influence we will see attested to by contemporaries in the first half of this study—the development of new criteria for literary evaluation, new genres, particularly the novel, a new public for literature—was systematically and deliberately redefined or erased in a process designed to ensure that France's literary canon and its luminaries not bear the imprint of female influence. Whereas many in the seventeenth century exalted women's participation in the literary field and proclaimed it a distinguishing and honorable characteristic of France itself, the nineteenth century in particular opted for another vision of the nation and its cultural heritage, one in which women played a more limited, traditional role, if any role at all. From salonnières who left indelible imprints on the literature and the writers of the period, women and the salons they created and dominated were transformed into purveyors of politeness.

In this examination of the history of the representation of seventeenth-century salon culture, I draw from and build upon the body of research and commentaries by historians and literary critics over the past three hundred and fifty years devoted to the salons and to the phenomena associated with them, such as *préciosité* and most recently *galanterie*, sociability and conversation. Literary scholars and historians have investigated the *ruelles* from many different angles, and new approaches are in fact arising at a rapid pace as the influence of the salons in history and literature is increasingly recognized. Two trends in scholarship, not unrelated to each other, have in particular contributed to our current knowledge of the salons and how they functioned in classical France: women's and gender studies and the very fruitful alliance between history and literature and the form it has taken in the field generally known as "cultural studies."[27] As early as the mid-1970s, scholars were revisiting the female-dominated *ruelles* in an effort to fill in the blanks of literary and social history by adding women's voices. Individual biographies of famous salonnières had been a staple of historical discourse in France from at least the nineteenth century, if not before. Many of these works have added to our knowledge of the salons and their functioning.[28] But scholars, particularly outside the hexagon, have increasingly turned to the salons as an institution. Dorothy Backer's *Precious Women* had the merit in particular of bringing into the forefront the principal players of the salon movement. Carolyn Lougee's *Le Paradis des femmes: Women, Salons and Social Stratification in Seventeenth-Century France* was the first to place the salons in the context of the seventeenth century in general and to attribute a serious effect to what had previously been portrayed as primarily polite, private gatherings. Lougee convincingly demonstrates, among other points, how the *ruelles* served to challenge the rigid social classes and hierarchies of traditional French society. After *Le Paradis des femmes*, it became impossible to examine the salons as entities that functioned on their own, separate from the important changes that took place in classical France.[29] Ian Maclean's *Woman Triumphant* provided an essential in-depth analysis of the relationship between women and knowledge in the years leading up to the reign of Louis XIV. He was one of the first to highlight the link between the salons and women's literary production, and to take women's efforts in the intellectual and literary realms seriously. More recently, Linda Timmermans has contributed to our knowledge of women's place in culture in the early modern period in her exhaustive *L'Accès des femmes à la culture*. Of special importance to my purposes is the in-depth portrait she gives of the salons and their influence on literary culture.[30] In her influencial *Ideology and Culture in Early Modern France*, Erica Harth included the salons and their productions, such as portraits and the novel, in her analysis and thus rehabilitates genres that had previously been seen as simply frivolous salon games. She continued her work in *Cartesian Women*, in which she straddles the domains of history, literature, and philosophy in order to show how women influenced the development of philosophical discourse, in large part through the salons. In "Preciosity or the Fear of Women," Domna C. Stanton provocatively argued that the phenomenon of the *précieuse*, more specifically the virulent critique of these women seen as the center of salon culture, indicates a very real perceived fear of women's influence on the literary and social field. Dena Goodman's monumental work on the eighteenth-century salons convincingly demonstrates how the institution was an intregral part of Enlightenment philosophy and historical events. In this plethora of important studies of the literary field that all take gender into account, Timothy Reiss has shown how the worldly milieu was an essential component in the development of a new public and new forms of literature. [31]

As these feminist scholars, often historians, were working to reintegrate the complex web of influences and functions of the salons into the history of France's classical past, many literary scholars were adding to our knowledge of the workings of the *ruelles* by focusing on the women writers who formed the nucleus of many of the *ruelles*, and resurrecting their important literary productions, which had been for the most part forgotten since at least the nineteenth century. Interestingly, like the historians drawn to the subject of women in early modern France, these literary critics were initially almost exclusively American or British and working outside of France. A new literary history of classical France was in fact being composed from outside France's borders, a history that gave voice to the female literary "shadows" alluded to by Yourcenar in her speech.[32] Nancy K. Miller, in the context of her general efforts to establish a poetics of women's writing, was particularly influential in having Lafayette's and Villedieu's literary productions not only taken seriously by scholars, but also taught in classrooms in new and old contexts. Joan DeJean's *Tender Geographies* offered an entirely new version of the literary history of the period most identified with France's literary canon, and returned the novel and its dominant female practitioners to the place of prominence they had occupied during the period. Other scholars have since added to this history. For example, Elizabeth Goldsmith's work on conversation, correspondence, and memoirs has furthered our knowledge of these crucial elements of the salon's productions. Patricia Cholakian's work on memoirs has been particularly inspirational.[33] Katharine Ann Jensen has focused on a genre associated in a particular way with women, letter-writing. Roxanne Lalande, Donna Kuizenga, and Gabrielle Verdier, among others, have resurrected Villedieu's influential voice, while Perry Gethner and Henriette Goldwyn have shown how women's literary efforts were not limited to narrative, but extended into the "male" domain of theatre. Lewis Seifert, among others, has offered a new vision of a genre associated with the salons, the literary fairy tale, and restored it to its place of importance. These efforts have helped to restore the salon and its practitioners to the important place they occupied during the period. At the same time, they have revitalized seventeenth-century studies by raising new and intriguing questions. The fruitful collaboration between historians and literary specialists, inspired in large measure by the growing interest in cultural studies, that has shed new light on the workings of the worldly milieu is especially well illustrated by the collection of essays entitled *Going Public*, edited by Elizabeth Goldsmith and Dena Goodman.[34]

By the end of the twentieth century, interest in the salons and the French female literary tradition spread from abroad to France itself. In addition to Timmermans's comprehensive study of women and knowledge, a number of scholars produced studies of specific women writers as well as of the seventeenth-century milieu in general. Sévigné and Lafayette had always received much critical attention. Roger Duchêne consecrated most of his scholarly career to these two women in particular. Micheline Cuénin was one of the first on either side of the Atlantic to take Villedieu seriously as a writer. Her work was indeed responsible for inspiring scholars to examine Villedieu more closely. In *Le Parnasse Galant*, Delphine Denis revitalizes the worldly milieu by focusing on "ouvrages de galanterie" and their importance in the evolution of the literary field. Myriam Maître has produced a comprehensive study of the phenomenon of preciosity, and Natalie Grande's work particularly on Scudéry has led to increased interest in this marginalized writer. Critical attention to women's activities during *le Grand Siècle* is relatively recent in France compared to abroad and can perhaps be attributed in part to a generalized effort to identity some of France's unique qualities during a time of European integration.[35]

Some French scholars have been drawn to analyzing the classical literary field in ways that elucidate female participation without explicitly taking gender into account. In *La Naissance de l'écrivain*, for example, Alain Viala examines the competing forces of literary legitimization in seventeenth-century France, analyzing modes of production, identifying literary tastes, and especially important for my purposes, giving a detailed portrait of the worldly or mondain literary scene. Hélène Merlin has focused on the literary debates of *Le Grand Siècle* as well as on the complex interplay of literature, monarch, and academy that marked the period.[36] Viala has continued his analysis of this worldly milieu by focusing on *galanterie* as a category of analysis and revealing its influence on literature and the century as a whole. In a similar vein, critics have been drawn to the construct of *sociabilité* in both the seventeenth and eighteenth centuries in France. Other critics have turned to *préciosité* and used a cultural approach to define this elusive concept essential to understanding the workings of the salons.[37] Christian Jouhaud's work on the public and notions of power during the seventeenth century is also illustrative of the general interrogation of the workings of the literary field during this important period.

In *Mastering Memory* I bring together these various strains of research, profit from their insights, and use them to develop a new literary and cultural history of the phenomenon of salon culture and its influence on the literary field. Through a series of close readings chosen to recreate the linguistic and literary milieu, I offer a new way of interpreting and understanding the salon movement itself by focusing on the definition of literary taste and the criteria for literary evaluation that emanated from the salons and their worldly public.[38] Incorporating this particular history of the salons into an analysis of the entire literary field of the period, instead of offering the salons as a separate facet of this literary history, alters the way we view and define France's classical literary past. *Mastering Memory* is a revisionist cultural history designed to interrogate the official shape of France's state-sanctioned cultural identity.

As shall become clear throughout this analysis, I am particularly intrigued by how the worldly culture associated with the salons was viewed as specifically French. In the seventeenth century, Frenchness was associated in part with the particular freedom accorded women in the social and cultural arenas. It is indeed this quality of Frenchness, or association with it, I will argue, that later led to the process of re-memorization of France's *Grand Siècle*. In the course of my research and in my own experience, I have been especially struck and intrigued by the differences in perceptions of the salons and the different scholarly perspectives that often seem to fall along national lines.[39] It is striking that foreign scholars have been at the forefront of resurrecting the influence of the female "shadows" on France's classical past, whereas French scholars until the late twentieth century have been more reticent to accord the salons and seventeenth-century French women writers any influence on the general literary field, opting instead to see them as separate entities and rarely taking gender into account in their studies of the overall French classical field. In the seventeenth century contemporaries often identified women's status in society and their role in the literary field as a uniquely French phenomenon. Interestingly, the focus of such discussions during the classical era was not whether the worldly milieu was a serious force in cultural politics—the answer was a unanimous yes that they were—but rather whether it should be. My readings of the seventeenth-century literary context in the first half of *Mastering Memory* reveal that the representations of the salons during the seventeenth century overwhelmingly portray this milieu as having the power to alter the literary landscape. The first half of this study culminates in the following intriguing question: Why was this memory of salon culture ostensibly written out of French literary history? For what reasons and following what processes did a particular representation of the salon and its relationship to literature win out in France over the efforts to integrate the salons into a general assessment of seventeenth-century France?

In the second half of *Mastering Memory* I turn to what posterity did with the representations of the unique institution of the salon, its participants, and in a broader sense, with the worldly milieu it was seen to embody. It is essential to understand seventeenth-century contemporaries' vision of this milieu in order to fully appreciate its transformation by succeeding generations. Thus this is not a book that can be understand by reading simply a few passages or chapters. It is best read as a complete narrative. I examine the complex dynamics of the interplay between history, memory, and France's cultural identity using the case of the salons and their relationship to literature. In a gradual process that accelerated after the Revolution and reached its apogee in the late nineteenth century and the Third Republic, seventeenth-century salons and their role in literary culture were redefined. Critics and historians turned from disputes in the seventeenth century over whether salon culture should be as dominant as it was to debates over whether it even existed at all. As some of the literature associated with the seventeenth century was designated as representative of official French national culture, the literary sphere that produced this canon was reconfigured, and in this historical revision, the salons and female literary influence were relegated to the shadows or erased altogether. I analyze the forces that propogated and strengthened a certain vision of the seventeenth century, namely the consecrating and overwhelming forces of education. In order for these representations to become engrained in France's collective memory, they had to be transmitted beyond the confines of the intellectual realm. The educational system proved to be the perfect vehicle for this transmission. The decision regarding what authors would be taught, how, and in what context was critical to the success of the specific vision advanced of the seventeenth-century literary scene. And far from being a historical vision limited to the past, this crucial reformulation of France's classical literary field remains imprinted upon the nation's collective memory today.

The focus of this study is thus the processes involved in the creation of a collective memory as defined by Pierre Nora: "What remains of the past in the lived reality of groups or what these groups make of the past."[40] I am less concerned with determining the historical "truth" of the salon, were that ever even possible, than with analyzing how the seventeenth-century salon has been interpreted, and reinterpreted, how it has been transmitted to posterity, how it has been re-membered, as Nora describes his own concept of writing history.[41] The case of the seventeenth-century salons allows one access to the complex dynamics of the interplay between memory, history, and collective identity. What has been included and excluded in the literary and social history of France's classical age illuminate facets of France's collective memory and the powers that constituted it in the past and are still working to define it today.

Notes

1   Marguerite Yourcenar, *Discours de réception à l'Académie Française* (Paris, 1981), p. 11.
2   Ibid., pp. 11–12.
3   It is interesting to note that in the first volume of his new French literary history published in 1997, d'Ormesson does not include a single woman writer, thus preserving the status quo he defended in this speech to the Academy. He does, however, include a few in the

second volume published a year later, specifically Sévigné, Lafayette, Marceline Desbordes-Valmore, Colette, and Yourcenar. I analyze his new history in Chapter 4.

4   Throughout this study, I will use the term salon interchangeably with the word *ruelle* to refer to the worldly gatherings of primarily the seventeenth and eighteenth centuries. Salon is actually an anachronistic term given that it was not coined until the nineteenth century to refer to these gatherings, but as it is much more common today than *ruelle*, for the sake of simplicity and clarity I will use both terms.

5   Louis Gillet, "Introduction," *Les Grands Salons littéraires (XVIIe et XVIIIe siècles): Conférences du Musée Carnavalet* (Paris, 1928), p. 11. Gillet calls the salons "une école de délicatesse."

6   Roger Picard, *Les Salons littéraires et la société française, 1670–1789* (New York, 1943), p. 12.

7   Ibid., p. 19.

8   At the same time, Picard also cites seventeenth-century contemporaries as referring to a salon as "the court for literary reputations" and "the temple of taste" (*goût*) without explaining the difference between his two different assessments. *Les Salons littéraires*, p. 27.

9   Marc Ferro, *Histoire de France* (Paris, 2001), p. 622. Yet like Picard, Ferro also refers to women's dominant presence in the salons, stating: "women govern the literary and political games" (p. 623), a position that is hard to reconcile with his general portrait of the salon as an institution.

10   See for example, Louis Batiffol, "Le Salon de la marquise de Rambouillet," in Gillet, *Les Grands Salons littéraires*, p. 44

11   Ibid., p. 11.

12   The "querelle des femmes" was an intellectual debate that occurred in France primarily during the fifteenth, sixteenth, and early seventeenth centuries. For an overview of this "quarrel" over the intellectual capabilities and even definition of woman, see Joan Kelly, *Women, History, and Theory* (Chicago, 1984).

13   See in particular David Bell, *The Cult of the Nation in France: Inventing Nationalism 1680–1800* (Cambridge, 2001).

14   Michel Winock, *Parlez-moi de la France*, 1995; (Paris, 1997), p. 17.

15   *Histoire de la France: Choix culturels et mémoire*, ed. André Burguière and Jacques Revel, 1993 (Paris, 2000), p. 295.

16   Ibid., p. 295.

17   Ibid., p. 303.

18   *Historia*, no. 9710, September 1997.

19   Ibid., p. 13.

20   Ibid., p. 128.

21   Ibid.

22   Ibid., p. 129.

23   This exhibit was a collaborative effort between the Library of Congress and the Bibliothèque Nationale de France.

24   *Creating French Culture* catalogue (New Haven, 1995), pp. ix–x.

25   Of course the "Carte de Tendre" was included in Scudéry's novel *Clélie*, but here it is presented alone, divorced from its novelistic context.

26   Joan DeJean analyzes "La Carte de Tendre" in *Tender Geographies* (New York, 1992).

27   In what follows, I wish only to give the general lines of the scholarship of recent years devoted to the salons, their participants, and their productions. Given the amount of research

produced, especially in the last twenty years, I cannot cite everyone who has added to this body of interdisciplinary work. I have tried to be somewhat complete in the bibliography, although even that is necessarily partial. I will have ample occasion in the pages that follow to add many of the other important and influential voices that have contributed to the portrait we have today of women's participation in seventeenth-century France.

28 Nicole Aronson, *Mme de Rambouillet ou la magicienne de la chambre bleue* (Paris, 1988); Nicole Aronson, *Mlle de Scudéry ou le voyage au pays de Tendre* (Paris, 1986); Roger Duchêne, *Naissance d'un écrivain: Mme de Sévigné* (Paris, 1996); Roger Duchêne, *Ninon de Lenclos, ou, La manière jolie de faire l'amour* (Paris, 2000); Roger Duchêne, *Mme de la Fayette* (Paris, 2000); Roger Duchêne, *Etre femme au temps de Louis XIV* (Paris, 2004).

29 These scholars, and others, were inspired by Natalie Zemon Davis, Joan Kelly, and Joan Scott, to name only three of the primary theorists in history, and their questioning of historiography and the place it had allotted women.

30 I am particularly grateful to Timmermans for this inspiring work and will have many opportunities to cite from it in the pages to follow.

31 Timothy Reiss, *The Meaning of Literature* (Ithaca, 1992).

32 Another example is the recent volume on women's literary history in France produced by Cambridge University Press. *A History of Women's Writing in France from the Middle Ages to the Present*, ed. Sonya Stephens (Cambridge, 2000).

33 Patricia Cholakian, *Women and the Politics of Self-Representation in Seventeenth-Century France* (Newark, 2000), as well as her articles on Montpensier.

34 *Going Public: Women and Publishing in Early Modern France*, ed. Elizabeth Goldsmith and Dena Goodman (Ithaca, 1995).

35 It is also possible that the interest in seventeenth-century women writers was inspired by work being done abroad, although this critical corpus remains often difficult to get in France. Still, important studies by foreign scholars often appear in French bibliographies, even if scholars in France do not often incorporate this work into their own.

36 New studies on the development and role of the public in seventeenth-century France also include Joan DeJean's *Ancients Against Moderns: Culture Wars and the Making of a fin de siècle* (Chicago, 1997).

37 Myriam Maître, *Les Précieuses: Naissance des femmes de lettres en France au XVIIe siècle* (Paris, 1999).

38 I deliberately provide extensive quotations from works that are often difficult to locate in order to make these texts accessible. I have also consciously avoided paraphrasing because direct quotation is the best way to recreate the cultural milieu, and illustrate the usage of terms and the specific linguistic formulations of the period. My English translations are very literal, for the same reasons.

39 To cite one example among many, in her analysis of the public in seventeenth-century France in *Public et littérature en France,* Hélène Merlin grants women and women writers little to no role in significantly shaping the literary field, despite the fact that she analyzes in depth one of the period's most important literary debates, that surrounding a novel penned by an active salonnière and woman writer, Lafayette's *La Princesse de Clèves.*

40 As cited by Jacques Le Goff in *History and Memory,* 1977 (New York, 1992), p. 95.

41 In "Comment écrire l'histoire de France," Pierre Nora describes a process much like the one I'm advancing here. Nora explains that "the way is open for an entirely different history; no longer the determining factors, but their effects; no longer actions that have been memorized or even commemorated, but the traces of these actions and the play of these commemorations; not events for themselves, but their construction over time; the

erasure and the rebirth of their significance; not the past as it occurred, but its permanent reuses, its uses and misuses, its influence on successive presents; not tradition but the way it has been constituted and transmitted. In short, not a resurrection, not a reconstruction, not even representation; a rememoration. Memory: not the memory but the general economy and governance of the past in the present. A history of France, but to a second degree." *Les Lieux de mémoire* (Paris, Quattro, 1997), vol. 2, pp. 2229–30.

Chapter 1

The Voices of Shadows: The Salons and Literary Taste

In 1664, when the genre of the *nouvelle historique* was just coming into its own in France, the erudite scholar Pierre-Daniel Huet composed a history of the entire novel form in which he tried to account for French supremacy in the genre. A salon habitué and friend of some of the century's most illustrious women, such as Mlle de Montpensier, Mlle de Scudéry, and Mme de Lafayette, Huet glorifies women's position in France and attributes the superiority of the French novel to their unique status:

> Il est vrai qu'il y a sujet de s'étonner que notre nation ayant cédé aux autres le prix de la poésie épique et de l'histoire, ait emporté celui-ci [the novel] avec tant de hauteur que leurs plus beaux romans égalent à peine les moindres des nôtres. Je crois que nous devons cet avantage à la politesse de notre galanterie qui vient à mon avis de la grande liberté dans laquelle les hommes vivent en France avec les femmes.[1]

> (It is true that it is surprising that our nation, which has allowed others to excell in epic poetry and history, has taken the prize with the novel, so much so that the best novels [of other countries] barely equal our minor ones. I think we owe this advantage to the politeness of our gallantry which is derived, in my opinion, from the great freedom with which men in France live with women.)

According to Huet's reasoning, women in France have created what he terms a "rampart" of virtue, to replace the real walls society usually builds around them, and men use language to climb these walls. Huet explains that "C'est cet art qui distingue les romans français des autres romans"[2] (It is this art that distinguishes French novels from others.) In Huet's assessment, sociability and gallantry, traits traditionally identified with France, have developed because of women's particular status and especially freedom in society. More important, women and the arts they cultivate and encourage affect the literary forms in which France is viewed as excelling, specifically the novel.

It is of course hardly revolutionary to underscore how the social institution that embodied female influence the most during the Ancien Régime, the salon or *ruelle*, was related to the development of the sociability and *galanterie* now so identified with French culture today. More striking is Huet's allusions to women's influence on literary expression and culture through this particularly French institution of the salon. If one sifts through the myriad correspondence, memoirs, commentaries, critical treatises, letters, and literary texts of seventeenth-century France in particular, and some of the histories and commentaries of succeeding centuries that attempt to illuminate France's classical past, it is possible to get glimpses of an association of the *ruelles* with much more than *galanterie* and sociability, athough these are always present. Dominated by the illustrious women who founded them, the *ruelles* of seventeenth-century France are often depicted as the spaces of supreme arbiters of literary taste and innovation and thus as an institution that constitutes a determining force of French culture.[3] For instance, in 1702, a commentator on the previous century gave the following description of the already renowned and applauded playwright Pierre Corneille's method for ensuring that his literary efforts would find favor with his public:

> Quand il avait composé un ouvrage, il le lisait à Mme de Fontenelles sa soeur, qui en pouvoit bien juger. Cette dame avait l'esprit fort juste; et si la nature s'était avisée d'en faire un troisième Corneille, ce dernier n'aurait pas moins brillé que les deux autres. Mais elle devait être ce qu'elle a été, pour donner un neveu à ses frères.[4]

> (When he had composed a work, he would read it to Mme de Fontenelles, his sister, who could judge it well. This woman's mind was very accurate (*juste*), and if nature had dared to produce a third Corneille, this one would not have shown less brightly than the other two. But she had to be what she was, to give a nephew to her brothers.)

Corneille's method was hardly unique for his time. Throughout the seventeenth century, one finds this type of collaboration between an author and his/her public. But it is not the kind of collaboration that comes to mind when today's readers turn to examining the creative processes of France's canonical minds. While one might feasibly envision Corneille asking one of his learned male colleagues for his opinion of his work, one would hardly think of him choosing his own sister as his ultimate arbiter and literary critic. And rather than seeking approbation founded upon knowledge of the ancient texts Corneille used as his sources, or the learned knowledge of rhetoric and rhyme associated with the established academic milieu, Corneille seems content to appeal to his sister's taste, rational mind, and good sense, her "esprit fort juste," hardly the criteria a modern reader would associate with proper literary criticism.

The process of literary evaluation described by Vigneul-Marville is not unique to Corneille. Throughout the seventeenth century, similar references are made to women's proficient ability to discern the quality of literature. For example, in 1633, Jacques Du Bosc states:

> J'en connais plusieurs [Dames de grande science] qui savent si bien juger des bonnes choses ... que leur conversation sert d'école aux meilleurs esprits; que les plus excellents auteurs les consultent comme des oracles, et qu'on s'estime glorieux de leur approbation et de leurs louanges.[5]

> (I know many very knowledgeable women who judge things so well ... that their conversation serves as a school for the best minds; the best authors consult them like oracles ... and they consider themselves fortunate to have their approval and their praise.)

Again, women are portrayed as the ultimate arbiters for the century's "meilleurs esprits" and its best authors, even though their critical criteria are elusive. These women are "oracles," not scholarly volumes that can be accessed easily to learn the formulae for literary success. In his preface to Vincent Voiture's *Oeuvres*, Martin de Pinchesne underscores women's position as literary critics: "Cette belle moitié du monde, avec la faculté de lire, a encore celle de juger aussi bien que nous, et est aujourd'hui maîtresse de la gloire des hommes."[6] (This beautiful half of the world, with the ability to read, also is able to judge as well as we are, and today is the master of men's glory.) As we shall see, women are responsible for creating an alternative system of values for literary evaluation and production.[7]

These representative voices from the past raise a number of issues that will be at the heart of the present study, questions that will help us to elucidate the complex cultural atmosphere surrounding literary production in seventeenth-century France. What role were women seen as playing in literary criticism? What were the criteria used to judge literary works? How did they develop and how did they shape the literary landscape? What was the relationship between author and public? What form did literary criticism take and what were its contexts? What was the relationship between what can be termed these "worldly" forms of literary debate and criticism and the more traditional, scholarly forms of literary evaluation?

My goal in this chapter is not to give definitive answers to such broad questions—an impossible task—but rather to delve into the relationship between women and the arena they developed for their cultural activities, the salon or *ruelle*, and the literary field of seventeenth-century France. As shall become clear, while the salons are typically viewed today as merely "schools for politeness," to return to Gillet's description, where social skills were honed, seventeenth-century depictions of this very French institution accorded them a much broader social function, and most important for my purposes here, a precise role with respect to literature. In this chapter, I will begin with an overview of the salon movement and its relationship to the literary field. Focusing on some of the most important "shadows," to use Yourcenar's formulation, I will elucidate the nature of these gatherings and especially the criteria associated with what I will term "worldly" critique as opposed to the voices of the learned scholars traditionally viewed as the purveyors of literary values. How are these criteria defined by the worldly milieu and to what ends? By the mid century, the status of the salon milieu as arbiters of literary value was so established as to incite intense opposition. An analysis of the voices of dissent will further elucidate the perceived nature of the relationship between the salons, and literary critique and production. I will further examine the influence of the worldly milieu on the building blocks of literature, that is, on the language of classical France. A reading of two representative texts of the period, Marguerite Buffet's *Nouvelles Observations sur la langue française avec Les Eloges des illustres savantes*, and Dominique Bouhours's *Entretiens d'Ariste et d'Eugène*, reveals not only the influence of the worldly milieu on language, but more importantly the stakes and even danger of allowing women to determine a politically-charged cultural product.[8]

The origin of what has become almost the mythical milieu of the salons, is usually associated with the famed *chambre bleue* of the marquise de Rambouillet.[9] Linda Timmermans's research has shown, however, that the marquise's gatherings were not an isolated social phenomenon. Two other salonnières, the vicomtesse d'Auchy and Mme des Loges, opened their doors and exercised power in the empire of letters before the famous marquise. Perhaps because the salons of d'Auchy and des Loges were openly academic, and posited themselves as serious gathering places for discussion and debate, especially with respect to literary matters, Rambouillet's *chambre bleue* is usually highlighted as the first to unite writers and worldly figures in the art of genteel conversation.[10] What has become the most celebrated model of the seventeenth-century *ruelle* began in approximately 1608 and remained a social institution until the marquise's death in 1665. Although scholars continue to debate when precisely the salon exerted the greatest influence, many identify the highpoint of the *chambre bleue* as the second quarter of the century, from 1624 until the beginning of the civil war referred to as "La Fronde" in 1648.[11] Contemporaries lauded Catherine de Vivonne not only for her abilities to assemble a fascinating group of people and facilitate social interaction, especially the art of conversation, but also specifically for her literary sensibility. The expressions "le rendez-vous de tous les beaux esprits" (the rendez-vous of cultivated minds) and "le souverain tribunal des ouvrages de l'esprit" (the ultimate court for works of the mind) are phrases that are often used by contemporaries to describe the marquise's gatherings.[12] Not simply a foyer for social refinement, the salon de Rambouillet exerted a strong influence on the development of the literary field in general.[13] The *chambre bleue* attracted authors and intellectuals such as Jean Chapelain and for many was an institution that could rival the French Academy founded by Richelieu at precisely the height of Rambouillet's influence. In 1725 when the duc de Langres was received into the French Academy, M. de Malezieu, the Academy's director, posited the *chambre bleue* as the inspiration for the Academy. Responding to the duc, Malezieu states:

> Je vous dirai simplement, Monsieur, que c'est avec une extrême satisfaction, que l'Académie Française reçoit aujourd'hui dans son sein un digne rejetton de la célèbre Julie et du grand Duc de Montausier. Elle n'oubliera jamais que ce fut à l'Hôtel de Rambouillet, maison célèbre, dont il sera parlé tant qu'il y aura des hommes de lettres sur la Terre, et sous les yeux de vos illustres Ayeux, que les Voitures, les Vaugelas, et les Balzacs tracèrent les premiers lineaments d'un dessein dont la perfection était réservée à un grand ministre qui n'était né que pour exercer des miracles.[14]

> (I will tell you simply, Sir, that it is with great satisfaction that the French Academy today receives into its bosom the worthy descendant of the famous Julie and the great duc de Montausier. It will never forget that it was at the hôtel de Rambouillet, famous place that will be talked about as long as there are men of letters on earth, and under the gaze of your illustrious ancestors, that the Voitures, the Vaugelas, and the Balzacs drew the first lines of a project whose perfection was reserved for a great minister who was only born to create miracles.)

Literature, philosophy, and politics were all subjects of discussion and debate and were equally if not more important than the games and practical jokes that Tallemant des Réaux in particular identifies as the hallmark of the *chambre bleue*.

To judge from many of the myths and histories surrounding the salons, especially the *chambre bleue*, one might be tempted to view the worldly public as diametrically opposed to the *doctes* and their academic norms, in particular to the illustrious, state-sanctioned French Academy. While their values may have differed, their habitués were the same. In reality the two spheres were emmeshed in each other, leading to a dynamic, but very complicated literary scene. Perhaps no one is more representative of this complexity than the secretary of the French Academy during its opening years, Jean Chapelain. Before being chosen to join Richelieu's illustrious forty, Chapelain was particularly well-known as a respected member of the marquise de Rambouillet's *chambre bleue*.[15] His extensive correspondance attests to his admiration of this worldly gathering as well as to his role as intermediary between the *chambre bleue* and the literary and cultural milieu at large. Chapelain's correspondance, like many others of its day, is especially valuable for its ability to shed light on how contemporaries viewed the marquise's *ruelle*, as well as for its capacity to enlighten us about what actually happened within the walls of the *chambre bleue* and other similar gatherings.[16]

To judge by his correspondance, Chapelain attended the salon de Rambouillet very regularly throughout the 1630s. He often highlights the literary activities of the salon, and his own participation. For example, in 1637 Chapelain invites his friend, M. de la Picardière, to the *chambre bleue* in order to hear the reading of his own epic poem, *La Pucelle*:

> Monsieur, je dois lire aujourd'hui le premier livre de *La Pucelle* à Mme la marquise de Rambouillet. C'est un banquet philosophique auquel je ne convie personne que vous. Les autres s'y sont conviées d'eux-mêmes et m'ont obligé à leur donner.[17]

> (Monsieur, today I am to read the first volume of *La Pucelle* to Mme la marquise de Rambouillet. This is a philosophical banquet to which I am inviting only you. The others invited themselves and have obliged me to give it to them.)

It is evident from these remarks that one of the activities directed by the marquise was literary evaluation. Chapelain thought highly enough of what he terms this "banquet philosophique" not only to participate but to submit his own literary production to its critique. Chapelain uses his correspondance to extoll the profitable virtues of the *chambre bleue* and to inspire friends, frequently academics, to join him. At one point, for example, he first promises to introduce his friend, Guez de Balzac, to the marquise, and then criticizes him for not exhibiting more interest in the salon:

28 novembre 1637: Si jamais vous venez à la cour, je veux nouer cette connaissance, [between the marquise and Balzac] ... C'est la plus estimable personne du monde, ... croyez m'en, si vous avez quelque opinion de mon jugement. ... 7 mars 1638 Je vous fais un reproche de n'avoir point eu de curiosité pour l'hôtel de Rambouillet où vous êtes parfaitement honoré, et d'avoir demandé des nouvelles de tant d'autres choses.[18]

(If you ever come to court, I want to introduce you to the marquise ... She is the most admirable person in the world ... believe me, if you have some faith in my judgment ... I reproach you for not having any interest in the hôtel de Rambouillet, where you are respected, and to have asked news of so many others things.)

In Chapelain's estimation, Balzac is doing himself a disservice by not profiting from the "banquet" offered by the marquise de Rambouillet. In another letter, he goes on to defend the *chambre bleue* and to qualify it as a space where reason reigns:

22 mars 1638: ... Au reste vous ne sauriez avoir de curiosité pour aucune chose qui le mérite davantage que l'hôtel de Rambouillet. On n'y parle point savamment, mais on y parle raisonnablement et il n'y a lieu au monde où il y ait plus de bon sens, et moins de pédanterie. Je dis de pédanterie, Monsieur, que je prétends qui règne dans la Cour aussi bien que dans les Universités, et qui se trouve aussi bien parmi les femmes que parmi les hommes ... l'hôtel de Rambouillet est l'antipathie de l'hôtel d'Auchy et le lieu du monde où votre vertu peut avoir une place qui lui soit la plus agréable, comme je suis assuré que vous me l'avouerez lorsque vous serez ici et que vous y aurez fait quelques visites.[19]

(Thus you could not be interested in anything that would merit it more than the hôtel de Rambouillet. People there don't speak with erudition, but with reason and there is nowhere else in the world with more good sense and less pedantry. I say pedantry, Monsieur, which reigns at court as well as in universities, and which can be found among women as well as men ... the hôtel de Rambouillet is the antithesis of the hôtel d'Auchy, and the place where your virtue would be right at home, as I'm sure you will admit when you're here and have come a few times.)

In order to further inspire Balzac to attend the salon, Chapelain describes the pleasure the group obtains from reading and commenting on Balzac's letters (24 December 1638). Knowing Balzac's antipathy towards anything pedantic, Chapelain goes to great lengths to distinguish Rambouillet's salon from other less desirable gatherings, such as that of the vicomtesse d'Auchy, where women try to emulate the *docte* discourse inspired by the founding of the French Academy.[20] Chapelain specifies that *raison* and *bon sens* are the hallmarks of the *chambre bleue*, that these salonnières are not "savantes" in the traditional sense. Yet in his letters, those who frequent the salon, the "palais des héroïnes," (the palace of the heroines) as he calls it, are worthy literary critics, as are those in the other salons he frequents.[21] In yet another letter to Balzac, Chapelain relates the worldly reception of one of Balzac's compositions:

> 24 July 1639: L'hôtel de Rambouillet, d'une voix commune, a applaudi à votre discours avec des acclamations sincères et toutes tellement pour vous seul ... Mais ce n'a pas été en ce lieu seul où cette belle pièce a été admirée. Je l'ai lu en quatre lieux différents et toujours à votre grande gloire et avec les mêmes effets qu'à l'hôtel privilégié.
>
> La dernière lecture que j'en ai faite a été à la marquise de Sablé, qui certes est une digne auditrice et qui sait bien peser toutes les beautés ... Je connais cette femme depuis deux mois seulement, et je suis bien marre de ne l'avoir pas connue, il y a vingt ans. C'est une Vittoria Colonna et au dela en matière de prose et sans doute il n'y a point de dame en France qui ait tant d'esprit ni tant de belles connaissances.[22]

> (The hôtel de Rambouillet unanimously applauded your speech with sincere acclamations all for you alone ... But this beautiful work was not only admired there. I read it in four different places, always to your glory, and produced the same effect as at the privileged salon.
>
> The last reading I did was to the marquise de Sablé, who certainly is a worthy listener who knows how to evaluate all its qualities ... I have only known this woman for two months, and I'm very vexed to not have met her twenty years ago. She is a Vittoria Colonna and even more on the subject of prose and without a doubt, there is no woman in France who has such *esprit* and so much knowledge.[23])

This image of Jean Chapelain running from *ruelle* to *ruelle* to have his friend Balzac's work judged does not seem to correspond to that of the Academician enforcing academic standards as he did in the quarrel over Corneille's *Le Cid*, an interesting literary event that we will examine in depth in Chapter 2.[24] But it is when we allow for both of Chapelain's literary worlds to exist that we start to recognize the true importance of Yourcenar's "shadows" and their influence on the seventeenth-century literary world. As Chapelain's letters relate, gatherings such as the marquise de Rambouillet's *chambre bleue* were not attempting to duplicate the workings or criteria of the *doctes* as epitomized by the French Academy. They were not all-female groups designed to counter the all-male Academy. As suggested by Chapelain, these worldly women were trying to establish another venue for literary evaluation and production, one founded upon collaboration and conversation, one where reason and *bon sens*, as defined by the group and founded upon worldly ideals, could be used to determine literary value.[25] This alternative space for literary evaluation did not, however, exist as an entirely separate entity. Its habitués and founders interacted with, or were often the same figures, as those in the literary sphere as it is traditionally defined. And the new critical values developed in the salons were designed to alter the entire literary field, not simply the literature produced by the *mondains*.

Chapelain's correspondance depicts a literary world that mirrors that of many of his contemporaries. While Richelieu was striving to establish cultural order with the creation of the French Academy, writers were seeking approbation not only from the academic realm but also, and even often primarily, from the worldly milieu. Indeed, as some critics have pointed out, many authors considered the opinion of the worldly public of the salons more crucial to their success. Alain Viala underscores the importance of the worldly public stating that: "this milieu of 'everyone who is anyone' creates a reputation that is worth as much as the approval of political and religious authorities."[26] Viala asserts that this public constituted "a new path to legitimation or recognition for writers."[27] In addition to the salon de Rambouillet, there were over fifty active salonnières in Paris alone throughout the seventeenth century.[28] The habitués' involvement with literary pursuits and interests varied according to the tastes of the hostess and her chosen guests, but it is clear from contemporaries that the major *ruelles* always had some relationship to the literary field, and their activities involved more than the simple composition of light verse often acknowledged today as the principal literary preoccupation of the salons. Saint Simon's description of the *chambre bleue* reflects the opinions of many of his contemporaries:

> L'Hôtel de Rambouillet ... était dans Paris, une sorte d'académie de beaux esprits, de galanterie, de vertu et de science ... et le rendez-vous de tout ce qui était le plus distingué en condition et en mérite, un tribunal avec lequel il fallait compter et dont la décision avait un grand poids dans le monde sur la conduite et sur la réputation des personnes de la Cour et du grand monde, autant, pour le moins, que sur les ouvrages qui s'y portaient à l'examen.[29]

> (The hôtel de Rambouillet ... was a kind of academy of cultivated minds, of gallantry, virtue, and knowledge in Paris ... it was the meeting place of the

most distinguished in merit and condition, a court that one had to contend with and whose decision carried great weight and [affected] the behavior and reputation of court figures and society at large, as much as [it affected] the works that were judged.)

The salon of the marquise de Rambouillet was thus not only a refined place dedicated to cultivating the art of sociability, but "a kind of academy," a "court that one had to contend with."

This verbal slippage between the words *ruelle*, *académie*, and *tribunal* appears relatively frequently in contemporaries' references to the salons and illustrates the conflation of the various worlds embodied by the habitués of the *ruelles*: writers, academicians, courtesans, intellectuals, and learned worldly figures were all drawn to certain salons and combined to create an alternative space to traditional academies or to the purely social space of the court. The primary characteristic that distinguishes the salon milieu from the court is its affiliation with the literary field. The arts of sociability and conversation could be pursued just as effectively at court, but not literary creation and arbitration. No contemporary, for example, would have thought to confound *cour* with *tribunal* or *académie*, understood in their cultural as opposed to juridical sense. This affiliation between literature and the salons only increased after the salon de Rambouillet. Indeed what can be called the second generation of *salonnières*, those that followed in the marquise's footsteps or had frequented her *chambre bleue*, were even more involved in literary pursuits.[30] Madeleine de Scudéry is the most obvious example. Her *samedis* were even more openly devoted to literature, due in large measure to the fact that Scudéry herself was one of the most celebrated novelists of her time.[31] By mid-century, the *ruelles* were more exclusively literary, and more frequently identified as tribunals for literary evaluation, provoking historians such as Roger Picard to conclude that

> from simple gatherings of cultured people, having no other objective than to see each other, have fun conversing and create a friendly ambiance, the [*ruelles*] were transformed into veritable literary academies, where authors went to try out their creations, and from which emanated critical assessments on literary works [*ouvrages d'esprit*].[32]

But as we have seen, contemporaries also viewed the origin of the salon movement, Rambouillet's *chambre bleue*, as a "tribunal" of literary value. Instead of a radical transformation, contemporaries might have viewed the more open emphasis on literature as a natural development of one of the salon's most important functions. A large number of the salons by mid-century had what can be viewed as a pedagogical mission: to teach habitués how to evaluate literature of all genres according to worldly standards. As a result, writers looked to these "foyer[s] intellectuel[s]," as George Mongrédien refers to Ninon de Lenclos's salon, for approval and wrote to please this particular worldly public.[33] And Mme de Sablé was recognized as a supreme arbiter of literary matters by Chapelain, as we have seen, as well as by her contemporaries in general. In the preface to his *Logique*, Arnault complimented Sablé for her literary acumen, stating "'Ce ne sont que des personnes comme vous que nous en voulons avoir pour juges.'"[34] (We only want people such as yourself as judges). Mme de Longueville, famous for her activities during the Fronde, viewed herself as an important literary critic, not hesitating to launch literary quarrels or to state openly her positions during these debates.[35] Similarly, while many women writers may have hesitated to actually sign their works, they were nonetheless known as writers and their works often circulated in the salons. Some of these same women were not in the least reluctant to take positions during literary debates, Mme de Lafayette and Mlle de Scudéry were often identified as being the most vocal and forceful in expressing their literary judgments.[36] Thus, as Ian Maclean has noted, "from the authors' point of view, the reception of their work in the salons was crucial to its failure or success."[37] He confirms Antoine Furetière's opinion as enunciated in his *Nouvelle Allégorie*, in which he equates the power of the salons' influence on literary taste and value with that of the official Academy.[38]

The progression towards worldly gatherings that were more devoted to literary evaluation and creation is closely and logically related to the growing number of women who were entering the literary field as writers themselves.[39] Many of the principal salonnières in the second half of the century resembled Mlle de Scudéry in that they were recognized and celebrated as important writers. Anne-Marie Louise d'Orléans, duchesse de Montpensier, for example, animated a well known salon at her château of St. Fargeau, where she was exiled after her seditious activities during the Fronde, and later in her Paris home at the Luxembourg Palace. La Grande Mademoiselle was known for her short stories such as *La Princesse de Paphlagonie*, her development of the genre of literary portraits, as well as her memoirs.[40] Mme de Sablé animated one of the most intellectual gatherings of the period and composed her own volumes of maxims, in addition to nourishing those of la Rochefoucauld, the role for which she is primarily known. La Rochefoucauld also frequented Lafayette's salon, reputed by many to be the most literary and intellectual, along with that of Mme de La Sablière.[41] Obviously the author of what is often touted as France's first modern novel was as involved in her own literary productions as she was with those of her guests. And the marquise de Sévigné, friend of all the above women, frequently heard her own letters read aloud in salon gatherings.

Thus the more one advances from the beginning of the century to the celebrated reign of Louis XIV, the more one finds salon habitués engrossed in creating and critiquing literature. This conflation of women writing, developing new literary genres, and animating worldly gatherings to this extent is unique to France and to this period of French history. Even eighteenth-century France cannot offer illustrations of literary salons that resemble those of the seventeenth in their fascination with literature and their pursuit of new literary values. Many historians today would be in agreement with Picard when he states that France's eighteenth-century salons are "encore plus brilliants" (even more brilliant) than their seventeenth-century predecessors.[42] Eighteenth-century salons are celebrated in official French national memory as more philosophical and political, and decidedly less focused on literature.[43] But with this change in emphasis came a change in the role of the female salonnière. From writer she becomes primarily hostess, an important shift to which we will return. If eighteenth-century salons are more acknowledged and recognized today, it is precisely because it became undesirable to link women to dominant roles in literary arbitration and creation. Seventeenth-century salons, especially those of the mid century, as we shall see, inspired an enormous body of satirical works designed in large measure to counter women's insurgency into the world of letters. In contrast, eighteenth-century salons provoked no such attacks. Before we turn to an examination of these revelatory voices of dissent, let us first examine more in depth the new literary values being propagated by the worldly milieu of the salons.

Advancing Worldly Values: *Goût*, *Bon sens*, and the *Je ne sais quoi*

How did the salons advance alternative literary values and go about arbitrating literary production in seventeenth-century France? While it is difficult to determine precisely how the participants in the worldly milieu functioned as literary critics, it is possible to discern how they were *viewed* as functioning, and the nature of their influence. Salon criticism was primarily an oral activity, but its practices surface in some written artifacts, for example, in correspondances such as Chapelain's and in descriptions of the process by which authors sought to have their works accepted by society. The collaborative nature of literary production and criticism is frequently underscored in such accounts, as in the description of Pierre Corneille's creative process previously cited. Commentators often remark upon the influential role of women and their particular qualities for literary evaluation. Like Corneille's sister, many women were characterized as having "a very sound mind," which they used to perform such literary evaluation, most often in the setting of a salon. Some intellectuals praise them as the ultimate literary arbiters. In the mid century, the abbé de Pure granted women authority in the empire of letters: "pour les règles de l'Art, ce sont les Dames qui aujourd'hui décident du mérite de ces choses[44] (as for artistic rules, women today determine the merit of such things). Yourcenar's choice of the term "sovereignty" to refer to women's position in the world of early modern French letters becomes particularly appropriate in light of such remarks. Women had acquired a status not only as readers, but as arbiters of literary taste. By the mid century, one critic asserts that "C'est la moindre chose que de plaire aux savants ... Il faut être du goût des dames pour réussir (The easiest thing is to please the intellectuals ... One must conform to women's taste to succeed).[45]

A principal characteristic of salon criticism is the collaborative nature of literary evaluation. Literary criticism is not done in isolation but rather in a group setting and through correspondances. The salons attracted not only women but many of the leading male writers and intellectuals of the day, such as Jean Chapelain, Paul Pellisson-Fontanier, and Daniel Huet.[46] Collective criticism reflected the process of literary creativity fostered by the salons. Many of the forms of the criticism during the period—letters, debates, and conversations, published or simply circulated—are also associated with the novel, the genre most identified with the salons. One example of this collective criticism is the series of letters between La Rochefoucauld and Mme de Sablé and other members of her salon regarding the composition of the maxims. As Joan DeJean has pointed out, writing was often a communal effort.[47] Similarly, the decision to accept or to reject a particular maxim or literary work was founded on a group sense of literary taste and value. Conversation was at the heart of this process that created literature and determined its value, and as we shall see, it was not uncommon for literary critics to use the dialogue form to contrast two opposing camps.[48] In choosing to stage debates as conversations, writers were trying to transmit another level of collective understanding of the salons, even though such documents were transcribed in literary form.

What are the defining characteristics of this worldly critical process? In seventeenth-century descriptions, common sense (*sens commun*) is frequently associated with the worldly arena of the salons. Taste becomes a principal category of literary criticism. Furetière states that *goût* "se dit figurément en morale des jugements de l'esprit ... cet esprit a le goût fin. M. Blondel a fait un traité du bon goût dans son livre d'architecture" (is said figuratively in moral treatises of judgments of *esprit* ... that *esprit* has elevated taste. M. Blondel wrote a treatise on good taste in his architecture book). The French Academy confirms this function, defining taste in part as that which "fait apprécier les beautés et les défauts dans les ouvrages d'esprit"[49] (makes it possible to appreciate the beauty and the faults in literary works). Other key terms of this criticism—*plaisir, goût, sentiment naturel, sensibilité, bon sens, le je ne sais quoi* (pleasure, taste, natural feelings, sensitivity, good sense, the *je ne sais quoi*)—reveal its nature: it cannot be defined with precision according to certain accepted models. In this context, Du Bosc's choice of "oracles" to describe women who evaluate works proves to be especially appropriate. The knowledge gleaned from oracles does not obey standard precepts of logic and reason. It cannot be explained, but it is considered to be more valuable and contains more meaning than other sources.

Throughout the century, it is evident that a tension existed between standard rules governing literary production, most often associated with Aristotle and other "Ancients," and this less easily defined but eventually equally authoritative form of criticism.[50] In 1671, in his work entitled *La Guerre des auteurs anciens et moderns*, Gabriel Guéret clearly identifies the adversarial poles in this conquest of critical mastery when he remarks that in literary circles "un certain goût de Cour [est] plus sûr et plus suivi que [les] règles de Poétique" (a certain court taste is more sure and more followed than poetic precepts).[51] This "certain taste" is in fact one of the key terms of worldly criticism. Critics, commentators, and authors frequently identify it as an important tool of the literary critic. As the principal attribute of salon criticism, taste merits an in-depth look.

The Gender of Taste

In *Le Parallèle des Anciens et des Modernes*, Charles Perrault has his character Monsieur le Président, a learned defender of "the Ancients," confront his "modern" counterpart, Monsieur l'Abbé, whom the author characterizes as a more liberated and worldly figure, "un homme savant, mais plus riche de ses propres pensées"[52] (a wise man, but having more of his own thoughts.) During the course of their discussion, the subject turns to taste, specifically to the literary taste of a female critic. M. le Président defends a classic poet who has been rejected by a certain "Madame la Présidente Mormet," with a categorical denunciation of the value of women's taste in literature: "Je ne pense pas ... qu'en général le goût des dames doive décider notre contestation"[53] (I do not think ... that in general women's taste should decide our debate). The Abbé responds by defending female judgment: "S'il ne l'a décide pas entièrement il est du moins un grand préjugé pour notre cause. On sait la justesse de leur discernement"[54] (If it [taste] doesn't determine it entirely, at least it is strongly favorable for our cause. Everyone knows the accuracy of their judgment). Perrault's fictional debate illustrates the status worldly salon criticism had achieved by 1687, when Perrault composed his manifesto for the Moderns. In categorically and matter-of-factly advancing that "everyone knows" women's critical acumen, Perrault is acknowledging their literary taste as a recognized critical category.

Following in Perrault's footsteps, another author and active member of the literary field at the end of the century, celebrated for her own salon, was also particularly attuned to the gendered politics surrounding taste and its role in literary criticism. At the beginning of the eighteenth century, having experienced the salons of the previous century, Anne Thérèse de Lambert composed two works, *Réflexions sur le goût*, in which she explores the various conceptions of this elusive quality held by her contemporaries, and *Sur les femmes*, a text designed to defend women's intellectual freedom. These texts provide a clear analysis of taste and its role in judgment as formulated in the mid to late seventeenth century, for Lambert draws upon this period for her discussion. When read together, these two essays prove to be especially useful for understanding what eventually becomes a tumultuous debate whose venom can be attributed to the important stakes associated with who can determine literary value, according to what means, and to what ends.

In *Réflexions sur le goût*, Lambert's main purpose is to define taste and specify its role in society. She begins by underscoring its pervasive presence and its enigmatic nature: "Tout le monde parle du goût: on sait que l'esprit du goût est au-dessus des autres; on sent donc tout le besoin qu'on a d'en avoir; cependant rien de moins connu que le goût"[55] (Everyone speaks of taste: everyone knows that the faculty of taste is superior to others; everyone thus feels the need to have it; yet nothing is less understood than taste). Lambert recognizes that taste is necessary, is highly-valued, and yet is open to interpretation and to debate. She goes on to suggest some elements that compose taste, drawing upon the proposals offered by seventeenth-century counterparts. Referring to Anne Le Fevre Dacier's learned treatise on taste, Lambert offers "esprit" and "raison" as the principal components of taste. Drawing on Le Fevre Dacier, Lambert explains that taste is "a harmony, an agreement between the mind—"l'esprit"—and reason—"la raison" (142). Others eliminate "reason" from their definition of taste, and replace this agent with a more elusive factor, "le sentiment" (emotions). Lambert explains:

> D'autres personnes ont cru, que le goût était une union du sentiment et de l'esprit; que le sentiment, averti par les objets sensibles, faisait son rapport à l'esprit ... et que l'un et l'autre d'intelligence, formaient le jugement. (142)

> (Others have believed that taste is the union of feeling and *esprit*; that emotion, touched by sensitive things, communicated this to the mind, and that together they formed judgment.)

In her own interpretation of taste, Lambert favors the latter definition and privileges "feeling," or subjective appreciation, over logical reasoning as the element that determines taste most directly. In fact, she explicitly valorizes "le sentiment," which I will translate as feelings and opinion, over reason, advancing that taste is "une espèce d'instinct, qui nous entraine, et qui nous conduit plus surement que tous les raisonnements" (142–3) (a kind of instinct, that carries us along, and guides us more surely than any reasoning.) According to Lambert, taste is thus a natural quality, an instinct, that is especially useful in matters requiring evaluation and judgment because it "guides us more surely." But although Lambert advances that taste is an innate, intrinsic quality, she stresses that it must be developed through contact with worldly society: "C'est la nature qui le donne; il ne s'aquiert pas; le monde délicat seulement le perfectionne" (144–5) (Nature gives it; it cannot be acquired; the civilized world simply perfects it). According to Lambert, taste once made perfect by worldly society can assume its primary function, that of determining value and guiding judgment. Taste's dominion is immense. It is called upon to judge everything, from matters of propriety—*bienséance*—to literary works, "les fleurs de l'esprit" (144) (the flowers of *esprit*).

Of particular importance in Lambert's argument is her disassociation of the concept of taste from any firmly established and scholarly rules or criteria. When guided by taste, one judges and appreciates according to intuition as refined by worldly society. Taste allows the critic to perceive the undefinable, what Lambert calls the "je ne sais quoi de sage et d'habile, qui connaît ce qui convient" (144) (*je ne sais quoi* that is wise and skilled, that knows what is proper). Taste is not part of a codified or even codifiable system of evaluation. Lambert argues that no specific rules can encompass taste: "le goût a pour objets des choses si délicates, si imperceptibles, qu'ils échappent aux règles"

(144) (Taste has as its subjects things that are so fine, so imperceptible, that they escape rules). She then posits the superiority of this uncodified taste over methods of evaluation that are formulated according to accepted precepts and official norms. She explains that taste enables the critic to detect qualities that please, the "agréable," not just the aesthetic properties of an object, its "beauté." For Lambert, beauty can be judged rationally, but pleasure cannot because no rules can contain it. Taste is superior to rational categories of evaluation because beauty alone is insufficient: "Le beau sans l'agréable ne peut plaire" (145) (beauty that isn't pleasant cannot please). And for a literary work, for example, to be perfect it must please, according to Lambert's critical standards.

Lambert ends her essay in a circular fashion by reiterating the bond between taste and feelings and opinions, as opposed to reason, and by clearly associating good taste with worldly society. Good taste is "un usage établi par les personnes du grand monde, poli, et spirituel. Je crois qu'il dépend de deux choses: d'un sentiment très délicat dans le coeur, et d'une grande justesse dans l'esprit" (146) (a tool [power] established by polite and witty society. I think it depends upon two things: refined emotion in the heart and great accuracy in the mind). Lambert's *Réflexions sur le goût* as a whole contains the main tenets of the debate over taste and its use in the evaluation of literary works. Lambert, like many of her worldly contemporaries, posits taste as the principal element of critical judgment, and offers a definition formulated by a specific public, the worldly public. She plays taste against standards, establishes it as primarily natural as opposed to learned, and associates it with pleasure. In valorizing taste in methods of judgment and pleasure as a desirable and necessary quality, Lambert takes a stand that is directly opposed to official norms espoused throughout the period by groups such as the French Academy, the defenders of the Ancients, and the *doctes* in general. Such proponents of scholarly categories frequently express a desire to eliminate the pleasure produced by a work from the consideration of its "true" value.[56] They thus undermine taste as a valid criterion. Lambert, on the other hand, elevates taste and the pleasure obtained by means of this method of evaluation over rules. She thus supports certain worldly practices in the general debate over the methods of literary criticism.

Lambert in fact writes in order to defend a specific public and its critical methods, the worldly public that frequents the salons. Her position becomes clear when her remarks on taste are placed in the larger context she created for them. The entire essay *Réflexions sur le goût* can be found verbatum in her longer work entitled *Sur les femmes*. When read as part of *Sur les femmes*, Lambert's

Réflexions take on another dimension. She discusses taste in order to underscore the gendered politics of literary criticism, and to denounce the validity of standards founded solely upon scholarly reason and official norms.

Significantly, it is within this defense of the salons and women's literary enterprises that Lambert inserts her discussion of taste. In the context of *Sur les femmes*, taste is inextricably identified with women and with their methods of critical judgment. Immediately following her remark criticizing those who reject women's own literary works simply because they do not conform to the standards identified with antiquity, Lambert associates taste directly with women:

> Un auteur très respectable (Malebranche) donne au sexe tous les agréments de l'imagination: Ce qui est du goût, est, dit-il, de leur ressort, et elles sont juges de la perfection de la langue. L'avantage n'est pas médiocre. (96–7)
>
> (A very respectable author [Malbranche] endows women with all the attributes of the imagination: that which concerns taste is, he states, within their competence, and they are judges of lingistic perfeciton. This advantage is not a minor one.)

In the context of *Sur les femmes*, Lambert discusses taste in order to defend women's judgment and what can be termed in general "worldly criticism." Her comments on taste begin with a line that does not appear in the *Réflexions*, a remark that clearly associates taste, judgment, and women: "Parmi les avantages qu'on donne aux femmes, on prétend qu'elles ont un goût fin pour juger des choses d'agrément" (98) (Among the advantages attributed to women is that they have a refined taste for judging pleasant things). She also expands her discussion of feelings and opinion as a component of taste with the design of defending women as critics. She addresses those who attack women's minds using the age-old axiom that women's mental capacities are less perfect than men's because women are dominated by feelings, emotions, and instinct, "le sentiment" (101). Lambert defends subjective appreciation as a valid quality in judgment, explaining that it is more natural, original, and unconstrained:

> Je ne crois donc pas que le sentiment nuise à l'entendement: il fournit de nouveaux esprits qu'illuminent de manière que les idées se présentent plus vives, plus nettes, et plus démêlées ... Nous allons aussi surement à la vérité par la force et la chaleur des sentiments, que par l'étendue et la justesse des raisonnements. (102)

(I thus don't believe that feelings are detrimental to understanding: they furnish new insights that make ideas brighter, clearer, and more sorted out … We arrive as surely at truth by the force and warmth of emotions as by the range and the accuracy of reasoning.)

As she develops her defense of feelings within the overall discussion of taste, Lambert more clearly associates taste with the feminine and valorizes women as critics. In defending the nebulous realm of feelings and opinion and in linking this realm to women, Lambert might appear essentialist to readers today. But her remarks must be read within their original seventeenth-century context of discussions over who has the authority to judge literary works and what standards are valid, as well as in the context of class. Lambert and other critics, both male and female, who espouse this definition of taste, all belong to a specific aristocratic milieu. Lambert is not relegating women to what might now appear to be the inferior sphere of feelings as opposed to the superior one of traditional reason and knowledge. Rather, she valorizes taste and subjective evaluation in order to validate the opinions of a specific public, the worldly, aristocratic public. She privileges "le sentiment" over a conventional concept of "la raison" in order to strengthen the affiliation between taste and women. As taste is identified as a valid, albeit contested criterion of judgment, this move qualifies worldly women as valid and natural literary critics. Moreover, good taste is learned through contact with "le beau monde," a milieu in which women play a dominant role. Taste does not follow the standards espoused by learned scholars, a milieu that for the most part excludes women. Lambert is defending the right of women and worldly culture in general to pass judgment on works and to determine literary standards according to different criteria.

Lambert can be seen to represent those who reject literary standards based on traditional, scholarly categories of evaluation. Her argumentation is part of the "Querelle des Anciens et des Modernes." In fact, Lambert's rhetoric has much in common with a defender of the Moderns, Perrault. In his *Parallèle*, Perrault offers a defense of those his critics conceive of as "tous les gens sans goût et sans autorité," (people without taste and without authority) that is, those who, "révèr[ent] les Anciens sans les adorer" (admire the ancients without idolizing them) to use Perrault's terms.[57] Central to his defense of the Moderns is a specific definition of taste that resembles Lambert's. Responding to the rigid Président's complaint that "modern" literary critics have no taste, the illuminated and worldly Abbé responds:

Mais je commence à comprendre ce que vous voulez dire pour n'avoir pas de goût, c'est de n'estimer pas les auteurs selon l'ordre du temps ou selon le rang qu'ils sont en possession d'avoir, mais selon la force et le génie que l'on y trouve. Cependant, j'appellerais plutôt cela avoir du goût que n'en avoir pas; car il en faut davantage, pour juger par soi-même et avec connaissance, que pour se conformer aveuglement au jugement des autres.[58]

(But I'm beginning to understand what you mean by not having taste; [it means] to admire authors not according to their place in history or rank, but according to the strength and the genius one finds in [their works]. Yet, I would call this to have taste rather than to not have it; one must have more taste in order to be able to judge for oneself knowledgeably, than to blindly conform to the judgment of others.)

For M. le Président, the representative of traditional and rigid criteria, "to have taste" in literary matters is to accept certain models, specifically those of "the Ancients," as representative of perfection and good taste. But as the Abbé points out, taste as advanced by such critics does not correspond to the conception of taste formulated by worldly society. For, as is evident in both Lambert's and in Perrault's definitions, taste is precisely that which cannot be contained by rules and models. It in fact corresponds to a liberation from such constraints, and is as such a valorization of individual judgment. This reorientation of critical authority allows for the evaluations of a type of critic, the worldly critic, and of an entire milieu, aristocratic society, where women have an equal and often dominant role.

Worldly taste is thus considered throughout the seventeenth century as a quality women possess innately which they can develop and pass on to men through social interaction. This salon taste cannot be codified, but must be felt, once it is learned. Nor can this taste be standardized and thus controlled. When formed by society, particularly by women, an individual can judge spontaneously and correctly, according to a "natural sense." S/he recognizes literary beauty and uses her/his own reasoning, informed by a worldly form of reason, to evaluate literature. Hubert Gillot sums up the qualities associated with society and cultivated in the salons as "well informed and spontaneous judgment, discernment, an ability to formulate a personal opinion on everything, a natural ability to penetrate anything, an innate sense of literary beauty, a sense of the finer points and nuances, a curiosity for intellectual things, wide-ranging culture."[59] Social education, not book learning, is valorized. Thus everyone has access to this creative process, and it can be governed by women who are excluded from traditional forms of education. The worldly public regarded education in society as equal to scholastic learning. As Antoine Adam has remarked, the *précieuses*, and I would extend his remarks to the worldly milieu of the salons in general, rejected the pedantic criticism associated with the *doctes* in favor of this vague category of taste developed by initiated habitués.[60] And while commentators such as Lambert may seem to be rejecting "raison" as a critical category, they are actually reformulating the concept in order to include the "raison" of female participants, a worldly form of reason. As we have seen, as early as the beginning of the century, Chapelain characterized the *chambre bleue* as the realm of *raison*: "On n'y parle point savamment, mais on y parle raisonnablement." "Raison" was often associated with worldly women. For example, upon the death of Lafayette, Sévigné praised her friend as the embodiment of reason: "Elle a eu raison pendant sa vie, elle a eu raison après sa mort, et jamais elle n'a été sans cette divine raison, qui était sa qualité principale"[61] (She possessed reason during her life, she had reason after her death; she was never without this divine reason that was her principal quality).[62] In a traditional sense, "goût" is not considered to be part of intellectual reasoning. But in the worldly salon milieu, taste is developed according to a worldly sense of reasoning.[63] In a broader sense, the salon milieu was offering a new way to reason and to construct value and knowledge.

Worldly activity in the empire of letters, guided and fashioned by salonnières, formed a kind of counter-culture. The primarily oral tradition of worldly criticism was a recognized and influential force in the empire of letters, as evidenced by the vehement opposition as many sought to weaken its power. Composing literature and critiquing it go hand in hand.[64] The danger perceived by many anti-worldly intellectuals lies in putting into practice the concept of literary value developed in the salons, for such criteria would not simply affect female literary production, but literature as a whole.

The Voices of Dissent: A Gendered Critique of Worldly Power

As the salons became increasingly identified as centers of literary critique and production, and the salonnières more recognized as writers with the ability to transform the literary field, the number of opposing voices swelled in an effort to drown out the worldly collaborative orchestras of innovation. Many of these satires and critiques raise age-old arguments one associates with the "querelle des femmes." But when one analyzes them in the context of the worldly milieu of the salons and their relationship to literature, such texts become a valuable source for understanding what was really at stake in the battle for influence and control over the literary field of classical France.

In *Sur les femmes*, Lambert not only examines the concept of "taste" used by the salons to evaluate literature, she also defends the benefits society derives from women when they are permitted to exercise their mental capacities. This essay is a direct reaction to the climate of dissent to which we now turn our attention. Lambert laments what she views as the current deplorable situation—she is writing around 1720—in which female creativity is the object of hostile criticism. Whereas a number of estimable works have been penned by women in recent years, particularly novels, women's literary initiatives have not received the critical acclaim Lambert feels they deserve. She launches an attack on the critical reaction to these works. Instead of taking female literary production seriously, many critics have indiscriminately heaped ridicule on women writers. Female creativity has been suppressed out of fear of this ridicule: "Il a tout déplacé, et met où il lui plaît la honte et la gloire" (86) ([Ridicule] has changed everything, and attributed shame and glory to whatever it wanted). In addition to literary production, this ridicule has been extended to include the intellectual activities of worldly society in general: "Pour ce qui est des personnes du grand monde, s'ils osent savoir, on les appelle pédants" (86) (As for people in society, if they dare to know something, they're called pedantic). Lambert devotes the rest of her essay to denouncing the society desired by women's critics: "J'attaquerai les moeurs du temps, qui sont l'ouvrage des hommes" (87) (I will attack society's customs, which are the work of men). She glorifies a time when women's influence on society was free from such disrespect and satire. In her discussion, the salons of the mid-seventeenth century emerge as foyers of artistic freedom, innovation, and discussion: "Il y avait autrefois des maisons où il était permis de parler et de penser; où les muses étaient en société avec les graces. On y allait prendre des leçons de politesse et de délicatesse" (93) (There used to be houses where one was permitted to speak and to think, where muses socialized with the graces. People went there to take lessons on civility and refinement). The salons fostered female creativity and created an ambiance that was receptive to women's works. Lambert accuses her present society of rejecting such worldly criteria and judgments. In her opinion, one author in particular is responsible for this lamentable state of affairs: Molière. By deriding women's desire to exercise their intellectual capacities, Molière discouraged them from laudable enterprises. One could also advance that he has made it very difficult to see salon culture as in the least bit influential or serious when it comes to literary matters. An analysis of the voices of dissent that reacted negatively to the salon movement reveals their recognition of the serious threat the worldly public, in their opinion, posed not only to the literary field but to societal order, and the intimate ties they perceived to exist between the two.

By the middle of the century, following the Fronde in which women had played a role as never before, the numerous *ruelles* and the literature they fostered were making an indelible mark on a nation in a period of transition, and offering new options for women in the society Louis XIV was in the process of inheriting.[65] My purpose here is not to review the social influence of the literary works women were producing, but rather to suggest that the worldly social structure that nourished them, the *ruelles*, was becoming more and more identified with literary pursuits. By the 1650s, there was a large body of works that explicitly recognized what many viewed as the literary "monde à l'envers" being fostered by the salons. Works such as Samuel Chappuzeau's *L'Académie des femmes* (1661) were designed to counter this worldly literary influence.[66] The term *"précieuse"* began to have the negative connotations it possesses today, which was not the case at the beginning of the century when *"précieuse"* was used as a compliment to describe a woman who wished to distinguish herself from the ordinary. It should be remarked that this was not a term salon women used to describe themselves.[67]

Today the two most well-known and detailed descriptions of the salons' activities, aside from Molière's comedies, are Michel de Pure's *La Précieuse ou le mystère des ruelles* (1656), and Antoine de Somaize's *Dictionnaire des précieuses* (1659). Critics and historians remain divided as to whether or not these two works are serious attempts to document a historical phenomenon or whether they are, like Molière's comedies, designed as satires whose purpose is ultimately to eliminate female literary influence through ridicule. What is important for my purposes here is that both authors censor women as literary arbiters, and reflect an atmosphere of growing hostility to women's incursions into the literary field. What I view as primarily satirical texts identify the salon activities that provoked the most critical fire: the evaluation as well as the composition of literature. Somaize in fact defines a *précieuse* as an arbiter of literature: "ce sont seulement celles qui se mèlent d'écrire ou de corriger ce que les autres écrivent" (they are only those women who are involved in writing or in correcting what others write).[68] The salon members of de Pure's text openly debate literary questions. One character states:

> J'ai un plaisir extrême à m'élever en autorité sur l'ouvrage d'un homme d'esprit qui se présente à mon tribunal, et qui est comme sur la sellette pour attendre mon jugement. Mon âme véritablement est ravie d'exercer cet empire de gloire et d'esprit, et de me voir l'arbitre de ces hauts sujets.[69]

(I take great pleasure in judging the work of a man of *esprit* who presents himself at my court, and who is on the carpet awaiting my judgment. I am delighted to exercise this glorious and intellectual power, and to be the arbiter of such lofty subjects.)

This power over literary production is the "principal purpose" of salons, according to de Pure.[70] De Pure describes critical discussions in the *ruelles* and identifies the criteria used to evaluate literature. One female critic explains that "Il n'est pas question de juger ... mais de goûter. Nous ne demandons pas ce que vous en pensez, mais ce qui vous plaît"[71] (It is not a question of judgment but of taste. We are not asking you what you think, but what pleases you). De Pure's vocabulary, especially his use of "taste" and "please" reflects the values we have seen associated with the worldly arena. Domna Stanton advances that censoring works such as those by Somaize and de Pure derive from the authors' recognition that the *précieuses'* "presumption to criticize and determine the fate of masterly productions [is] an intentional reversal of divinely ordained roles."[72] Many other seventeenth-century commentators join Somaize and de Pure in rigorously opposing or denying this state of literary affairs, adopting the strategy of rejecting the worldly public of the salons and advocating conventional rules. Even Daniel Huet, an habitué of the salons and friend and admirer of Lafayette in particular, expressed his uneasiness over women's power in the empire of letters, primarily because it was not founded on principles derived from traditional scholarly learning:

> Parmi nous la galanterie a rendu les femmes arbitres du mérite des choses qui dépendent, non seulement des sens, mais aussi de l'esprit, elles abusent du droit qu'on leur laisse usurper; et du plus bas genre de la poésie, qui est de leur ressort, elles s'élèvent au plus sublime, qui demande avec les talents naturels le secours de l'étude et de la méditation, dont elles sont entièrement dépourvues.[73]

> (Among us, gallantry has made women the arbiters of the merit of things which depend, not simply upon the senses, but also on the mind, they abuse the right that they are allowed to usurp; and from the lowest genre of poetry, which is within their capacities, they elevate themselves to the most sublime, which demands, along with natural talent, the help of education and meditation, which they do not possess at all.)

According to Huet, "natural sense" can and should only go so far.

The 1650s and 1660s witnessed intense debate regarding what if any influence the worldly arena should exert on the literary field, proof of the identification of the worldly milieu as a force to be reckoned within the literary field. For Lambert as well as for many critics, Molière's influential comedies were the works that put nails in the coffins of women's attempts to influence the literary field. Whatever his actual intentions, Molière's *Les Précieuses Ridicules* and his *Les Femmes Savantes* reflect the complex literary climate and attest to the role women were viewed as playing. Perhaps more than any other works, these two plays are responsible for today's collective memory of *préciosité* and the salon movement in general, especially the negative connotations associated with their incursion into literature. As we shall see later, the canonization of Molière will play a large role in determining the nation's collective conception of the entire period. Molière's satires reveal what were perceived during the period as the dangers of worldly influence on literature, and thus merit a closer look.[74]

Molière's Critique of Worldly Taste

As early as twenty-five years after the playwright's death, Molière was recognized as the consummate satirist of his society. In *Les Hommes Illustres*, Charles Perrault identified the two very considerable faults that Molière viewed the French in particular as possessing: the first, that children were disgusted with the status of their fathers and sought to define themselves in new terms and the second, "que les femmes avaient une violente inclination à devenir, ou du moins, à paraître savantes, ce qui ne s'accorde point avec l'esprit du ménage"[75] (that women have a strong inclination to become, or at least to appear, learned, which goes against the spirit of a household). According to Perrault, Molière set out to correct his compatriots of these two national vices. Like Lambert after him, Perrault attributes the virtual eradication of women's desire to be learned to Molière's very effective satires:

> Ces comédies firent tant de honte aux dames qui se piquaient trop de bel esprit que toute la nation des précieuses s'éteignit en moins de quinze jours, ou du moins elles se déguisèrent si bien là dessus qu'on n'en trouva plus, ni à la Cour, ni à la Ville, et même depuis ce temps-là, elles ont été plus en garde contre la réputation de savantes et de précieuses, que contre celle de galantes et de déréglées.[76]

(These comedies made women who took too much pride in their minds so ashamed that the whole *précieuse* nation was extinguished in less than two weeks, or at least it became so hidden that it was no longer found either at court or in the city, and since this time, women have been more careful to avoid the reputation of learned or *précieuse* than that of gallant or crazy.)

Thanks to Molière, France quickly rid itself of one of its distinguishing characteristics: learned women. It is curious, however, that Perrault grants such power to Molière's comedies that in less than fifteen days women preferred to be called "crazy" rather than "learned," especially given the fact that the two comedies to which Perrault is referring, *Les Précieuses Ridicules* and *Les Femmes Savantes*, were produced thirteen years apart. One wonders why, if *Les Précieuses* was so effective, Molière felt the need to satirize women's foray into the domain of learning thirteen years later. One thing is certain: today Molière's comedies depict for many women's status under the Sun King.

In 1659 Molière decided to inaugurate his definitive return to Paris with a one-act farce designed to reflect the turbulent atmosphere surrounding the relationship between the salons and literature. *Les Précieuses Ridicules* was an immediate success and in fact launched Molière on his comedic career. In deciding to take on the subject of "precious" women, Molière knew he was treading on dangerous territory, for the public he was addressing was closely affiliated with the one whose values he was satirizing, and may, indeed, have been the same public. Molière's preface to the second edition (the first was published without his permission) reveals his awareness that he was walking a fine line between amusing the influential salon public and insulting them. To defend his production, Molière creates a distinction between a true *précieuse* and the provincial imitation he presents in his play, stating that the worldly public would be wrong to see themselves in the ridiculous figures of Magdalon and Cathos.[77] That Molière felt the need to explain and defend his satire illustrates the power the worldly milieu was exerting over literary values. The play proved to be very popular, but its production was also suspended twice when influential members of the worldly public questioned Molière's choice of subject for his satire.

In *Les Précieuses ridicules, préciosité* is first presented by the two rejected suitors, who describe it as a disease that has not only "infecté Paris, il s'est aussi répandu dans les provinces"[78] (infected Paris, but has also spread to the provinces). Magdalon and Cathos have caught the disease primarily through contact with Madeleine de Scudéry's novels. They carefully explain the "Carte de Tendre" to their uncle, Gorgibus, and implore him to "Laissez-nous faire à loisir le tissu de notre roman," (Sc. 4, l. 113) (let us freely compose our novel). The play offers a catalogue of all the general characteristics associated with many of the salons, such as women's desire to control marriage or reject it altogether, and to exert power over comportement and language according to models advanced primarily in Scudéry's popular novels, to which Molière explicitly refers. As *préciosité* is associated specifically with Scudéry and her literary production, it is difficult to entirely dismiss the play as simply a satire of an extreme provincial version of salon culture. As many critics have pointed out, the names Magdalon and Cathos evoke those of Madeleine de Scudéry and Catherine de Vivonnne, marquise de Rambouillet. Most important for our purposes here, since Molière posits in *Les Précieuses* that the literature produced by and for the worldly public, according to their values, is responsible for the disorder in the patriarchal realm of Gorgibus's house, Molière is clearly criticizing writers such as Scudéry who produced such works, as well as the salon public who supported them. Indeed the last line of the play is an overt condemnation of this literature. Gorgibus addresses himself to this very literature and states "Et vous, qui êtes cause de leur [that of his nieces)] folie, sottes billevesées, pernicieux amusements des esprits oisifs, romans, vers, chansons, sonnets et sonnettes, puissiez-vous être à tous les diables!" (Sc. 17, ll. 9–12) (And you, who are the cause of their madness, foolish nonsense, pernicious amusements of idle minds, novels, verse, songs, sonnets, go to the devil!).

As will also be the case in his later comedy, *Les Femmes Savantes*, the principal aspect of the salon movement satirized by Moliere is the control over language and literary production. Cathos and Magdelon speak a jargon incomprehensible to their valet. The salon scene (Sc. 9) continues this critique of the *précieuses'* pretention to linguistic purity as Magdelon and Cathos, seated on their "commodités de la conversation" (Sc. 9, ll. 21–2) (commodities for conversation) become literary critics, "arbitres souverains des belles choses" (Sc. 9, l. 63) (supreme arbiters of beautiful things) for Mascarille's literary attempts. The scene passes in review the literary genres associated with the *ruelles*, discussing poetry, novels, and portraits. In reality Mascarille is the disguised valet of one of the rejected suitors. He thus obviously has no authentic claims to literary proficiency. Nevertheless, he promises to transform their humble gathering into "une académie de beaux esprits" (Sc. 9, ll. 99–100). Mascarille's attempt at poetry is obviously less than mediocre, yet the two women are in awe over his rhymes. The scene consists of a word-by-word dissection of the four lines, with Mascarille provoking the women to exclaim their pleasure over what the audience clearly perceives to be an entirely worthless rhyme, as is evident in the following passage:

Mascarille: Avez-vous remarqué ce commencement: Oh! Oh! Voilà qui est extraordinaire: Oh! Oh! comme un homme qui s'avise tout d'un coup: Oh! Oh! La surprise, Oh! Oh!
Magdelon: Oui, je trouve ce oh! oh! admirable.
Mascarille: Il me semble que cela ne soit rien.
Cathos: Oh! mon dieu! que dites-vous? Ce sont là de ces sortes de choses qui ne se peuvent payer.
Magdelon: Sans doute; et j'aimerais mieux avoir fait ce oh! oh! qu'un poème épique.
Mascarille: Tudieu! vous avez le goût bon.
Magdelon: Eh! je ne l'ai pas tout à fait mauvais. (Sc. 9, ll. 145–55)

(*Mascarille*: Did you remark the beginning : Oh Oh. That is extraordinary. Oh Oh. Like a man who suddenly realizes something. Oh Oh. Surprise. Oh. Oh.
Magdelon: Yes, I find that Oh Oh admirable.
Mascarille: It seems like nothing to me.
Cathos: Oh my goodness! What are you saying? It is the kind of thing has has no price.
Magdelon: Without a doubt. I would prefer to have composed that Oh Oh than an epic poem.
Mascarille: My goodness! You have good taste [le goût bon].
Magdelon: True, it's not all that bad.)

Mascarille's ultimate compliment to Magdelon on her "goût bon" identifies Molière satire to be against the worldly criteria of literary evaluation developed in the salons. The focus of his attack is made clearer when Mascarille later proudly announces that "Les gens de qualité savent tout sans avoir jamais rien appris" (Sc. 9, ll. 179–80) (People of quality know everything without having learned anything), thus making a clear distinction between the foundations of scholarly and worldly critical values. *Bon goût, sensibilité*, and *bon sens* founded upon the collective values of the worldly public lead only to a ridiculous sense of what constitutes acceptable and laudable literature.

Les Femmes Savantes can be viewed as a companion piece to *Les Précieuses Ridicules*. Composed near the end of his career in 1672, Molière revisits the same theme and again denounces worldly salon taste as dictated by women. Molière actually began work on the play as early as 1668, when he announced that he was writing a comedy "tout à fait achevée" (the perfect comedy). It was presented for the first time in 1672 and enjoyed moderate success, but perhaps not the popularity Molière had hoped his "perfect" comedy would have. This work is more refined, elaborate, and carefully composed in verse, revealing Molière's tenacity, if not obsession, with addressing the question of literary values. Once again a household has been turned into chaos by women who opt against the traditional roles prescribed to them by society, and as in *Les Précieuses*, their control of language and their taste in literature, as well as their desire to control knowledge, prove to be at the heart of this disorder. In Act II Scene 3, almost exactly the middle of the play, Molière stages another salon scene in which the female characters exhibit their literary sensibility. In this instance the scene has even greater ties with the reality of Parisian salon life and thus cannot be dismissed as the imperfect mirroring of this life by "pecques provincales"(country bumkins) Molière has his fictional poet, Trissotin, recite a poem that had in reality been composed by the abbé Cotin, a celebrated salon habitué of the time, a poem his seventeenth-century public would probably have recognized.[79] In any case, it certainly resembles the types of poetry composed and read aloud in the salons. Molière expands the scope of his critique and satirizes not just provincial women who have supposedly been infected by *préciosité*, but women drawn to learning and the *ruelles* that are their spaces. As in *Les Précieuses*, the intrigue revolves around the question of marriage and women's attempt to govern its practice, or even to reject it altogether. But the thrust of the satire is leveled at the literary and intellectual occupations of the learned ladies. As in *Les Précieuses*, the women's attempt to influence language is revealed as totally unreasonable by a servant.[80] In Act II, Sc. 7, Chrysale's tirade against women's pretention to learning is a summary of the arguments of the sixteenth-century "querelle des femmes" placed within the seventeenth-century context of the salons. What distinguishes Chrysale's female relatives from previous versions of *bas bleues* is their desire to write: "Les femmes d'à présent sont bien loin de ces moeurs: Elles veulent écrire et devenir auteurs" (Act II, Sc. 7, vv. 585–6) (Today's women are far from these morals [behavior]. They want to write and become authors). It is this desire to have an effect on literature that provokes the greatest amount of venom from the satirist's pen.

In the central salon scene of Act III, Sc. 2, Molière exposes the emptiness of the women's literary taste and utter lack of *raison*. Trissotin assures the women that they will find his poem "d'assez bon goût" (Act III, Sc. 2, v. 754) (fairly good taste) which they of course do, only confirming their inability to discern literary quality. As in *Les Précieuses*, the women take the sonnet apart word by word. Philaminte is overwhelmed by the originality of "quoi qu'on die" (whatever they say) and exclaims "Ah! que ce quoi qu'on die est d'un goût admirable!" (Ah, that "whatever they say" is of admirable taste) (Act III, Sc. 2, v. 783). They applaud his poem and exclaim that "On n'a que lui qui puisse écrire de ce goût" (Only he can write with such taste) (Act III,

Sc. 2, v. 838). Molière's reiteration of the term "goût" as the principal criteria to discern literary value is a clear reference to the "goût" associated with the worldly milieu. He is not simply satirizing women who dare to tread in the literary world or the world of learning but more importantly the very processes, methods, and values associated with worldly literary evaluation as practiced in the *ruelles*. Not only is the women's "goût" faulty, they are wrong to use it to evaluate a poem. The criteria of "goût" is thus revealed as invalid, as are other worldly literary values such as pleasure and emotion or *sentiment*. Molière goes to great lengths to illustrate the emotional effect the sonnet has on its female public. In *Les Femmes Savantes*, the women are so carried away by their emotional reaction to the poem that they are rendered almost incapable of listening to the rest.

> *Philaminte*: On n'en peut plus. (We can't stand it any longer.)
> *Bélise*: On pâme. (We're fainting.)
> *Armande*: On se meurt de plaisir. (We're dying of pleasure.)
> *Philaminte*: De mille doux frissons vous vous sentez saisir. (You can feel a thousand sweat shivers.) (Act III, Sc. 2, vv. 810–14)

Philaminte's daughter Henriette, who rejects her mother's learning and prefers to embrace the traditional roles allotted to women, is admonished for not participating emotionally in the literary feast: "Quoi! sans émotion pendant cette lecture!" (What? No emotion durng this reading!) (Act III, Sc. 2, v. 819) her Aunt exclaims. It is interesting to remark that, as in *Les Précieuses Ridicules*, the salon Molière recreates is entirely female, with the exception of the poet who offers his "aimable repas." This intentional deformation of the salon milieu in which the male component of the worldly public is effectively eliminated is designed to place the blame for such laughable literary practices solely on women's shoulders.

In both plays, poetry is presented as the only genre composed and evaluated by the worldly public in the salons. In limiting their literary endeavors to poetry, Molière curtails the breadth of this influence by circumscribing it into an area of relatively little importance given the status of poetry in the seventeenth century. Yet the widespread reaction to the worldly public's influence, an influence that will become even clearer in the next chapter, on the literary field attests to the perception that this influence could not be so narrowly contained. Molière himself acknowledges at least the intent of the salons to have a more widespread influence. In *Les Femmes Savantes*, Molière extends his critique to philosophy and even science that were often the subjects of discussion.

Through the milieu of the salons, women sought to impose worldly values founded upon a collective sense of taste, pleasure, *bienséance*, and *bon sens* (good sense) on the world as a whole. They sought to restructure knowledge itself. Armande voices the women's objectives: "Nous approfondirons, ainsi que la physique, / Grammaire, histoire, vers, morale et politique" (In addition to physics, we will delve into grammar, history, verse, ethics, and politics) (Act III, Sc. 2, vv. 893–4). At the end of Act III, Sc. 2, Armande predicts the extent of their power and verbalizes the ultimate fears of the critics of the worldly arena:

> Nous serons par nos lois les juges des ouvrages.
> Par nos lois, prose et vers, tout nous sera soumis:
> Nul n'aura de l'esprit, hors nous et nos amis.
> Nous chercherons partout à trouver à redire,
> Et ne verrons que nous qui sache bien écrire. (Act III, Sc. 2, vv. 922–6)

> (By our laws we will be the judges of literary works
> According to our laws, prose, verse, everything will be under our control:
> No one will have *esprit* besides us and our friends
> We will try to correct everything
> And will consider only ourselves capable of writing well.)

Armande hopes to take sole possession of the literary realm, as underscored by her use of "our" and "we."[81] The academy proposed by Armande will be above all a foyer of linguistic and literary tyranny. It is this project that attracts the most satire from Molière. He devotes over twenty lines to Armande's and Philaminte's descriptions of what they intend to do to the French language during their "doctes conferences" (erudite conferences) (Act III, Sc. 2, v. 906) in their "académie" (Act III, Sc. 2, v. 909). Clearly those who have the linguistic tools and control over literary values are also viewed as possessing the power to change society itself. In Molière's plays, women who aspire to such power merit satire, censorship, and containment.

Determining the Language of a Nation: Bouhours and Buffet

Molière's comedies are just two of the many texts that sought to comment upon the influence the *ruelles* were perceived as having on what what would become one of the hallmarks of Frenchness: the French language itself. An analysis of a few of these representative texts pertaining to language will allow us to see the further infiltration of the worldly milieu upon French culture, and its inscription in some of the texts most associated with a nascent sense of French national identity and a collective sense of its exemplary culture.

French literary culture and especially the language used to create it are arguably two of the most important characteristics associated with French national identity. In a recent survey done in France, when asked the question "To be French, in your opinion, is above all ..." 24 per cent of those responding chose "speak French."[82] Not only does language play a role in uniting the nation within the hexagon, but it also is viewed by the French as a powerful and indeed necessary tool that enables France to maintain an influential place in the world at large. One of the current challenges facing the French language is its relationship to the internet and the accompanying new technologies. Philippe Douste-Blazy the former ministre of culture, said in a speech in 1996 that "the rapid development of new technology represents a true challenge for our language and our culture."[83] As is often the case these days, the "challenge" is coming from the US and specifically from English, which threatens to dominate these new technologies. Douste-Blazy underscores the necessity of making the web "plurilingual." As he states it, it is a matter of keeping not just the French language alive, but France's importance to the world in general.

> If we want to be able to continue to express and to maintain our vision of the world in our language, it is because our language constitutes for us the most efficient tool for our thoughts ... It is by assuring a dynamic presence for francophone countries on the information highways that the French language will continue to play its role as a great language of international communication, a language of access to knowledge and to cultures.

The role and presence of France's language mirrors the identity of the country itself. Seventeenth-century France witnessed the same recognition of the power inherent in language and culture and many of the discussions were focused on determining who would share in this power and according to what terms. Two texts, Marguerite Buffet's *Nouvelles Observations sur la Langue Française avec les Eloges des Illustres Savantes, tant Anciennes que Modernes* (1663), and Dominique Bouhours's *Les Entretiens d'Ariste et d'Eugène* (1671), reflect particularly well their century's preoccupation with defining women's cultural roles. In addition, each author is keenly aware of the crucial stakes of this participation.

Curiously, Buffet begins by characterizing participation in literary culture as a dangerous endeavor: "c'est une chose étrange que l'on prenne tant de plaisir de se mettre en danger, et que le péril soit agréable aux personnes de lettres, comme aux soldats"[84] (It is strange that people take such pleasure in putting themselves in danger, and that peril is pleasing to writers as well as to soldiers). These provocative words appear in the "Au Lecteur," the opening address to the reader, and immediately mark the *Observations* as both a pleasurable and a perilous effort. Buffet recognizes that as a female soldier in what will become a war over literary territory, and eventually even national identity, the danger and peril are doubled. She is both proud of her enterprise, dedicating it to the queen, and nervous about its reception, hence the decision to solicit royal patronage. She tells her royal patron that she considers these remarks on language to be "aussi curieuses que nécessaires" (as curious as they are necessary) (Epistre n.p.). It is as though she recognizes that her *Nouvelles Observations* is an intriguing and even unique portrait of the status of language during the 1660s and a pedagogical treatise designed to augment the new language being cultivated by worldly society.[85] Her text illustrates to an exceptional degree the influence the *mondains* were exerting on the development of language. When one thinks of such an influence, Molière's ridiculous *précieuses*, with their "commodités de la conversation" first come to mind. Buffet's text, however, brings us back from such fictional exaggeration and allows us to comprehend the nature of this worldly influence in a more reasonable and rational and most likely more realistic portrayal. In the first half of the treatise, Buffet seeks to arm her contemporaries, especially women, with the power of language. The first two hundred pages are devoted to instruction in the mastery of language. The one hundred pages that follow can be viewed as an example of one of the literary portrait galleries in vogue at the time, but a portrait gallery with a specific theme: to inscribe into cultural memory female contemporaries who are examples of what can be achieved when one learns the linguistic lessons Buffet tries to impart in the first two-thirds of the text, or more generally, when women decide to achieve linguistic excellence and to cultivate it to realize their own objectives.[86]

We know little about the elusive Buffet. Much of what we can perceive is derived from the *Observations*, the only text by her that survives today. From the title page, Buffet establishes her authority as an expert on language and as the perfect pedagogue for women. The title page not only includes her name, but goes on to identify her as "faisant profession d'enseigner aux Dames l'art de bien parler et de bien écrire sur tous sujects, avec l'Orthographe française par règles" (whose profession is to teach women the art of speaking and writing well on all subjects, and French spelling according to rules). It is clear that Buffet puts speaking on a par with writing, neither one being viewed as superior to the other. In the "Epistre" to the Queen, she describes herself as "une fille de condition qui s'est vue obligée de se soutenir par la profession des Lettres" (a young woman of quality who has found herself obliged to support herself by the literary profession) (n.p.). Later she states that the written text is a transcription of what she has done in reality, that is, she has actually taught other women of quality to use language properly. Buffet thus affirms the professional identity she stated on the title page, and endows the written text with the authority of personal experience. Her text is a result of worldly experience and her teaching method, first oral and here written, is founded upon her personal experiences as a "young woman of quality" and a pedagogue for others like herself.

Les Observations is the result of Buffet's personal observations: "les fautes qu[elle] voi[t] commettre tous les jours à quantité de gens de condition, et principalement aux femmes" (the mistakes [she] see[s] made everyday by a number of people of quality, and especially women) (6) have inspired her to rectify what she considers to be an embarassing situation.[87] Buffet characterizes her text as a new, unique attempt to improve linguistic competence, especially among women. While "beaucoup d'excellents esprits ont travaillé sur cette matière," (many excellent minds have worked on this subject) the female public in particular "n'a point lu leurs livres, ou que si on les a lus, on n'a point profité" (hasn't read their books, or if they have, they didn't learn from them) (6–7). Buffet's method is different: she will be concise, and will strive to be entertaining as well as edifying. Her work consists of four parts: 1. to identify and banish "termes babares et trop anciens" (dated and barbaric terms) (7); 2. to address how to speak concisely; 3. "regarde les termes corrompus et mal prononcés" (addresses corrupted terms and those that are mispronounced) (8); and 4. to correct the confusion over genders (8). The most distinguishing feature of her work, however, is that she will cater specifically to a female worldly audience of the period and use a contemporary style as opposed to a traditional scholarly one addressed to a generic, non-time specific public: "J'ai developppé toutes ces choses de la manière la plus en usage et la plus intelligible: c'est ce qui me fait espérer qu'elles en tiront de l'instruction" (I have developed all these subjects according to the method that is the most used and the most understandable, which is why I hope women will learn from it) (8–9). She later describes her lessons as "instruction, que j'ai rendue aisée et familière pour les femmes" (lessons that I have made simple and approachable for women) (119). Her text is designed to enhance the already strong position she views women as occupying in the cultural sphere:

Je sais qu'elles aiment les belles choses, et qu'elles ne sont pas moins capables d'en bien juger que les hommes, ayant les mêmes dispositions pour les apprendre. Ceux qui savent connaître la vivacité et l'excellence de leur esprit, n'ignorent point que dans toutes les sciences où elles voudraient s'appliquer, elles s'y rendraient aussi habiles que les hommes. (9)

(I know they appreciate beautiful works, and that they are no less capable than men of judging them, having the same dispositions for learning. Those who know how to recognize the sharpness and excellence of [women's] minds, are not at all unaware that in all the fields in which they apply themselves, they become as skillful as men.)

By characterizing her female contemporaries as proficient judges and masters of "esprit," Buffet reveals her pedagogical manual to be a product of its time and an effort to further enhance the cultural status she, like many around her, viewed women as having already achieved.[88]

Buffet allies herself with the female worldly public she is addressing while at the same time augmenting her authority by exhibiting her extensive knowledge of the traditional sources of linguistic competence. Her authorial persona is thus a unique combination of a *docte* scholar and worldly "fille de condition" speaking from personal experience. For example, Buffet goes into great scholarly depth when describing the origin of the written alphabet (14–19). At the same time that she establishes her credibility by exhibiting this knowledge, she stresses the accessibility of the knowledge due to her simple and direct style, her project to explain "avec toute la facilité imaginable"(with all the ease imaginable) (19), "avec le plus de facilité qu'il m'a été possible"(with the most ease I could) (27). She serves as a bridge between the *doctes* and the *mondains*.

As a participant in the worldly milieu, Buffet's text is a product of this particular arena and shows its provenance in a variety of ways. First, Buffet takes the study of language out of the academy and transfers it to the salon, drawing upon examples she has heard, and punctuating her text with phrases such as "plusieurs disent" (many say) and "d'autres disent souvent"(others often say). *Les Observations* is thus a text generated from the oral, especially worldly, milieu and destined for that same public. It is not a general treatise on French usage but rather an attempt to inculcate polite, specifically Parisian, society with the desire and ability to speak a polished, worldly version of French. To reinforce the bond between the forms of language she is advocating and polite society, Buffet frequently cites provincial usage, always with condescension and in order to condemn it. She senses that given her chosen public, this particular admonition would be a fast cure—for what salonnière aspires to speak like a provincial?

Moreover, the rules she uses to correct language come from her own milieu and not the academic spheres dominated by the *doctes*. It is this association with the worldly milieu that makes her text "familiar," to use Buffet's own term, to the female audience she views herself as primarily addressing. The fact that these worldly rules are transmitted orally, as opposed to the written grammar books to which the traditional grammarians adhere, further accentuates Buffet's valorization of the worldly milieu and of the oral culture associated with it. She strenuously corrects barbarisms, words that she qualifies as "anciens" (dated) and others that she pronounces as "pas francais" (not French) (27).[89] Her method is one that is designed with her selected public in mind. As a member of that society, Buffet knows that by using admonishments such as "c'est ridiculement parler" (that's a riduculous way to speak) and stating that a word is "fort ancien and hors de l'usage" (very dated and no longer used) (30–31), and by labeling expressions as bourgeois or provincial or stating that only "le petit peuple" (common people) would speak in a certain manner (73) she will draw upon her particular public's desire to conform to their societal values.[90] Her values are thus worldly, as opposed to scholarly. She is especially concerned with style, saying, for example, "On dit dans le beau style, un régal de conversation, on nous donne un regal de musique." (It is said, in elegant style, a conversational treat, we are given a musical treat) (36–7). It is this "beau style" (elegant style) that constitutes the most failsafe rule, in spite of its obvious vagueness, a vagueness it has in common with the rules governing literary taste with which we are already familiar.

Just as for literature, the ultimate arbiters of language are "les gens polis," (polite people) that is, worldly society dominated by women (12). Her experts are above all "tous ceux qui font profession de bien parler la langue française" (all those who profess to speak French well) (102–3), a vague category that elevates oral linguistic competence to the level of official rules. She frequently uses contemporary worldly figures as examples of people who should be recognized for their linguistic competence and achievements.[91] The examples Buffet provides of correct usage, or the examples she offers that need correction, are most frequently those that would find a place in polite, worldly conversation, as illustrated by the following passages:

> Belle comme un astre, ou comme un ange, l'un est aussi bon que l'autre.
> Ce mot d'en vérité est fort en usage, il est fort bien reçu en parlant et en écrivant.

Ce terme est encore fort en usage, et nouveau, quand une femme a quelque chose d'agréable, on dit, elle a bien du revenant.

Cette femme parle regulièrement de toutes choses, ou pertinemment, regulièrement est meilleur.

Quand une femme est savante, on peut lui dire de bonne grâce qu'elle mérite le premier rang au parnasse, et non pas de la faire passer pour un Platon et un Aristote, comme quelques-uns. (34–5)

(As beautiful as a star, or as an angel, both are equally good.

This word in truth is very often used. It is very well received in speaking and in writing.

This term is very popular, and new, when a woman is pleasing, people say she is really *revenant*.

This woman speaks regularly of everything, or pertinently, regularly is better.

When a woman is learned, one can politely say that she deserves the first rank in Parnassus and not liken her to a Plato or to an Aristotle, as some do.)

As in the above passage, women are often the chosen examples. Moreover, the majority of the examples she uses to correct usage have to do with how people describe each other, how people interact, how to speak of learned women, how to compose letters, types of love, or other such subjects that were among the preoccupations of the salons. [92] One in fact has the impression when reading *Les Observations* that one is observing a salon discussion on language, not that one is reading a language textbook designed to correct bad usage.[93] *Les Observations* has much in common with Scudéry's *Conversations* which are usually viewed to be accurate representations of salon *entretiens*. Buffet makes it a point to stress that her rules are valid for oral as well as for written language, because in her estimation, oral expression has the same status as written. She often distinguishes between what is valid in conversation and what is correct in writing, thus valorizing the art of conversation as the equal of written compositions when it comes to linguistic usage.[94]

Buffet's overriding purpose at the heart of *Les Observations* is to make the "bel usage" of language known and followed. Her measuring stick to determine whether or not a phrase or a word is "bien reçu" (well received) or "en usage" (used) in "le beau style" (elegant style) or belongs to "bel usage" (elegant usage) is worldly society, not learned grammarians. The vague category of "de bons Auteurs" (good authors) also provides an authoritative reference to determine "bel usage."[95] This is a treatise that emerged out of worldly experience and is addressed above all to a worldly public, but whose author remains cognizant that in producing a document on language she is entering a terrain that is traditionally associated not with worldly society but with learned scholars. Her text is a counterpoint to the scholastic treatises on language that in her opinion have failed to have an effect on worldly language. *Les Observations* addresses the problem of linguistic incompetency from a completely different perspective. Instead of imposing rules generated outside of worldly society upon ways of speaking, Buffet relies on "bel usage" and "usage" in general to generate correct speech.[96] Buffet proposes new models of correct French usage, and even new words so that her public can learn what is acceptable.[97] She substitutes her "bel usage" which she clearly associates with contemporary society for the authority associated with the *doctes* and specifically "les Anciens" with whom she is clearly familiar.[98]

The importance of such a feminization of culture is underscored by Buffet's opening chapter in which she develops the relationship between the creation and use of language and nationhood. The chapter title is "De la nécessité de bien parler sa langue, et combien la française est estimée de toutes les nations" (Concerning the necessity to speak one's native language well, and how the French language is valued by all nations). To speak French well, a language recognized by others as exceptional, is a source of national pride; the speaker thus contributes to France's glory. According to Buffet, France uses this language for cultural dominance: "cette langue est estimée non seulement dans toute L'Europe, mais même dans toutes les autres parties du monde. Il n'y a point de veritable courtisan dans les cours voisines, qui ne l'entende, et qui ne la parle, puis que cela suffit pour se faire aimer du Prince et pour se maintenir auprès de lui" (This language is valued not only throughout Europe, but even in all the other parts of the world. There is not a single true courtisan in neighboring courts who does not understand it, who doesn't speak it, because this is sufficient to be liked by the souverain and to remain close to him) (4–5). To speak French is a political act. For foreigners at least, it is to recognize the influence of the Sun King. Thus to define what this language should be has political consequences.[99] Buffet depicts the international status the French language was achieving during the period. People outside of France's borders choose to master French not only for political reasons, they also do so because it is quite simply, in Buffet's view, a beautiful language. As an example of the magnetism of French, Buffet offers Mlle de Scurman, a learned woman who converses freely in twenty-two languages. When Scurman chooses to write, however, she opts for French exclusively: "Elle travaille à la composition, et ses plus beaux ouvrages sont en langue française qu'elle estime plus que les autres langues" (She composes, and her most beautiful works are in French, which she values more than other languages) (3). The exceptional status of

French is even more reason for the native speaker to practice it correctly and well. While much of her effort is devoted to ridding her society of words she qualifies as "pas français," Buffet also gives the sense that her century has reached a point of correctness that merits emulation. One must avoid "un vieil mot," (an outdated word) (76) or "vieil style" (outdated style) (83) for example in order to achieve "le bel usage," a form of language that is clearly evolving within the conversational salon milieu and being dictated by those salon practitioners.

Implicit in Buffet's text is the idea that to enable women to master and define French is to empower them to transcend their traditional sphere of influence. She equates eloquent French women, whom she describes as "puissantes," (powerful) with public orators who praised Roman emperors. Buffet's emphasis on the power to be derived from language reflects the shift in the mid seventeenth century away from military prowess as a source of power to power in the cultural sphere. Many of the same women who were active military figures during the Fronde, such as Montpensier, turned to literary occupations afterwards, channeling their efforts to defy the limits imposed on their sex into the realm of culture. Buffet strives to inspire her contemporaries to a linguistic competence and greatness that would rival or even surpass that of the Ancients recognized as proficient. Armed with language and "le beau style," Buffet's contemporaries would rival the famous orators of old and potentially wield as much power:

> Il n'est pas difficile de se persuader, que toutes celles qui possèdent ce riche avantage de parler juste, ne soient infiniment estimées, puis qu'on les appelle les protectrices de l'éloquence. Elles brillent avec autant de gloire et de pompe, que les plus fameux orateurs, et reçoivent le même honneur; leur conversation est recherchée des plus habiles; il semble qu'elles portent avec elles, comme une autre Tullia, tout le trésor du bien dire, s'étant acquis le secret de se rendre aussi célèbres, et de se faire écouter, de même que l'on faisait autrefois ces grands Orateurs Romains, qui avaient l'art de gagner, et persuader ce qu'ils voulaient par la force et les charmes de leur bien dire. (119–20)

> (It is not difficult to be persuaded that all the women who possess this rich advantage of speaking correctly are infinitely valued, since they are called the protectors of eloquence. They shine with as much glory and ceremony as the most famous orators, and receive the same honor; their conversation is sought out by the most clever people; it seems as though they carry with them, like another Tullia, all the treasure of speaking well, having acquired the secret to make themselves equally famous, and to make themselves heard, just as the

great Roman orators did previously, who had the art of winning people over and the ability to persuade and convince others by the force and the charm of their speech.)

Women who possess the art of eloquence reign as the Roman orators did, and, even more important, merit the same praise as their ancient counterparts: "ces illustres sont puissantes, j'ose dire qu'il s'en faut peu, qu'on ne leur fasse encore le même honneur que l'on faisait autrefois à ceux qui ne pouvaient assez louer les empereurs de Rome, quand ils entraient en triomphe, après avoir dompté les ennemis de leur patrie" (These illustrious women are powerful; I dare say that they almost merit the same honor given to those who could not praise Roman emperors sufficiently when they entered in triumph, after having conquered their nation's enemies) (121). In this view, linguistic power is the equivalent of military prowess and merits the same praise. More specifically, verbal linguistic competence is the highest form of power: "je tiens impossible de pouvoir exprimer ce que peut le bien dire sur les esprits: il en est souverainement le maître" (122) (It is impossible to describe what effect good speech can have on the mind; it is the supreme master). Women who possess the art of speaking are viewed as "astres" in the "cercles" and in "les ruelles," stars that "vont éclairer toute l'assemblée … bref elles y reçoivent toute la gloire et l'encens qu'on donnerait aux plus parfaites du monde" (will enlighten the whole assembly … in short they receive all the glory and praise that are given to those who are the most perfect in this world) (120–21). Eloquence is recognized as the supreme power in this century of *ruelles*.

* * * * *

The last third of *Les Observations* provides examples, past and present, of "illustres savantes" (illustrious learned women), or "parfaites," whom Buffet offers as models to inspire her contemporaries. In her examples, mastery of language, specifically of the French language, is prized as the key to exemplarity, which accounts for the marriage of what at first glance appear to be very disparate texts.

The *Eloges des Illustres Savantes, anciennes et modernes* is prefaced with a relatively lengthy treatise on women and knowledge during which Buffet develops a logical argument to prove that women are not only men's equals in matters of the mind, but their superiors.[100] In this preface, she strives to illustrate that since the soul does not have a gender, one can logically conclude that there is no difference between a woman's or a man's mind.[101] Women are by nature at least men's equals, if not their superiors. She praises women's minds as "natural, agreeable," saying that they possess an "unforced style" which is a product of both art and nature.[102] The myriad examples Buffet uses to support her arguments are drawn primarily from the past, and specifically from Antiquity, although she does insert a few contemporary references. In many respects, she uses the preface to rehearse past arguments regarding women's position vis-à-vis men, mirroring previous contributions to the centuries old *querelle des femmes*. But rather than offering vague philosophical or religious argumentation as her predecessors had, Buffet grounds her remarks in the actions of real women, past and present. For example, she points to Hedvvige, Queen of Poland, in order to show that christianity was much advanced through women's efforts:

> Les savants n'ont pas ignoré qu'Hedvvige Reine de Pologne, fille puisnée de Louis dit le Grand, Roi de Hongrie et de Pologne. Cette charitable et illustre princesse, que l'histoire appelle la mère des savants, ayant fondé un collège, en l'Université de Cracovie, elle fit plusieurs belles actions dans tout ce pays pour la défense et le maintien de la foi catholique qui témoignèrent ce grand zèle qu'elle avait pour la conversion de ces peuples, qu'elle gagne par sa doctrine et par une conduite merveilleuse dont elle se servait ordinairement. (204–5)

> (Learned people are not unaware of Hedvvige Queen of Poland, daughter of Louis the Great, King of Hungary and Poland. This charitable and illustrious princess, whom history calls the queen of the learned, having founded a college at the University of Cracovie, did many worthy actions throughout the country for the defense and maintenance of the Catholic faith which shows the great zeal she had to convert these people, whom she converted by her doctrine and by her marvelous behavior which she always displayed.)

By inscribing the names of such figures as Hedvvige into her text, Buffet strives to ensure that they will be known and admired by more than simply "les savants." She hopes to inspire the worldly women who are the readers she privileges throughout the text. Buffet uses her preface to pay hommage to "un très grand nombre de savantes et de courageuses heroïnes qui ont paru avec admiration dans tous les siècles" (a great number of learned women and courageous heroines who were admired throughout the centuries) in order to counter the general argument handed down by the likes of Plato and Aristotle that women are men's inferiors in every respect.[103]

The portrait gallery that follows her treatise is devoted entirely to Buffet's female contemporaries, many of whom Buffet actually knows personally.[104]

Such a decision emphasizes Buffet's effort to break with the past, for while she obviously knows this history as she has just evidenced in the preface, her decision to foreground female contemporaries underscores her desire to augment her own personal authority as well as advance her own century as offering something new with respect to women, their experience, and their influence on the world. Among all the women she could have chosen, Buffet specifies that she will end her treatise on language "par les noms de quelques-unes que j'ai estimé des principales pour la science et les belles lettres," (with the names of a few that I have considered the principal ones for knowledge and literature) (237), thus again showing her elevation of intellectual qualities over all others, and the imprinting of her work with her own opinion: "j'ai estimé." These women are what she calls "illustres savantes," (illustrious learned women) a term she coins to refer to women who merit recognition primarily and often solely for their contributions to the intellectual realm. By identifying knowledge as the distinguishing characteristic of these illustrious women, Buffet offers a new definition of a "femme illustre," as well as of "heroïne," a term she uses frequently with reference to accomplishments in writing as opposed to the more traditional definition.[105] Previous galleries such as Père Le Moyne's *Femmes Fortes* in her own century and earlier Boccaccio's *Famous Women* and Christine de Pizan's *La Cité des Dames* inspired by Boccaccio, all included women who could be honored for military heroism, physical strength, political acumen, as well as intellectuel prowess. Buffet, however, chooses only those women whose power and control over language and matters of the mind make them players in the intellectual realm and thus worthy of emulation.

Even when one might identify one of the portraits' subjects as worthy of remembrance for other qualities, Buffet shows how all merit is derived from the mind. For example, Buffet's choice to lead off her gallery is someone who has achieved political recognition and leads her own country. But instead of extolling Christine de Suède's political capabilities, Buffet explains that the strength of this "illustre savante" emanates from her "sagesse" and her espousal of knowledge as the ultimate gift a souverain must possess and use to guide her/his people. Buffet explains:

> Cette auguste princesse a toujours cru que rien ne relevait davantage les souverains de la terre que leur sagesse … Elle a cru que ceux que la divine Providence a élevés au dessus des autres hommes étaient indispensablement engagés par les lois de l'honneur et de la conscience à devenir savants pour servir d'exemple à leur peuple, et les conduire à la félicité publique par de bonnes loix. Ses premières victoires sur les Allemands et sur les autres peuples

du Nord, sont les fruits de sa première sagesse et de ses conseils; et toutes les batailles que les généraux ont gagnées sous sa conduite, font bien voir que Mars n'est jamais plus heureux que quand il est conduit par Pallas. (238–9)

(This esteemed princess always believed that nothing elevated rulers of the world more than their knowledge. She believed that those whom divine Providence had elevated above other men were indispensibly obliged by laws of honor and conscience to become learned in order to serve as an example for their people and lead them to happiness through good laws. Her first victories over the Germans and over other Northern peoples are the fruits of her knowledge and her advice; and all the battles that the generals won under her guidance illustrate well that Mars is never as successful as when he is guided by Pallas.)

With the example of Christine, Buffet proves that even women who could be honored for more traditional qualities, like rank, achieve a more important kind of greatness by privileging intellectual pursuits.

Buffet's next portrait is devoted to someone who is qualified for immortality due entirely to her mental capacities. Just as she did in the first half of her text, Buffet cites Mademoiselle de Scurman for her linguistic prowess and her knowledge in a variety of subjects such as theology and philosophy. She uses Scurman as a transition to what will become her primary focus in the rest of the portraits: all the various facets of knowledge as illustrated by her French female contemporaries. And Buffet stresses that the rest of her examples will be French because, in her words:

Ce serait en vain que j'aurais cherché d'illustres preuves du mérite et du savoir des dames chez les étrangers, si je ne faisais voir que la France n'est pas plus au dessus des autres nations par la gloire de ses héros, que par la science et la vertu de ses héroïnes. Que la Suède admire son illustre reine, la Hollande sa docte Scurman, nous trouverons en la Sapho de nos jours, l'incomparable Mademoiselle Scudéry, plus de science, de doctrine, et d'esprit que dans la Sapho des Grecs tant vantée dans l'Antiquité. (244–5)

(It would be a pointless effort to search for illustrious proof of the merit and knowledge of women among neighbors, if I didn't show that France is not only superior to other nations due to the glory of its heros but also due to the knowledge and virtue of her heroines. Let Sweden admire its illustrious queen and Holland its erudite Scurman, we will find in the Sappho of our time, the incomparable Mlle Scudéry, more knowledge, more doctrine and more *esprit* than in the Greek Sappho so praised in Antiquity.)

Thanks to Scudéry, the France of Buffet's time—"de nos jours"—surpasses Antiquity just as France excells militarily beyond any other country. As is evident in this portrait of Scudéry as well as those of her other contemporaries, Buffet's emphasis on language and *esprit*, and her espousal of the worldly values of the salons reflect her particular context and ally her with those who defended women's participation in literary culture. She considers these roles quintessentially French, stating that she would be remiss if she didn't show how "France is not more superior to other nations due to the glory of its heroes but also by the knowledge and virtue of her heroines." Again, "heroine" in this context is associated uniquely with the intellectual realm. She echoes many of her contemporaries, both male and female, who associate a particular status of women founded upon "science" and mastery of language in writing and conversation with a concept of Frenchness. Buffet describes how Scudéry has achieved prominence not only in France but beyond its borders:

> Aussi voyons-nous que tous ceux qui savent parler et écrire en français lui ont donné une estime si universelle, qu'ils la prennent pour un modèle achevé de bien parler et de bien écrire. Tout le monde lit ses ouvrages avec autant de profit que de plaisir: en sorte que nous pouvons avancer … qu'elle ne peut être inconnue ou méprisée que par des pédants ou des babares, et que la cour trouverait plus à se plaindre dans le silence de cette éloquente fille, que dans le retranchement d'une des académies du Royaume. (247–8)

> (Thus everyday we see that all those who speak and write in French so universally esteem her that they take her as a perfect model for good speech and writing. Everyone reads her works for profit as much as for pleasure; thus we can advance that … she can only be unknown to or scorned by pedants or barbarians, and the court would find more to lament in the silence of this eloquent woman than in the elimination of one of the academies of the kingdom.)

When one remembers that in the beginning of her treatise Buffet underscores how the French language is universally admired and spoken, it is clear that Buffet is offering Scudéry as a model not only for France but for Europe as a whole.

Many of the women she chooses embody the precepts she had advanced in the first part of her text. Buffet isolates la duchesse de Montausier, for example, because one can see her in letters "toute la gravité et la politesse du plus beau style qui ait jamais paru entre les auteurs les plus célèbres" (all the seriousness and politeness of the most elegant style that has ever appeared in the most famous authors) (248–9). With such language, and by valorizing letters as a genre, Buffet highlights the values of the worldly milieu and by extension asserts that modern *savantes* surpass all those of Antiquity. For example, she praises Madame la comtesse du Plexis stating that "elle possède plus de vertu, d'esprit et de science, que les anciens n'en ont vanté dans toutes leurs héroïnes" (she possesses more virtue, *esprit* and knowledge than the Ancients praised in all their heroines) (260). Du Plexis, whom Buffet identifies as a friend, possesses the gift of eloquence, and Buffet inscribes her into history for this oral prowess, a strength that is usually ignored by historians. Such traditionally ephemeral strengths are the focus of Buffet's record of her world. "L'éloquence" and "la beauté de l'esprit" (282) are traits that are included in the "savoir" or knowledge Buffet is singling out for praise. Describing Mademoiselle Dupré, for example, Buffet writes:

> Cette illustre fille est une des galants esprits du siècle, et de qui on ne peut assez estimer la conversation. Personne n'y sait mieux entrer et sortir avec plus d'avantage qu'elle fait: Elle sait parler de toutes choses fort agréablement, et avec toutes la grace et l'éloquence qu'il faut avoir pour se bien faire rechercher ... bref il faut la connaître pour en pouvoir parler assez avantageusement, et lui rendre la justice qu'elle mérite. (280–81)

> (This illustrious young woman is one of the gallant *esprits* of the century, and her converstaion cannot be admired enough. No one knows how to enter or withdraw from a conversation better than she. She knows how to speak of everything very pleasingly and with all the grace and eloquence necessary for one to be sought after ... in short, one must know her to be able to speak of her so advantageously, and to give her the justice she deserves.)

The shadowy, ephemeral, worldly, salon milieu of conversation is thus valorized and rendered immortal by Buffet's written word and reevaluation of the qualities that merit historical inscription. And as Buffet's personal experience serves as one of the foundations of the *Eloges* just as it did for the *Observations*, she often transcribes her experience as an audience member transfixed by the eloquence of one of her "savantes héroïnes," as she does with du Plexis:[106]

> Comme elle est fort éloquente et éclairée sur les plus belles matières, il y a une satisfaction qu'on ne peut exprimer, dans le bonheur de la pouvoir entendre raisonner si solidement, et si universellement de toutes choses. Elle parle avec tant de grâce, et d'éloquence, que l'on souhaiterait qu'elle parlat toujours pour avoir de nouveaux désirs de la pouvoir imiter. (261–2).

(As she is very eloquent and enlightened about beautiful, important subjects, one cannot express the satisfaction one has when one has the good fortune to be able to hear her reason so solidly and so universally about all subjects. She speaks with such grace and eloquence, that everyone wishes she would always speak in order to have new reasons to be able to imitate her.)

Here and elsewhere, Buffet transforms her personal experience into that of a general public, that of "on." Her entire century is in admiration of such women.

But Buffet goes one step farther in her praise of "illustres savantes" by not only inscribing their greatness and her century's admiration, but by elevating her female subjects above their male contemporaries and even the male models of antiquity. Of the Comtesse de la Suze, for example, she states:

Que l'on ne vante plus les poètes de l'antiquité, au desavantage de notre sexe, depuis que nous avons vu briller notre Minerve française, l'incomparable Madame la Comtesse de la Suze, l'ornement de la Cour, et la merveille de son siècle, qui sait si bien parler le langage des Dieux, qu'elle mérite d'être au dessus des hommes ... On ne lui peut disputer le premier rang entre les plus beaux esprits du siècle, sans faire paraître qu'on n'a pas le goût des bonnes choses, et qu'on est tout à fait ignorant en l'art de bien parler et de bien écrire, si le chant de ses Odes est plus charmant que celui d'Horace. Je puis ajouter qu'elle ne se plaint pas moins agréablement qu'Ovide dans ses élegies. (262–3)

(No one should praise the poets of Antiquity to the disadvantage of our sex since we have witnessed our French Minerva shine, the incomparable Mme comtesse de la Suze, the ornament of the court and the marvel of her century who knows how to speak in the language of the gods so well that she deserves to be elevated above men ... One cannot argue against her being given the first rank among the most outstanding *esprits* of the century without showing that one has no taste for good work and that one is completely ignorant of the art of speaking and writing well, as the recitation of her odes is more charming than Horace's. I can add that she laments no less pleasingly than Ovid in his elegies.)

Buffet accords worldly taste, "le goût des bonnes choses," a privileged status in determining worth, thus identifying her text with the worldly milieu. In this new order, women figure among "les plus beaux esprits," and oral accomplishments merit as much recognition as written ones, for in many instances it is this ephemeral, oral worldly milieu that Buffet is striving to immortalize. Buffet refers to unpublished works, "pièces de cabinet" (works composed in a study) with which she is personally familiar, and describes other contributions such as "un ton de voix" (tone of voice) in order to inscribe such new values of the worldly milieu for posterity. A certain Madame de Miramminy, for example, merits inclusion because of her "pièces de cabinet" that she refuses to publish out of humility.[107] In another portrait Buffet describes the oral interventions of another "savante Minerve" in philosophical discussions as expressed with "tant de doctrine et d'éloquence, qu'elle le prenait aussi facilement le coeur que l'estime de ses Auditeurs. Elle a une grâce et une facilité à exprimer si belle, une prononciation si libre, un ton de voix si agréable, qu'on ne peut rien ajouter à cette incomparable" (273) (such doctrine and eloquence, that she possesses the heart as well as the esteem of her listeners. She has such grace and ease of expression, such a fine pronunciation, such a pleasing tone of voice that nothing can be added to this incomparable woman). Another woman is among "celles qui possèdent la Philosophie naturelle, puis qu'elle parle de toutes choses avec un raisonnement si fort et si admirable, qu'on le peut croire toute Philosophe" (those who possess a natural sense of philosophy, because she speaks with such strong and admirable reasoning that she seems a complete philosopher) (282–3). This "natural philosophy" is reminiscent of the "natural taste" women used to judge literary productions. And as we have seen previously, reason and reasoning are not banned from this brand of knowledge. They are simply redefined and contextualized to reflect worldly values and practices. With such descriptions Buffet attempts to inscribe this influential, female-dominated world of the salons into posterity.

In addition to often surpassing the linguistic prowess of their male contemporaries, many of the women Buffet describes, women for the most part forgotten by posterity, aid the men familiar to today's readers. Buffet praises Madame de Bonnevant, for example, as:

> le plus bel esprit, et le plus éclairé qui ait jamais cultivé la Philosophie. Elle est très savante dans celle de Monsieur Descartes, personne ne l'a jamais comprise avec plus de facilité que cette illustre. Lors qu'il s'est fait des conférences chez elle des plus savants hommes de France, cette docte Philosophe paraissait comme un flambeau pour leur donner des lumières … Jamais la philosophie de M. Descartes n'a reçu plus d'honneur et n'a été plus estimée que depuis l'approbation en cette illustre Dame, qui en a dissipé les ténèbres. (265–6)[108]

(the most beautiful *esprit*, and the most enlightened that has ever cultivated philosophy. She is extremely knowledgeable about Monsieur Descartes, no one has ever understood him more easily than this illustrious woman. When the most erudite men in France had meetings at her home, this erudite philosopher [in the feminine] appeared liked a torch to give them light ... Never has Descarte's philosophy received more honor nor been more highly regarded as since the time that this famous woman gave it her approbation, [this woman] who dissipated its shadows.)

In another portrait, Buffet praises Descartes's sister and her "belles productions d'esprit qu'elle a mises au jour" (excellent literary works that she has given to the public) because her "style est élégant et pompeux, et rempli de doctrine" (style is elegant, elevated and filled with doctrine) (279). Such descriptions of seventeenth-century worldly gatherings and their participants offer an alternative portrait of France's classical literary past. Women such as Bonnevant were not content to simply remain on the sidelines and revel passively in the insights of the male contemporaries they gathered at their homes. Buffet echoes the other contemporaries we have seen who grant women a very active role as critics, and offer us portraits of women who appeared as "torches" to illuminate the writings we consider today as France's literary legacy.[109] The fact that very few names of the women in Buffet's portrait gallery are recognizable to us today attests in part to the strength of the detractors of these "illustres savantes," and what we will see later as posterity's omission of the world Buffet inscribes in the eventual reformulation of a conception of classical France.[110] Her text proves that one can have an effect by being eloquent. She describes the power of immortality through language, in this case especially oral language.[111] Buffet's ideas are clearly a product of her time. Her female exempla do not follow any ancient models but rather create new ones based on contemporary worldly traits. While Buffet begins her treatise by alluding to the fact that everyone wants to emulate France by speaking French, the rest of her text reveals that France's linguistic superiority is due in large measure to the place alloted conversation and *esprit*, not just language, and the role of women in creating this superiority.

* * * * *

The originality of Buffet's *Observations* is especially apparent when one compares it with a text that enjoyed wider circulation and more visibility both during the seventeenth century and later. Le Père Dominique Bouhours's many works on literature and in particular on language established him as one of the foremost intellectuals of his day. One of Bouhours's most well-known texts, his *Entretiens d'Ariste et d'Eugène*, reflects the redistribution of power in the cultural sphere due to the growing influence of the worldly public.[112] This text, like Buffet's before it, bears witness to the intense interest, especially in the latter half of the century, in the development of French as a means of communication and artistic expression and the status this language could and should hold in the world. It is an especially intriguing document for our purposes because it inscribes worldly influence on the cultural sphere, while simultaneously revealing a shift in the evaluation of this influence and in particular its associations with women and the worldly milieu they were seen as orchestrating.

Bouhours is an intriguing figure who, much like Chapelain, spent his existence traveling between various often contradictory intellectual spheres. He was born in 1628 in Paris and entered the Jesuit order at the age of sixteen. After studying theology in Bourges and rhetoric in Tours, he returned to Paris and became the preceptor first for the illegitimate son of La Rochefoucauld and the duchesse de Longueville, the celebrated *frondeuse*, and then for Colbert's oldest son. In the 1660s, Bouhours became an active member of worldly Parisian circles, such as Scudéry's *samedis*, while retaining his ties with the arenas more officially recognized as academic such as the Académie de Lamoignon. On the one hand his associations include writers and intellectuals such as Boileau, La Fontaine, la Bruyère, Bossuet, and Racine and on the other worldly figures such as Bussy-Rabutin, Sablé, and Sévigné.[113] Racine, among others, submitted literary works to him for review and revered his taste that was clearly a product of the mixed milieus he frequented. Bussy-Rabutin reflects the opinion of many of his contemporaries when he complimented Bouhours on his exceptional literary and linguistic acumen and taste, stating to him in a letter: "La France vous aura plus d'obligations qu'à l'Académie Française; elle ne redresse que les paroles, et vous redressez le sens"[114] (France owes you more than [it owes] the French Academy; it [the French Academy] only corrects words, you correct meaning). Sévigné describes him in her letters as the quintessential salon figure: "l'esprit lui sort de tous les côtés"[115] (*esprit* emanates everywhere from him). Even in the eighteenth century Bouhours still occupied a place of prominence in intellectual history. For example, in his *Temple du goût*, Voltaire places him just after today's more recognizable figures, Pascal and Bourdaloue. I would contend that if he is less well-known than others today, it is perhaps because of his overt ties with the world of the *mondains*. Whatever his status today, however, it is clear that in the mid-seventeenth century, Bouhours was a strong intellectual voice and acknowledged expert on linguistic and literary matters, and reflected particularly well the complex nature of the intellectual climate due to his many different affiliations.

Bouhours's *Entretiens d'Ariste et d'Eugène*, like Buffet's *Observations*, is very much a product of the literary field of the mid-seventeenth century and mirrors many of the preoccupations of both traditional intellectuals and the newer worldly public. Begun in the early 1660s and published in 1671, *Les Entretiens* was an immediate success, going through several reprintings, and was translated into many languages.[116] The work's popularity was due in large mesure to Bouhours's adroit ability to combine scholarly knowledge and worldly interests. *Les Entretiens* are conducted by figures who could easily have found their place in Scudéry's *samedis*. Bouhours addresses topics familiar to *ruelle* habitués, such as *le bel esprit* and *le je ne sais quoi*, subjects that one also finds in Scudéry's *Conversations*. What distinguishes Bouhours's text from Scudéry's, and others, is this author's ability to combine what today we might term the "ancient" and "modern" stances of the classical literary field, which I have been roughly equating with *docte* and *mondain*. In defining classical taste, for example, he straddles the fence between Boileau and the worldly taste we have examined.[117]

Of particular interest for our purposes is the chapter in the *Entretiens* entitled "La Langue française" in which Bouhours explores the importance of his native language to his era, discusses its development, and ruminates on its particularies. Like Buffet, Bouhours has as one of his objectives to teach his contemporaries proper usage in both speaking and writing. And like Buffet, Bouhours begins by underscoring the supremacy of the French language:

> On parle déjà français dans toutes les cours de l'Europe. Tous les étrangers qui ont de l'esprit se piquent de savoir le français; ceux qui haïssent le plus notre nation aiment notre langue … le peuple même … apprend notre langue presque aussitot que la sienne, comme par un instinct secret qui l'avertit malgré lui qu'il doit un jour obéir au Roi de France, comme à son légitime maître … si la langue française n'est pas encore la langue de tous les peuple du monde, il me semble qu'elle mérite de l'être. (35–8)

> (French is already spoken in all the courts of Europe. All foreigners who possess *esprit* are proud to know French; those who hate our country the most love our language … even the people … learn our language almost as soon as they learn their own, as if by a secret instinct that warns them unconsciously that they must one day obey the King of France as their legitimate master … if French is not yet the universal language of the world, it seems to me that it deserves to be.)

France's exceptional monarch is directly responsible for this perfect and conquering language: " La gloire du Roi y contribue peut-être autant que celle de ses prédécesseurs. Les langues suivent d'ordinaire la fortune et la réputation des Princes ... Que doit faire présentement pour une langue polie et parfaite la grandeur d'un monarque comme le nôtre" (The glory of the King perhaps contributes as much as that of his predecessors. Languages usually reflect the fortune and the reputation of sovereigns. What must the grandeur of a monarch such as ours do [for language] today?) (36–7). French has become perfect: "cette perfection où la langue française devait parvenir sous le règne du plus grand monarque de la terre" (this perfection that the French language was destined to reach during the reign of the greatest monarch on earth) (117).

French owes its status in the world not only to its monarch's superiority but more precisely to its "génie," and it is this "génie de la langue française" that Bouhours identifies and elaborates upon in the *Entretiens*.[118] This text is less of a manual of correct usage than Buffet's, although Bouhours does offer page upon page of expressions and words that have entered the language, which he then consecrates as correct or banishes from desirable usage. Words and expressions are acceptable if they are "ces façons de parler qui ont cours parmi les personnes polies" (the ways polite people speak) (79), that is, if they are used in worldly society.[119] Unlike Buffet, however, Bouhours makes no effort to establish conversation as equal to written French. Although responsible for the introduction of new words, conversation is in Bouhours's estimation inferior to written expression.[120] But what seems to primarily interest Bouhours is the question of what the French language is and how it differs from other, often related, languages. In Bouhours's opinion, French bears the unique imprints of its monarch as well as of its polite, worldly society. Many of the qualities Bouhours highlights as typical of the French language are those that are most often associated with the polite society of the salons. "Le bon sens et la bienséance l'accompagnent [French] partout" (Good sense and propriety accompany [French] everywhere) (40). It is "le langage des hommes raisonnables qui n'ont rien de grossier et de barbare" (the language of reasonable men who have nothing uncouth or barbaric [about them]) (63). "Que de noblesse, que d'élévation, que de bon sens" (what elevation, what good sense, what nobility) he says of the French vocabulary. In his estimation, French is above all "reasonable," and "natural." It is marked by "clarté" (clarity), "naiveté" (58) and "simplicité" (54).[121] In fact, Bouhours says it is the only language that follows "l'ordre naturel, et qui exprime les pensées en la manière qu'elles naissent dans l'esprit" (the natural order and which expresses thoughts in the way they are born in the mind) (55). Bouhours consistently underscores this "natural" quality of French explaining that "les termes trop recherchés, les phrases trop élégantes ... lui sont insupportables. Tout ce qui sent l'étude, tout ce qui a l'air de contrainte la choque" (terms too sought-after, phrases that are too elegant ... are unbearable [to French]. Everything that resembles study, that seems constraining shocks it) (52).[122] In his estimation, French is unique in this respect: "Il n'y a que la langue française qui suive la nature pas à pas" (only French follows nature step by step) (56).[123] In addition to all these estimable qualities, the French language also has "un talent particulier pour exprimer les plus tendres sentiments du coeur" (a particular talent for expressing the most tender emotions of the heart) (57).

   Given Bouhours' description of the nature of French, it would follow that women would be especially polished practitioners of the French language. In fact, Bouhours identifies women who speak well as one of France's distinguishing characteristics: "Mais d'où vient ... que les femmes en France parlent si bien? N'est-ce pas parce qu'elles parlent naturellement et sans nulle étude? ... il n'y a rien de plus juste, de plus propre et de plus naturel que le langage de la plupart des femmes françaises" (But how is it that women in France speak so well? Is it not because they speak naturally and without study ... there is nothing that is more exact, more proper and more natural than the language of the majority of French women) (57). Women's language and French in general would seem to obey the same laws of nature. Bouhours's choice of vocabulary to characterize it reveals implicitly the influence of worldly, salon culture on its formation.[124] The models he offers for emulation, such as Conrart, Balzac, Voiture, Sarrasin and Pellisson, are primarily those associated with the worldly milieu, as opposed to didactic, scholarly texts or even the texts of those writers we today would judge to be models of linguistic perfection.[125] Bouhours singles out Vaugelas in particular for his positive and determining influence on French, an influence founded upon consecrating the usage of "des meilleurs écrivains du temps et des plus honnêtes gens de la Cour" (the best authors of the time and the most *honnête* people of the court) (117) as opposed to the preceptes of scholarly grammarians. In answer to the question "que faut-il faire ... pour bien parler et pour bien écrire" (what must one do in order to speak and to write well) (124), one finds polite society singled out:

   A vous dire la vérité, repartit Eugène, je dois le peu que je sais au commerce des honnêtes gens et à la lecture des bons livres. Ce sont, à parler en général, les deux voies qu'il faut tenir, ce me semble, pour savoir bien la langue française: l'une ne suffit pas sans l'autre. En fréquentant les personnes polies, on prend insensiblement je ne sais quelle teinture de politesse que les livres ne donnent point; ce n'est guère que dans les belles conversations qu'on apprend à parler noblement et naturellement tout ensemble. Mais aussi ce n'est guère que dans les bons livres qu'on apprend à parler juste, et selon toutes les règles de l'art. (124)

(To tell you the truth, responded Eugène, I owe the little I know to involvement with *honnêtes gens* and to reading good books. In general, these are the two roads to follow, it seems to me, in order to know the French language well: one is insufficent without the other. In frequenting polite people, you unconsciously pick up shades of politeness that books don't give. Only in conversation can one learn to speak nobly and naturally. But only from good books can one learn to speak correctly and according to artistic rules.)

And the "good books" Eugène cites as necessary for a proper linguistic education are Vaugelas, Balzac, and Voiture.

But while, unlike Buffet, Bouhours accentuates the need for books, this salon habitué voices the opinion associated with the *mondains* that there are those in the worldly milieu who have no need for the traditional means of education and can function at a superior linguistic level simply because of their natural gifts. We have already seen how many associated these gifts specifically with women. In the *Entretiens*, Bouhours uses the same reasoning and vocabulary as those who praised women's natural talents of *bon goût* and *bons sens* to describe the intricacies of language used during his time period, but does not associate such gifts specifically with women. The following lengthy passage is especially intriguing in this regard, as one finds the same terms Lambert uses approximately forty years later to describe worldly influence and linguistic *goût* and *bon sens*. These are also the qualities Buffet underscored in the portraits of her "illustres savantes" where she replaced scholarly knowledge with worldly *sagesse*:

Car enfin on veut aujourd'hui dans le langage des qualités qu'il est assez difficile d'allier ensemble: une grande facilité et une grande exactitude; des paroles harmonieuses, mais pleines de sens; de la brièveté et de la clarté; une expression fort simple, et en même temps fort noble; une extrême pureté, une naïveté admirable, at avec cela je ne sais quoi de fin et de piquant ... On a beau lire les bons livres et voir le grand monde, on ne fait rien, si la nature ne s'en mêle. Pour bien profiter de la lecture et de la conversation, il faut avoir du naturel pour la langue, beaucoup d'esprit, beaucoup de jugement et même beaucoup d'honnêteté ... j'entends par honnêteté une certaine politesse naturelle, qui fait que les honnêtes gens ne gardent pas moins de bienséances dans ce qu'ils disent que dans ce qu'ils font. En un mot, il faut avoir ce qu'un de nos bons auteurs a appelé le talent de la parole. Ceux qui ont ce talent-là n'ont pas besoin, comme les autres, d'une longue étude et d'un grand usage pour avoir une connaissance parfaite de notre langue: leur génie leur tient lieu de tout; ils n'ont qu'à le suivre pour bien parler. (144–5)

(Today people want language to possess qualities that it is fairly difficult to join together: a great ease and great precision, harmonious words but full of meaning; brevity and clarity; simple yet very noble expression; extreme purity, admirable naiveté and *je ne sais quoi* that is refined and witty. However much one reads good books and lives in society, all is useless if nature doesn't contribute something. In order to profit from reading and conversation, one must have a natural gift for language, lots of *esprit*, much judgment and even a lot of *honnêteté* ... by this I mean a certain natural politeness, which compels *honnête* people to maintain propriety in what they say more than in what they do. In a word, one must have what one of our esteemed authors has called a talent for speech. Those who have this talent do not need to study long or practice for a long time in order to have perfect knowledge of our language: their genius takes the place of everything. They need only to follow it in order to speak well.)

It is perhaps this inscription and praise of the worldly milieu, and Bouhours's attempt to equate it with the *docte* world of grammarians, that inspired Bouhours's contemporary, Barbier d'Aucour, to take up the pen and denounce the *Entretiens*.[126] Bouhours would seem to be describing in particular the female salon participants and seconding Buffet in her choice of "illustres savantes," many of whom lacked formal education but profited from worldly commerce due to their "natural politeness." But when he turns to an example, Bouhours chooses the person celebrated by the most scholarly of all assemblies, the French Academy, and thus the person least likely to be associated with the salon, worldly milieu: Louis XIV himself:

Mais savez-vous bien que notre grand monarque tient le premier rang parmi ces heureux génies et qu'il n'y a personne dans le royaume qui sache le français comme il le sait ... Comme le bon sens est la principale règle qu'il suit en parlant, il ne dit jamais rien que de raisonnable; il ne dit rien d'inutile. (146)

(But you know well that our great monarch is first among these fortunate geniuses, and that no one in the realm knows French the way he does ... Because *bon sens* is the principal rule that he follows when speaking, he never says anything unreasonable or useless.)

Bouhours effectively divorces his discussion of *bon sens* and the *naturel* from the milieu in which it had developed: the worldly milieu of the salons. And while the *Entretiens* has much in common with Buffet's text, Buffet proves herself to be much more controversial for modern-day readers, while at the same time reflecting perhaps better than Bouhours the recognition in the seventeenth-century of women's influence on the literary field.

Bouhours's glorification of the linguistic prowess of his monarch is perhaps attributable to his desire throughout the *Entretiens* to highlight a specific function of language. Not only is language a conquering tool making other countries subservient to one monarch, it defines the essence of its own country. Bouhours compares French to a variety of other languages in an effort not only to show the superiority of the French language, but more importantly of French national character. According to Bouhours, "le langage suit d'ordinaire la disposition des esprits; et chaque nation a toujours parlé selon son génie" (60) (language usually follows a mind's disposition; and each nation has always spoken according to its *génie*). In his depiction, the French language, like the French people, is direct and spirited, in addition to being clear and polite:

> Il faut donc que les Français, qui sont naturellement brusques, et qui ont beaucoup de vivacité et de feu, aient un langage court et animé, qui n'a rien de languissant ... au reste, nous avons trouvé le secret de joindre la brièveté non seulement avec la clarté, mais encore avec la pureté et la politesse. (60–61)

> (Thus the French, who are naturally abrupt and have a lot of spirit and fire, must have a language that is direct and animated, that has nothing languishing about it ... we have found the secret for combining brevity not only with clarity but also with purity and politeness.)

> ... cet air facile, naturel et raisonable qui est le caractère de notre nation et comme l'âme de notre langue. (123)

> (... this easy, natural and reasonable manner, which is our nation's character and like the soul of our language.)

Such descriptions illustrate the clear link between polite, worldly society and the development of this perfect, soon-to-be universal language. To judge by Bouhours's text, worldly polite society was determining the language of Europe's most formidable political power as well as the character of this nation.

In the chapter entitled "Le Bel Esprit," Bouhours further underscores the influence of worldly culture on national identity: "[C'est] l'étoile de la nation française d'avoir présentement ce beau tour d'esprit que les autres nations n'ont pas" (182) (It is the glory of the French nation to currently have this elegant way of thinking that other nations don't have). Later he states: "On dirait que tout l'esprit et toutes la science du monde soient maintenant parmi nous et que tous les autres peuples soient barbares en comparaison des Francais ... je ne sais rien de plus commun dans le royaume que ce bon sens délicat qui y était si rare autrefois" (188) (It is as if all the world's *esprit* and knowledge were now among us, and all other people were barbaric in comparison with the French ... I know nothing more common in the kingdom than this delicate *bon sens* that used to be so rare). Bouhours's temporal identification of these distinguishing qualities of the French language—it is happening "currently," "now,"—and his emphasis on the fact that *esprit* and *bon sens* are now common whereas they "used to be so rare" can be viewed as further evidence of the worldly milieu's pervasive influence by the 1660s.

Bouhours would thus seem for the most part to be praising the influence of the worldly milieu. But while his *Entretiens* reveals the influence of worldly society, this text also reflects the growing opposition to this influence, especially its female component. While many would hold women responsible for the spreading of *bon sens* and *esprit*, Bouhours refuses most women the title *bel esprit*:

> Ce beau feu et ce bon sens ... ne viennent pas d'une complexion froide et humide. Le froideur et l'humidité, qui rendent les femmes faibles, timides, indiscrètes, légères, impatientes, babillards ... les empêchent d'avoir le jugement, la solidité, la force, la justesse que le bel esprit demande ... elles ne sont pas trop raisonnables. (190–91)[127]

> (This fire and *bon sens* ... does not come from a cold and humid make up. Cold and humidity, which make women weak, timid, indiscreet, flighty, impatient, chatterboxes ... make them unable to have the judgment, firmness, force, and accuracy that *bel esprit* requires ... they are not very reasonable.)

In the final analysis, just as he did earlier by elevating Louis XIV as the natural master of language, Bouhours attributes the polished state of French not to worldly culture but to the official French Academy, thus eliminating worldy cultural influence.

> Ainsi pour polir, pour épurer, pour embellir notre langue, il a fallu nécessairement en retrancher tout ce qu'elle avait de rude et de barbare. Nous devons un si utile retranchement aux soins de l'Académie française, qui se proposa pour but dès

sa naissance de nettoyer la langue des ordures qu'elle avait contractées dans la bouche du peuple et parmi des courtisans ignorants ou peu exacts. (77)

(Thus in order to polish, purify and embellish our language, it was necessary to remove everything that was uncultured and barbaric. We owe this very useful removal to the work of the French Academy which from its inception proposed as its goal to clean the language of the garbage it had contracted in the people's mouth and among ignorant or imprecise courtisans.)

Bouhours is thus more critical of society and its influence than Buffet. Unlike his female contemporary, Bouhours does not use his text specifically to pay tribute to women and their influence, but rather works to inscribe the French language in general into history and offer it as a universal model, one that can be associated with worldly influence but is more importantly affiliated with a particular and unique monarch. He wants to offer French as a universal model for linguistic excellence, a move that in turn would establish the French character as also worthy of emulation given that language is a direct reflection of the national psyche. Given this conception of language, women's importance in determining this national language should not be over emphasized. Buffet, on the other hand, would work to do just the opposite: empower women linguistically and develop their current influence in order to offer a model that would grant "illustres savantes" their natural place. Thus, where one author highlights female influence the other eliminates it.

How can one explain what can appropriately be called the backlash, intimated by Bouhours's text? If language and cultural production are to define a nation, then their use must be carefully monitored, and their development must be put in safe hands, such as those of the government-sponsored, all male French Academy. The terms associated with the worldly milieu, taste and *bon sens*, for example, must be appropriated and redefined in order to weaken or even sever their connection with a worldly public dominated by women. A certain "good taste" must be advanced, not one founded on nature, *bon sens*, and sentiment, but on a brand of reason carefully defined as male. This is precisely the move seen in the debates at the end of the century. While the marquise de Lambert, for example, continues to defend the qualities of nature and emotion, associated with women, over learned reason, stating that "nous allons aussi surement à la vérité par la force et la chaleur des sentiments, que par l'étendue et la justesse des raisonnements" (102) (we arrive at truth as surely through the force and the warmth of feelings as by the breadth and accuracy of reasoning), others seek to eradicate the influence of the *mondains*. For many, the state-sanctioned *doctes* must prevail over the salon.

The end of the seventeenth century witnessed an effort to redefine what constituted acceptable criteria for literary judgment, and in this reformulation, the qualities associated with women from the beginning of the century are most often rendered gender neutral, reconstituted as male, or rejected altogether. "Natural talents" must have "the help of studies," to return to Huet. There is a move to defeminize qualities such as *bon sens* by disassociating them from nature and thus women. Timothy Reiss contends further that the debate over women's reason at the end of the century was an effort to ensure that women's reason was "peculiar to their sex" and not part of universally admired "French" reason.[128] This shift in the roles women were seen as playing in the literary field and with respect to language is particularly apparent when one examines a textual corpus unique to France: the *discours de réception*, or acceptance speeches, and their responses given at the French Academy from 1640 to 1715. These speeches allow us to reconstitute the image of the French Academy and of its functions and power as formulated by its members, considered officially to be the most influential figures in French culture. A reading of the speeches, precursors to Yourcenar's speech with which we began, reveals a gradual redefinition of the Academy, a restructuring of the literary and political empires. The speeches are historical documents that reflect this reconfiguration as well as literary texts whose rhetoric works to create a mythology of the French Academy, as these authors collectively narrate the story of the politicization of culture during the most classic of French literary moments. As shall become apparent, while *bon sens* and *bon goût* continued to be identified as French traits that distinguish the celebrated century of Louis XIV from all previous ones, and elevate France over its neighbors, a Rambouillet or a Sablé are no longer at their origins nor are they universal models to be followed.

Appropriating Worldly Taste: The French Academy Rules

During the early years of the Academy, founded by Richelieu in 1634, what acceptance speeches there were addressed a privileged few and thus were not published. But by 1640 the Academy was a recognized and authoritative, albeit fledgling, cultural regulator and barometer, its renown enhanced in particular by its role as the ultimate arbiter in the quarrel over *Le Cid*. The speeches reflect this gradual entry into the public realm, a process that culminated in 1672 when the induction ceremonies were opened to the public. Throughout the century, the form of these speeches changed as they became pieces to define the Academy to the public, to explain its purposes, and overall to specify for the public and its own members the nature of the "empire" the Academy was to exercise over letters. The speeches of the period are very different from today's speeches. When a new member is inducted today, her/his purpose is to extoll her/his predecessor. This was not the case in the seventeenth century. The speeches were somewhat formulaic, with the predecessor's outstanding qualities figuring as only one element of the formula. The newly-elected academician stressed why he was not worthy to belong, then gave a history of the illustrious group to prove his point, a narrative that included much praise for the founder. Each speech thus provided a portrait of the institution, with the accomplishments of individual members only briefly evoked.

The definitions and functions of the Academy as expressed in the speeches vary immensely as the century progresses. In 1640, for example, M. Patru specifies that this illustrious group to which he belongs is composed of "ces grands ouvriers qui travaillent tous les jours à l'exhaltation de la France"[129] (these great laborors who work every day for the glory of France). In 1643, M. de Besons values the Academy as the place where one "pouvait rencontrer les règles assurées" (I, 7) (can encounter the accepted rules). A year later M. Salomon reinforces his colleague, praising the Academy as "l'abrégé et le receuil de tout ce que la raison peut produire d'excellent et d'achevé quand elle est rectifiée par une méditation bien réglée, et qui a le plus purement découvert les règles que le bon sens doit tenir" (I, 10) (the condensation and receptacle of everything that is excellent and accomplished produced when reason is corrected by a carefully regulated meditation, and that has the most purely discovered the rules that *bon sens* must maintain). Salomon's use of the superlative here—"the most purely"—introduces a note of competition. As we have seen, the Academy was not the only group engaged in advancing literary and linguistic preceptes.[130] This sense of opposition between the Academy and other rule makers will surface again.

In his acceptance speech of 1647, Pierre Corneille acknowledges the Academy as the ultimate arbiter of value: "vous savez si exactement discerner le prix et le rang de toutes les choses" (I, 25) (you know how exactly to discern the merit and rank of everything). He views the Academy as having been founded by Richelieu to purify the French language so that it could then be used as a political tool of subordination: "Richelieu [a confié] à vos soins la pureté d'une langue qu'il voulait faire entendre, et dominer par toute l'Europe" (I, 19) (Richelieu [confided] to your care the purity of a language that he wanted to make understandable and dominant throughout Europe). It is important to note here that when the dictionary project comes up in these early speeches, the purpose is defined above all as one of refinement. The political function of the refinement is expressed only in vague terms. This conforms to Chapelain's original formulation of the Academy's purposes in the founding statutes for the Academy. He views the Academy's function as to "rendre la langue capable de la dernière éloquence ... Il fallait dresser un dictionnaire qui fut comme le trésor et comme le magasin des termes simples, et des phrases reçues"[131] (make the language as eloquent as possible ... A dictionary had to be created that would be the treasury and the repository of simple words and accepted phrases).

The rhetoric of self-definition in the speeches of the 1650s contains a surprising adversarial tone. It is as though the Academicians felt compelled to define their institution in opposition to a rival group perceived as having equal power in the same domain of letters. Phrases incorporating the comparative and superlative modes abound. In 1651, for example, l'Abbé Tallemant clearly opposes the Academy to its worldly counterpart:

> C'est ici où les savants deviennent polis, et où les polis deviennent savants, où l'on apprend à penser, et à dire, et où les moeurs se forment aussi bien que le langage ... le bon goût, la pureté, et les beautés véritables qui ne se trouvent point ailleurs que parmi vous. (I, 56–8)

> (This is where learned people become polite, and polite people become learned, where one learns to think and speak, and where customs as well as language are formed ... good taste, purity, and true beauty are only found among you.)

"Good taste" is an obvious reference to the salons, the foyers of good taste. Tallemant's attempt to affirm that true beauty can only be found in the confines of the Academy underscores the power of the rival legitimizing space. As the century advances, the implicit and occasionally explicit comparisons with other recognized forms of beauty, purety, good sense, and reason become more prevelant in the speeches, as the Academicians strive not only to define the Academy, but to do so in opposition to other such bodies, subtly discrediting them in the process. In 1661, the rhetoric of the speeches seems to declare the battle over false authorities won. M. Cassagnes portrays a worldly consensus acknowledging the Academy's authority: "Qui ne voit maintenant que votre estime est toujours suivie de l'estime publique, et que vous êtes les maîtres de la réputation" (I, 133) (Who doesn't now recognize that your esteem is always followed by public esteem, and that you are the masters of reputations). To make the group he is opposing even clearer he continues:

Je me déclare contre cette erreur vulgaire, qui persuade à tant de gens qu'il n'y a point de règles, ... et que si on veut exprimer heureusement ses pensées ... on n'a qu'à laisser faire son esprit. (I, 136)

(I declare myself against this vulgar mistake that persuades so many people that there are no rules ... and that to express thoughts well, one only has to rely on *esprit.*)

In defining the Academy, these initiates like Cassagnes usurp the position and rhetoric associated with the *mondains* and in particular with the salons. M. le Clerc in 1662 declares the Academicians "les justes et fidèles arbitres de tout ce que la science, l'art et la politesse peuvent produire de délicat, de fort, et de magnifique" (I, 150) (the just and faithful arbiters of everything that knowledge, art, and civility can produce that is delicate, strong, and magnificent). The choice of these terms—"arbiters," "civility," "délicate"—are not arbitrary, for they are the same ones associated with the salons and the *précieuses*. Here the terms are appropriated by the state-sanctioned and legitimiziing body in an effort to disenfranchise worldly institutions from arbitrating literary value and establishing standards. It is also not coincidental that this type of rhetoric appears particularly in the speeches of the 1650s and 1660s, precisely the moment when the salons were both recognized as influential arbiters and under attack by the satirical and censuring pens of the critics of the salons and the worldly public's influence on literature and language.

By the 1670s, the usurpation of the *mondains'* position as arbiters of good taste and *esprit* seems complete according to the speeches. Tallemant le Jeune in 1675 severs *politesse* from the worldly salon milieu with which it had been associated and in fact rewrites cultural history to attribute this civilizing process uniquely to the Academy:

Demandez quelle est la cause de la politesse du langage et des moeurs ... toute cette pureté de langage qui est répandu dans les écrits des particuliers, et cette justesse de style qui est presque universelle dans le royaume sont venues, insensiblement des conférences de l'Académie. (I, 445)

(Ask what is the cause of the politeness of language and customs ... all this purity in the language that has spread to the writings of individuals, and this stylistic precision which is almost universal in the kingdom, came from the Academy's meetings.)

He concludes by stating that "c'est elle [the Academy] qui ... a formé le goût, et donné de l'esprit presque à tout le monde" (I, 445) (the [Academy] established taste and gave *esprit* to almost everyone). In an even more surprising appropriation of salon and worldly values, he establishes *galanterie* as the force at the heart of the Academy's effectiveness: "nous trouvons parmi nous de la galanterie, et c'est ce mélange heureux, qui fait la douceur et l'utilité de nos assemblées" (I, 443) (We find gallantry in our midst, and it is this fortunate combination that creates the pleasure and usefulness of our assemblies). One is reminded of Huet's identification of *galanterie* as one of the distinguishing characteristics of French culture. But in the case of Huet, "gallantry" maintains its first connotation, that is, as the commerce of men and women. Huet specifically noted that it developed because of the "liberty" with which women associated with men in French society. In the case of the Academy, however, the definition of gallantry is as devoid of women as the Academy itself. One is left to wonder what indeed Tallemant understands by the term. His valorization of gallantry like his identification of taste and *politesse* with the Academy, however, underscore the extent to which these values were recognized as desirable traits and thus needed to be associated with the official legitimizing body, the Academy, as opposed to the worldly salon society that gave birth to them and first defined them.

Various critics have maintained that by the 1670s, the modernist faction of the Academy was gaining ground over the *doctes* and indeed that worldly language was infiltrating the dictionary project of the Academy itself. According to Antoine Adam, for example, the "Moderns" triumph over the grammarians and assert that the French language had reached its point of perfection, due in large measure to the civilizing influence of *honnêtes gens*. Adam recounts how the first edition of the dictionary, which appeared in 1692, "had so many scandalous mistakes that even the academicians themselves were ashamed of it, prohibited its circulation, and quickly proceeded to republish it" precisely because the "grammarians" had been defeated in favor of worldly usage.[132] Critics such as Adam and more recently Marc Fumaroli, thus acknowledge the influence of the worldly public on language usage, but fail to account for the appropriation by the Academy of the same values of this worldly public and their attribution uniquely to the French Academy. The Academicians viewed as belonging to both camps, the Ancients and the Moderns alike, co-opt taste in particular, as well as *bon sens* and other worldly values and trace their origins to the Academy, thus seeking to elide the institution most identified with these values, the salon, from the legitimizing institution and discourse of the nation.

Why was it so important for the Academy to portray itself as the sole institution endowed with the right to control language, legitimize taste, and define *esprit*? As the century progresses, again looking solely at the rhetoric of these speeches—which project a totally unified front despite our own knowledge of the internal strife—one perceives how the academicians recognized the importance of this control. The Academy becomes more and more closely associated with Louis's political agenda. The concept of language as an arm of government and a reflection of its strength was even more the case when Bouhours was writing in the 1670s than when Buffet composed her text in 1668. At precisely the time Bouhours published *Les Entretiens*, Louis XIV was taking the French Academy under his wing.[133] This shift in function—from purifying the French language and establishing standards to glorifying the reigning monarch—reflects a crucial change in the historical contextualization and status of the Academy. In 1672, Louis XIV actually took over as the protector of the Academy, upon the death of Séguier. This change in protectors was accompanied by a change in the actual location of the group's assemblies. Until 1672, the Academy had always met in a *hôtel particulier* (private mansion) primarily at Conrart's, and then Séguier's. When Louis XIV took over this function, the Academy was moved to the Louvre. In a speech in recognition of Louis's supposed generosity, Charpentier, spokesperson for the group, emphasized the uniqueness and the significance of the move:

> Mais qu'un Roi ait assez aimé les lettres, pour loger une Académie dans sa propre maison; c'est ce que la posterité n'apprendra guère que parmi les actions de Louis le Grand. Il ne se contente pas de nous attacher à sa protection toute puissante, il veut nous attacher à titre de domestiques. Il veut que la majesté royale et les belles lettres n'aient qu'un même palais. (I, 350)

> (But that a King loved letters enough to lodge an Academy in his own home; this is what posterity will only see in Louis le Grand's actions. He is not satisfied with granting us his all powerful protection, he wants to attach us to him as servants. He wants royal majesty and the literary realm to have the same palace.)

Charpentier's use of the term "servants" to describe the Academicians under Louis's protectorate is particularly apt and correctly expresses the function of the Academy after 1672 as formulated in the speeches. According to the speeches, Louis not only wanted the "royal majesty" and "the literary realm" to have the same home, he wanted letters and majesty to become fused, with letters reifying and promoting majesty. From 1671, the transitional year, the speeches reflect this altered vision of the Academy's purpose and function.

Even the history of the group is rewritten to express this symbiotic relationship with the monarchy. In the formulations of the latter part of the century, the Academy is depicted as having been born out of Richelieu's desire for his own immortality. In 1670, for example, Quinault explains that the Academy "fut l'ouvrage de l'admirable cardinal de Richelieu, qui la voulut établir comme la dépositaire de l'immortalité qu'il avait si bien mérité" (I, 176) (was the work of the admirable Cardinal de Richelieu, who wanted it to be the repository of the immortality he so merited). From a body running parallel to the monarchy the Academy becomes portrayed as a very limb of the monarchy. Letters become a weapon to fight the battle against erasure from history. In his historization of the Academy, Perrault attributes this same goal to its founder. In his words, Richelieu considered the creation of the Academy as "celle de ses actions qui conserverait la gloire de toutes les autres. Il savait que les louanges de la Cour et les acclamations du peuple ne laissent aucune trace après elle" (I, 282) (the action that would conserve the glory of all his other [actions]. He knew that the praises of the court and the people's acclamations do not leave any trace). The explanation of the assembly's principal project, the dictionary, is also imbued with a rhetoric of immortality.

> Et parce que le temps altère toutes choses, [Richelieu] souhaita par un effort de sa prudence, que la Compagnie s'occupat sans relache à polir notre langue et à la fixer autant qu'il se pouvait, pour empêcher de vieillir les ouvrages de son temps. (I, 282–3)

> (And because time alters everything, [Richelieu] prudently wished that the company be constantly occupied in polishing and stablizing our language as much as it could, in order to prohibit the works of his time from aging.)

This formulation of the purposes underlying the dictionary does not appear in the speeches predating 1671. The Academy's role as defined here is to reflect Louis's glory back to him and to ensure his renown for centuries to come. In his response to La Fontaine, the Abbé de la Chambre ennumerates the functions of the Academy: "travailler pour la gloire du Prince, consacrer uniquement toutes ces veilles à son honneur, ne se proposer point d'autre but que l'éternité de son nom, rapporter là toutes ses études; voilà l'âme et la vie de nos exercices. Voilà ce qui nous distingue de tous les autres gens de lettres" (II, 111) (Work for the glory of the Prince, dedicate all its work to his honor, to have as its sole purpose the eternity of his name, to dedicate all its studies to this; this is the soul and life of our work. This is what distinguishes us from all other people of letters).

This immortality can only be ensured if control over language is seized. Towards the end of the century, the dictionary becomes the principal preoccupation, as it finally nears completion after almost forty years of work. This intellectual monument is to be valued above all as a major weapon in Louis's arsenal, for it is created not only to purify the French language, as we saw earlier, but to ensure that Louis's renown will live on forever. By means of the dictionary, the Academy takes control over language and impedes it from changing. Their works, and others, dedicated to the glory of Louis XIV will thus be understood by the following generations. In 1693, M. Bergeret explains the dictionary project as an effort to:

> fixer le langage que nous parlons aujourd'hui et l'empêcher de vieillir. Ce serait avoir servi utilement l'église et l'état, si avec le secours du Dictionnaire ... la langue n'était plus sujette à changer, et si les grandes actions du Roy qui pour être trop grandes, perdent beaucoup de leur éclat par la faiblesse de l'expression, n'en perdaient plus rien dans la suite par le changement du language. (II, 403)

> (stabilize the language we speak today and impede it from aging. [To do this] would be to have served the church and state usefully, if with the aid of the Dictionary, the language was no longer subject to change and if the King's great actions, which because they are so great lose this brilliance by the weakness of expression, did not lose more later because language had changed.)

Following the logic expressed here, to compose a dictionary is the best thing these "servants" can do, for by controlling language and establishing standards, they ensure the monarch's immortality through writing. Given this context, it is easy to understand why the Academy impeded the publication of Furetière's dictionary which was ready in 1685, nine years before the Academy's magnun opus.[134] The arbiters of language had to be those officially sanctioned, in this case protected, by the subject of discourse. The empire of the Academy and Louis XIV's empire embody the same notion of power, as each strives to immortalize the monarch. In what appears to be a moment of linguistic liberation, M. de la Chapelle declares in 1695 "N'en doutons donc plus, et ne craignons plus de le dire; l'Académie est comme le gage et le sceau de l'immortalité au nom français. Sa fortune a marché d'un pas égal avec celle de la monarchie" (III, 17) (Let us doubt this no longer, and no longer fear to say it; the Academy is like the guarantee and the seal of immortality for the French name. Its fortune has followed that of the King's step by step).

By defining and stabilizing the French language, the Academy will render their monarch immortal. The academic linguists become subordinate within the royal household. Language is not merely for self-expression. It serves an overtly political function. The clear link between language and monarchical power explains in large part why the question of who controls language is so essential. Salons can be seen as rival homes for linguistic precepts and literary values without royally sanctioned "servants."

By the 1670s, the relationship between the Academy and political power becomes clearer and more elaborated upon in the rhetoric of the speeches. Instead of praising fellow Academicians for their ability to establish standards, the emphasis is placed on the function of the Academy in the political realm. In 1670, the abbé de Montigny states that Richelieu's founding of the Academy was "le chef-d'oeuvre de sa politique" (I, 181) (his political masterpiece). The Academicians begin to portray the Academy as a microcosm of monarchy, a body expressing the same notion of "political" as the government. Quinault in 1670 explicitly draws this parallel:

> Il en est du Royaume des lettres ainsi que des autres Empires; il y doit avoir de la subordination, et l'harmonie ne s'y trouverait jamais parfaite si tous les génies s'y rencontraient également élevés. (I, 176)

> (The same is true in the kingdom of letters as in other empires; subordination must exist, and harmony will never be perfect there if all geniuses are equally exalted.)

Quinault thus justifies the "empire" exercised by the French Academy. They, like the monarch of any empire, possess the power to dominate.

Like Richelieu, Louis XIV and his ministers recognized the power inherent in literary culture and language itself, and sought to harness this power for their political interests. Like many before him, Bossuet in fact fuses the intellectual and military battlegrounds when he explains the birth of the French Academy in his acceptance speech of 1671:

> [Richelieu] entreprit de faire en sorte que la France ... fut en même temps docte et conquerante, qu'elle ajoutait l'empire des lettres à l'avantage glorieux qu'elle avait toujours conservé de commander par les armes. Et certainement, Messieurs, ces deux choses se fortifient et se soutiennent mutuellement. (I, 268)

> ([Richelieu] tried to make France scholarly and conquering ... [he wanted it] to add the empire of letters to the glorious advantage it had always had to

command by weapons. And certainly, Sirs, these two things mutually strengthen and uphold each other.)

Later, in his acceptance speech of 1693, the abbé Bignon characterizes the illustrious group he is joining as "cette élite de savants, nouveaux héros de l'empire des lettres" (II, 409) (this elite of learned people, the new heros of the empire of letters). Through his use of a warlike rhetoric, Bignon echoes and reinforces the discourse of many of his fellow Academicians who also endow the Academy with a power equal to or even surpassing military power. Bignon's and Bossuet's uses of "empire" to qualify the intellectual world as epitomized by the Academy reflect the two principal meanings ascribed to the term. In the first instance, "empire" is the equivalent of "monarchy," thus corresponding to Furetière's first definition: "Monarchie, étendue de pays où quelqu'un commande" (Monarchy, the expanse of land that someone rules). Bossuet's usage corresponds to Furetière's explanation of the term in its figurative sense: "se dit figurément en morale, de la domination, du pouvoir qu'on a sur quelque chose" (is said figuratively of the domination, the power, one has over something). Heterogeneity of thought and views could only present a threat to this effort to control. By having the Academy legitimized as the ultimate arbiters of taste and literature, Louis could appropriate such cultural values as tools for his empire. The Academy serves as a mirror of monarchy, and these Academicians are the monarchs of letters in Louis's image. In 1684, La Fontaine subserviently bows to this defeat of the public, as he glorifies the Academy:

> Il ne faut pas s'étonner si vous exercez une autorité souveraine dans la république des lettres; quelques applaudissements que les plus heureuses productions de l'esprit ayent remportées, on ne s'assure point de leur prix, si votre approbation ne confirme celle du public ... en France, le peuple ne juge point après vous; il se soumet sans réplique à vos sentiments. Cette juridiction si respectée, c'est votre mérite qui l'a établie. Ce sont les ouvrages que vous donnez au public, et qui sont autant de parfaits modèles pour tous les genres d'écrire, pour tous les styles. (II, 102)

> (It is not surprising that you exercise such absolute authority in the republic of letters; whatever applause the best works receive, their worth is not assured if your approbation does not confirm the public's ... in France, the people do not judge after you they submit themselves without a word to your opinion. This jurisdiction that is so respected was established because of your merit. It is due to the works that you give to the public, and that are perfect models of all genres, for all styles.)

"The people" as judges are silenced, or at least that is the desire expressed in the writings of the Academicians. Moreover, given that novels do not enter into the Academy's purvue, that genre, like other worldly compositions, is eradicted from the official literary scene, as the Academy does not offer any "models" to be followed.

The speeches at the end of the century are imbued with a clear sense of having won a battle, not over ignorance but over undesirable influences and standards. These speeches seem to look back and historicize this battle and subsequent victory. In 1693, L'abbé de Fénelon states:

> Ainsi on ne donne plus le nom d'esprit à une imagination éblouissante; on le réserve pour un génie réglé et correct qui tourne tout en sentiment, et qui suit pas à pas la nature toujours simple et gracieuse, qui ramène toutes les pensées aux principes de la raison, et qui ne trouve beau que ce qui est véritable ... le vrai sublime dédaignant tous les ornements empruntés, ne se trouve que dans le simple. (II, 390)

> (Thus we no longer give the name *esprit* to an outstanding imagination. We reserve it for a genius that is regulated and correct and that comes from feeling, and that follows simple and gracious nature step by step, that reduces all thoughts to the principles of reason and that finds beautiful only that which is true ... the true sublime disregards any borrowed ornaments and is found only in the simple.)

Esprit is redefined according to the Academy's standards. One Academician in particular is portrayed as the finest warrior in this battle over literary influence and power: Boileau. In his acceptance speech of 1694, Boileau pronounces the Academy "les arbitres souveraines de l'eloquence" (II, 487) (the sovereign arbiters of eloquence). At the beginning of the eighteenth century, Boileau is praised for having reinstated taste into a chaotic literary world. This adoption of Boileau as a kind of "father of the Academy" is indicative of the direction and function the Academy had taken, especially with respect to the worldly public and women. The history the abbé d'Estrées creates regarding Boileau's influence is striking, given the relationship we have seen many contemporaries establish between women and taste. Speaking of the illustrious Boileau he is replacing, d'Estrées states in 1711:

> C'est par lui qu'on a vu renaître dans la composition ce goût exquis qui s'était presque perdu. Il fallait instruire, détromper, détruire les préjugés, rectifier les idées sur le style, sur l'éloquence, sur la poésie, donner des précautions

contre la contagion du faux bel esprit qui s'était répandue dans la République des lettres. (III, 485)

(It is through him that exquisite taste, which was almost lost, was reborn in writing. It was necessary to teach, enlighten, destroy established ideas, correct ideas on style, eloquence, poetry, caution against the false *bel esprit* that had spread throughout the Republic of letters.)

Il ôta le voile de dessus les yeux du public, qui commença à se savoir mauvais gré ... de s'être laissé éblouir par de fausses lueurs, et d'avoir admiré l'esprit destitué de bon sens. (III, 486)[135]

(He took the veil off the public's eyes, which had begun to regret ... having let itself be blinded by false light and having admired *esprit* divorced from *bon sens*.)

In the end, Boileau, perfect representative of the Academy's ideals, was "pour l'établissement du bon goût dans la litterature" (III, 486) (for the establishment of good taste in literature) but a *bon goût* decidedly different from that attributed to women by Lambert and others. This set of standards and notions of taste and judgment are the legacies the Academy sought to impose and judged to be its overall purpose during those influential years. The immortality of these goals, like that attributed to the dictionary, is an obsession in these speeches, as the Academy seeks to control the literary culture of their day and the history of that culture for the future. Embedded in this constructed history is the exclusion of origins and influences, the erasure of other voices, in particular those of the *mondains* and women. Perrault proved to be an accurate fortune teller when he predicted this silencing in his own speech of 1671, saying "je sais que vous êtes les véritables dispensateurs de la gloire ... car, Messieurs, je suis persuadé que la posterité éloignée ne parlera que de vous, ou de ceux dont vous avez parlé" (I, 281) (I know you are the true dispensers of glory, for Sirs, I'm persuaded that posterity will only speak of you or of those you spoke about). In the history of the social legitimization of literary and cultural practices in general, we have only spoken seriously of this particular group. These speeches of the Academy are the first example of a cultural history that has been constructed to eliminate the salon, especially its female members, as cultural institutions of serious consequence. The reaction against the salons and the worldly public, so well documented that it has become canonized, is legitimized in these speeches, even as their influence subtly surfaces.

The debates over taste, its definition and ownership, and the efforts evident in these academic speeches to redefine taste in order to exclude the worldly public illustrate the threat perceived in worldly standards. Such methods of evaluation could in fact lead to the acceptance of questionable works, even the novels of which the worldly public was so enamored and that Boileau worked so hard to condemn.[136] In an effort to rid the literary field of worldly influence, Boileau exorted his fellow Academicians in 1698: "Cherchons ce qui est vrai, ce qu'un lecteur froid approuve, ce que les reflexions des siècles à venir ne démentiront point" (III, 124) (Let us seek what is true, what a cold reader can approve, what the reflections of centuries to come will not prove wrong). Boileau's "cold reader," would readily reject the literary practices of the worldly public, as opposed to the "warm" worldly reader who relies on sentiment and taste to judge and create these works. As we shall see, Boileau was perhaps justified in fearing the literary processes emanating from the salons, for their influences were designed to extend far beyond the pages of a book and alter the very fabric of society.[137]

Notes

1   Pierre-Daniel Huet, *Traité de Pierre-Daniel Huet sur l'Origine des romans*, 1669; ed. Fabienne Gégou (Paris, 1971), p. 139.

2   Ibid., p. 139.

3   In her illuminating and comprehensive study of the relationship between women and culture in early modern France, Linda Timmermans explores in depth the roles salon women played as aribiters of literary productions, as writers, and as cultural forces from 1598-1715. Timmermans provides a wealth of information drawn from contemporary sources. In my discussion of the role of women in the *champs littéraire*, I will often have occasion to draw upon Timmermans's insights. My own perspective is similar to hers, in that I also view women as having exercised a large influence on the seventeenth-century literary field. My perspective on these questions differs in part in that I am examining them in light of a burgeoning sense of French collective identity. Linda Timmermans, *L'accès des femmes à la culture (1598-1715)* (Paris, 1993). See in particular Chapter 2, "Le Débat sur le rôle des femmes dans la vie littéraire," pp. 133–76.

4   M. de Vigneul-Marville (Argonne), *Mélanges d'histoire et de littérature*, 3 vols (Rotterdam, 1702), I, p. 156.

5   Jacques Du Bosc, *L'honneste femme*, as cited by Ian Maclean, *Woman Triumphant*, p. 149.

6   As cited by Gustave Reynier, *La Femme au XVIIe siècle* (Paris, 1929), p. 20. Régnier is one of a few historians who attribute much importance to women's influence on literature during the period. See in particular pp. 17–20. He does not limit their arbitrage to worldly genres, stating that "there is not a genre, even the most austere, that does not fall within the jurisdiction of the salon. It is their votes that assure the success of treatises on morality as well as comedies" (p. 67).

7   According to Roger Chartier, aristocratic and bourgeois women actually had a higher
    literacy rate than men during this period.

8   It should be remembered that the seventeenth century witnessed the creation of the French
    Academy by Richelieu, a state-sponsored institution whose purpose was to set standards
    for literature and especially to produce a dictionary of the French language. Even in 1635
    Richelieu recognized the political power of language. Louis XIV will further develop this
    relationship. We will return to the Academy at the end of this chapter.

9   Rambouillet's *ruelle* was called the *chambre bleue* because of its blue walls.

10 See Timmermans pp. 71–9 for a discussion of the importance of the salons of des Loges
    and d'Auchy. We will return later to possible explanations of why these two salons have
    been overshadowed by that of the marquise de Rambouillet.

11 Roger Picard, *Les Salons littéraires et la société française* among others. By identifying
    the principal period of influence as long before Molière's arrival in Paris, scholars such
    as Picard shield Rambouillet from Molière's satire. I will return to the reasons for the
    creation of this particular myth, and others like it, in Chapter 3.

12 Timmermans, p. 77.

13 As Alain Viala remarks of the salon de Rambouillet, "It is simple ... all well-known writers
    of the first half of the century ... tried to obtain from this group a kind of acknowledgement
    of their literary merit." As cited by Timmermans, p. 77.

14 *Discours de l'Académie Française*, vol. 3, p. 11. Roger Picard states that the salon de
    Rambouillet was "another Academy which for a time was no less influential than the
    official [one] and whose literary judgments were no less awaited and followed than those
    of the forty." *Les Salons littéraires*, p. 52. Picard, however, identifies the poet Voiture, not
    the marquise herself, as the motivating force behind the intellectual qualities associated
    with the *ruelle*.

15 Chapelain also frequented Marie de Gournay's salon between 1625 and 1635. I wish to
    thank Allison Stedman for this precision.

16 See Christian Jouhaud's illuminating study of Chapelain in his *Les Pouvoirs de la
    littérature: Histoire d'un paradoxe* (Paris, 2000). It is important to note that much of what
    we know about the salons is derived from such correspondances as well as memoirs from
    the period, in addition to the satires and derogatory portraits of salon critics from the mid
    century on. Salon organizers such as the marquise de Rambouillet did not keep records
    of what happened. Much of the historical documentation regarding Scudéry's salon that
    was composed by her friend Pellisson was lost in a fire. We thus do not have the sources
    traditionally associated with "historical truth" when it comes to the salon movement and
    must derive our portrait from less officially-sanctioned and traditional sources. This is one
    reason why the image of the salon has been so easy to manipulate.

17 Correspondance de Chapelain from *Documents Inédits sur l'Histoire de France*. éd. Ph.
    Tamizey de Larroque (Paris, 1983), vol. 222, pp. 148–9.

18 Ibid., vol. 221, pp. 149 p. 209.

19 Ibid., vol. 221, pp. 215–16.

20 In characterizing the *chambre bleue* as a space that banned pedantry, Chapelain was
    appealing to Balzac's traditional vision of women's place. In response to this letter, the
    editor of Chapelain's correspondance notes that Balzac composed a letter in which he
    denounced women who would pretend to traditional knowledge: "Il y a longtemps que
    je me suis déclaré contre cette pédanterie de l'autre sexe, et que j'ai dit que je souffrirais
    plus volontiers une femme qui a de la barbe qu'une femme qui fait la savante ... Tout de
    bon si j'étais modérateur de la police, j'enverrais filer toutes les femmes qui veulent

faire des livres" (Long ago I declared myself against this pedantry of the other sex, and I said I would rather suffer a woman with a beard than one who pretended to be learned ... if I governed the police, I would get rid of all women who want to write books). vol. 221, pp. 215–16.

21   Letter of 2 october 1638 to Balzac, vol. 221, p. 298.

22   Chapelain, vol. 221, pp. 462–3.

23   *Esprit* is a very difficult word to translate. According to the Robert Historique, from the twelfth century it has been used to designate "le principe de la vie intellectuelle, l'intelligence" (the concept of intellectual life, of intelligence). In the seventeenth century, the expression "bon esprit" refers to the "aptitude à juger sainement" (the ability to judge properly). Also in the seventeenth, "bel esprit" refers to a cultured person, but by the eighteenth century this term was used pejoratively. It can thus be translated, for example, as "mind," "intelligence," "intellect," "thought," "a cultured person." Given all these valences, I prefer to leave the term in French.

24   In fact, to judge by the dates, Chapelain was doing both simultaneously.

25   In *Le Parnasse galant*, Delphine Denis examines the creation of this worldly public that she characterizes above all as "galant." She examines the salons in particular as foyers of literary creation founded upon the new values of *galanterie*. Denis does not focus on the relationship between this public and the literary world at large, as I am advancing here. See her discussion of the salons and collective writing, pp. 153 and following. *Le Parnasse galant: institution d'une catégorie littéraire au XVIIe siècle* (Paris, 2001). In a similar vein, Myriam Maître discusses the relationship between women and literary criticism, but separates them from the literary milieu as a whole. Maître does not allow the *précieuses* a definitive influence on the entire literary field. *Les Précieuses*, pp. 275 and following.

26   Alain Viala, *La Naissance de l'écrivain* (Paris, 1985), pp. 150–51.

27   Ibid., p. 151. Viala, however, does not go so far as to put this new public on a par with the literary authority of the *doctes* and the Academy.

28   Georges Mongrédien gives an estimate of sixty-two. As cited in Aronson, *Rambouillet*, p. 30.

29   As cited by Roger Picard, *Les Salons littéraires*, p. 62.

30   See Timmermans for a detailed discussion of the salons that made up this second phase of salon life, pp. 95–111.

31   Roger Picard remarks that "Mlle de Scudéry's salon was less aristocratic and more literary than Mme de Rambouillet's ... it was above all a literary gathering." *Les Salons littéraires*, pp. 77 and 79.

32   Picard, *les Salons littéraires*, p. 101.

33   Of Ninon de Lenclos's salon Mongrédien states: "Her salon on the rue de Tournelles is more than a *précieuse ruelle*; it is an intellectual gathering that shines above an unconformist society. All those who frequent it learn to think correctly and freely." *Les Précieux et les précieuses* (Paris, 1963), p. 145.

34   Cited by Antoine Adam, *Histoire de la litterature francaise au XVIIe siècle* (Paris, 1948), vol. 1, p. 273. Adam elevates Sablé above all her female contemporaries, with the exception of the marquise de Rambouillet. In his words: "But of all the female figures around Mme de Rambouillet, the most striking, the one who deserves a place in literary history is the marquise de Sablé ... she has a great soul and a lively intelligence. She even has something virile about her. Politics is a real passion for her ... She was interested in literature" (pp. 272–3). Roger Picard also extolls the intelligence of Mme de Sablé, whose reputation has fallen into oblivion today. For Picard, Sablé is responsible for some of the

literary genres that are unique to France, especially maxims: "A new literary genre was born, enriching this literature so particular to our country, that of essayists and moralists. It is Mme de Sablé who inspired this movement and awakened La Rochefoucauld's genius." *Les Salons littéraires*, p. 113. As is often the case in Picard's descriptions of the salons, women's roles are primarily to inspire male writers. He does not mention, for example, Sablé's own maxims. Adam praises Mme de Sablé: "She had great influence ... An inspiration for writers, an authority in literary circles, she played many roles. She inspired the taste for detailed analyses of emotions. The taste for portraits and maxims also came from her" (vol. I, pp. 272–3). Actually, Mlle de Montpensier is usually identified as the creator of the written portrait genre.

35 Timmermans, p. 108.

36 As Timmermans states, "No more than Mme de Lafayette, Mlle de Scudéry never hesitated to give her opinion of works being debated." *L'accès des femmes*, p. 114.

37 Ian Maclean, *Woman Triumphant 1610–1652* (Oxford, 1977), p. 149.

38 Alain Viala disputes Furetière's assessment, stating that "[Furetière] excessively valorizes the salon de Rambouillet by making it the point of perfection of the art of literature ... he gives the salons a place that is equal to the academies because they are, in the decade 1650–1660 very active and capable of opening the door to success." *La Naissance de l'écrivain*, p. 155.

39 Historians have had a tendency, when they even acknowledge the literary importance of the salons, to attribute this interest to the association of a man of letters to a particular salon. Voiture, for example, is viewed as the motivating literary force behind the *chambre bleue*. Segrais is said to have inspired Montpensier, La Fontaine is the major influence at La Sablière's salon, La Rochefoucauld inspired Mme de Sablé, and Segrais, Huet, and La Rochefoucauld dominated Lafayette and were responsible for the quality of her works. See for example, Picard's discussion pp. 106 and following. While male writers did indeed frequent the salons, their participation should not overshadow women's own literary endeavors, interests, and abilities in our reconstruction of the salon milieu.

40 For an interesting reading of Montpensier's literary importance, see Juliette Cherbuliez, "Performing Print, Forming Print: Montpensier and the Politics of Elite Textual Production" in *Actes de Dartmouth*. Patricia Cholakian has contributed a lot to our knowledge of Montpensier. See in particular her *Women and the Politics of Self-Representation*. She has recently edited an edition of Montpensier's *Histoire de Jeanne Lambert d'Herbigny, marquise de Fouquesolles* (Delmar, New York, 1999).

41 Mme d'Auchy's salon at the beginning of the century was also considered to be primarily intellectual. She, however, was not a writer herself, a fact that distinguishes her version of the salon from that of her successors such as Lafayette and Scudéry.

42 Roger Picard, *Les Salons littéraires*, p. 136.

43 Picard, pp. 136 and 139.

44 As cited by Roger Lathuillère, *La Préciosité: Etude historique et linguistique* (Geneva, 1969), p. 655. Abbé Michel de Pure, author of *La Précieuse ou le mystère des ruelles*, was a critic of this *monde à l'envers*.

45 De Villars, *Entretiens*, as cited by Hubert Gillot, *La Querelle des Anciens et des Modernes en France* (Paris, 1914), p. 362.

46 This collaboration is especially apparent in correspondences, such as those between Chapelain and Balzac or Scudéry and Huet.

47 For a discussion of what Joan DeJean has termed salon writing, see her *Tender Geographies*, pp. 22 and 43 especially.

48   For an in-depth analysis of the role of conversation during the period, see Elizabeth
     Goldsmith, *Exclusive Conversations* (Philadelphia. 1988). The two primary critical
     works in the quarrel over *La Princesse de Clèves*, for example, Jean-Baptiste Trousset de
     Valincour's *Lettres à Madame la Marquise de * * * sur le sujet de la Princesse de Clèves*,
     and Jean Antoine de Charnes's *Conversations sur la critique de la Princesse de Clèves*
     both use the salon milieu as the setting for their debates. Bouhours's *Entretiens d'Ariste
     et d'Eugène* (1671) and Perrault's *Parallèle des Anciens et des Modernes* (1692) are also
     examples of the conversational form adopted for criticism.
49   The example chosen by the Academy to illustrate the relationship between taste and literary
     judgment, however, casts doubt upon the importance and seriousness of this role. The
     dictionary cites Molière's imposter poet, Mascarille, in *Les Précieuses Ridicules* when
     he compliments Magdelon and Cathos for their tasteful appreciation of his sonnet, saying
     "Vous avez le goût bon" (You have good taste). As shall become apparent, by the end of the
     century, when the dictionary first appeared, *goût* had already undergone a transformation
     as critics such as the Academy tried to combat worldly influence on the literary field.
50   In her important study of the *précieuses*, Myriam Maître discusses the association
     contemporaries made between the *précieuses* and literary arbitration, and especially the
     rejection of traditional scholastic rules. I would extend her observations to include the entire
     worldly milieu, as opposed to simply the female *précieuses*. See in particular pp. 244 and
     following and pp. 275 and following. Timmerman remarks that "women played a role in
     the devalorization of scholarly culture." *L'Accès des femmes au savoir*, p. 70. She explores
     the role of literature in worldly culture, pp. 94 and following.
51   Gabriel Guéret, *La Guerre des Auteurs anciens et modernes*, 1671 in *Les Auteurs en belle
     humeur* (Amsterdam, 1723), p. 21.
52   Charles Perrault, *Le Parallèle des Anciens et des Modernes*, 1692; ed. Hans Robert Jauss
     (Munich, 1964), p. 3.
53   Ibid., p. 30.
54   Ibid., pp. 31–32.
55   Anne-Thérèse de Lambert, *Réflexions sur le goût*, in *Oeuvres* (Paris, 1748), vol. I, p. 141.
     All references will be to this edition, with page numbers inserted paranthetically in the
     text.
56   I will analyse in depth this criterion of pleasure in Chapter 2.
57   Perrault, *Parallèle des anciens et des moderns*, Preface.
58   Ibid., 1er Dialogue, pp. 40–41.
59   Hubert Gillot, *La Querelle*, p. 344.
60   Adam explains "the importance of this new form of criticism created by the *précieuses*. If
     they give no motive for their judgments, it's because they believe in the immediate effect
     of taste. So much so that here again, as in the domain of oral ideas, one perceives that they
     fashioned the last generation of the seventeenth century and the decisive step that liberated
     esprit classique from the servitude of pedantry must be attributed to them. There was an
     act of faith in pure reason or in the excellence of the nature of *esprit*, that rendered the
     traditional teachings of dogma unnecessary ... The *Précieuses* thus established themselves
     as the adversaries of *pédants* (scholars)." Antoine Adam, *Histoire de la littérature française
     au XVIIe siècle*, vol. II, p. 30.
61   Letter to the comtesse de Guitaut, 3 June 1693, as cited by Marcil Hervier, *Les Ecrivains
     français jugés par leurs contemporains* (Paris, 1922), p. 300.
62   "Elle a eu raison" can also be translated as "she was right," creating an interesting play
     on words.

63   Linda Timmermans specifically separates taste from the realm of reason (*L'accès des femmes*, p. 168). I would argue, however, that the salons were seeking to reevaluate all categories of reason and logic, and develop new models that would be more amenable to female input.

64   Domna Stanton identifies the fear of female authorship as one of the forces that provokes virulent reaction to the salons. She remarks that, in the eyes of the *précieuses*' critics, "the ultimate step in the presumptuous usurpation to name is the pretention to authorship." "The Fiction of Préciosité and the Fear of Women," p. 130.

65   For an overview of women's activities during the Fronde, see my *Revising Memory*, pp. 42–7. For an in-depth examination of the French female literary tradition developing at this time, see Joan DeJean, *Tender Geographies*, as well as her other numerous studies. There is a large body of recent work devoted to the women writers of this period. Please consult my bibliography for these works, too numerous to mention here.

66   For an overview of this literature, see Albistur and Armogathe, *Histoire du féminisme*.

67   The literature on *préciosité* is vast and daunting. The positions of historians and literary critics with respect to the word, and the phenomenon associated with it, are contradictory, revealing the impossibility of ever really seizing the full meaning and importance of this uniquely French phenomenon of the seventeenth century. For a brief description of *préciosité*, see my entry in *The Molière Encyclopedia*, ed. James Gaines (Westport, CT, 2002), pp. 389–90. Lathuillère's study is usually recognized as one of the most exhaustive and important works on *préciosité*. For other studies, consult my bibliography.

68   Antoine de Somaize, *Dictionnaire des précieuses*, 1659 (Paris, 1861), vol. I, p. 23.

69   Michel de Pure, abbé de, *La Précieuse ou le mystère des Ruelles* (Paris, 1656), p. 49.

70   Ibid., p. 191.

71   Ibid., p. 360.

72   Domna Stanton analyzes the construction of *préciosité* and the vehement reaction against the *précieuses*, focusing on de Pure's, Somaize's, and Molière's depictions. "The Fiction of Préciosité and the Fear of Women," p. 120.

73   Pierre-Daniel Huet, *Huetiana* (Paris, 1722), pp. 175–6. As Timmermans remarks, Huet eventually came to the conclusion that women were responsible for the perversion of taste in the French literary field because love and gallantry inspired genres that were not of the same order as the epic, which in his opinion should have been more cultivated by his contemporaries. Timmermans, *L'Accès des femmes à la culture*, p. 171.

74   My goal here is not to determine Molière's personal opinions regarding women's influence on the literary realm, but rather to rehearse some of the characteristics of the satire directed against this influence as most famously found in Molière's two plays.

75   Charles Perrault, *Les Hommes Illustres*, 1696.

76   Charles Perrault, *Les Hommes Illustres*, 1696, vol I, pp. 79–80, as cited by Georges Mongrédien, *Recueil des textes et des documents du XVIIe siècle relatifs à Molière* (Paris, 1965), p. 701.

77   In *L'Accès des femmes à la culture*, Timmermans rehearses the arguments of the debate over the concept of true and false *précieuses*, without coming to any conclusions as to the validity of the terms. See her illuminating discussion pp. 117–23.

78   Molière, *Les Précieuses Ridicules*, ed. Brigitte Diaz (Paris, 1998), Scene I, ll. 26–7. All further references will be to this edition.

79   In following centuries, commentators elaborated upon the origins of Molière's choice of salon poetry and offered explanations for his inspiration, especially his use of Cotin's poem and the quarrel scene between Trissotin and Vadius. Some viewed these scenes as

the result of a conspiracy between the playwright and Boileau. Monchesnay explains that "M. Despréaux gave Molière the idea for the scene between Trissotin and Vadius in *Les Femmes savantes*. The same scene occurred between Gilles Boileau, the satirist's brother, and the abbé Cotin. Molière was having a hard time finding a bad work to criticize and M. Despréaux brought him abbé Cotin's sonnet with a madrigal by the same author, which Molière used so well in his incomparable scene" (*Bolaeana*, 1742, p. 34 as cited by George Mongrédien, *Recueil des textes et des documents*, p. 413). Similarly, in his *Mémoires*, Louis Racine attributes the inspiration of the quarrel scene to Boileau: "It was [Boileau] who furnished Molière with the scene in the *Femmes savantes* between Trissotin and Vadieux. The same scene occurred between Gilles Boileau and Abbé Cotin." *Mémoires*, 1747, p. 270 as cited by Mongrédien, ibid., p. 413.

80   Martine retorts: "Mais je ne saurais, moi, parler votre jargon" (But I don't know how to speak your jargon), to which Philaminte replies: "L'impudente! Appeler un jargon le langage fondé sur la raison et sur le bel usage!" (Impudent girl! Calling a language founded upon reason and proper usage jargon!) (Act II, Sc. 6, vv. 475–6).

81   Given the role that seventeenth-century literature will eventually be called upon to play, that is, the role of France's classics, Armande's words are especially subversive to later generations. Women want to take control of what will become the literary *patrimoine*.

82   *L'Histoire*, no. 100, May 1987, p. 77. This response was fifth after "to be born in France," "to defend freedoms," "to defend the country," "to have the right to vote" and "to be attached to tradition or a common history."

83   Speech to the Haut conseil de la Francophonie, 2 May 1996 (Internet).

84   Marguerite Buffet, *Nouvelles Observations sur la langue française* (Paris, 1668), "Au Lecteur," n.p. All further references will be to this edition, with page numbers inserted parenthetically in the text.

85   Dena Goodman offers a very comprehensive and enlightening analysis the relationship between women, language, and spelling in "L'ortografe des dames: Gender and Language in the Old Regime," *French Historical Studies*, vol. 25, no. 2 (Spring 2002), pp. 191–223.

86   Montpensier's portrait galleries, *Les Divers Portraits* and the *Galeries des Portraits*, both appeared only a few years before Buffet's text, in 1659 and 1661. For analyses of the literary portrait genre, see Erica Harth, *Ideology and Culture in Seventeenth-century France* (Ithaca, 1985), pp. 70–73; Allison Stedman, "A Gallery of Authors: The Politics of Innovation in Montpensier's *Divers Portraits*," in *Genre*, XXXIII, Summer 2000, pp. 129–50; and my "Rescripting Historical Discourse: Literary Portraits by Women," in *Papers on French Seventeenth-Century Literature*, 14 (1987), pp. 521–35.

87   Later she reiterates this connection between her text and personal, lived experience: Entre la diversité des personnes que je vois tous les jours il se trouve peu qui savent leur langue" (Among the many different people I see every day, there are few who know their language) (p. 11).

88   Buffet destines her work above all to the worldly women who animate the salons. It is, in her view, not just an advantage for them to speak correctly, but a necessity: "ce n'est pas que je veuille obliger toutes les femmes à ne s'attacher qu'à l'étude de bien parler; je sais qu'elles doivent penser aux occupations qui leur sont plus importantes. Il y en a que leur condition appelle tous les jours dans les belles conversations, celles-là semblent être obligées de se cultiver un peu plus que les autres qui sont plus retirées du grand monde" (it is not that I want to oblige all women to only study how to speak well; I know they must think about other things that are more important to them. There are those whose social position demands that they enter into conversation every day, these women seem

obligated to learn more [about correct usage] than those who are more distanced from worldly society) (pp. 124–5).

89   For example, "hormis c'est un mot qui n'est pas Francais" (*hormis* is not a French word) (p. 33).

90   Indeed ridicule seems to be the most influential force Buffet relies upon to incite her contemporaries to repent of their corrupt linguistic ways. She frequently cites a phrase she has heard and pronounces such usage as "très ridicule" (very ridiculous) (p. 85), comprehending that this is perhaps the most effective way to have worldly participants mend their speaking habits.

91   For example, she praises Mademoiselle de Scurman for her knowledge of languages: "l'antiquité n'a rien qui lui soit comparable, et que la posterité ne produira jamais rien qui lui puisse disputer le titre glorieux d'incomparable qu'elle s'est légitimement acquis, pour parler aussi de vingt-deux sortes de langues." (Antiquity has no one comparable to her, and ... posterity will never produce anything that can dispute her glorious title of uncomparable that she legitimately acquired for speaking twenty-two different languages) (pp. 2–3).

92   Buffet is expecially conscious of defining how one should speak of learned women. There are numerous other examples, such as the following: "Une femme qui se plaira à cultiver les sciences, on dira souvent c'est une femme de lecture, il faut dire, c'est une femme de cabinet" (of a woman who chooses to cultivate the sciences, people often say she is a reading woman; one should say, she is a woman of the study) (pp. 36–7). Other examples that illustrate Buffet's penchant for what I would term "worldly" examples are, among many others "Voyant une personne qui n'a pas sa gaieté ordinaire, on dira qu'elle est toute désorientée, le terme est fort bon ... Parlant de la beauté d'un visage qui sera en ovale, on ne dit plus dans le beau stile, c'est un visage long, il faut dire c'est une ovale achevée, quand il est tout beau; étant rond on dit, c'est une beauté à la Romaine" (seeing someone who is not in his/her ordinary good mood, one would say that he/she is very disoriented, the term is excellent ... Speaking of the beauty of a face that is oval, it is no longer said, in proper style, that it is a long face; one must say it's a perfect oval, when it is beautiful; if it is round, one says that it is a Roman beauty) (pp. 40–41).

93   Interestingly, a few of the words Buffet finds acceptable are those that Molière mocked in *Les Précieuses Ridicules*, a play that appeared just a few years before Buffet's text. For example, she states "Il est superbement, ou magnifiquement meublé, l'un est autant bon que l'autre, on s'en peut servir" (it is superbly or magnificently furnished, one is as good as the other and can be used) (p. 42). Thus, although Molière states in his Preface that he is only mocking provincial usage, Buffet's defense reveals that Parisian polite society found such words acceptable.

94   For example, "Il n'y a rien tel, il n'y a rien de tel, sont bons, le premier se dit dans la conversation, et le second en écrivant" ("Il n'y a rien tel, il n'y a rien" the first is used in conversation and the second in writing) (p. 70).

95   As is evident in explanations such as the following: "Il est incliné à cela, ou encliner, de bons auteurs ont écrit encliner on doit les suivre" ("incliné" or "encliner", good authors have written "encliner." They must be followed) (p. 72).

96   For example, she states "recouvert pour recouvrer, est bon, parce que l'usage l'a introduit" ("recouvert" for "recouvrer" is acceptable, because usage introduced it) (p. 75).

97   As for example, "sériosité est un mot nouveau, dont on se sert, et qui est bien reçu à la Cour" ("sériosité" is a new word that people use and that is well received at court) (p. 69).

98   She often refers to such authorities as Pythagore, the Lacedemoniens, or even Numa Pompiluis, among many others one could characterize as "the Ancients" (pp. 95–6).

99 And Buffet is indeed very concerned with defining the French language for posterity. For example, she views French as above all intolerant of superfluous expression. She characterizes "true" French as a language that carefully avoids the superfluous: "il est important dans les rencontres, de parler, et d'écrire, d'éviter les termes superflus, qui est une des plus grandes fautes que l'on puisse commettre contre la langue française" (It is important when speaking or writing to avoid superfluous terms, which is one of the greatest mistakes one can make in French) (p. 102).

100 Her argumentation in many ways resembles that of Madeleine de Scudéry's harangue devoted to Sapho in her *Les Femmes Illustres*. In that harangue, Scudéry has her protagonist Sapho use logic to convince Erinne that women need to achieve fame by writing, and not just through the traditional means of beauty.

101 Buffet states: "les âmes n'ayant point de sexe, il s'ensuit par conséquent que la beauté d'esprit ne connaît point cette difference d'homme et de femme" (Because souls do not have a gender, it follows that *la beauté d'esprit* (beauty of the mind) does not know the difference between a man and a woman) (p. 200).

102 For a discussion of this passage of Buffet's text, see Timothy Reiss, *The Meaning of Literature*, p. 195.

103 Buffet explains Plato's and Aristotle's hostility towards the female sex in much the same way as Christine de Pizan did over 200 years earlier in her *La Cité des Dames*. According to Pizan, because women were not physically attracted to these philosophers, they attacked the entire female sex out of spite and frustration (pp. 232 and 235 for example).

104 For example, when she turns to Madame la comtesse du Plexis, she states: "puisque je sais que cette illustre Dame n'aime les louanges que pour les distribuer, ayant l'honneur de la connaître si parfaitement que je fais; je ne puis refuser à moi-même la satisfaction que j'ai de lui rendre justice …" (because I know this famous lady does not like praise, except to distribute it herself, having the honor of knowing her as well as I do, I can't refuse myself the satisfaction of doing her justice) (pp. 259–60).

105 Of the duchesse de Montausier, for example, she says "Toute la Cour est fort persuadée que cette incomparable héroïne n'a pas moins de beauté et d'éloquence dans ses écrits pour persuader ce qu'elle veut, qu'en avait autrefois cette fameuse Romaine [Cornelia]" (the whole court is totally persuaded that this incomparable heroine has no less beauty and eloquence in her writing to make her case than that famous Roman [Cornelia] had in the past) (pp. 249–50).

106 At one point she explains that, while she could have included many more women in her *Eloges*, "J'ai voulu ne parler que de celles qui sont dans ma connaissance" (I only wanted to talk about those I know personally) (p. 282).

107 "Son humilité ne veut pas que ses ouvrages soient mis en lumière, ce sont des pièces de cabinet fort précieuses, qu'elle laisse en manuscrit. Ce travail étant si beau, j'ose dire qu'il y a de l'injustice à le vouloir cacher." (Her humility does not want her to publish her works, which are very exquisite *pièces de cabinet* that she leaves in manuscript form. This work is so beautiful that I dare say it is unjust to want to hide it) (p. 270).

108 In *Cartesian Women*, Erica Harth offers a detailed investigation of the relationship between Descartes and women such as Bonnevant.

109 In another portrait, Buffet relates the story of Mlle Despinasse and a "grand poète" she identifies as Monsieur de Lauret. Lauret "la consultait souvent, quand il avait à travailler aux pièces les plus importantes de sa poésie" (consulted her often when he was working on the most important examples of his works) (p. 282).

110 Buffet herself recognizes learned women's detractors during her time period, and alludes to them in order to render her female *exempla* even more noteworthy due to their ability to counter public opinion. Buffet states: "Si celles qui sont sur le throne ont leurs ennemis, il semble être inévitable que les habiles femmes n'en soient exemptes; ce qui ne m'étonne point que le caprice de quelques hommes par une injuste jalousie se rendent leurs ennemis, leur faisant une guerre continuelle. Ils veulent qu'elles soient enfermées dans l'ignorance, qu'elles soient éloignées de posséder et l'esprit et la disposition propre à recevoir les sciences" (If those who are on the throne have their enemies, it seems inevitable that capable women would not be exempt; so it doesn't surprise me at all that the capriciousness of a few men, that unjust jealousy makes them their enemies, are constantly at war against them. They want them to be locked way in ignorance, and [maintain] that they are far from possessing the *esprit* and the make up to receive knowledge) (pp. 270–71).

111 In contrast, Scudéry in *Les Femmes illustres* identifies immortality with writing. See her harangue, "Sapho à Erinne."

112 An intellectual who was an authority on language, Bouhours straddled both worlds, in his position as the precepteur for Colbert's son and an avid guest at Madeleine de Scudéry's salon.

113 For an overview of Bouhours's life and associations, see Mireille Gérard's entry "Bouhours, Dominique" in the *Dictionnaire des littératures de langue française*, vol. 1, eds Jean-Pierre de Beaumarchais, Daniel Couty, and Alain Rey (Paris, 1994,), p. 313. See also Peter France's entry in *The New Oxford Companion to Literature in French*, ed. Peter France (New York, 1995).

114 As cited by de Noual la Houssaye in "Bouhours, Dominique" in *Biographie universelle ancienne et moderne*, ed. M. Michaud (Paris, 1854–65), p. 212.

115 As cited by Gérard, *Dictionnaire des littératures de langue française*, p. 313.

116 The *Entretiens* was reprinted three times between 1671 and 1673, 7 more times in Paris and elsewhere between 1683 and 1691. In addition, the eighteenth century witnessed seven more editions between 1703 and 1768, which attests to the work's appeal well beyond Bouhours's intended audience. *Entretiens d'Ariste et d'Eugène*, ed. René Raouant (Paris, 1920), p. 25. All further references will be to this edition, with page numbers inserted parenthetically in the text.

117 As the editor of the 1920 edition of the *Entretiens* remarks, "Il donne la main à Boileau, mais en même temps il sourit, et de toutes ses grâces à Mlle de Scudéry" (He shakes hands with Boileau, but at the same time he smiles, with all his charm, at Mlle de Scudéry). *Entretiens d'Ariste et d'Eugène*, p. 20.

118 For an analysis of this *génie*, see Marc Fumaroli's article, "Le Génie de la langue francaise," in *Les Lieux de Mémoire*.

119 Like Buffet, many of Bouhours's examples emanate from the worldly milieu. See, for example, his discussion of "tourner" and "tour," among many others (p. 83).

120 Bouhours describes the genesis of language as passing from the oral to the written. If a term is worthy, it will survive in written form after its introduction in what Bouhours's implies to be the inferior medium of conversation: "Néanmoins en (sic) n'emploie guère ces façons de parler hors de la conversation, et elles ont lieu tout au plus dans les billets … comme c'est dans la conversation que naissent d'ordinaire les termes nouveaux, ils y demeurent quand ils ne périssent pas un peu après leur naissance, ce qui leur arrive assez souvent. (Nevertheless these ways of speaking are barely used except in conversation, and at most they're used in notes … as new terms are usually born in conversation, they remain if they don't die soon after their birth, which often happens) (p. 85).

121 Furetière underscores this clarity associated with the French language. Under "Français" he writes: "On dit adverbialement, en bon français, pour dire franchement et en paroles claires et nettes" (As an adverb people often say "in good French" to mean frankly and in clear and direct terms).

122 In this vein, Bouhours denounces what he terms "fausses Précieuses" (p. 52). It is interesting that he critiques only "fausses Précieuses," leading one to the conclusion that "vraies" *précieuses* do exist but do not merit such critique. It would thus follow that true precious women are like other *honnêtes gens* and use French correctly and even add to its glory. As we have seen, the distinction between "false" and "true" *précieuses* and even the definition of *préciosité* itself is unclear and debated. See Domna Stanton's discussion in "Préciosité and Fear of Women."

123 Indeed, the only language that comes close to French is its "mother," Latin. In Bouhours's opinion, "Pour peu qu'on les examine toutes deux, on verra qu'elles ont le même génie et le même goût, et que rien ne leur plaît tant qu'un discours noble et poli, mais pur, simple, naturel et raisonnable" (If you examine both of them, you will see that they have the same *génie* and the same taste, and that nothing pleases them as much as a noble and polite speech, but [at the same time] pure, simple, natural, and reasonable) (p. 68).

124 Bouhours, however, straddles the fence on women's influence. He censures "certaines femmes qui se servent à toute heure d'expressions extraordinaires, et qui dans une conversation disent cent fois un mot qui ne fera que de naître ... Pour plaire ... il ne faut point avoir trop envie de plaire, et pour parler bien français, il ne faut point vouloir trop bien parler" (certain women who constantly use extraordinary expressions, and in a conversation say a word that has just been coined 100 times ... In order to please ... you shouldn't want too much to please, and to speak French well, you must not want to speak it too well) (p. 53).

125 The editor of the 1920 edition critiques Bouhours for precisely this point. In this editor's opinion, Bouhours's failure to name such writers as "Corneille, Pascal, Molière, Boileau and Racine," and his advice to follow the examples of Conrart and Pellisson reveal the faultiness of Bouhours's taste: "He didn't name them, and this omission judges him. We reach the limits of his taste (*goût*)" (pp. 22–3). One sees here the disparity between twentieth-century assessments of good taste and those of Bouhours's own century.

126 It is interesting to note that following the publication of d'Aucour's critique, he was hired by Colbert as the preceptor of his second son, leading one to believe that Aucour's remarks must have been more to Colbert's liking than Bouhours's. Later in the early nineteenth century, La Harpe will praise Aucour's critique: "it is almost the best literary criticism of the seventeenth century." As cited by Rauount, introduction to the *Entretiens*, p. 26. We will return to the figure of La Harpe and his taste later.

127 There are exceptions, however: "Ce sont celles qui de côté de l'esprit n'ont rien des imperfections de leur sexe" (Those are the ones who in terms of *esprit* don't have any of the imperfections of their sex) (p. 191). Bouhours's remarks resemble those of Rousseau in his *Lettre à d'Alembert*. I wish to thank Katharine Ann Jensen for pointing this out.

128 Timothy Reiss, *The Meaning of Literature*, pp. 99 and 106.

129 *Recueil des Harangues prononcés par Messieurs de l'Académie française* (Paris: Coignard, 1714), vol. I, p. 2. All further references will be to this edition, with page numbers inserted parenthetically in the text.

130 Salomon's remarks are especially laden with meaning given that the pronouncement over *Le Cid* was too recent not to be in the minds of his listeners. In that instance, Corneille's *bon sens*—supported by the *mondain* public—had been severely reprimanded by the

more "reasonable" and meditating Academy. We will analyze this quarrel in depth in Chapter 2.

131 Paul Pellisson-Fontanier, *Relation contenant l'Histoire de l'Académie française* (Paris, 1653), pp. 228–9.

132 Antoine Adam, *Histoire de la littérature française au XVIIe siècle*, vol. V, pp. 22–3.

133 A history of the French Academy is beyond the scope of the present study. See Marc Fumaroli's article "La Coupole" in *Les Lieux de Mémoire*. Hélène Merlin has examined the power of the French Academy in *L'Excentricité académique: Littérature, institution, société* (Paris, 2001).

134 Abbé A. Fabre, *Chapelain et nos deux premières académies* (Paris, 1890), p. 350. Fabre explains that the Academy had Furetière's privilège revoked. The work appeared in Holland in 1690.

135 In the eighteenth century, the triumph of a good taste associated with Boileau over the "false" taste of the worldly public continues to gain credence. Louis Racine states: "Il [Boileau] fut parmi nous comme le créateur du bon goût; ce fut lui, avec Molière, qui fit tomber tous les bureaux du faux bel esprit. La protection de l'Hôtel de Rambouillet fut inutile à l'abbé Cotin, qui ne se releva jamais du dernier coup que Molière lui avait porté" (Among us Boileau was the creator of good taste; it was he, with Molière, who demolished all the offices of false *bel esprit*. The protection of the hôtel de Rambouillet was useless for abbé Cotin, who never recovered from the last blow Molière inflicted on him). *Mémoires*, 1747, p. 337–8, cited by George Mongrédien, *Recueil des textes et des documents du XVIIe siècle relatifs à Molière* (Paris: CNRS, 1965), p. 413. In Racine's view, the salons were struck down by the combined efforts of Boileau and Molière. Racine's chronology is somewhat questionable, however. Cotin would not have expected the protection of the hôtel de Rambouillet in 1672, when *Les Femmes savantes* appeared, the marquise having been dead for almost a decade.

136 Boileau's "Dialogue des Héros de roman" is an especially virulent diatribe against the heroic novel, in particular Madeleine de Scudéry's extremely popular examples. For an analysis of Boileau's attack on the novel, see Joan DeJean, *Tender Geographies*.

137 Timmermans, like many other historians and critics, stresses that literature is often a game in the salons (p. 181). While this may be true in part, the other roles literature played in these worldly gatherings, and other attitudes toward literature, should not be overshadowed by this one role too often identified as the main one when it comes to a salon public.

Chapter 2

Defining a Literary Culture:
The *Ruelles* and Literary Innovation

When Madeleine de Scudéry died in 1701, one contemporary succinctly voiced the sentiments of many of the illustrious novelist's contemporaries, inscribing the following poem under her portrait:

> De la sage Sapho l'ornement de la France
> Tu vois dans ce portrait l'exacte ressemblance.
> On connaît son mérite, on connaît ses écrits
> Partout où l'on connaît la gloire de Louis.
> La modestie en elle au savoir fut unie,
> Et son coeur seul était plus grand que son génie.[1]

> (Of the wise Sapho, adornment of France
> You see in this portrait the exact resemblance
> They know her worth, they know her writings
> Wherever they know of Louis's glory.
> Modesty was united in her with knowledge
> And only her heart was greater than her genius.)

Such praise, which was not rare throughout the seventeenth century, underscores how contemporaries valued not only the person but her writings, and, even more surprising perhaps for us today, equated "la sage Sapho" with French excellence and deemed her a figure as renowned as her monarch.

Scudéry's status reflects the indelible imprint the worldly public and the women writers she epitomized had made on French culture in general by the end of the seventeenth century. The new forms of "writings," "genius," and "knowledge" Scudéry represented and that were cultivated in the worldly milieu of the salons were being used to define a new culture, one founded upon new literary genres such as the novel, alternative criteria for literary evaluation, such as *bon goût, bon sens,* and collaboration, a new worldly public with the power not only to produce this literature but to impose its taste on the literary field at large, and even innovative roles for literature, such as the use of fiction to offer new roles for women. As we have seen, commentators and critics recognized the power of this public educated in the salons and identified the real danger as not simply the existence of alternative modes of writing and criticism, but as putting into practice the values that were espoused in the salons. As Somaize's critique of the *précieuses* illustrates, one of the biggest fears was that women would write. These new literary practices would not simply affect worldly literary production, but the literature of the state as a whole. The new literary field that developed parallel with and in opposition to traditional, scholarly values and texts exerted great force on the shaping of France's collective sense of identity. Of course France was known for its all powerful monarch and for the academies and artistic creations he controlled, but as is evident in the preceding praise of Scudéry, "wherever they know of Louis's glory" one knows Scudéry's writings and genius. The novel, *galanterie*, conversation, and the status of women were all perceived as traits as specific to France as Louis XIV. And in the development of a sense of national culture, literature was accorded a central role. An influence on literature thus constituted a determining force on the representation of the entire culture identified with France.

One would expect that the worldly milieu would have left a strong mark in terms of structure, content, and public on the new genre of the *nouvelle historique* or *galante*, for the authors who developed this form of fiction were also the principal participants in salon culture. What is perhaps less evident and more surprising is the fact that literary culture at large in the seventeenth century felt the influence of the *mondains*, in particular their taste and their collaborative methods. By the 1660s not only were the genres associated with the salons changing the literary scene, so too were their creative and critical methods making their mark on the literary field. The precise nature of this worldly force becomes clear when one delves into the literary productions of the period, both imaginary and critical, as well as in some of the intense debates that accompanied these productions. In this chapter I will examine four examples that illustrate particularly well the profound and determining effect the salons and the worldly milieu exercised on the seventeenth-century literary field. In the first reading, I return to the beginning of the century and the well-known quarrel surrounding Corneille's *Le Cid*. Much more than a debate over the rules governing tragedy, this discussion offers a fascinating portrayal of the emerging conflicts over worldly taste and scholarly standards, and the publics associated with each. A second quarrel later in the century, that surrounding Lafayette's *La Princesse de Clèves* in 1678, is a continuation of this conflict, as well as a provocative illustration of how the new critical methods associated with the worldly milieu inspired new literary genres and critical methods to evaluate those genres. While both these debates have elicited much critical commentary, no one has yet examined them in light of the salons' influence on literary taste and criteria for literary evaluation, nor have critics taken gender into account in their analyses.[2] From these two quarrels I turn to analyses of the works of two of the most influential members of the worldly milieu, Lafayette and Villedieu. Their novels as well as the specific trajectory of Villedieu's career as a writer illustrate particularly well the ways in which the worldly literary climate determined the shape of literary production and criticism during the period. The innovations of these two novelists go beyond the development of a new genre, the novel. Both Lafayette and Villedieu inscribe new ways of obtaining knowledge, ways inspired by the milieu of the salons.

A Monstrous Public

In 1637, a young and audacious Pierre Corneille decided to test the theatrical conventions of his time by producing a hybrid play that defied the accepted notions governing both genre and subject. His tragi-comedy, *Le Cid*, was an immediate hit and Corneille, emboldened by his new-found notoriety, published a poem entitled "Excuse à Ariste" in which he was viewed as flaunting his success and crowning himself the public's newest creative genius.[3] Irritated by such arrogance, as well as by the success of *Le Cid*, Georges de Scudéry, a rival playwright and Madeleine de Scudéry's brother, composed a lengthy and detailed attack of the play, criticizing in particular Corneille's violation of generic principles and the essential concept of *vraisemblance*, or plausibility and propriety, founded upon Aristotle's Poetics but redefined by the seventeenth century. Scudéry's diatribe inspired a number of responses from many learned members of the literary milieu. The debate continued for almost a year, until the newly-formed French Academy, following orders by its founder, Richelieu, stepped in to give the final and unequivocal assessment and end all further discussion.

At first glance, the furore surrounding *Le Cid* would seem to have little to tell us specifically about the worldly milieu and its particular influence on literature. No female salonnière left her written opinion; indeed, all the participants were male. The various discussions over the play's sources, over rules governing genres, and the conventions dictating plausibility and propriety would not seem to be areas in which the worldly public would have the expertise or the desire to make their opinions known. But upon closer examination of the texts themselves, the quarrel over *Le Cid* reveals the changing nature of the literary public at the beginning of the seventeenth century, in particular the growing power of the worldly public to affect literary creation by establishing new critical criteria to rival the ones expounded by those traditionally viewed as the experts, the *doctes*. And in this public, women were already being recognized as an influential force to be reckoned with. A number of critics have recently been drawn to this quarrel and have contributed to our understanding of its historical and literary significance. Hélène Merlin in *Public et Littérature en France au XVIIe siècle* was among the first to underscore how this debate illustrates the changing nature and definition of literary public.[4] In his study of power in the literary field, Christian Jouhaud has focused attention on Jean Chapelain, the spokesperson for the French Academy's definitive contribution to the quarrel, and shown the complexities of the literary public through this figure who, as we have seen, straddled the worldly and academic milieus.[5] None of these studies, however, has analyzed the influence that a newly-developing salon public, dominated by women, had on the rhetoric of the quarrel. As shall become apparent, Corneille was acutely aware of and catered to a particular gender when he composed his masterpiece. An analysis of the inscription of this female worldly public illustrates the place that women were beginning to occupy in France's literary field.

While the various critiques or defenses of Corneille's actual play comprise the main action on the battleground of the quarrel, the playwright's egocentric poem "Excuse à Ariste" was in fact the text that inspired the initial shots of this verbal war.[6] Inebriated by the success of his play, Corneille composed a self-congratulatory poem in which he crowned himself the principal arbiter of his own works and, even more audaciously, questioned the authority of the revered *doctes* of "Le Parnasse littéraire" to judge any literary production. He fashions an account of his success according to which the public, charmed by the quality of his verse, elevates him to the position he enjoys:

> … Je sais ce que je vaux, et croy ce qu'on m'en dit:
> Pour me faire admirer je ne fais point de ligue …
> Mon travail sans appui monte sur le Theâtre,
> Chacun en liberté l'y blâme ou l'idolâtre
> Là sans que mes amis prèchent leurs sentiments
> J'arrache quelque fois trop d'applaudissements
> Par d'illustres advis je n'éblouïs personne
> Je satisfais ensemble et peuple et courtisans
> Et mes vers en tous lieux sont mes seuls partisans

Par leur seule beauté ma plume est estimée
Je ne dois qu'à moi seul toute ma Renommée ...[7]

(I know what I am worth, and believe what people say about me
To make myself admired, I do not create any cabales
Without any help my work appears on stage
Everyone is at liberty to condemn or to praise it
Without my friends preaching their opinions
I sometimes inspire too much applause
I dazzle no one by illustrious opinions
I satisfy both the common people and the court
And my verses are everywhere my sole supporters
By their beauty alone is my pen valued
I owe my renown to myself alone.)

Corneille explains that he has no need to influence public opinion by hiring friends to applaud at his plays, as was common practice at the time. He is perfectly capable of judging his own worth—"I know what I am worth"—and of listening to the approbation of an unbiased public that recognizes and applauds the "beauty" of his verse. When Corneille daringly states "I owe my renown to myself alone," a line that infuriates his critic Scudéry, he is paying homage to his own literary genius, as well as ratifying a certain public's opinion of this genius. This stance would be provocative enough. Corneille compounds this provocation by specifying the nature of the public he is aiming to please: "I satisfy both the common people and the court." He thus completely obfuscates the traditional arbitrating body, the learned critics. The public Corneille aims to please is decidedly more generic and worldly. He then goes on to specify the source of his genius and thus popularity by associating his inspiration with love:

J'ai brulé fort longtemps d'une amour assez grande,
Et que jusqu'au tombeau je dois bien estimer,
Puisque ce fut par là que j'appris à rimer:
Mon bonheur commença quand mon âme fut prise,
Je gaignai de la gloire en perdant ma franchise,
Charmé de deux beaux yeux, mon vers charma la Cour,
Et ce que j'ai de nom je le dois à l'amour.
J'adorai donc Philis, et la secrète estime
Que ce divin esprit faisait de notre rime
Me fit devenir Poète aussi tôt qu'amoureux.

(I was consumed for a long time by a fairly great love,
That I must respect until the grave,
Because that is when I learned to compose:
My happiness began when my soul was captured,
I achieved glory while losing my freedom,
Charmed by two beautiful eyes, my verse charmed the court,
And whatever reputation I have I owe to love.
I thus adored Philis and the secret esteem
That this divine spirit created in our rhyme
Made me become a poet as soon as I fell in love.)

Corneille is thus a product of the worldly milieu, in which love can serve as inspiration for the poet and which can then judge the merit of the work that it has inspired. This literary world accords women the position of honor, not only with respect to inspiration, a role they had traditionally held, but more provocatively, in terms of judging the quality of the work created, the "beauty" of the author's "pen."

Throughout the quarrel, Corneille consistently has recourse to the opinion of this particular public in his defense. In fact, the only real defense he offers to counter the attack that his play is defective, both in form and content, is that the play is pleasing to the public, specifically a female public. In his response to Scudéry's attack, Corneille does not attempt to counter Scudéry's arguments based on his own interpretation of traditional, learned doctrine. He simply replies to Scudéry's erudite attack by stating and restating the obvious: the public liked the play so it must be good. In a letter to Scudéry Corneille writes:

Ne vous êtes-vous pas souvenu que le Cid a été représenté trois fois au Louvre et deux fois à l'Hôtel de Richelieu: Quand vous avez traité la pauvre Chimène d'impudique, de prostituée, de parricide, de monstre; ne vous êtes-vous pas souvenu, que la Reine, les Princesses et les plus vertueuses Dames de la Cour et de Paris, l'ont reçue et caressée en fille d'honneur? (148)

(Do you not remember that Le Cid was presented three times at the Louvre and two times at the hôtel de Richelieu: When you called poor Chimène a prostitute, shameless, a monster, didn't you remember that the Queen, the princesses, and the most virtuous women of the court and in Paris received her and pràised her as a woman of honor?)

Je me contente pour toute Apologie, de ce que vous avouez qu'il a eu l'approbation des savants et de la cour; C'est éloge véritable ... détruit tout ce que vous pouvez dire après. (151)

(I need no other apology than your admitting that [Le Cid] had the approval of the learned scholars and of the court; This true praise ... destroys everything you can say afterwards.)

Such a response infuriates Scudéry, and not just because it inspires professional jealousy. Scudéry is acutely aware that Corneille is trying to alter the nature of literary power by redefining the public that counts in literary evaluation and by changing the criteria according to which literature can and should be judged. Where Corneille recognizes the worldly public as literary authorities, and pleasure as a valid, guiding principle, Scudéry is determined to exclude this uneducated public and to force authors to conform to learned doctrine based in large part on classical models, specifically those of Aristotle. In this respect, the quarrel can be seen as a barometer of the influence the worldly public was beginning to exert on the literary field.

Scudéry in fact begins his lengthy critical treatise by negating the public's authority to judge and by ridiculing pleasure as a critical concept:

Tout ce qui brille n'est pas toujours précieux ... souvent l'apparence du bien se fait prendre pour le bien même. Aussi ne m'étonnai-je pas beaucoup que le Peuple qui porte le jugement dans les yeux, se laisse tromper par celui de tous les sens, le plus facile à decevoir: Mais que cette vapeur grossière, qui se forme dans le Parterre ait pu s'élever jusqu'aux Galleries, et qu'un fantôme ait abusé le savoir comme l'ignorance, et la Cour aussi bien que le Bourgeois, j'avoue que ce prodige m'étonne, et que ce n'est qu'en ce bizzare événement que je trouve Le Cid merveilleux. (71)

(Everything that shines is not always precious ... often the appearance of value is mistaken for value itself. Thus I'm not very surprised that the common people, who judge by their eyes, allow themselves to be fooled by the sense that is the easiest to deceive. But that this fog, which formed in the lower classes [le parterre] could rise up to the galleries, and that this ghost took advantage of knowledge as well as ignorance, and the court as well as the bourgeoisie, I admit that this extraordinary event does shock me, and it is only [in its ability to produce] this bizarre event that I find Le Cid marvelous.)

According to Scudéry, the public has not used its head in evaluating the play, and instead has permitted "this fog," that is, admiration founded upon the mere appearance of merit, to envelope it. His mission throughout the *Observations* is to bring reason back to literary evaluation, a reason founded upon rules that he knows and understands because he is a privileged member of the erudite public that would never allow itself to be so enveloped. The principal rules he asks the public to remember are the traditional "three unities" or "trois unités" drawn from Aristotle's Poetics. Using these well-rehearsed, precise dogma, Scudéry is able to condemn Corneille's success because it obviously does not scrupulously adhere to such scholastic criteria.

But Scudéry's attack is inspired by more than a desire to reiterate the rules to Corneille and his public. As Scudéry knew only too well, Corneille obviously knew his play was not composed in full accordance with *docte* policy. What author desirous of pleasing by traditional means would opt to have a daughter lose her father in a duel with her fiancé, have this fiancé win a war for a king, and have the orphaned daughter marry her fiancé in spite of his choice of honor over love all in the space of a single day? What author respectful of these unities would advance that such events are *vraisemblable*, that is, plausible and morally acceptable, according to seventeenth-century interpretations of Aristotle's notion of verisimilitude?[8] Scudéry throws all the established rules at Corneille and the public that admired the play, only to have Corneille and the public shrug their shoulders and say "It's a great play because it's enjoyable to watch." Scudéry is furious because Corneille sought to achieve theatrical success according to different rules, and succeeded. Scudéry's primary objective is not to prove how the play violates standard practice, even though he meticulously does so over the course of a hundred pages. He desires above all to elevate learned criteria such as the three unities and a certain notion of *vraisemblance* over the vague notion of pleasure and other such criteria that were becoming powerful critical tools in the hands of the public.

In addition to denouncing its means of evaluation, Scudéry uses his attack to denigrate the public itself and attempt to re-establish the learned public as the only one truly capable of judging literary productions. One aspect of the play that draws much of his critical fire is the character of Chimène, who marries her father's murderer. Scudéry locates Corneille's most reprehensible violations in this character, and is particularly appalled by the fact that the public applauded her rather than condemning her. The character of Chimène violates all established poetic principles, which are designed not only to ensure compositional coherence, but also to ensure that a production is morally acceptable and a good example, given literature's goal at the time to "please and instruct." According to Scudéry, there is nothing that can be done to make Chimène *vraisemblable*, that is plausible and conforming to rules of propriety. Even though the story is drawn from history, it is a history that has no place on the stage given that it cannot be made morally plausible (76). Scudéry is horrified by Chimène, whose behavior renders the play a production that "choque la raison et les bonnes moeurs" (shocks reason and good standards of behavior) (77). He rails against her, repeatedly calling her a "monstre" (monster) (82), "cette dénaturée" (this unnatural woman) (82), a "Furie" (95), an unnatural daughter who does not honor her father (92), who is "indigne de la lumière" (unworthy to see the light of day) (94), to cite only a few of the flattering depictions. Scudéry offers extensive and detailed reasoning in order to show why the public was wrong to accept a play with such a character. For example, he uses Act III, in which Rodrigue visits Chimène just after killing her father, in his attempt to reestablish the "reasonable" poetic rules the public has chosen to forget, and to critique the public in this process. After first condemning Chimène's actions in Act II, Sc. III, where she speaks instead of simply retiring to her room after her father's death—"ce discours est plus extravagant que généreux, dans la bouche d'une fille, et jamais aucune ne le dirait, quand même elle en aurait la pensée" (this speech is more extravagant than generous, in the mouth of a young woman, and never would a single young woman utter it, even if she were to think it) (89)—he turns to the central act of the play, which he qualifies as

> celui qui a fait battre des mains à tant de monde; crier miracle, à tous ceux qui ne savent pas discerner, le bon or d'avec l'alchimie, et qui seul a fait la fausse réputation du Cid. Rodrigue y paraît d'abord chez Chimène, avec une épée qui fume encore du sang tout chaud, qu'il vient de faire répandre à son père ... Cette épouvantable procédure, choque directement le sens commun: et quand Rodrigue prit la résolution de tuer le Comte, il devait prendre celle de ne revoir jamais sa fille. Car de nous dire qu'il vient pour se faire tuer par Chimène, c'est nous apprendre qu'il ne vient que pour faire des pointes: les filles bien nées n'usurpent jamais l'office des bourreaux; c'est une chose qui n'a point d'exemple; et qui serait supportable dans une Elegie à Philis ... mais non pas dans le grave Poème dramatique, qui représente sérieusement, les choses comme elles doivent être. (89)

> (the one that made everyone applaud, cry that it was miraculous, everyone, that is, who cannot distinguish between good work and alchemy, which is the only thing that created Le Cid's false reputation. Rodrigue first appears at Chimène's house, with a sword still dripping with the warm blood of her father ... This appalling act directly shocks common sense: when Rodrique decided to kill the count, he was supposed to decide to never again see his daughter. To tell us that he goes to Chimène's in order to be killed by her is really to tell us that he only goes there in order to go over the top: Young women who are well-bred never take on the role of executioner; there is not a single example of such a thing; it might be acceptable in an elegie to Philis, but not in a serious dramatic work that represents seriously things as they must be.)

Scudéry uses his *Observations* to elevate "les judicieux" (judicious people) over "everyone who cannot distinguish between good work and alchemy." The "injudicious," worldly public that applauded Chimène's behavior has to be brought under control, and the judicious, erudite public's taste founded upon conventional notions of *vraisemblance* must reign. Scudéry calls upon the public's "reason" to denounce this "unnatural daughter" and is particularly appalled by Chimène's reasoning when she states to Rodrigue that she understands the trap he was in and thus his motivation for killing her father. Chimène explains that she indeed does not blame him because he chose honor over love, since she would not have been able to love anyone who would have done differently, to which Scudéry exclaims: "O jugement de l'Auteur, à quoi songez-vous? O raison de l'Auditeur, qu'êtes-vous devenue?" (Oh author's judgment, what were you thinking of? Oh reason of the listener, what happened to you?) (91). In Scudéry's opinion, true reason has been replaced by a false reason conjured up by "alchemy." He attempts throughout the *Observations* to state what the reception of the play should be, and counter what it actually was.

The quarrel over *Le Cid* illustrates that worldly reason was indeed a force to be reckoned with as early as 1637. It is not coincidental that Scudéry reserves most of his venim for the character of Chimène. Corneille's complex female protagonist was especially appreciated by the worldly public whose taste Corneille was courting. As we have seen, Corneille in fact defends Chimène by calling upon the taste of a specifically female public. It is likely Scudéry knew only too well that the public had appreciated the bold character of Chimène. Indeed, this is precisely the critic's fear: that this public would permit alternative examples to be exhibited on stage because the criteria of poetic composition would be different. Scudéry feels he must remind the public of conventional rules, and in fact impose these rules, in order to ensure that a protagonist such as Chimène would not have a place in literature at all. Scudéry sees his role and that of the literary criticism he is composing to be that of the moral guarantor of society. Since the public, especially the uneducated female public, does not know the rules that ensure the morality of literature, it is up to the critic Scudéry to teach those rules and make sure that they remain the sole criteria governing the literary imagination. Corneille, on the other hand, represents the new worldly author/critic who wants pleasure to supercede other criteria and wants to grant more poetic liberty to both authors and the public.

Corneille's supporters recognized that the debate over *Le Cid* was less over the play itself than over who had the authority to judge literature and according to what criteria. One response entitled "La Voix Publique" echoed Corneille's defense of pleasure as a critical category (152) and defended the right of "honnêtes gens" to evaluate a literary production according to their own personal rules: "Les bons esprits connaissent assez le mérite des uns et des autres sans l'aide de vos [Scudéry's] observations ... Les honnêtes gens vous condamnent" (Good minds can recognize merit without the help of your remarks. Worldly people condemn you) (153). In another response usually attributed to Sorel, the critic allows for the judgment of the non-erudite public and condones the use of pleasure (231). In a bold move, this critic rejects the rules of the *doctes* that serve as Scudéry's primary critical reference, and states that it is possible to judge without having recourse to such rules (239). He, like Corneille, thus defends the worldly taste responsible for the playwright's success.

It can be argued that it is above all to denounce this worldly taste that Scudéry calls upon the nascent French Academy to pass judgment on Corneille's masterpiece. Scudéry implores the Academy to replace the public as judges and by so doing reestablish erudite *raison* belonging to an exclusive learned public in the world of French letters. When Richelieu ordered the French Academy to respond and indeed put an end to the quarrel, he was acknowledging the importance of the stakes of this debate, stakes that went far beyond Corneille's actual play. Richelieu took this response very seriously, not only because it was the Academy's first official pronouncement, but because the criteria governing literary production were at stake. Jean Chapelain, an erudite academician but also, as we have seen, an active member of the marquise de Rambouillet's salon, penned the final response, which did not meet Richelieu's demanding criteria until the third version, proof, in part, of the serious nature of the task in Richelieu's eyes.

The opening arguments of Chapelain's/the Academy's *Sentiments* illustrate clearly that like Scudéry the Academy understands the quarrel to be over much more than Corneille's actual play. The forty male immortals begin by addressing the act of literary criticism itself, defending the practice in the interest of "utilité commune" (the common good). It is to serve society as a whole that literary critics undertake the task of evaluation and occasionally censorship. Continuing this line of thought, the Academy states that its purpose is to aid the public in its literary evaluation, not discourage it or dismiss its approbation for Corneille's play. In fact, the writers defend pleasure as a necessary quality for literature, but with an important caveat. This pleasure must be "conforme à la raison" (in conformity with reason) (359). It becomes clear that this "raison" is derived more from the conventional rules advocated by Scudéry than from the relatively vaguely defined pleasure used by Corneille and others in defense of the play and the public's judgment. Thus while the Academy acknowledges the influence of pleasure in literary evaluation, it does so in order to define it according to its own criteria. The goal of the *Sentiments* is to determine "pas tant si elle (the play) avait plu, que si en effet elle avait dû plaire" (not so much if the play pleased, but if it should have pleased) (359). As shall become apparent, the verb "devoir" here represents the Academy's reinstitution of learned doctrine as the only acceptable criteria for criticism. A play may please, but how it pleases and according to what criteria determines whether the pleasure is truly acceptable.

The Academy establishes different degrees of pleasure, and elevates only one as acceptable and truly "utile" or useful:

> ... nous pouvons dire tous ensemble qu'une pièce de théâtre est bonne quand elle produit un contentement raisonnable. Mais comme dans la musique et dans la peinture nous n'estimerions pas que tous les concerts et tous les tableaux fussent bons, encore qu'ils pleussent au vulgaire, si les préceptes de ces arts n'y étaient bien observés, et si les experts qui en sont les vrais juges ne confirmaient par leur approbation celle de la multitude. De même, nous ne dirons pas sur la foi du peuple, qu'un ouvrage de poésie soit bon parce qu'il l'aura contenté, si les doctes aussi n'en sont contents. Et certes il n'est pas croyable qu'un plaisir puisse être contraire au bon sens, si ce n'est le plaisir de quelque goût dépravé. (360)

> (... we maintain that a play is good when it produces a reasonable satisfaction. But as with music and painting we do not judge all concerts and paintings good, even if the common people find them so, if the precepts governing these arts have not been observed, and if the experts who are the true judges, do not confirm the people's acceptance by their own. Similarly, we would not say, based on the people, that a work of poetry was good because it was pleasing to them if scholars were not also pleased. Certainly it is unbelievable that pleasure could be contrary to good sense, unless it is pleasure deriving from some depraved taste.)

It is clear in this passage and throughout *Les Sentiments* that the *doctes* and not the "common people" are the "true judges" of literary quality, and their judgment is founded upon certain "préceptes de ces arts" that only "les experts" are trained to know. While the Academy does not vindicate Scudery's every point, it does side with him on this essential point of literary politics: not everyone can judge and only certain criteria are valid. The public must be corrected by the learned *doctes* such as the Academy in order to avoid being duped by false poetic beauty, as the public was with *Le Cid*. The Academy recognizes that Corneille's play has its strong elements, especially moving passion, but the play's strengths have blinded the worldly public to its enormous flaws:

> Ce sont ces puissants mouvements, qui ont tiré des spectateurs du Cid cette grande approbation, et qui doivent aussi la faire excuser. L'Auteur s'est facilement rendu maître de leur âme, après y avoir excité le trouble et l'émotion; leur esprit flatté par quelques endoits agréables, est devenu aisément flatteur de tout le reste, et les charmes éclatants de quelques parties leur ont donné de l'amour pour tout le corps. (414)

> (These strengths, which made the spectators approve of Le Cid, should also excuse it [their approbation]. The author easily became the master of their souls, after having evoked strong emotions; their minds, finding some parts pleasing, were lulled into finding the rest pleasing, and the striking charms of a few parts made them love the whole thing.)

The Academy concurs with Scudéry that one of the chief flaws is indeed the character of Chimène. In the Academy's estimation, Chimène does not act as a woman should (372). Among her many faults, she is too egotistical in choosing love over allegiance to her father (373); she doesn't represent acceptable moral values (379) , and she is not "natural" (392). Only a woman "la plus dépouillée d'honneur et d'humanité" (the most stripped of honor and humanity) would accept to marry her father's murderer on the same day as the murder (368). In attempting to satisfy the rule of twenty-four hours, Corneille went beyond all *vraisemblance* and thus offered a heroine who could never serve as an example.

In the end, the Academy comes to the opinion that while the play did indeed please, it should not have. As literature must serve as an example, one must please according to the rules that ensure this exemplarity (360). For the good of society, the public must allow itself to be guided by the learned "good sense" of experts and of bodies such as the Academy. In the *Sentiments*, the Academy, headed by Richelieu, recognizes the power of this new worldly public and works to control it. This new public for whom learned rules are simply false constraints on poetic genius constituted a real danger, for their influence could engender new rules, new genres, and new subversive heroines. When Scudéry called upon the Academy to enter the quarrel, he framed his request in political terms, calling the Academy's intervention a move to defend France itself:

... prononcez, O mes juges, un arrêt digne de vous, et qui fasse savoir à toute
l'Europe, que *le Cid* n'est point le chef-d'oeuvre du plus grand homme de
France, mais oui bien la moins judicieuse pièce de Monsieur Corneille même.
Vous le devez, et pour votre gloire en particulier, et pour celle de notre nation
en général, qui s'y trouve intéressée: vu que les étrangers qui pourront voir ce
beau chef-d'oeuvre, eux qui ont eu des Tassos et des Guarinis, croyaient que
nos plus grands maîtres, ne sont que des apprentifs, C'est la plus importante et
la plus belle action publique, par où votre illustre Académie puisse commencer
les siennes: tout le monde l'attend de vous. (217)

(pronounce, my judges, a verdict worthy of you, one that shows all of Europe
that *Le Cid* is not the masterpiece of the greatest man in France, but rather
the least judicious play of a mere M. Corneille. You must, both for your own
glory and for that of our nation in general, which finds itself involved. Given
that foreigners who could see this beautiful masterpiece, those foreigners
who themselves have had Tassos and Guarinis, could believe that our greatest
masters are mere apprentices. This is the greatest and most important public
action by which your illustrious Academy can begin its actions: everyone is
expecting it from you.)

Plays such as *Le Cid* are dangerous because they can incite questionable
behavior, given a malleable public's tendency to emulate whatever it sees.
Literature is also a direct determinant of the status of the French nation and
for this reason also must conform to certain rules. According to Scudéry's
reasoning, to produce a questionable text and see it circulated among foreigners
as an example of French genius is to threaten France's reputation and status.
Scudery calls upon the Academy to denounce *Le Cid* as a product of a "the
greatest man in France," thus representing the best France has to offer, and
instead reduce it to the status of an imperfect play by a mere citizen not
recognized as having any particular affiliation with France itself. Only certain
kinds of literature, sanctioned by a specific, carefully selected, public, can be
sent out in the world to represent France. The role of the Academy, in Scudéry's
formulation, is thus to serve as a watchdog over literary production. Its actions
are public in the sense that they are political and destined to "publicize" a
particular vision of France and at the same time maintain control over the
"public" in the sense of populace.

In trying to replace the voice of the worldly public with that of the French
Academy, Scudéry was attempting to determine the shape of French literature
and displace the worldly public from any input into the form this literary
production would take. He saw his actions as not simply for the good of
literature but more importantly for the good of France as a nation. In his eyes,

French literature could not be seen as being shaped by the tastes of a worldly public. The Academy, at the urging of one of France's most powerful political luminaries, Richelieu, heeded Scudery's call to arms in the defense of France's glory. In the *Sentiments*, it is clear that the Academy recognizes the power of this new worldly public and the danger its criteria, principally pleasure, might pose to society and to France's image. The power of pleasure as a criterion, especially in the hands of an "injudicious" female public, could be used to create new heroines, new genres, and consequently new social mores. It is largely for this reason that the Academy used the debate to establish itself as the ultimate governing body for literature. The Academy managed to squelch any further debate over *Le Cid* itself, but the debate over the worldly public, in particular over women's influence, was far from over.

Putting Values into Practice: Valincour, Charnes, and the Worldly Public

Just as the quarrel over Corneille's *Le Cid* at the beginning of the century can be viewed as a revelatory moment that allows us to glimpse the beginnings of new criteria for literary evaluation and creation, another quarrel illustrates the influence of the public that Corneille had valorized almost fifty years previously, and reveals just how influential this worldly public had become. In 1678, Lafayette published *La Princesse de Clèves*, the historical novel that today is regarded as the first "modern" French novel. Before it even appeared, Lafayette's masterpiece provoked controversy due in particular to the heroine's *aveu* or declaration to her husband that she was in love with another man.[9] The novel's surprising ending in which the heroine rejects her "lover" even after her husband's death and opts to live out her life alone, also inspired passionate responses, as indeed it continues to do even today. The worldly newspaper, the *Mercure Galant*, published a series of letters responding to the editor's provocative questions regarding the forthcoming novel. When the novel finally appeared, it was immediately hailed a masterpiece of the new genre as well as an exceptional addition to the literature of *Le Grand Siècle*. In addition to numerous letters commenting on the novel that circulated throughout the realm, two lengthy critical texts appeared that analyzed the work's merits and faults in often painstaking detail. The first of these texts was Valincour's *Lettres à Mme la marquise *** sur le sujet de la Princesse de Clèves*. Valincour's critique of the novel was almost as long as the work itself. Six months later another lengthy volume was added to the debate. The abbé de Charnes published *Conversations sur la critique de la Princesse de Clèves*, a work that systematically refutes all the charges leveled at the work by Valincour. *La Princesse de Clèves* is the only prose work to have elicited so much critical furor during the classical period.

Critics have long been attracted to these two texts in particular for their ability to shed light on the public's expectations and for their value as documents that trace the evolution of the novel and generic norms. More recently, Valincour's and Charnes's texts have been analyzed in light of what they reveal about attitudes towards women, as much of the discussion revolves around the princess's behavior and whether or not it was socially acceptable.[10] The texts thus shed light on the culture of the early years of Louis XIV's reign, as well as on the literary history of the period, especially the development of the novel. But these texts are also valuable for their ability to elucidate the influence of the worldly milieu on the literary field, for both authors are acutely aware of the tastes and literary expectations of the worldly milieu and their effect on more traditional scholastic values associated with literary composition. The quarrel over Lafayette's novel is both representative of the questions surrounding the literary influence of the salons, and an exemplary, singular debate due to the intensity and the widespread influence of the discussions it elicited. Much more than a controversy around a novel, this quarrel represents in many respects the apogee of discussions surrounding the forms and functions of literary criticism and who determines them.[11] Valincour's and Charnes's texts both illustrate how by 1678 any critic had to take worldly taste into account, and how the world of the *ruelles* had infiltrated the forms used to discuss literature.

If this particular novel inspired such carefully crafted and often emotional responses, it is partly because it was one of the most popular works of its day. The question of the public and its taste and pleasure are thus the catalyzing forces behind the debate. Both the major participants recognize the importance of the public to their own works. Valincour identifies the almost inimitable relationship between this work and its readers when he remarks "Je crois qu'il est peu de livres en notre langue, qui soit plus capable d'attacher le lecteur, et de faire impression sur son esprit[12] (I think there are few books in our language that are more capable of attracting a reader and making an impression on his mind). The novel proves to be the perfect battlefield for determining the power of the worldly public as literary critics as well as for examining in depth its criteria for judgment of literary value. In both texts, the public, its authority, and its pleasure are among the critics' primary preoccupations. But an analysis of these texts reveals that while both Valincour and Charnes seem to have in common a desire to valorize worldly public opinion, in reality their views of this public and its criteria for judgment are very different. While Valincour would seek to limit the influence the worldly public could exercise on literary creation, Charnes embraces it and extolls the new creativity this public fosters.

The influence of the worldly public is immediately evident in the form of both critical texts. Just as Buffet takes the study of language out of the academy and locates it in a salon, Valincour and Charnes transfer the power to judge literature from the Academy to the worldly milieu of the salon. They recognize that the principal public for their critical works is indeed the worldly public and both inscribe this public into the actual form of their texts. Valincour recreates the worldly literary universe by addressing his series of three letters, the worldly genre par excellence, to a fictional marquise. The narrator renders himself subservient to the marquise by stating that he is only writing because she compelled him to do so. Throughout the *Lettres* Valincour constructs a narrator persona that is completely identified with the worldly milieu. He depicts himself as a man of society whose only role is to report the conversations he has had with a wide variety of people who could all have been participants in a *ruelle* of the period. To give an epistolary form to this series of conversations is to privilege doubly the worldly milieu. To enhance this relationship to worldly society, Valincour adds a strong female presence and voice. This highlighting and extolling of the salon milieu has led the modern day editor of the *Lettres* to advance that "Valincour propose une lecture mondaine de *La Princesse de Clèves* ... un dialogue délicat avec le public des 'honnêtes gens'" (Vaincour offers a worldly reading of *La Princesse de Clèves* ... a subtle dialogue with the public of *honnêtes gens*) (vi).

The world Valincour creates in the *Lettres* seems to contain every possible salon participant. He relates their various opinions and observations on the novel, as is evident in the following brief exerpts:

> Les femmes prudes ne peuvent pardonner ... (8)
> Les femmes habiles soutiennent que ... (9)
> La lettre a semblé un peu longue à bien des gens. (31)
> ... un homme que vous estimez infiniment et qui est assurément un des plus agréables et des plus polis esprits de son siècle ... (126)

> (Prudes cannot forgive ...
> Clever women maintain that ...
> The letter seemed a bit long to a lot of people.
> ... a man you infinitely esteem and who is surely one of the most agreeable and polite minds of his century ...)

One has the impression that one is reading a critical work in which great effort has been expended to include all voices and opinions, especially a collective, worldly voice emanating from a salon.

In response to Valincour, Charnes composed a literary critique that also valorizes the worldly reader as a judge of literary value. Charnes's text is a series of fictional conversations between the marquise of Valincour's *Lettres* and two friends, Cléonte and Damon. Charnes purposefully uses the same marquise as Valincour in order to better denounce that commentator's critical fiction and to reappropriate the female voice associated with the salons for different ends. Charnes creates a society that is more intimate than Valincour's, but the reader of the *Conversations* again finds him/herself in a worldly milieu dominated, even more so than in Valincour's text, by a woman. The group is meeting at her home, and she clearly leads the discussion by asking the questions.[13] Her "private" space is transformed into a public one in the sense that it is from this newly public space that the principles governing literary composition emanate. Charnes also situates himself vis-à-vis the discussion differently than does Valincour with respect to his fictional letters. In the preface to the *Conversations*, Charnes identifies himself as a member of the worldly public who was privileged to hear the novel read aloud before its publication, reflecting the process of worldly literary critique that will be emphasized in the *Conversations*.[14] He thus positions himself as the voice of worldly collective opinion.

Valincour's and Charnes's contributions to the debate over Lafayette's novel are not only imbued with the world of the salons on the level of form. More important, the rhetoric and criteria used to describe and evaluate the novel reveal these critics' preoccupation with taking into account and indeed playing to worldly concepts of literary value. Valincour begins the quarrel by limiting his critique to things that a worldly public would find interesting to judge, and indeed would at first glance be most qualified to render a verdict on: the "conduite" (plot), or how the novel is constructed, "les sentiments," or emotions and behavior of the principal characters, and "le style" or the written style of the work, especially the language. Valincour's worldly critics, for example, judge using the criteria of *bon sens, le goût* and *le plaisir* produced by various passages of the text, as when Valincour remarks: "Ces mots de Mme la dauphine ont un agrément et un air de naturel qui ne se peut exprimer. Je n'ai vu personne qui n'en ait été charmé, sans pouvoir dire précisément en quoi; et ce sont de ces beautés qui se font sentir, et qu'on ne saurait faire connaître" (Mme la dauphine's words possess a charming and natural air that cannot be described. I haven't met anyone who hasn't been charmed, without being able to say precisely why; these are beautiful moments that make themselves felt, but that one cannot describe) (197). Valincour's inclusion of such criteria illustrates the extent to which they were considered acceptable critical coin by at least some of the literary critics of the period.

In an intriguing strategy, Valincour simultanously incorporates worldly criteria in his literary analysis and works to cast doubt upon their true value. Just as he does with the voices of the worldly critics, Valincour includes them only to better denounce such literary values. For example, Valincour's interlocutors often cite the pleasure they obtained from a particular scene or character in the novel. On the one hand, then, Valincour would seem to be in a similar position to Corneille, valorizing pleasure as an essential value of a literary work. But at the same time, Valincour mitigates his valorization of pleasure by negating it. His critical voices accept, for example, the digressions in the work even though they are the mark of the outdated heroic novel: "Ses digressions ne sont pas extrêmement longues, et sont toujours si agréables, que si ce sont des fautes, au moins ce sont des fautes qui donnent du plaisir" (its digressions are not too long, and are always pleasing, so if they are mistakes, at least they are mistakes that give pleasure) (22). But then he goes on to criticize the digressions because in his view they have no useful relationship to the main story. Pleasure cannot take precedence over the rules of poetic composition. While pleasurable, in the final analysis, the critic valorizes generic utility over the more vague criterion of pleasure: "Il me semble que la marque d'un excellent ouvrage est de n'avoir rien d'absolument inutile" (it seems to me that the mark of a great work is to have nothing that is absolutely extraneous) (22).

Valincour goes even farther and rejects pleasure as a literary value by associating it with negative consequences for society at large. In one intriguing passage of the *Lettres*, the narrator interrogates a worldly woman of society about the true importance of pleasure as a literary criterion. He recounts that

> Madame de *** qui lit assez exactement toutes ces sortes d'ouvrages, et qui n'en avait point encore trouvé qui eut fait impression sur elle, a été pénétrée de celui-ci. Il y a des livres, me disait-elle l'autre jour, que l'on ne lit point, parce qu'ils sont mal écrits, et que l'on craint de s'ennuyer en les lisant. Je ne sais si par une raison toute contraire on ne ferait pas bien de s'empêcher de lire celui-ci. Est-ce que l'on doit craindre d'y avoir trop de plaisir, lui dis-je? C'est une crainte, me répondit-elle, que peu de gens s'avisent d'avoir, et qui cependant n'est pas si peu raisonnable qu'elle paraît. De la manière dont cette histoire est écrite, je suis assuré (sic) qu'il se trouvera plus d'une femme, qui

après l'avoir lue, se sentira le coeur plus tendre qu'elle ne l'avait auparavant. (277–9)

(Mme de ***, who reads fairly precisely all these kinds of works, and who had not yet found one that made a great impression on her, was filled with admiration for this one. There are books, she told me the other day, that no one reads because they're poorly written and one is afraid of getting bored by reading them. I'm not sure if this particular book shouldn't be avoided for the opposite reason. Should one fear getting too much pleasure [from a book]? I asked her. This is the fear, she answered, that few people dare to have, yet it is not as unreasonable as it appears. Because of the way this story is written, I'm sure there will be more than one woman, who after reading it, will feel more open to love than before.)

In this passage, Valincour employs the worldly voice of a female reader to uncharacteristically denounce pleasure as a valid criterion for literary evaluation. He presents her opinion as surprising, and thus perhaps as more valid because she is not simply mouthing collective public opinion associated with her milieu. In this moment, which Valincour presents as penetrating and illuminating because of its surprise and originality, the female reader expresses her fear that too much pleasure can in fact be harmful, a view that she characterizes as more reasonable than it might first appear, in this way accentuating the fact that what she is voicing goes against the collective opinion of the worldly public. She fears the pleasure produced by this text for precisely the same reason Scudéry denounced the public's approbation of *Le Cid*: pleasure in the text will cloud the judgment of the public and, even more dangerous, inspire them, due to such obscured vision, to accept behavior such as that exhibited by both Chimène and the Princesse de Clèves as not only acceptable but as exemplary and worthy to be followed. For Valincour's fictional female reader, the fact that the princess combats her passion for Nemours is not enough to counter the fact that she expresses that passion in the first place. In her view, it is not reasonable for a reader to condemn such illicit passion when the story is so pleasurable. An author who deliberately chooses to write such a fiction is thus an enemy of society, as Valincour's marquise explains:

dans ces sortes d'ouvrages, où l'on n'en prend que des idées qui nous plaisent, où l'on va même jusqu'à faire passer cette folie pour une vertu, et pour une marque de grandeur d'âme, il est bien difficile d'être toujours en garde contre elle, et de ne pas se laisser surprendre à un ennemi, qui nous tend des pièges si agréables. (280)

(in these kinds of works, which contain only pleasing ideas, and in which this folly [illicit passion] is passed off as a virtue and as a mark of great character, it is very difficult to always be on the defensive and to not be overwhelmed by an enemy that presents us with such pleasurable traps.)

Both the passion portrayed so beautifully in the text, and the author who composed such lines are traps that will influence a public and have a direct effect on society. Here and throughout the *Lettres*, Valincour recognizes the worldly critical category of pleasure, then works in conjunction with his supposedly worldly interlocutors to control this pleasure and undermine it.

In place of pleasure, Valincour advocates "le bon sens" or good sense as the principal characteristic that determines the true value of a text. At first glance, this would seem to be a valorization of another criterion that is associated more with the worldly public than with the *doctes*. But in Valincour's formulation it is clear that his *bon sens* is defined in relation to a set of rules established primarily outside of the worldly realm. When Valincour recounts his lengthy conversation with the "savant" or learned man, for example, it is evident that *bon sens* in this context has more in common with George de Scudéry's formulation than with any worldly concept. Valincour first states that the "savant" is too qualified to render a judgment on a trivial novel: "Ces sortes de bagatelles ne sont point de votre compétence; il faut les renvoyer aux Dames, et aux Cavaliers, qui en jugeront mieux que vous" (These sorts of trifles do not require your competence. They should be sent back to women and courtiers, who appreciate [judge] them better than you) (92). The expert responds: "Je n'ai point d'autres règles, que celles du bon sens ... et je prétends que l'on est obligé de les garder aussi bien dans une petite nouvelle, que dans un plus grand poème épique" (The only rule I have is that of good sense ... and I maintain that it is just as necessary to adhere to it in a short story as in an epic poem) (92), thus giving the impression that he would judge the way "women" and "courtiers" would. Just as Scudéry views Corneille as offering a heroine who lacks *bon sens* as well as constructing a play that transgresses all established rules, so too Valincour stresses that an author cannot shock the reader, no matter how blinded by pleasure, into accepting behavior that goes against a notion of *bon sens* established outside of the text and according to strict societal and generic criteria. Valincour's expert brings Valincour, playing the role of worldly critic, into line, stating that while some poetic license is permissible, "il ne leur est pas permis d'en abuser, jusques à faire des monstres et des chimères, ni jusques à inventer des choses qui choquent l'esprit de tous ceux qui les lisent" ([a writer] can't abuse it in order to produce monsters and chimera, nor to invent things that shock the mind of everyone who reads them) (90). When Valincour, playing the devil's advocate, seemingly dismisses the scholar's rules as too scholarly, the reader is made to agree with the scholar as opposed to his interrogator. Valincour asks "mais enfin, un ouvrage en est-il moins bon, pour n'être pas tout à fait conforme à ces règles si sévères, que la moitié du monde ne connaît point, et n'a guère d'intérêt de connaître? N'est-ce pas assez que l'on y trouve du plaisir: Si vous jugez que les aventures ne soient pas justes, les unes par rapport aux autres, considérez-les à part" (yet, is a work inferior because it doesn't conform to these strict rules that half the world doesn't know and has no interest in knowing? Isn't it enough to find it pleasurable: If you judge certain actions to be incorrect when read together, then consider each one separately) (119). The scholar responds with disdain:

> C'est justement ... comme si dans un concert où il y aurait de très belles voix, qui ne seraient pas d'accord entre elles, ni avec les instruments, vous m'alliez conseiller d'écouter avec application et de m'attacher à chaque voix, ou à chaque instrument ... Croyez-vous que cela fut fort raisonnable? (119–20)

> (That would be as if there were a concert with beautiful voices that did not go with each other or with the instruments and you advised me to listen to each voice or to each instrument. Do you think that is very reasonable?)

Reason is clearly allied with the scholar as opposed to the worldly critic. Valincour defines good taste or *bon goût* so that is can be controlled by judgment founded upon established literary conventions, not by the "fantasy" of a worldly public.[15]

Similarly, Charnes has recourse to worldly taste and the rhetoric of worldly literary criticism. And like Corneille before him, he posits pleasure as the principal quality with which to judge the value of the work. Charnes systematically defends the passages critiqued by Valincour as those that the readers found most pleasurable. In this manner, Charnes valorizes this worldly critical value par excellence and endows the worldly public with absolute authority over the value of a literary work, and indeed over his own work of criticism. Charnes accuses Valincour of not reflecting public opinion: "... le Critique n'avait pas suivi le sentiment du public, en faisant ses trois Lettres" (... the critic did not respect public opinion when he wrote his three letters) (vi). Charnes is inspired by this fault to compose his own critique:

Et je me serais peut-être résolu à entreprendre la défense de la Princesse de Clèves, si je n'eusse appris, qu'on avait vu en manuscrit quelques conversations qui pouvaient servir de réponse au Critique. Je les ai recouvertes, et j'ai cru que je devais les donner au public. C'est à lui de juger ... et je ne veux pas prévenir son jugement, en lui donnant le mien sur ces conversations. (vii–viii)

(I would have perhaps decided to defend La Princesse de Clèves myself if I hadn't learned that someone had found a manuscript of a few conversations that could serve as a response to the critic. I found them and thought I should give them to the public. It is up to the public to judge ... and I don't want to prejudice its judgment by giving [the public] my opinion of these conversations.)

In Charnes's explanation of the fictional genesis of his *Conversations*, he was inspired as a singular critic to respond to Valincour, but in the end had no need to do so because the collective voice of the worldly milieu had already formulated a response. Charnes's critical act thus consists solely of publishing the conversations he found. He erases himself from the critical act in order to privilege the public's judgment of the novel as well as the critical act reflecting this judgment created entirely by this public. Whereas Valincour positions himself as one voice in the collective, Charnes takes a more radical stance. He presents himself as not intervening at all in the public assessment of the novel.

Charnes's text is in fact designed to offer a new way of reading and determining the value of a literary text. In his view, Valincour's approaches are false interpretations of worldly critical methods, so he works to unveil and reveal this duplicity. He advances that while on the surface Valincour may use the same vocabulary of *bon sens* and *plaisir* associated with the worldly milieu, in reality Valincour is only a *docte* in worldly clothing, a traditional critic who can read and judge only according to and using methods that cannot adequately evaluate the new genre this novel represents. Charnes accuses Valincour of not thinking, a loaded charge that identifies the critic as an outsider to the worldly community he pretends to represent:

... mais il (le critique) n'y pense pas, et si cette histoire avait été faite sur les maximes qu'il établit, il s'en faudrait bien qu'elle n'eut donné à ses lecteurs le plaisir qu'elle leur a donné. Pour bien juger de cette variété, et de la beauté de l'imitation qui fait le grand charme de ces fictions: il faut être autre chose que Grammarien: Il faut un sens exquis et relevé: Il faut avoir appris par une grande expérience du monde à bien juger des bienséances, et avoir étudié les passions que l'on représente. (xvi–xvii)

(... but [the critic] isn't thinking; if this story had been composed according to the maxims he establishes, it would never have given its readers the pleasure it did. In order to correctly judge this variety and the beauty of imitation that creates the charm of these fictions, one must be more than a grammarian. One must have exquisite and an elevated sense [of judgment]. One has to have learned, by means of a great deal of worldly experience, how to judge propriety, and have studied the passions that [authors] represent.)

In Charnes's opinion, Valincour is not the right person to critique the novel because he is not schooled in the worldly values necessary to appreciate this type of literary work. He does not know how to "think" like the worldly collective, which entails feeling as opposed to merely comparing to "maxims" established outside the worldly milieu and outside the text itself.[16]

According to Charnes's critical method, one must read the novel as its own world rather than comparing it to an ideal existing outside of its cover. Thus Charnes's critics do not, for example, denounce the use of digressions simply because they are supposedly outmoded. They justify their inclusion by carefully examining how such supposed digressions function in the context of this particular work.[17] Charnes's critics work to establish new rules for the genre of the *nouvelle historique*, explaining that reliance on former models is useless. And they formulate these rules using *La Princesse de Clèves* itself and its relationship to its public. In their view, Valincour's critique is totally off the mark because he has not even recognized that this is indeed an example of a new genre. He is mired in outdated comparisons with the epic that have no place in this critical evaluation. Charnes defines the *nouvelle historique* as

> une troisième espèce, dans laquelle, ou l'on invente un sujet, ou l'on en prend un qui ne soit pas universellement connu; et on l'orne de plusieurs traits d'histoire, qui en appuient la vraisemblance, et réveillent la curiosité et l'attention du lecteur. On pourrait dire, que j'invente la description que j'en donne. Je ne fais pourtant que la tirer du sujet même, et je ne suis pas en aller chercher une chez les Anciens, puisque ces sortes d'ouvrages sont une invention de nos jours ... si je voulais me mêler de faire des règles pour ceux qui veulent écrire des histoire galantes, je ne voudrais pas en chercher ailleurs que dans cet ouvrage, et j'en tirerais tous mes exemples. A quelques critiques et à quelques bizarres près, il a eu l'avantage de plaire à tout le monde. (130; 145)

> (a third type, for which either one invents a story or one takes one that is not well-known; and one adorns it with many traits of history, which give a foundation of *vraisemblance*, and awaken the curiosity and get the attention of the reader. One could say that I'm inventing the previous description. Yet

I'm only drawing it out of this novel itself, and I didn't try to find an example among the Ancients because these sorts of texts are an invention of our time … if I wanted to try to compose rules for those who wanted to write novels, I would look only in this work and would take all my examples from it. With the exception of a few critics and a few bizarre people it has had the advantage of pleasing everyone.)

According to these new rules established by worldly society, one should examine the novel itself to determine if behavior or motivations are "reasonable" in the context of the story at hand. One must examine the motivations provided within the story, not simply whether or not one would find an *aveu* (declaration) reasonable according to a limited view of acceptable behavior.[18] Charnes urges the critic Valincour to analyze the princess's actions, for example, in the context of the fictional story, not according to the norms set by society at large.[19] In addition, he urges Valincour to evaluate the novel as a product of "our time," that is, of current French society, and not as a text that reflects supposedly universal norms of behavior. The public itself, in Charnes's opinion, recognizes this because the novel "has had the advantage of pleasing everyone." Charnes allies generic innovation with the public, thus explicitly underscoring the fear perceived by the *doctes* of the public's critical power: new worldly ideas will engender new texts with alternative values. "Reason" and "reasonable" are a constant refrain in Charnes's text and provide the benchmark for deciding whether or not a character or an event merits being defended against Valincour's critique. Charnes's formulation of reason is defined according to human nature, which makes it much more fluid and vague than Valincour's related concept of *bon sens*, which he defined more rigidly and allied with strict morals of human conduct. Charnes's "reasonable behavior" is not necessarily perfect; it is "natural." He thus applauds the author for having created a fiction that he views as perfectly reflecting natural human nature:

On ne voit nulle obscurité dans ses tableaux ni dans son style. On n'y voit nul effort ni rien d'outré. Tout y est naturel au dernier point … On ne le peut accuser d'autre affectation, que de celle de n'en point avoir … Il parle de toutes choses sainement et habilement. Il paraît partout vrai et juste. (xxii–xxiii)

(There is no opacity in his portraits and his style. There is nothing forced or extravagant. Everything is as natural as possible. He [the author] can't be accused of any affectation other than that of having none. He speaks of everything soundly and cleverly. He appears true and correct throughout.)

Charnes defends the author on the basis that he has produced a work that is as naturally worldly as he himself is:

> Le mérite de l'Auteur de ce Livre, est de connaître parfaitement ceux qu'il fait parler, d'avoir une grande science de la Cour et du coeur de l'homme, une grande beauté et une grande netteté de l'esprit, et ce qui est encore plus rare une délicatesse et une politesse, où peu de personnes peuvent atteindre. (xx)

> (The merit of the author of this book is to know its characters perfectly, to have deep knowledge of the court and of the heart of humankind, a great and clear mind, and even more rare, a subtly and refinement that few could hope to attain.)

Charnes analyzes the novel much as one would in the confines of the *ruelles*, carefully studying the emotions and characters depicted in the fiction in much the same manner as one finds Madeleine de Scudéry doing in her *Conversations* modeled on those she animated in her *samedis*. The characters in Charnes's *Conversations* explain the fiction and interpret it according to the often nebulous rules of their own society, by what is "naturel," for example.[20] They explain the author of *La Princesse de Clèves* and cite the text frequently, which they feel authorized to do because the novel's author has been characterized as a worldly intimate who knows the science of the court.[21] It is thus no surprise that, given their depiction of Valincour as an outsider to the worldly milieu, their concept of *bon sens, raison* and *nature* differ considerably from his. Charnes's voices reject Valincour's entire critical act because it is not in accord with worldly processes or principles. As such, it is simply "inutile (useless):" "S'il (Valincour) avait raisonné sur ces principes établis sur la nature même, il ne se serait pas étendu, comme il fait par tout, en des questions inutiles" (If he had reflected on these principles established on nature itself, he would not have elaborated upon, as he does throughout, useless questions) (219). In short, Valincour as a critic is "unreasonable" because he is incapable of reasoning as a worldly member of society would, or indeed the novelist him/herself did.[22]

Charnes thus uses his rebuttal to define and valorize worldly criticism and its methods. He shows what this criticism is, and who such a critic is, by unmasking Valincour, specifying what worldly critical values are by revealing what Valincour is not. The debate over *La Princesse de Clèves* is thus much more than a discussion over a novel. It is a forum to address more wide-ranging concerns: What is the role of a literary critic and from what realm should the legitimate critic emanate? Is the role of a critic such as Valincour or Charnes to reflect public opinion, or should the critic's role be more pedagogical? Should the critic actually guide and form the reader and consequently control the pleasure of the reader by defining it according to certain criteria? Such a discussion harkens back to Scudéry's critique of *Le Cid* and the Academy's response where it was determined that a work could please, but only according to rules established by the scholarly public. The answers to such questions reveal just how much worldly concerns were making themselves felt by 1678, as well as the unsettled atmosphere worldly literary criteria were creating.

In many ways, the voice of Valincour's critic, while donning a worldly exterior, has more in common with a traditional scholar than with the values associated with the salons. In the *Lettres*, the fictional author acts as an arbiter in the discussions, opposing the various opinions of the interlocutors and playing them off against each other. This is the voice of traditional *raison*, a discrete but ever present voice that examines the others' judgments of literary value, but reason defined very differently from Charnes's worldly conception. Thus, while Valincour seemingly reports the collective judgment of the worldly establishment, he in reality constructs a text designed to put into question the authority and validity of that voice, and valorize instead a singular scholarly voice more resonant with Huet's presence in *De L'origine des Romans*, which we will examine shortly. Valincour facilitates the discussion between individuals such as "les femmes prudes" (prudish women) and "les femmes habiles" (clever women), by constantly asking questions of these fictional interlocutors. But rather than letting their opinions stand, Valincour subtly manipulates the discussion in order to have everyone agree with one opinion, an opinion that in most cases reflects not a worldly sensibility but that of the scholarly singular critic Valincour is in reality. As a critic, Valincour wants everyone to agree with him (33). While he seemingly invites discussion and differing interpretations, in reality it is the *docte*'s singular voice that prevails.

In a similar strategy designed to endow the singular voice with greater authority over a worldly collective one, Valincour cites this society and reveals them to be in disagreement over the value of the text. In this way he casts doubt upon their ability to come to a consensus over literary value and indeed to offer anything useful to a public. The only voice that can be followed with certainty is that of the narrator/critic himself, whose role seems to be to serve as a guide to the reader through this maze of worldly public opinion. Valincour gives voice to worldly criticism in order to denounce the vague criteria on which its evaluations are founded and assert that such worldly rules cannot ultimately serve to determine literary value. He shows that worldly values are not objective or reproducible, that they cannot be categorized and that the methods for judgment are not always systematic, unlike his own approach which analyzes the novel carefully almost line by line. At one point, for example, Valincour's narrator-critic explains one particular episode stating that: "Comme la plupart du temps l'on condamne, ou l'on approuve les choses par rapport à son humeur, et à son inclination, j'ai vu d'autres personnes, qui ne se sont pas tant arrêtées à blamer les sentiments de Mme de Clèves en cette rencontre que ceux du Duc de Nemours" (Since people usually condemn or approve of things according to their own feelings, I met other people who in this instance didn't blame the emotions of Mme de Clèves as much as those of M. de Nemours) (192). Valincour's objective seems to be to offer a remedy to the elusive criteria illustrated by "humeur" (humour) and "inclination," by giving a more in-depth analysis and a "reasoned" response to the work. Thus while he ends his *Lettres* by again stressing the fact that he has included the opinion of many people (282), in the final analysis it is the voice of the critic that echoes in the reader's mind and strives to form his/her opinion of the novel.

Charnes in many respects reverses this situation in order to privilege the collective voice of the worldly critical milieu. Charnes's *Conversations* are recorded by an omniscient narrator who never intervenes, as opposed to Valincour's overriding narrative voice. Charnes displaces critical authority from one central voice and disperses it among the intimates of a worldly gathering. All the participants share the responsibility for this critical reading. If there is any central voice—and the various participants all seem to be equal—then it is the Marquise herself. Charnes thus uses his *Conversations* not only to defend Lafayette's novel, but to more wide-reaching ends: he writes in order to refute a critical voice that would supercede worldly opinion.

The *Lettres* and the *Conversations* in fact differ radically in their conception of the literary critic. It is clear that for Valincour, the role of the critic is to correct a wayward public, to aid that essentially worldly public in determining true literary value. While Valincour at times seems simply to relay the opinions of others, more often than not he, through the voice of his narrator, imposes his own. For example, when analyzing one particular scene of the novel, he pronounces categorically his personal judgment: "Je tiens cet endroit le plus difficile de l'histoire; et je crois que tous ceux qui voudront bien y faire reflexion, se trouveront de mon avis" (I find this place in the novel the most difficult, and I believe that anyone who really thinks about it will find him/herself in agreement with me) (33). The role of the critic as envisaged by Valincour in the *Lettres* is thus that of a guard dog. The critic is presented as the one who possesses the true keys to the value of a literary work, and these keys, like those in the Academy's *Observations sur le Cid*, are founded upon scholarly as opposed to worldly knowledge. The role of a critic such as Valincour is to make a reading public reason and come to its senses, to force it to "really think about it" instead of letting itself be blinded by the external beauty of a work of literature and in particular by the pleasure, often false, it produces.

In his response, Charnes shows an awareness of the stakes of the polemic present in Valincour's text, and categorically refutes his definition of the critic and his role vis-à-vis the public. In the preface to the *Conversations*, the author advances that the worldly public, especially when it comes to novels, are the best and most qualified critics: "Les personnes de bon sens qui ne se piquent point d'écrire, sont plus disposées à rendre justice au mérite. Ils ne sont guidés que par le plaisir qu'ils goûtent, ou par l'utilité qu'ils trouvent dans l'ouvrage qu'on leur présente" (People with good sense, who don't write, are more inclined to recognize merit. They are only guided by pleasure or by the usefulness they find in a work) (xv–xvi). He draws a portrait of the ideal literary critic that crowns the worldly public as critics and validates its taste. According to Charnes, one must be a part of the worldly public in order to adequately estimate the value of a literary work. "Il faut être autre chose que Grammarien: Il faut un sens exquis et relevé: Il faut avoir appris par une grande expérience du monde à bien juger des bienséances" (One must be more than a gammarian. One must have refined and elevated taste. One must have learned from worldly experience to judge propriety properly) (XII). It is this "worldly experience" that endows the critic with his/her capacity for evaluating a literary work. Charnes totally rejects Valincour's entire critical project: "Et pourquoi juger et blamer un ouvrage à qui la plus saine partie du monde a donné son approbation?" (Why judge and condemn a work that the most sound part of the public approved of?) (XXVII). He goes even farther and denies Valincour any authority as literary critic precisely because Valincour goes against public opinion instead of valorizing its judgment. Valincour's greatest weakness, in Charnes's eyes, is not belonging to the worldly milieu. The *Lettres*—and Charnes would disagree with Valincour's modern-day editor—are not a reflection of the worldly milieu that is better qualified than any other to judge *La Princesse de Clèves*. Charnes accuses Valincour of the worst critical sin, that of having composed the *Lettres* totally alone: "C'est une critique qu'il a faite tout seul dans son cabinet" (This is a critique that he composed all alone in his study) (24). This fact in itself is sufficient reason to discount Valincour's critical opinion. Charnes then dismisses Valincour's entire text, including any praise Valincour extends to the novel, as totally unnecessary: "son approbation ... n'est pas fort nécessaire. Les beaux endroits de *La Princesse de Clèves* se font assez sentir d'eux-mêmes" (his approval is not really necessary. The beautiful parts of *La Princesse de Clèves* make themselves felt without any help) (189). According to Charnes, only the public has the legitimacy to consecrate this type of literary work.

As Charnes states, *La Princesse de Clèves* was composed for "les honnêtes gens et les gens raisonnables" (*honnêtes* and reasonable people) (71), a group whose taste Valincour clearly does not represent because as Charnes carefully points out throughout the *Conversations*, Valincour is not a *mondain*. In the *Conversations*, any ad hominem attacks on Valincour are related to what Charnes views as Valincour's greatest fault: he has no right to critique a work beyond his purview, and worse, he has the audacity to pose as a worldly *gentilhomme* in order to appear more convincing to a public even Valincour recognizes as influential in literary matters. Charnes offers a sustained critique of the critic himself in order to establish the authority of the worldly critical voice. He takes off Valincour's worldly mask, questioning his identity and his right to pronounce judgment on Lafayette's novel. Whereas Charnes expected a worldly member of the public to have dared to express his opinion of the novel, someone with "un goût exquis, et un génie extrèmement élevé" (exquisite taste and extremely rare genius) (vi), the ultimate worldly critical qualities, instead Charnes discovers that this is "une Critique de guet-à-pens" (an ambush critique) (25) composed by someone who does not exhibit "un caractère si élevé" (a very lofty character) (xxiv). Charnes even has Valincour's own marquise reject his claim that he writes following her orders. She exclaims "Il prétend donc que c'est moi qui l'ai chargé de faire une Critique de la Princesse de Clèves? Ah! qu'il ne prenne point un si mechant prétexte; je saurai bien l'en désavouer, lorsqu'il le faudra" (He claims that I asked him to write a critique of la Princesse de Clèves? Ah! He shouldn't advance such a pretexte. I'll know how to disavow it when I have to) (8). Charnes further severs any relation between Valincour's critical voice and the worldly public from which he supposedly emanates by stating that the characters he supposedly cites to denounce the novel are only inventions of his own mind: "toutes ces personnes, dont le Critique parle, sont le critique même travesti" (all these people the critic talks about are the critic himself in disguise) (53). The entire world Valincour creates is thus revealed to be false, and its authority is undermined. He represents one voice, not the collective that has already given the novel its approbation. Charnes accentuates the singularity of Valincour's opinion, thus underscoring its limitations and valorizing collective public opinion in its place.

Il se loue et s'approuve à chaque trait. La satisfaction qu'il a de lui même, et l'approbation qu'il se fait donner par les personnages qu'il introduit, pour autoriser ses jugements, lui donnent une joie ridicule, qui est répandue dans tout son livre, et qui marque un esprit fort borné. Ainsi l'on ne doit pas être surpris qu'un homme qui n'a de vu que pour se regarder lui-même, n'ai pas vu toutes les beautés et le mérite d'une fiction aussi agréable que celle de la Princesse de Clèves. (xxiv–xxv)

(He constantly praises and pats himself on the back. His self-satisfaction and the approval he gives himself through the characters he introduces in order to lend authority to his judgments give him a ridiculous joy, which is spread throughout his book and characterizes a very limited mind. Thus we shouldn't be surprised that a man who can only see himself could not see the beauty and the merit of such a pleasing fiction as La Princesse de Clèves.)

With his "lumières toutes particulières" (personal insights) (178–9), Valincour does not represent collective worldly opinion. Thus this critic who "a prétendu passer pour un homme du grand monde, et pour un galant de profession" (claims to be a man of the world, and a gallant by profession) (17) is unveiled as the singular *savant* he is, the outsider incapable of original thought who dares to judge "un ouvrage excellent, sans avoir la moindre tienture de la délicatesse et de la politesse que toute la France y a remarquées" (an excellent work without himself possessing the least bit of refinement and politeness that all of France remarked) (xxix–xxx) in the novel. The new genre requires a new type of critic, specifically a worldly one.

Throughout the *Conversations*, Charnes goes to great lengths to point out the gulf that exists between the worldly evaluation of the novel and Valincour's opinion that is usually opposed to it. Charnes thus recognizes that the debate over the novel goes far beyond simply determining the merit of this particular work. The true debate is over the public's authority to judge literature. At the heart of the quarrel is the quest for power—who holds it and who can wield it, and to what ends. Both Valincour's and Charnes's works illustrate that the general interrogation surrounding the developement of literary criticism is intimately related to the concept of power, and more precisely to the power of survival. They both understand that critics consecrate knowledge and its forms, and are endowed with the power to determine what works, what images, and what perceptions of the world will be transmitted to posterity through literature and ideology. Valincour wants to assure that this knowledge will be determined by a certain type of critic, and not by the public at large. He creates an elaborate scenario that he uses to please the general public, to seduce it, and to a more subtle degree, to denounce it. It should not be forgotten that twenty-one years after the publication of the *Lettres*, Valincour would be named to the French Academy, succeeding Racine. In preparing for this honor, he thus distinguishes himself from the public that he pretends to represent in the *Lettres*, and elevates himself above this critical voice.

When examined closely, it is clear that his text is a series of subtle refutations of worldly public opinion and authority. The critic first praises the work, thus positioning himself as seemingly in accord with the public, only to then retrace his steps in order to undermine the opinion that he has just seemingly valorized. This conflict between the worldly and the non-worldly critic culminates in a conversation that Valincour establishes between his supposed *"honnête homme"* and a "scholar," a discussion that in reality is a debate over the criteria of literary criticism and a trial to decide who can best pronounce judgment on a work of literature. Valincour's learned authority shows himself to be very harsh with respect to the novel. The "I" of the critic then takes the position of devil's advocate in order to entice the "scholar" to enunciate precisely his criteria for literary evaluation, provoking him, as we have seen, by seemingly advancing pleasure as the most important criterion. The scholar rejects this worldly criteria as completely unreasonable: "Ceux qui n'y penseront pas ... dit-il, pourront y prendre du plaisir, comme ceux qui ont un diamant faux, sans le connaître, se croient riches ... l'esprit raisonnable ne peut s'attacher à rien qui soit visiblement faux" (Those who don't reflect could obtain pleasure, like those who have a false diamond, without knowing it, think themselves rich ... a reasonable mind cannot be attracted to anything that is visibly false) (105, 107). According to this argument, pleasure cannot be used to discern the true value of a work. One must employ a certain form of scholarly reason founded upon recognized precepts of literary value. One must use accepted rules to separate "false diamonds" from true ones. Valincour thus reiterates the same arguments we have already seen in the general quarrel over what criteria of judgment should be used. His method throughout the *Lettres* indicates that, while admitting the influence of the worldly public and its primary criteria of pleasure, Valincour intends to reestablish the rules associated with the scholarly milieu. He hopes to denounce the worldly milieu as uncertain and capricious, as he allies himself, at least indirectly, with the scholarly critic he presents. Valincour's severity with respect to *La Princesse de Clèves* derives from the fact that he sees in the novel, and in its success among the public, an unparalleled occasion to enforce a more authoritarian form of criticism that would eliminate the power of the worldly public to consecrate a work.

Charnes recognizes that the true inspiration for Valincour's critique is his desire to destroy the power of the worldly critic and its corresponding criteria for judgment, thus his defense of the worldly critic is completely unambiguous. In the *Conversations*, he fights for the recognition of the public as a legitimate authority in literary matters, revealing himself to be the defender of the worldly milieu. He establishes pleasure as the absolute criteria, to the detriment of the rules proposed by Valincour. According to Charnes, "Si cette histoire avait été faite sur les maximes que [Valincour] établit, il s'en faudrait bien qu'elle n'eût donné à ses lecteurs le plaisir qu'elle leur a donné" (If this story had been composed according to the maxims [Valincour] establishes, it would not have given its readers as much pleasure) (XVII). And it is pleasure that according to Charnes determines the true value of a work, and a pleasure that is not defined according to certain rules. He rejects Valincour's criteria, and explains that worldly criteria should take precedence over such rules: "C'est aux règles à s'accomoder au goût d'un siècle aussi poli que le nôtre; et puisque les observateurs scrupuleux des règles du poème épique ne plaisent point, il faut croire que ces règles ne sont plus à notre usage et s'en faire de nouvelles" (Rules must be made to conform to the taste of such a polite century as ours; and since those who scrupulously observe the rules for epic poems do not please at all, one must come to the conclusion that these rules are no longer useful to us and create new ones) (145). In advancing the cause of new rules, rules established by worldly society, "polite" rules that "conform to the taste of a polite century" Charnes is attacking the constraining rules advocated by Valincour and the *doctes*. At the same time, he is identifying the important forces underlying this quarrel. In effect, the whole quarrel is founded upon a conflict over liberty and power—to write, to critique, to advance new criteria of evaluation—and the desire to control the creative genius of authors and the critical power of the worldly public. Ultimately this quarrel is also over who is going to define the literature that this most "polite" century is offering to a world desirous of emulating the nascent cultural capital, France. Charnes is taking an extremely bold position that will be defined as the "modernist" stance par excellence. He even uses this particular vocabulary. With respect to ancient models, Charnes explains that:

> Ces règles qu'on nous a laissées, étaient excellentes pour les anciens ... mais pour nous qui avons d'autres lumières, et qui voyons les choses avec d'autres yeux, tout cela ne saurait nous surprendre ni nous divertir longtemps. Nos modernes ont suppliée à la fable ancienne, qui n'est plus à notre usage ... Enfin nos derniers auteurs ont pris une voie qui leur a semblé plus propre à s'attacher le lecteur, et à le divertir; et ils ont inventé les Histoire galantes ... (133–5)

(These rules we inherited were excellent for the Ancients ... but for us, who have different insights and who see things differently, these cannot surprise or entertain us for long. Our most recent authors have adopted a direction that has seemed to them more likely to engage and entertain the reader. They invented *histoires galantes*.

In advancing and defending the new worldly values of an alternative critical public, Charnes is also defending the innovative genre that is the ultimate product of this public and its values, the historical novel as best illustrated by *La Princesse de Clèves*. He is careful to point out that this novel is a product of "a century as polite as ours," qualifying the time period as "polite," a worldly adjective, and separating "our" century, this worldly century, from all previous ones, especially those ancient ones consistently held up as literary models by the scholarly establishment. To extend Charnes's logic, new genres and new tastes require new criteria, specifically worldly and specifically French, since the genre he is evaluating has no antecedents in preceding centuries or countries. In his rhetoric, "our way of doing things" and "our century" can be seen as valorizations of phenomena he associates uniquely with his own country, a country that has as one of its distinguishing characteristics the influence worldly society has on its culture.

Charnes's effort to defend a new genre as he defends the new society that produced it is especially apparent in his response to Valincour's critique of the literary qualities of *La Princesse de Clèves*. Valincour recognizes that the *nouvelle galante* is indeed a new genre, but in his version, it still needs to conform to the same, if not more strict, traditional generic conventions such as those of the epic. As his "scholar" states, authors such as Lafayette "sont bien plus obligés à garder l'exacte régularité, que ceux qui font de grands poèmes" (are even more obligated to maintain generic regularity than those who compose great epics) (113). Charnes, on the other hand, would prefer to liberate the author from the models of antiquity: "Et je ne sais si outre le plaisir que ces ouvrages donnent, il ne serait pas utile de leur donner un plus libre cours" (I'm not sure if given the pleasure these works give, it wouldn't be useful to give them more artistic freedom) (147). It is precisely this authorial liberty, linked as it is in Charnes's text to the public's pleasure and influence, that provokes critics such as Valincour to invoke "ancient" rules to govern literary creativity. The worldly public, especially given its female influence, must not be given too much liberty. At the heart of the quarrel is the fear, expressed by Valincour and combatted by Charnes, of what is uncontrollable, that is in this instance, pleasure. To make pleasure the overriding criteria for literary creation is to risk losing control over this creation. The politics of literary creation thus reflect state politics, and the ideal critic in Valincour's eyes is in the image of the all-powerful monarch. The public, especially one dominated by women, cannot be granted a legitimate place in such a conception of the critic. The values associated with the salon milieu and especially the women writers working within this milieu—*bon sens*, what is "naturel," *vraisemblance*, authorial invention and liberty—were perceived as being at odds with the conventional social order by critics such as Valincour.[23]

New forms of literature, with alternative models, could bring about a new national literary culture. The stakes are indeed much higher than one would have first imagined.

Zaïde: Modes of Knowledge and Worldly Taste

It can be argued that the development of the novel required a new type of critical method to appreciate it, or even more radically, that new critical methods made it possible for the novel to come into being, that a certain critical climate can make works possible. An analysis of another of Lafayette's novels, *Zaïde*, allows us to see how the salon milieu is inscribed into the fabric of many of the works emanating from it. As we have seen, Lafayette was one of the most engaged figures in the salons throughout the century. As a young girl, she attended Rambouillet's *chambre bleue* with her friend, the future marquise de Sévigné. By mid-century, Lafayette had become an influential member of Madeleine de Scudéry's *samedis*. She also had her own salon on the rue de Vaugirard. At the same time, Lafayette frequented Montpensier's circles, as well as the court, where she was a close friend of Henriette d'Angleterre, the wife of Louis XIV's brother. As she was actively involved in worldly activities, Lafayette was writing what would become some of the best examples of historial fiction of the period, in particular her celebrated *La Princesse de Clèves*, as well as historical memoirs in which she imparted her vision of the time period to posterity. For Lafayette, as for many of her female contemporaries, active participation in the salons was fused together with literary creativity and composition, with each activity consciously and constantly nourishing the other. It is thus not surprising that Lafayette's works, as products of the worldly milieu, bear the signature of that world in a particularly intense manner.

While many critics and historians have pointed out the ways in which Lafayette's works reflect her own vision of the seventeenth century, no one has isolated the precise nature of the influence of the critical climate of the salon milieu on the fabric of her novels. One novel in particular illustrates to an exceptional degree Lafayette's engagement with the worldly milieu and especially her inscription of the critical processes associated with it. This worldly critical climate can be perceived in Lafayette's provocative novel, *Zaïde*, especially when the instances of its publication and production are taken into account. Lafayette's novel did not appear on its own. When the novel was published in 1669, it was accompanied by a lengthy critical treatise that served as its preface. This preface, entitled *Traité sur L'origine des Romans*, was composed by Huet in 1666 and was addressed to Segrais, Lafayette's friend who lent his name to the cover of *Zaïde*. Huet's *De L'origine* and Lafayette's novel can be seen to comment on the processes of literary debate as they were developing in the mid seventeenth century. Both texts identify modes of interpretation by offering a portrait of the critic engaged in this process, and both reveal the influence of a worldly public on the development of literary taste. While Huet's very lengthy and intensely learned treatise on the origins of novels is a critical text that conforms to scholarly expectations, Lafayette's novel can be read as a corollary to the act of literary criticism so overtly represented by Huet's text, one that advocates another approach to knowledge as it highlights the salon milieu to which Lafayette belonged. Together both texts reflect many of the preoccupations of seventeenth-century worldly critics as well as scholars as they sought to develop criteria for literary taste and methods for determining literary value.

Huet's *Sur L'origine des romans* is clearly the critical text that conforms most to scholarly expectations and thus could, at least on the surface, be viewed as emanating from the voice of the *docte* as opposed to the worldly community. Interestingly, this literary history of the novel not only attracted the attention of scholars, but was equally appreciated by the worldly public. It was first composed in 1666 when Huet was with Eléanore de Rohan, the abbesse de Caen. In true worldly style, he would read to her in the evening what he had written during the day (46).[24] Yet Huet's treatise is above all a very erudite exploration that reflects in content as well as structure the preoccupations and views of the institutionalized voices of scholarly critics. I will focus my attention on Huet's act of criticism within this text, his creation of a critical voice, and what effect this voice is meant to have on the novel for which it serves as the preface.

As his title implies, Huet attempts to uncover the origin of the novel. He rehearses all the past forms of the genre from almost every country imaginable. Huet begins by offering a carefully phrased, very categorical definition of the novel. In his words:

L'amour doit être le principal sujet du roman ... il faut qu'elles [les histoires feintes] soient écrites avec art et sous certaines règles ... La fin principale des romans ou du moins celle qui le doit être et que se doivent proposer ceux qui le composent, est l'instruction des lecteurs ... Ainsi le divertissement du lecteur que le romancier habile semble se proposer pour but n'est qu'une fin subordonnée à la principale qui est l'instruction de l'esprit et la correction des moeurs.[25] (47)

(Love must be the main subject of the novel ... these fictions must be written artistically according to certain rules ... The principal purpose of novels, or at least what should be the purpose and what every author should aim for, is to instruct readers ... Thus the entertainment that the clever novelist seems to offer as his/her purpose is subordinated to the main one, which is to instruct the mind [*esprit*] and correct behavior.)

In this definition, Huet legitimizes the genre by stressing that the author's purpose is primarily to instruct.[26] He chooses to depict novels as more than fluffy musings on love deriving from a mind with no other purpose than to entertain. Pleasure is subordinated to education; a worthy novelist pretends to offer merely "entertainment" but in reality instructs, a point Huet stresses repeatedly. Huet's comment is striking because pedagogy is not usually associated with the novel, but rather is ascribed to serious genres such as the theatre. Moreover, in this definition, like any serious literary genre, novels must follow "certain rules" and be composed "artistically."[27] According to Huet, novels can be distinguished from other imaginative genres because they are "fictions de choses qui ont pu être et qui n'ont point été" (fictions that could have happened, but didn't) (95), evoking the standard rule of *vraisemblance*.[28]

In his definition, Huet underscores the primary characteristic of the novel which then becomes the guiding tenent of his treatise as a whole: it is intricately related to society. Its lofty object is "to instruct *l'esprit* and to correct behavior," not merely to reflect reality. At the end of the treatise, Huet posits a symbiotic relationship between the novel and society. He credits the genre's present day excellence to the role of women and identifies seventeenth-century France as the time and place most conducive to producing premier examples of this literary form. Instead of attributing the superiority of this branch of French letters to the erudition of his contemporaries, Huet thus steps out of his academician's robes to compliment not the intellectual but the social climate. This is the context for the passage that we have examined previously in which Huet asserts:

Je crois que nous devons cet avantage à la politesse de notre galanterie qui
vient à mon avis de la grande liberté dans laquelle les hommes vivent en France
avec les femmes. Elles sont presque recluses en Italie et en Espagne, et sont
séparées des hommes par tant d'obstacles, qu'on les voit peu et qu'on ne leur
parle presque jamais.[29]

(I think we owe this advantage to the civility of our gallantry which derives in
my opinion from the great freedom in which in France men live among women.
[Women] are almost reclusive in Italy and in Spain, and are separated from
men by so many obstacles that they are rarely seen and never spoken to.)

According to Huet, the social commerce of women and men, in particular
their conversations, influences the style of novels, and accounts for France's
excellence.[30] Huet formulates his overall purpose according to this belief in the
relationship between society and literary creation: "je dis qu'il faut chercher
leur première origine dans la nature de l'esprit de l'homme inventif" (I say that
one must look for their origin in the nature of the mind [*esprit*] of inventive
man) (51). Throughout the text, it is apparent that this "nature de l'esprit" that
leads to the novel is generated by an author's society and the value it accords
to creativity. What follows is more of a sociological than a literary exposition
of cultures across the centuries. In this literary journey, Huet travels across
immense territories of time and space, from Egypt to Persia, Syria to Greece,
and Spain to France, among others. The second stage of his trip is devoted
to the diffusion of the novel.[31] He occasionally stops to give a more detailed
description of a particular work, revealing the depth of his knowledge.[32]

Throughout the treatise, Huet is careful to lend a structure to his work,
to give order to the vast, even overwhelming, amount of information he is
presenting. In addition to creating an intelligible literary history for the novel,
this structure, underscored by Huet's use of the first person, highlights the
voice of the critic himself. Order is indeed one of the main themes.[33] When
perceived as a critical act, *De L'origine* provides an example of the masterful,
expert scholarly critic belonging to the institutions of criticism. Huet does not
hesitate to interject his own opinion, authorized by the erudition he exhibits.[34]
He portrays himself as a trustworthy guide through the many countries of
literary history. He builds a case that defies contestation because few would
have the expertise in all the literatures he cites. This knowledge allows him
to make often sweeping generalizations because he appears to master all
literatures of every country and every time. Huet often refutes the opinions
of others. [35] He does not, for example, locate the origin of the novel in France
of the middle ages. The critic takes control over scholarly as well as literary

texts, just as he controls his own text by giving it explicit order. This control extends to knowledge itself, as evidenced by Huet's use of the verbs "falloir" and "devoir" throughout the text. Overall Huet conveys a sense of purpose. The quest for truth and the presentation of a certain scholarly method to arrive at this truth seem to be at the heart of his critical enterprise. He advocates a method wherein the singular critic threads his way through the maze of literary history and others' erudite opinions and constructs a truth founded on authoritative texts. His treatise thus portrays the critical act as that of a scholar, working alone in contact with sources and literary texts, and transmitting the knowledge gleaned with an authoritative, masterful voice.

Huet accentuates this conception of the critical act in a lengthy passage concerned with the role of the public in the reception of a work. This obvious digression from his search for the origins of the novel focuses attention on the act of criticism itself, bringing up many of the issues of the general debate in the seventeenth century over who can judge and by what standards. In the persona of the scholarly critic, Huet offers one point of view:

> Il ne faut pas juger d'un livre par le nombre mais par la suffisance de ses approbateurs. Tout le monde s'attribue la licence de juger de la poésie et des romans, tous les piliers de la grande salle du palais et toutes les ruelles s'érigent en tribunaux où l'on décide souverainement du mérite des grands ouvrages; on y met hardiment le prix à un poème épique ... quelquefois, l'on y pourra perdre de réputation. Un sentiment tendre y fait la fortune d'un roman. (87–8)

> (A book must not be judged by the number but by the quality of its admirors. Everyone feels permitted to judge poetry and novels, all the pillars of the court and all the salons establish themselves as courtrooms where people supremely decide the merit of great works. They audaciously decide the worth of an epic poem ... sometimes people can lose their reputation. A tender emotion can make a novel's fortune.)

Huet's argument seems to rejoin those of the salons' detractors who, as we have seen, put these "courts" that judge so "absolutely" on trial. Huet goes on to elucidate the "suffisance" that worthy critics must possess. He relies on the authority of ancient authors seemingly to right this democratization of the critical act, stating that

> l'estime des poèmes [selon Cicéron] dépend du jugement d'un petit nombre de personnes, et de cette [maxime] d'Horace, qu'il n'appartient pas à tout le monde d'en remarquer les défauts ... ils [auteurs] se contentent de plaire à de

plus fins connaisseurs, et qui ont d'autres règles pour en juger. Et ces règles sont connues de si peu de gens, que les bons juges sont peut-être plus rares que les bons romanciers ou les bons poètes ... Je reviens au roman. (88)

(the value of literary works depends upon the judgment of a small number of people and upon the following maxim by Horace, that not everyone has the ability to remark mistakes ... [authors] are content to please the most discerning connaisseurs, who have other rules by which to judge. And these rules are known by so few people that good judges are perhaps more rare than good novelists or good poets ... I return to my discussion of the novel.)

Huet seems to promote the kind of criticism his *De L'origine* represents, one in which the best judges are not the uneducated public but the "most discerning connaisseurs" who know "other rules with which to judge." His argument echoes that of Scudéry and the French Academy in the debate over how *Le Cid* should be evaluated. In this acknowledged aside, as well as in his own critical act, Huet seems to side with such *doctes* as opposed to the worldly critics.

But is this passage really so categorical, or is there perhaps a touch of irony? We should not forget that Huet was an active member of worldly society and frequented the *ruelles*. His aside is composed in such a way as to allow for an opposing reading that acknowledges the legitimacy of worldly criticism. This conflict in perspective glimmers through the imprecise vocabulary. Although he refers to the Ancients, he does not specify that these "most discerning connaisseurs" and their rules are the scholarly critics who rely on ancient models. Similarly, his remark that "these rules" again imprecise, are known to "so few people" can be interpreted as either rules known by scholars or worldly criteria and the elusive taste known to the elite of the salons. Huet thus enters the debate over critical methods and does not adopt one categorical position. While his learned treatise and his critical persona can be characterized as traditional and scholarly, the influence of the worldly public surfaces as Huet alludes to other forms of criticism and to other judges. This undercurrent of worldly empathy is especially evident when Huet expounds on the creativity at the heart of novels. He asserts that the desire to invent, common to everyone, does not derive from reasoning, imitation or custom, but rather from nature. It follows from this that the appreciation of the products of this "natural inclination" also employs innate characteristics as opposed to learned, customary doctrine founded on reason: "... il ne faut point de contention d'esprit pour les [novels] comprendre, il n'y a point de grands raisonnements à faire, il ne faut point se fatiguer la mémoire; il ne faut qu'imaginer ... C'est pourquoi ceux qui agissent plus par passion que par raison ... y sont les plus sensibles" (it is not necessary to have a *contention d'esprit* to understand novels, it doesn't take a lot of reasoning, one doesn't need a lot of memory; one need only imagine ... That's why those who act more out of passion than reason are the most sensitive to novels) (132). With such remarks, Huet joins the side of the debate that acknowledges women as natural judges, and stresses that the new genre needs new critics.

By allying the novels with society and its sense of taste, Huet seems to legitimize a critical method that emanates from the same society that produces the novel, the worldly milieu, even while he offers an example of scholarly criticism. Perhaps this format is necessary in order to convey his messages of tolerance both for the new genre and for worldly critics. Huet in fact defends the novel, advocating that it be at least tolerated by censors.[36] In a final gesture he returns to their pedagogical function, calling them "des précepteurs muets" (silent teachers) (142). He praises d'Urfé and Scudéry, and then elevates *Zaïde*, "dont les avantures sont si nouvelles et si touchantes, et dont la narration est si juste et si polie" (whose adventures are so new and touching, and whose narration is so exact and polite) (149).[37]

Thus, on the one hand, Huet's text can be seen to represent the voice of the learned, authoritative critic, the one to whom Georges de Scudéry appealed to join him in denouncing *Le Cid*. Yet concurrently, Huet reveals himself to be another Chapelain, a learned figure schooled in the classical scholarly taste but also an integrated member of the worldly milieu. Huet's preface invites us to read *Zaïde* as much more than a text of "new and touching adventures." On an implicit level, this novel is a corollary to Huet's commentary on the critical act of literary evaluation. Huet suggests that the new genre may require different methods of evaluation, as well as different critics. *Zaïde* continues the exploration of this cultural debate and, as shall become apparent, it is a clear endorsement of a worldly critical method.

It is especially significant that Lafayette's and Huet's hybrid text appeared at the height of the debate over the forms of criticism and the identity and function of the critic, in particular the place of the salons and the worldly public in the critical process. Lafayette and Huet seem to want to provide a commentary not just on novels but on the act of evaluating literature. Moreover, the conjoined text itself is a product of the salon milieu. In a letter and in his *Mémoires*, Huet describes a collaborative creative process and stresses that Lafayette was indeed the novel's author, even though *Zaïde* was published under Segrais's name:

Qui peut mieux être informé de la vérité que moi, qui ai été dans une étroite liaison avec cette dame, qui lui ai vu composer ce livre, et à qui elle l'a communiqué pièce à pièce à mesure que son travail s'avançait.[38]

(Who can be better informed of the truth than I, who was very close to this women, who saw her write this book, and to whom she gave it little by little, as her work advanced.)

Tandis que Madame de Lafayette composait son charmant roman de *Zaïde*, auquel Segrais a mis la main et son nom, ce dernier me demanda un jour qui étaient selon moi les premiers auteurs de romans ... je travaillais donc avec ardeur, et ce que j'avais écrit dans le jour, je le lisais le soir, à la savante abbesse [Marie-Eléonore de Rohan, abbesse de Caen]. J'achevai enfin (1666) cette lettre à Segrais, qui depuis fut publiée et mis en tête de *Zaïde*. C'est pourquoi Madame de Lafayette aimait à me dire que nous avions marié entre eux nos enfants.[39]

(While Mme de Lafayette was composing her charming novel *Zaïde*, with which Segrais helped and which he signed, the latter asked me one day who in my opinion were the first novelists ... I wrote with much fervour, and whatever I wrote during the day I read in the evening to the knowledgeable abbess [Marie-Eléanore de Rohan, abbesse de Caen). I finished this letter to Segrais, which was since published as a preface to *Zaïde*. That's why Mme de Lafayette liked to say to me that we had married our children together.)

Just as the process of literary creation is one of collaboration, so too is the critical method espoused to determine the value of such texts. Lafayette's novel, when analyzed in this context, inscribes the critical act of collective salon criticism that is in direct contrast with the singular voice of the learned male scholar in Huet's preface. It is an exploration of modes of interpretation and possible means of attaining understanding. Through her choice of structure and themes, Lafayette inscribes a subtext that valorizes worldly critical acumen. She publicizes and valorizes the salon's critical process.

The first thing that strikes the reader of *Zaïde* is the novel's structural complexity. Whereas Lafayette's previous work, *La Princesse de Montpensier*, is a textbook example of the *nouvelle historique*, *Zaïde* seems to harken back to the *roman héroïque*, the novel form that was gradually replaced by the *nouvelle historique*. Lafayette emphasizes the ties with the heroic novel, whose most celebrated practitioner was her friend, Scudéry, by incorporating the technical hallmark of the genre, the interpolated narrative (*histoire intercallée)* structure, as well as all the commonplaces of the heroic novel—portraits, every possible love configuration, mistaken identities, and almost innumerable twists of fate. To make matters even more complicated, all these characteristics of the heroic novel are telescoped into a narrative the length of a *nouvelle*, thus forcing the reader to pay close attention and become acutely aware of the actual structure. Lafayette can be viewed as choosing this particular form because it provides a unique way to comment on the act of criticism.

The variety of perspectives created by the constant succession of internal narratives is an essential component of Lafayette's commentary. Each internal narrative explores a different facet of passion. Each illuminates, sometimes very obliquely, the principal story of Consalve and Zaïde, the main characters who meet at the beginning of the novel when Zaïde is washed up on a beach after a shipwreck. Consalve immediately falls in love with her, and for the rest of the novel tries to discover her identity and her story. His quest is made especially difficult by the fact that they do not speak the same language. The theme of communication and interpretation is what joins all the various interpolated narratives to the main story, and allows Lafayette to address the salon's methods for attaining knowledge and understanding and determining the value of literary texts.

The multiplicity of narrative voices in *Zaïde* can be interpreted as Lafayette's inscription of the collective voice of the salons. A brief summary of these voices and their narratives reveals the intentional and intense scattering of point of view in the novel. *Zaïde* begins with the main story presented by an omniscient narrator who resurfaces occasionally thoughout the novel. S/he relates that Consalve joins Alphonse in exile after an unhappy love affair. Both characters flee the company of others. Consalve then recounts his past misfortunes to Alphonse. Next Alphonse attempts to top Consalve's tale of woe with an account of his own tragedy. Consalve's friend, Don Garcie, tells his story to Consalve, whom he finds in exile. Don Olmond, also a friend of Consalve, then retells the story of Zaïde and her friend and confident Félime to Consalve, a narrative he learned from Félime. Inbedded in this story is that of Alamir, who is in love with Zaïde. This account was told by Mulziman, a friend of Alamir, to Félime who then related it to Don Olmond who tells it to Consalve. There is a brief return to the main story, then the rest of Félime and Zaïde's story told through don Olmond to Consalve as related by Félime. Félime's internal narrative constitutes a third of the novel. Finally Zaïde repeats to Consalve much of the story told by Félime, although this is not inscribed in the text. Zaïde is never granted her own narrative. She is the kernal of truth to be discovered. Most of these stories contain something to help Consalve learn the truth about Zaïde, that is, her identity and her narrative.

The various narrators thus provide complementary pieces of the puzzle. Knowledge and understanding are revealed to be best served by a mode of interpretation founded on a collaborative creative process. This collaboration reflects the composition of the novel itself, for Lafayette, Huet, Segrais, and La Rochefoucauld each had some hand in its production. I would contend that Lafayette inscribes this collaboration in *Zaïde* in order to valorize it, and by extension the act of worldly criticism. The steady stream of internal narratives reflects the activity of the salons.

In *Zaïde*, the collaboration of multiple voices representing the art of conversation is revealed to be the only method of discovering the truth about Zaïde, or indeed for understanding any of the minor puzzles of the novel. In contrast, the singular voice is shown to be totally ineffective. This is especially well illustrated by the main character, Consalve. Even his own past, which he relates to Alphonse, has been supplemented by knowledge obtained through someone else.[40] When he stumbles upon the mysterious Zaïde, he attempts to construct a narrative of her identity and her amorous past and present on his own and without the aid of linguistic information. The omniscient narrator details the composition of this story derived solely from Consalve's interpretation of appearances. With every fragment Consalve renders himself more miserable because he becomes convinced by his own fabricated story that Zaïde loves someone else, that that person died in the shipwreck, that he himself resembles the person she loved, and that she is devastated by her loss and tormented by his resemblance to her lover. The story cannot be confirmed through a conversation with Zaïde due to the language barrier and thus becomes more and more elaborate and, as we shall see, erroneous. The narrator relates, for example, that

> enfin il crut savoir, comme s'il eût appris d'elle-même, que l'amour était la cause de ses pleurs (finally he believed he knew, as if he had learned it from Zaïde herself, that love caused her tears). (49)

> il s'imagina qu'il ressemblait à cet amant qu'elle lui paraissait regretter (he imagined that he resembled this lover that she seemed to him to regret). (50)

> Il crut que, quand il serait aimé de Zaïde, ce ne serait toujours que son rival qu'elle aimerait en lui (He believed that, when Zaïde would love him, she would really only love his rival whom she saw in him). (100)

Lafayette's use of the verbs "believe" and "imagine" with Consalve as the sole subject underscores Consalve's process of individual creation, a process that is not enlightened with others' interpretations and understanding. The situation becomes even more complicated later in the novel when Consalve, now out of exile and at war for his country, encounters Alamir and decides that he is the one whom Zaïde loves ... and he is not just a rival ghost. Until the final pages Consalve remains tortured by his conclusion that "elle est entre les mains d'un rival, et d'un rival aimé" (she is in the hands of a rival, and of a rival she loves) (106).[41]

Consalve's reading of signs illustrates that individual reasoning must be supplemented with the knowledge of others to make a complete narrative and to interpret events. His creation of a narrative informed by only one mind is echoed by his friend Alphonse's tale of personal tragedy. Alphonse relates that he fell in love with Belasire, primarily because she conformed to his demand that the woman he would marry would never have loved another. But he is so determined to guarantee that Belasire is uniquely his that he begins to misinterpret her every word and gesture, and like Consalve, creates a narrative on his own. He allows no one else's reasoning or interpretation to penetrate or influence his construction of truth. His mistake leads to his killing of his own friend out of jealousy that is totally unfounded.

Consalve does not learn his friend's lesson, and spends most of the novel adding to his faulty account. Finally, Consalve and Zaïde overcome all obstacles, especially Consalve's false narrative, and are united in marriage. Lafayette underscores that a process of collaboration allows the characters to arrive at knowledge. Step by step the various narrators and their interpolated stories and other perspectives on events undo the story Consalve has developed regarding Zaïde's history. Félime's account of the same events Consalve constructed into his narrative of misery proves Consalve to have been a lousy interpreter and in fact incapable of coming to the truth on his own. With the help of Félime and don Olmond, voices for Zaïde's story, Consalve learns that his narrative is wrong. Each of his narrative fragments is taken up by Félime, and each fails the test for truth. Lafayette uses Félime's account to illustrate that a collaborative effort, with a female voice at its foundation, leads to knowledge and understanding.[42]

Lafayette compounds her inscription and valorization of the collaborative nature of the salon's approach to creativity and to understanding by commenting on the need not only to adopt a different method but also to use different tools for interpretation. In this equation, language, the ordinary means of attaining knowledge, can be equated with the accepted rules of poetic precepts of scholars. In *Zaïde*, Lafayette elevates the qualities we have seen associated with salon culture—good and common sense, sensitivity—over language as she advocates a different sort of reasoning. Throughout the novel, language is at the heart of Consalve's torment. He needs linguistic means for communication and knowledge. When he does attempt to read other signs, or combine them with language for understanding, he proves to be incompetent. Nonverbal signs only add to the faulty narrative he has already constructed because he cannot interpret them. He immediately transforms them into language to add to his story. "Il s'imagina" is a constant refrain as Consalve constructs a narrative from what he sees. Lafayette underscores that knowledge, represented by Zaïde, cannot be attained only through traditional means, that is, through language. It must be supplemented with other tools of interpretation. Indeed, throughout the novel, language is portrayed as untrustworthy and misleading.[43]

Some characters rely on means other than linguistic ones to find the truth. The characters who are most successful at using these alternative tools are women. The gender-marked nature of interpretation, indeed the indispensability of female participation in the act of interpretation and even in the search for knowledge and understanding, is underscored by the fact that in Félime's account, Zaïde is shown to be a good interpreter because she is not trapped on the surface of linguistic signs. For example, Zaïde correctly interprets Consalve's actions when he tries to show his affection by taking a bracelet she made from her hair (222). Consalve completely misinterprets these actions. Overall she has the ability to read Consalve correctly despite the language barrier because she interprets other signs; she is not limited to language. Félime relates that Zaïde sensed that Consalve "avait de la passion pour elle; quoiqu'elle n'en pût juger par ses paroles, il y avait un air dans ses actions qui le lui faisait soupçonner" (felt passionately about her; even though she couldn't judge by his words, there was something about his actions that made her suspect this) (220). She attempts to communicate with him without words because she recognizes the value of non-verbal means of communication: "Comme elle ne pouvait se faire entendre par ses paroles, ce n'était quasi que par ses regards qu'elle expliquait à Consalve une partie des choses qu'elle lui voulait dire" (Since she couldn't make herself understood through words, she explained some of the things she wanted to say to Consalve through her gaze) (96). As we have seen, Consalve is incapable of interpreting such signs and longs only for words.

Interestingly, when the two are finally able to speak, each having learned the other's language, the mystery continues. After a separation, Consalve encounters Zaïde, or rather, her voice, as he walks past a walled garden. Consalve does not recognize Zaïde because she speaks Spanish, accenting again language's ability to deceive. Deprived of any other means of communication, for they are separated by a wall, Consalve is unable to arrive at the truth: "La grande ressemblance de cette voix avec celle de Zaïde lui causa de l'étonnement, et peut-être aurait-il soupçonné que c'était elle-même, sans que cette personne parlait espagnol" (This voice's great resemblance to Zaïde's surprised him, and maybe he would have suspected that it was she, except for the fact that this person spoke Spanish) (135). Their reunion is thus thwarted because of the very thing Consalve desired: that they be able to communicate through language. When they are finally reunited, Consalve discovers that linguistic signs, the conventional method of interpretation and communication, are not enough. He laments: "Je suis bien destiné au malheur de ne vous pas entendre ... puisque, même en me parlant espagnol, je ne sais ce que vous me dites" (I am destined to the misfortune of not understanding you, ... since, even when you speak Spanish to me, I don't know what you are saying) (153).

The events of the novel and its structure underscore that when language is supplemented with other methods and tools of communication, knowledge can be attained through collaboration. When viewed in light of the context of the debate over criticism, this provocative novel offers an epistomological critique: it advocates reaching knowledge, evaluating the world and by extension a literary work, by other than the traditional means of institutionalized written precepts and stringent rules. The novel's structure and themes offer a commentary on conventional criticism epitomized by Huet's preface, which is dominated by the singular voice of the traditional scholar. In this commentary, language can be equated with models, the written precepts of the Ancients. Non-verbal signs that ultimately lead to understanding in the novel, including *bon sens* and *sensibilité*, are the foundation of salon criticism, which Lafayette valorizes in her novel as a better means for understanding the events of her story and by extension of valuing literary works in general. In addition, the oral tradition associated with women and epitomized by salon activities is imbedded in *Zaïde*'s structure with its succession of voices, and valorized.

Harriet Stone remarks that "the real tension of the novel is between two aspects of the French identity: the accessible, or classifiable, and the inaccessible, or unknown."[44] I would agree, and argue that, in this instance, the "accessible, or classifiable" can be equated with *docte* or scholarly criticism, whereas "the inaccessible, or unknown" is the elusive criteria of worldly criticism. Lafayette stresses that one must listen to other voices, other forms of communication, other means toward knowledge, especially those associated with women, for it is the collaboration of these divergent approaches that leads to knowledge and understanding. It is through the collaborative processes and values associated with the salons that the new French genre of the *nouvelle* can be best evaluated, appreciated, and understood. A new French literature and a new French public mutually reinforce each other.

With the development of the novel and the influx of women onto the literary and social scene, came a new way of writing and especially a new approach to evaluation. Women and men collaborated in this literary and critical enterprise. Huet's preface and Lafayette's novel are designed to juxtapose the old with the new, and highlight the innovations taking place in seventeenth-century literary culture. In *Taste and Ideology in Seventeenth-Century France,* Michael Moriarty remarks that "the salons could foster cultural knowledge of a different type."[45] Lafayette's novel enumerates and highlights means to achieving this "cultural knowledge" via non-traditional venues, such as collaboration and non-verbal communcation. Her novel plays out aspects of the debate over standards of criticism and deliberates on who has the ability or the authority to judge.

Villedieu: Creating a New Public for Literature

One of Lafayette's contemporaries, Marie-Catherine Desjardins, Mme de Villedieu, was acutely aware of the emerging worldly public and sought to reinforce and create its influence and capitalize upon its power. An exploration of her work, and especially her relationship to this public, underscores its growing influence on the literary field. Like Lafayette, the dyamics of worldly values are imprinted deliberately on her corpus. But for Villedieu, the act of putting pen to paper was fundamentally different than it was for Lafayette or for any of her female literary contemporaries, or indeed for many of her male colleagues in the literary arena. Villedieu knew she had to be successful. Her very livelihood depended on the favor of the public. As the first woman of letters to earn her living by writing, Villedieu actively courted this public esteem.[46] She molded her literary personae and her works to conform to the changing tastes of the public. More important, her work illustrates the evolution of the literary public, and the emergence of a new sphere of influence, that of the worldly public.

Villedieu's literary trajectory was unique for a woman writer, and reflects the changing system of literary patronage during the period as well as the growing importance of the worldly public.[47] Upon her arrival in Paris from Normandy, she was immediately received into the circle of the Rohan family, where her mother was a lady-in-waiting.[48] She composed poetry in various Parisian salons and quickly received a reputation for her *esprit*. From poetry she turned to the novel and published a few volumes of *Alcidamie*, a heroic novel like those of Scudéry. During this period of literary initiation, Villedieu was nourished, both literally and figuratively, by the salon milieu. Her circle included the duchesse de Nemours, who was her patron but also an author in her own right, as well as former participants in the civil war known as the Fronde, such as the duchesse de Chevreuse, Mme de Montbazon, and Mlle de Montpensier. But Villedieu was also aware of the limitations of this feminocentric milieu in the late 1650s. Perhaps in reaction to the various critiques of the *précieuses* and the salon milieu, Villedieu decided to extend her repertoire and cultivate the more recognized genres of comedy and tragedy. Villedieu's experimentation with these genres attests to her self-conscious management of her literary career and her concern with her public reception and image. She became the protégé of the abbé d'Aubignac, the learned Academician and author of *La Pratique du Théâtre*, the pedagogical manual for dramatists. Under his tutelage Villedieu produced *Manlius* which was critically acclaimed when it was presented by the Hôtel de Bourgogne in 1662. Moreover, this tragedy involved its author in a literary debate featuring some of the most recognizable names of the day, principally d'Aubignac, Donneau de Visé, de Villiers, and Corneille.[49] She also courted royal favor by producing ballets and even a comedy, *Le Favory*, which was presented by Molière's troupe for Louis XIV and the royal family.[50] Villedieu thus became part of what we now consider to be the more official literary establishment.[51] In the opening years of Louis XIV's reign she worked above all to secure this academic public's favor. And, while always associated with the worldly public, she seems to have succeeded in being recognized as an important authorial voice by her learned contemporaries. In 1668 she even took on the role of literary critic at the request of J. Herauld de Gourville and defended Boileau's *Satires*.[52] This woman writer, whom modern critics associate almost exclusively with novels and a female public, thus worked to win over the academic as well as the worldly public.

Ultimately, though, Villedieu returned to the novel, or more precisely, worked on developing the new, shorter genre of the *nouvelle historique* that had attracted the worldly public's interest and approbation. Villedieu never returned to the theatre and devoted the rest of her career to pleasing the worldly public by composing a plethora of novels that she published with Barbin, the publisher associated above all with worldly genres. She dedicated *Lisandre* to one of the most powerful female court figures and a writer in her own right,

Mlle de Montpensier. Why this relatively sudden shift back to a genre she had deserted? I would speculate that Villedieu recognized that the worldly public's opinion and influence had grown strong enough to support her as a writer. She could now focus on cultivating and nourishing their literary taste and authority.[53]

Villedieu's huge corpus, produced primarily in the late 1660s and 1670s, reflects this growing critical voice and her own effort to nurture, develop, and legitimize it. Already in 1668 during the quarrel over Boileau's *Satires*, Villedieu identified herself with worldly critical values. Micheline Cuénin remarks that Villedieu's letters are especially intriguing because "c'est une des seules voix connues qui s'éleva alors en faveur du jeune insolent, ensuite parce qu'elle est celle d'une 'mondaine,' non formée aux habitudes scholastiques" (hers is one of the few voices to defend the young insolent man and because it is the voice of a worldly person who was uneducated in the scholastic sense).[54] Above all, Villedieu chooses to defend Boileau for not following ancient models, a modernist stance shared in the quarrel by her friends Molière, Furetière and Chapelle. She writes "N'est-ce pas un grand crime pour lui ... que de surpasser les Maîtres de l'Art même?" (Is it such a crime for him to surpass even the masters of the art of satire?).[55] As Cuénin remarks, to defend Boileau in this case is to defend the right to self-expression, to be oneself in the literary realm, liberated from the slavish imitation of ancient models, which was the modernist stance par excellence.[56] As the primary practitioner of a new genre, Villedieu's position could hardly be anything but "modern."

In order to initiate her public into the literary territory of the novel, and thereby gain acceptance for her innovations, Villedieu engaged her readers in dialogue. In fact, few other authors of the period carry on a conversation with their readers as Villedieu does. An analysis of Villedieu's efforts to address her public in her numerous dedications and prefaces, reveals her nurturing and careful tutelage of this public to accept the new genre of the historical novel.[57] In these critical texts, Villedieu strives to secure the protection of the worldly public by simultaneously developing and conforming to their tastes. Interestingly, even her foray into the more reputable genre of tragedy bears the imprint of her concern for this public. In 1662 she dedicated *Manlius* to Montpensier, an intriguing choice given Villedieu's affiliation with d'Aubignac and other *doctes*. By choosing this particular patron, Villedieu seems to acknowledge the power of the worldly public and pay homage to a fellow woman writer who was a central force in this public, especially with respect to literary matters.[58] She again chose to secure Montpensier's favor when she dedicated *Lisandre*, her second novel, to her in 1663. Curiously, in this dedication Villedieu presents herself as an intermediary between the novel's true author and the duchess: "Je crois que votre Altesse-Royale se divertira mieux, à la lecture d'une petite histoire qui m'a été écrite depuis quelques jours par une de mes amies" (I think your Royal Highness will be more amused by reading a story that was written to/for me a few days ago by one of my female friends).[59] Here Villedieu emphasizes female literary solidarity. Dedicated to a woman writer, the "petite histoire" is the work of a writer identified as female, which is then presented by a woman, who usurps the traditional male position of publisher/editor. The author's objective is solely to "divertir" (amuse), a worldly criterion, as opposed to the traditional *"plaire et instruire"* (please and instruct) demanded of literary works by the official scholarly public.

A few years later, Barbin sought to solidify Villedieu's relationship to what he viewed as the female-dominated worldly public.[60] In 1668, he published, without Villedieu's consent, her *Recueil de quelques lettres et relations galantes*, a collection of letters written primarily from Brussels. In order to guarantee their acceptance, and thus protect his commodity, Barbin called upon the marquise de Sévigné to give her blessing to the project:

> L'estime particulière que je sais que Mlle Desjardins fait de vous, m'oblige à vous présenter ce recueil de quelques-unes de ses lettres, et à vous demander en leur faveur, une protection, que le beau sexe est obligé (en quelque sorte) d'accorder à tous ces ouvrages. Ceux-ci sont d'un caractère à dépendre du jugement d'une ruelle galante, plûtot que de celui de l'Académie. Et comme je les imprime en son absence, et sans son ordre, je me trouve chargé de leur succès.[61]

> (The particular esteem that I know Mlle Desjardins has for you obliges me to present to you this volume of some of her letters, and to ask you for your patronage, which the fairer sex is obliged, in some way, to accord to all such works. These works depend on the judgment of salons, rather than that of the Academy. And as I am printing them [these letters] in her absence and not at her command, I find myself responsible for their success.)

Barbin's remarks underscore the clear association of certain genres with women, "le beau sexe" (the fairer sex), and with the geographical location where they practiced literary criticism, "une ruelle galante" (a salon), a space he opposes clearly to the French Academy. Barbin, like many of his contemporaries, is trying to keep women in their place by giving them an area of expertise that does not intersect with "official literature." As we shall see,

while Villedieu courts the salon public, she does not limit their authority as
Barbin would do. She will even call upon them to judge the venerable genre
of History.

Even though Villedieu did not authorize the publication of these letters,
one can nonetheless see the preoccupation with her public literary persona
that circulates through all her works. In one letter, she responds to her
interlocutor's demand that she publish her letters: "Quoi! bon Dieu, rendre
mes lettres publiques, moi, qui pour l'ordinaire ne prends pas la peine de les
relire avant que de les cacheter, moi, qui ne sais aucune langue étrangère, qui
n'ai jamais lu d'auteur plus ancien que M d'Urfé, et M de Gomberville, et
qui n'ai pour toute science qu'un peu d'usage du monde, et une expérience de
vingt-sept années de vie" (What! Good God, make my letters public, me, who
ordinarily does not even reread them before sealing them, me, who does not
know a foreign language, who has never read anyone before M. d'Urfé and
M de Gomberville, and whose only knowledge consists of society's customs
and twenty-seven years of life experience).[62] While one can understand her
hesitation in publishing works she has not reread, her excuse that she is not
learned enough seems to be very tongue-in-cheek. After all, by 1667, when this
letter was composed, Villedieu was already an accomplished and recognized
author. She had published poetry, theatre, and novels under her own name,
without the aid of anything but "un peu d'usage du monde, et une expérience"
(a knowledge of society and experience) of life. Rather than being read as
an excuse for not publishing, these lines can be interpreted as Villedieu's
valorization of her authority to publish, an authority founded on worldly
experience, knowledge of novels and "usage du monde" as opposed to learned
values: the same worldly criteria salon critics used to judge literary works.[63]
She identifies herself as a new type of writer whose works conform to different
criteria for success. This interpretation is reinforced by the fact that in this
same letter, Villedieu expounds upon the act of writing and the relationship
between writer and public. She states: "il y a une grande différence (selon
moi) entre le style des romans et des nouvelles, et celui des lettres: quand on
fait un livre, qu'on sait qui doit être vu de tout le monde, on tache d'y traiter
de matières générales, dont le public puisse être satisfait" (I personally believe
that there is a big difference between the style of novels and stories, and that of
letters. When one writes a book, which one knows will be seen by everyone,
one tries to deal with general subjects that can satisfy the public).[64] Public
satisfaction and pleasure are the motivating forces that guide Villedieu's pen.
No other writer of the period composes so "publicly," that is, is so conscious
of her own reception as author as well as of the reception of her works.

Villedieu often explains her writing process, even her philosophy of writing, in her prefaces and dedications. She seems desirous of involving the reader in the interpretation and judgment of her works. While this is obviously a commonplace in prefatory remarks, especially by the eighteenth century, Villedieu's addresses are unique and innovative given her historical context and the public she is specifically addressing, the worldly public. She attempts to draw them into her creative processes in order to gain their approval. Her dedication of *Cléonice, ou le roman galant* to the duchesse de Nemours in 1669 is interesting in this regard because she involves the duchesse, and the reader in general, in the creation of a new genre, the *nouvelle galante*. Villedieu begins by evoking the old heroic genre that had fallen out of favor by the mid 1660s:

> Déjà le soleil commençait à dorer de ses rayons ... Mais pardon, ma grande Princesse, je le prends sur le ton d'un roman dans les formes, et c'est une nouvelle galante que j'ai résolu d'écrire ... Je vous déclare par avance, que si mon héros est attaqué par vingt cavaliers, et qu'il ne soit défendu que par trois ou quatre, il sera contraint de leur céder, comme s'il n'était point le héros de ma nouvelle. Accomodez, s'il vous plaît, vos idées au vraisemblable ... et souffrez que je m'éloigne de la fable et du prodige, puisque c'est d'une aventure de nos derniers siècles dont j'ai à vous faire le récit ... il faut exciter la curiosité du lecteur, pour divertir son imagination.[65]

> (The sun had already begun to shine its rays ... But excuse me, my great Princess, for beginning this story as I would a novel, when I have decided to write a *nouvelle galante* ... I declare to you in advance that if my hero is attacked by twenty soldiers, and is only defended by three or four, he will be obliged to surrender, as though he were not the hero of my *nouvelle*/story. Please adapt your ideas to what is plausible (*vraisemblable*) ... and permit me to distance myself from fables and the marvelous, because I am telling you a story from the recent past ... one must excite the curiosity of the reader in order to entertain his/her imagination.)

In contrasting her novel to the heroic genre, Villedieu calls upon her readers' literary experience and asks them to set it aside for something new. She draws the reader in and asks for his/her approval of this new genre. She is not addressing all publics, but specifically the public familiar with the heroic novel, thus primarily the worldly public with which she associates herself when she says she has only been nourished by d'Urfé and Gomberville. And once again, her primary goal is to "entertain," this time by offering them something new.

Villedieu has a clear sense that she is treading on new literary and critical territory. In *Les Amours des grands hommes*, published in 1671, she explains her creative process in an effort to gain approval through instruction. She seems aware that in order for the genre to be accepted, she needs to create a public for it and initiate readers. The *épître*, however, is addressed to a higher source of authority, the king himself, in a clear effort to legitimate her transformation of the literary means used to reflect the monarch's power: history. She explains her rewriting of history:

> Les grands hommes n'ont été traduits à la posterité que sous des figures terribles: les auteurs se sont imaginés les élever au dessus de l'homme quand ils les ont dépouillés de tous les sentiments de la nature: ils nous représentent les philosophes insensibles, et les conquérants ne se montrent à nous que les armes à la main. Quant à moi, Sire, qui suis persuadée que l'amour est aussi vieux que le monde, j'ai cru pouvoir le démêler dans les incidents, où il semble avoir le moins de part ... Je ne doute pas que les savants ne se révoltent contre cette métamorphose, et je crois déjà les entendre dire, que je viole le respect dû à la sacrée antiquité. Mais je ne sais s'ils trouveraient autant d'exemples pour soutenir leur censure, que j'en ai pour autoriser ma licence.[66]

> (Great men have been conveyed to posterity only as terrible figures; authors imagined they were elevating them above the common man when they stripped them of all natural feelings: they show us insensitive philosophers, and conquerors come before us only with weapons in their hands. As for me, Sire, who am persuaded that love is as old as the world, I believed that I could discern it in incidents where it would seem to have had the least effect ... I have no doubt that scholars will revolt against this metamorphosis, and I think I can already hear them say that I am violating the respect due to sacred Antiquity. But I do not know if they will find as many examples to support their censureship as I have to authorize my liberties.)

Villedieu endeavors to adapt the public to this new genre founded on a rewriting of history.[67] By carefully explaining her relationship to official history and the genesis of her works, she seeks to gain the public's acceptance. As we have seen elsewhere, she is most concerned with the worldly public and here even openly rejects the opinion of "scholars." Her "metamorphosis" of history is authorized by "examples" of love's involvement in historical events, which she substitutes for the traditional models of historical composition.

Nowhere is Villedieu a more forceful pedagogue than in the preface of *Les Annales galantes*, published in 1670.[68] Villedieu remains more faithful to her historical sources in this novel than in her previous works, and employs the preface to prepare the reader for this new method of composition. She begins by stressing the veracity of *Les Annales*: "Je lui déclare donc, [to the reader] que les Annales Galantes sont des vérités historiques, dont je marque la source dans la table que j'ai insérée exprès au commencement de ce tome" (I declare to [the reader] that *Les Annales Galantes* are historical truths, for which I cite the source in the table I have intentionally inserted at the beginning of this volume).[69] She facilitates the collaboration of her literary public in verifying the novel's veracity by citing her sources. But Villedieu is careful to stress her deviation from these authoritative sources, explaining her method while creating her own literary authority.

> J'avoue que j'ai ajouté quelques ornements à la simplicité de l'Histoire. La Majesté des matières historiques ne permet pas à l'Historien judicieux de s'étendre sur les incidents purement galantes ... J'ai dispensé mes *Annales* de cette austérité. J'augmente donc à l'Histoire quelques entre-vues secrètes et quelques discours amoureux. Si ce ne sont ceux qu'ils ont prononcés, ce sont ceux qu'ils auraient dû prononcer. Je n'ai point de mémoires plus fidèles que mon jugement: quand on m'en fournira quelques-uns, où mes héros parleront mieux que dans mes *Annales*, je consens à rapporter leurs paroles propres. Mais tant que les Historiens les rendront muets, je croirai pouvoir les faire parler à ma mode.[70]

> (I admit that I have added a few ornaments to the simplicity of History. The majesty of historical subjects does not permit the judicious Historian to elaborate on incidents that are purely galant ... In my *Annales* I have dispensed with this austerity. I have added some secret conversations and discussions of love to History. If these are not what [historical figures] said, this is what they should have said. I do not have any memoirs more faithful than my judgment: when someone gives me some, in which my heros speak better than in my *Annales*, then I will transcribe their own words. But as long as Historians make them mute, I will believe that I can make them speak in my way.)

Villedieu's use of the first-person voice is especially striking. As she teaches her public what to expect, she forcefully states her right to revise history. Because history does not include "secret conversations and discussions of love" Villedieu feels authorized to invent them. She valorizes her inventions as in fact more authoritative than anything real events could offer: "this is what they should have said." She grounds her inventions in her personal reading of history, in her "judgment." That this is a personal, interpreted vision of history, not just an imagined version, and as such a deviation from standard narratives, is emphasized by Villedieu's use of the possessive, "*my* heroes" and "I will believe that I can make them speak in *my* way."

Villedieu goes on in this preface to instruct the readers on how to receive this work: "Ils [readers] trouveront dans cet ouvrage des Portraits du vice assez naïvement représentés; mais ils observeront, s'il leur plaît, qu'on ne l'élève que pour le détruire ... et l'air enjoué qui est répandu sur les matières les plus sérieuses, doit paraître assez divertissant aux gens qui le remarqueront, pour les obliger à ne pas trahir l'intention d'un auteur qui les aura si bien divertis" (In this work, [readers] will find portraits of evil fairly naively represented; but they will observe, if it so pleases them, that it [evil] is only brought up in order to destroy it ... and the cheerful quality that infuses even the most serious subjects must appear entertaining enough to the people who remark it that they will not betray the intention of an author who will have entertained them so much).[71] Above all, readers should be pleased, "entertained" by a writing style that she characterizes as "divertissant" (entertaining), the same term that is almost a refrain in all Villedieu's exonerations to her readers. In drawing attention to the pleasure of the text, Villedieu marks her difference from history, which must instruct more than please, as she indicates that her text should be judged according to worldly as opposed to learned criteria. She rejoins, among others, Corneille's argument in defense of his Cid. Pleasure takes precedence over all else.

With *Les Annales galantes*, Villedieu seeks to legitimate the new genre she is developing by offering its philosophy.[72] Her works are designed to complete history as they compete with it. In framing her historical narratives with pedagogical tools, Villedieu elevates the "particular" history she is composing to the level of a universal history with pedagogical value, the goal of all official histories.[73] Villedieu grounds her authority as *historienne* in her own experience, beliefs, and meditations on history. In the preface to *Les Annales galantes de Grèce*, published posthumously, she defends her decision to focus on famous Greek women by citing her own opinion, one that her public could no doubt agree with: "Cependant il *me* [my emphasis] semble que les nations étant composées de deux sexes, on ne peint la Grèce qu'à demi, quand on n'en peint que les grands hommes; ajoûtons quelques traits à cette peinture et disons aujourd'hui quelque chose des dames" (Yet it seems to me that, nations being composed of two sexes, that only half of Greece is depicted when only great men are described; let us add a few strokes to this painting and today say something about the women).[74] Once again she draws her readers into the creative process by explaining her methods and through her use of the first person plural.

In addressing the worldly public, Villedieu is doing much more than flattering them. Through her prefaces she takes control of the critical act and indicates how her works should be interpreted. But at the same time, Villedieu establishes a dialogue with the worldly public and involves the reader in the process of interpretation. She creates a collaborative group of worldly critics and writers who can support the new novel genres, the *nouvelle historique* and *histoire galante*. Her prefaces and *épîtres* reveal Villedieu's awareness and cultivation of new ways of reading and writing, and of consecrating authors. It is enough for an author to please based on worldly taste. And in this literary territory women can be both critics and writers.

* * * * *

Like Lafayette, Villedieu can be viewed as inscribing the worldly critical process and its values in the culmination of her literary career, *Les Désordres de l'amour*. This particular historical novel reveals her obsession with the act of interpretation—with being interpreted herself, with the reception of her works, and with interpreting the world around her for her readers. But unlike Lafayette who never openly enters her text as a critic/writer, Villedieu inscribes herself as critic into this text in order to control the interpretation of her novel and to train her public in this new genre. In addition, she creates a conversation with the reader, reminiscent of the salon milieu, with herself as the principal female figure who guides the discussion.[75]

Les Désordres is the culmination not only of Villedieu's literary career, but also of the *nouvelle historique* as a genre. It is the text that remains the most faithful to its historical sources. Villedieu carefully weaves her fiction into the political history of sixteenth-century France. She clearly identifies her text as a novel that illustrates her theory of history according to which all historical events, even those on the royal stage, are determined by the passions of individuals.[76] The strong narratorial/authorial presence throughout the text ensures that the reader will not interpret these stories as they would any other history. [77] *Les Désordres* consists of four parts, with parts III and IV together comprising one story. To create unity among the three stories, the narrative is punctuated by maxims in verse, interspersed and numbered sequentially, such as the following:[78]

MAXIME I
Mais l'Amour, ce tiran des plus illustres âmes.
Cet ennemi secret de nos prosperités,

Qui, sous de faux plaisirs, nous déguisant ses flames.
Nous fait passer des maux pour des félicités;
Aux yeux du nouveau Roi fait briller ses chimères.
Il se laissa charmer à leur vaine douceur,
Et leurs voluptés mensongères
En séduisant les sens, amolissent le coeur. (5)

(But Love, this tyrant of the most illustrious of souls
This secret enemy of our prosperity
Which, underneath false pleasures, conceals from us its flames and
Which deceptively represents evils to us as good;
It shines its idle fancies in the eyes of the new king.
He allowed himself to be charmed by its vain sweetness
And its deceitful delights, by seducing the intellect, weaken the heart.) (11)

In addition, short maxims such as the following are strewn throughout the text:

les mouvements de l'amour sont rapides (23) (love develops rapidly). (19)
La personne qui faisait ce discours devait le rendre suspect; mais l'amour et ses effets, se règlent rarement par la raison. (32) (Because of who was uttering these words, they should have been suspect, but love and its effects are rarely ruled by reason.) (23)
La jalousie de la beauté grave des ressentiments éternels dans le coeur d'une jeune personne. (48–9) (Jealousy of the beauty of another woman can engrave an eternal grudge into a young woman's heart.) (33)
Le parfait amour rend si docile que d'abord cet amant consentit à tout ce qu'on souhaitait. (105) (True love is so powerful that, at first, this suitor consented to everything that was desired of him.) (63)
C'est une douce tentation pour un homme de 21 ans, que les avances de galanterie d'une belle et grande princesse. (130) (It is, after all, a sweet temptation for a man of twenty-one to be exposed to the amorous advances of a beautiful and noble princess.) (78)
On ne guérit pas de ce mal [l'amour] aussi aisément qu'on en devient malade. (191) (Unfortunately, it is far easier to become infected with love's germs than it is to be cured of the malady.) (110)

Both types of maxims can be viewed as Villedieu's attempt to explain the particular fictional universe she is creating, a world in which events are determined entirely by emotions.[79] She endows her invented world with laws. Because she remains so close to her sources, Villedieu expects her readers to be familiar with this history and even to have their own interpretations of events, which might be at odds with the one she is advancing. As she is offering an alternative history, she must somehow make it believable, *vraisemblable*, to use the seventeenth-century lexicon.[80] The maxims serve this purpose, for they explain the often exaggerated actions of the characters. Arthur Flannigan remarks that particularly in the second part, the imbedded maxims often justify what seems to be an infraction of the rules of *vraisemblance*.[81] And as these pronouncements are in the form of maxims, they are more authoritative than some of the other authorial interventions. The resulting text is *vraisemblable*, that is, it conforms to a concept of plausibility and propriety, but this *vraisemblance* is created within the text itself. Villedieu strives to divorce her reader from his/her previous knowledge of the past in order to advance a different *vraisemblance*, a different "reality." As Flannigan remarks, "there is a kind of 'dialogue' between the *récit historique* and the narrator's *discours* that postulates a new logic or a different meaning for the past events. This 'dialogizing' is how the *nouvelle historique* is born."[82]

Villedieu also guides her reader's interpretation in less impersonal ways than by enunciating maxims. Throughout *Les Désordres* she establishes a unique rapport with the reader in which she orients his/her interpretation of this *H/histoire*. This relationship is already apparent in the opening maxims when Villedieu uses the first person plural. She establishes herself as a presence in the text with much in common with the public, in particular at the end of the first part of *Les Désordres*. Of the war she has just examined she concludes:

> ... il demeure constant qu'elle prit naissance dès l'année 1577, et il ne l'est pas moins, comme les mémoires sur lesquels je fais ce commentaire en font foi, qu'elle eut sa source dans les intrigues d'amour que je viens d'écrire ... tout cela a sa principale cause dans l'amour. Il n'est que trop suffisamment prouvé par les diverses intrigues qui composent cet exemple, que l'amour est le ressort de toutes les passions de l'âme ... Je vais tâcher à prouver de même, que s'il est funeste dans ses excès, il n'est pas moins à redouter dans ses commencements; l'histoire du Maréchal de Bellegarde ... s'offre à propos à ma mémoire pour fournir cette seconde preuve ... elle me sert à joindre aux galanteries de mon sujet les vérités importantes de l'histoire générale. (65)

> (It remains irrefutably true, however, that it was conceived in the year 1577. It is equally true, just as the memoirs on which this account is based prove, that the war stemmed from the love intrigues that I have just described ... All of this, I affirm, was caused principally by love. The diverse intrigues that comprise this story prove convincingly that love is the force behind all the other human passions ... I shall try to prove that just as it is fatal in its conclusions, it is to be feared no less in its beginning stages. The story of Marshall de Bellegarde

... comes to mind appropriately as a second verification ... it serves also to complement these love stories with the important, general truths to be extracted from History.) (40–41)

Villedieu describes the composition of her novel as she guides her readers' interpretation. The stories appear as theorems she is intent on proving, rather than as whimsical fictions. The maxim upon which the fiction is founded, that love is at the center of all historical events, is the guiding maxim of the *nouvelle historique* as a genre. Villedieu uses these authorial interventions not only to determine the *vraisemblance* of her own text, but of the genre as a whole. The reader is initiated into this new genre by the maxims and by such guiding remarks as "j'ai dit ailleurs" (97) (I have recounted elsewhere) (58), "dont j'ai déjà dit un mot dans la premiere partie" (102) (whom I have already mentioned in the first story) (60), "le même duc de Guise dont j'ai parlé dans le premier de mes exemples" (119) (the same Duke of Guise of whom I have spoken in the first of my examples) (73), seemingly superfluous remarks that underscore the work's composition and create a bond with the reader. She portrays the *nouvelle* as real history, as when she explains the provenance of a letter she inserts in the text: "Une lettre à Mlle de Guise, qui m'a étée donnée en original, et dont voici mot par mot la copie" (206) (I have seen the original; here is an exact copy of it) (119). In addition, she occasionally comments upon a character, in this way also governing the reader's interpretation, as when she refers to "la dame coquette" (39) (the flirtatious woman) (27), and "cette belle affligée" (73) (this beautiful but distraught woman) (46).

Villedieu's bonding with her readers is especially apparent in the authorial intervention at the end of the second part.[83]

Ainsi ce même amour qui dans la première partie de cet ouvrage a produit les semences de la Ligue, met dans celle-ci un obstacle secret à la paix générale du royaume et nous a coûté une étendue de terre qui ne pourrait être reconquise qu'au prix de beaucoup de sang et de beaucoup de travaux ... .J'espère ne rapporter pas de moindres preuves, que non seulement il [l'amour] fait agir nos passions, mais qu'il mérite souvent tout le blâme que ces passions peuvent attirer; qu'il nous conduit jusques au desespoir, et que les plus parfaits ouvrages de la nature et de l'art dépendent quelquefois d'un moment de son caprice ... Je ne doute point qu'en cet endroit plus d'un lecteur ne dise d'un ton ironique que je n'en ai pas toujours parlé de cette sorte, mais c'est sur cela même que je me fonde pour en dire tant de mal, et c'est pour en avoir fait une parfaite expérience que je me trouve autorisée à le peindre avec de si noires couleurs. (117–18)

(Thus, this same passion, love, which in the first part of this work produced the seeds that led to the League, in this part secretly obstructs the general peace of the country and costs us a stretch of land which could not be regained except at a bloody and costly price ... I hope to provide equally convincing evidence that not only does it activate our other passions but also that it deserves often all of the blame directed towards these passions. I hope to prove equally that it pushes us to the edges of despair and that the most beautiful works of nature and art depend often on a moment of its caprice ... I am sure that at this point more than one reader is saying, somewhat ironically, that I have not always spoken in this manner. That is precisely why I am now justified in speaking so negatively. And, finally, it is because [of my own experience, (my translation)] that I am authorized to paint love with such dark colors.) (70–71)

Through her use of the first person plural, Villedieu allies herself with her specifically French readers: "nous a coûté une étendue de terre" ([cost] us a stretch of land).[84] She reinforces this more personal relationship by stressing that everyone is subject to love's power: "il nous conduit jusques au desespoir" (it pushes us to the edges of despair). In addition, she draws upon her personal reputation to reinforce the bond with the reader as well as the *vraisemblance* of the text she is offering. "More than one reader" will remember her previous works in which she presented less dismal descriptions of love, and more importantly they will recall her own life, during which she hardly rejected love's advances. But this new negative vision of love's power is drawn from "une parfaite experience/her own experience." It is this personal experience that constitutes Villedieu's literary authority and authorizes her interpretation of historical events. And Villedieu seeks to show that this experience has much in common with that of her readers.

Throughout *Les Désordres*, Villedieu enunciates maxims the public can agree with so they can concur on the interpretation of the novel, thus underscoring the need for collective interpretation. She joins her readers as members of the reading/interpreting public. And while Villedieu on the one hand determines the interpretation of the narrative by the maxims, on the other she uses them to draw the reader into the text, to make the reader a partner in her transformation of history. The "nous" (we) underscores the collective nature of the interpretive act.[85] All readers can concur with such maxims because they are founded on the readers' own experience, which the narrator/author shares.

That Villedieu views her readership as the worldly, and not the academic, literary milieu is evident in the nature of the maxims and the authorial interventions, all of which express the experiences and values of the worldly milieu. The official historical narrative is shown to function solely according to the particular realm of passions and intrigue so familiar to Villedieu's projected readers. As Flannigan remarks, the maxims become less and less related to the text itself and more universal. Whereas in the first part the opening maxim is proved by the story, the second advances more of a "universal truth," in Flannigan's words, and in the third and fourth parts "the maxims have all but lost their specific narrative connection with the prose" (75).[86] By advancing "universal truths," associated with the worldly milieu, Villedieu reflects the readership she is courting. One could even go so far as to advance that she is highlighting the more private activities of the nobles, the realm to which they were relegated under Louis XIV, an arena traditionally viewed as devoid of real power. Villedieu caters to her readers by advancing this sphere as the source of all political actions and power. Through her authorial interventions, she calls upon her readers to validate this revision of history, and thus her act of writing and the resulting new literary genre.[87]

The maxims and authorial discourse with the public derive from a collaboration between author and public that Villedieu inscribes in her text. By openly drawing the reader into the interpretive act, Villedieu stresses the worldly critical process. This valorization embedded in the structure of the narrative is reinforced further by the actual events of the fiction. Flannigan has advanced that communication is at the heart of *Les Désordres*. I would agree that language is the central focus of all four parts of *Les Désordres*, but I would argue that the focus of the narrative is not communication but the act of interpretation. In fact, Villedieu's characters are obsessed with interpretation, much as Villedieu herself is in all her works and in her literary career in general. An examination of a few key passages reveals this obsession, and Villedieu's valorization of the processes of worldly criticism.[88]

Throughout *Les Désordres* Villedieu composes scenes that could be considered *mise-en-abîmes* of the creative act and the corresponding interpretive process required to decipher it. In the first story, for example, the characters compose a ballet with the intention of disgracing the main female protagonist, Mme de Sauve: "La Reine de Navarre se chargea de celui d'un ballet, dont le Duc de Guise donna le plan, et qui, dans leur idée, devait être un coup mortel pour la vanité de Mme de Sauve" (21) (The Queen of Navarre took charge of creating a ballet which the Duke of Guise directed and which they intended to be a mortal blow to Mme de Sauve's vanity) (18). The enemies of de Sauve plot the ballet to have her publicly humiliated by the Roi de Navarre, whom she has been courting, but who supposedly feigns to reciprocate her sentiments only the better to humiliate her later. But their plans fail when the Roi de Navarre, their supposed ally in crime, secretly falls in love with de Sauve. During the presentation of the ballet, instead of adhering to his scripted part, the Roi de Navarre rewrites it to glorify de Sauve, and "mit tant de confusion dans l'ordre du ballet qu'on ne sçut ce qu'il devait représenter" (24) (caused so much confusion in the structure of the ballet that no one knew anymore what it was supposed to represent) (19).

This complex scene can be read as mirroring the writing and critical practices of the worldly public, which were often collective in nature.[89] Collective interpretation is also inscribed as the scheming group as a whole works to make "order" out of "confusion." The collaborative methods of the salon public prove to be more efficient than the interpretation of the single critic, or the lone individual as represented by one character, Monsieur. Monsieur, also in love with de Sauve, is unable to interpret the scene on his own and needs the enlightenment of the other characters (29–30; Flannigan 22). Finally "la Reine sa soeur le tira ce cet aveuglement" (30) (the Queen, his sister, disabused him of this error) (22). Complicity in composition as well as comprehension is thus valorized.

Villedieu inserts a similar scene into her second story. The mareschal and marquise de Bellegarde, after being passionately in love, find themselves married and despising each other. The mareschal decides that the only way he can get rid of his wife is to prove that she is unfaithful: "il n'en espérait plus que d'une galanterie de sa femme, et il résolut de se retrancher sur une apparence, s'il ne pouvait parvenir à une vérité" (106) (He could hope only for his wife's infidelity and resolved to save himself by exploiting this appearance of misconduct, even if no such misconduct took place) (64). Again, through a collaborative effort with his wife's duplicitous lady-in-waiting, the mareschal resolves to stage a scene to unveil his wife's supposed infidelity with Bussi, who is in love with her.

La vieille femme de chambre fit croire à Bussi que Mme de Bellegarde vaincue par ses importunités lui en accordait un, [rendez-vous] et il fut arrêté pour le lendemain … Le mareschal espéra de pouvoir supposer la Piemontaise [a woman who resembles Mme de Bellegarde] à la place de sa femme, et ensuite de donner sous main tant de faux avis à Bussi, qu'il se croirait dispensé d'être discret, et publierait la faveur qu'il penserait avoir obtenue. (107)

(The elder chambermaid convinced Bussi that Mme de Bellegarde, giving in to his insistence, had agreed to see him. He was told that the meeting would take place the following day … The marshall wished to be able to present the woman in question as his wife and in this underhanded way, to give such false

declarations to Bussi that he would no longer consider himself obliged to be
discreet but would make known to others the favors that he had received, so
he was to think, from Mme de Bellegarde.) (64)

But Mme de Bellegarde learns of the plot by intercepting a letter between
her husband and the woman he has enlisted to impersonate her. As in the
previous story, collaboration leads to knowledge. But in this instance, Mme
de Bellegarde's own interpretive capabilities are also valorized: "Mais il était
écrit dans les astres que Mme de Bellegarde démêlerait toutes les intrigues de
son mari, et son génie familier l'assista dans cette occasion comme en plusieurs
autres" (107) (But it was written in the stars that Mme de Bellegarde should
unravel all of her husband's plots; her well-known ingenuity helped her in
this instance as in several others) (64). The narrator joins in the process of
interpretation of the theatrical scene by explaining the protagonist's sentiments:
"Mme de Bellegarde n'aimait plus assez son mari pour être capable de grande
jalousie. Il n'y a point d'amour si violent qu'un long mépris ne chasse d'un
bon coeur" (109) (Mme de Bellegarde no longer cared enough for her husband
to be jealous. There is no love so strong that a continuous contempt will not
eradicate from a noble heart) (65). By inserting a maxim, Villedieu involves
the reader in the interpretive process. The reader is drawn out of the fiction
and asked to either agree or disagree with the maxim using his/her knowledge
of the world to do so. Once again the maxim is designed to express collective
worldly values. The reader, together with the author and Mme de Bellegarde,
correctly, and collaboratively, understand the staged scene and the reasons
for its creation.

Like the Roi de Navarre in the previous story, Mme de Bellegarde rewrites
the scene composed by her husband and his co-conspirators. She herself goes to
meet Bussi and unveils the plot in which he unwittingly finds himself. But her
scheming husband, who is secretly watching, "était si prévenu au désavantage
de sa femme qu'il crut que, malgré ses ordres, elle avait été avertie de son
arrivée, et qu'elle avait tenu auparavant des discours contraires à ceux-là"
(114) (had so expected to find his wife compromised that he was sure that,
in spite of his orders, she had been forewarned of his arrival and that prior to
this moment she had said to Bussi exactly the opposite of what she was now
saying) (69). Left to his own interpretation, the mareschal, like Monsieur in Part
I, cannot correctly interpret the scene, giving Villedieu yet another occasion
to demonstrate how collaboration alone leads to knowledge.

It is interesting to note that in this second story, a woman dominates both
the creative and the interpretive acts. Mme de Bellegarde re-authors her

husband's theatrical script, much as Villedieu rewrites history in *Les Désordres*. In both cases, a woman goes beyond appearances, the superficial, to unveil the truth. Villedieu continues to emphasize female creativity in parts 3 and 4 of the novel, which together comprise one story. As in parts 1 and 2, she foregrounds and expands upon the need to interpret creative compositions. The whole second half of the novel is constructed to glorify the worldly literary and critical process.

We have seen how Villedieu disseminates maxims throughout *Les Désordres* and creates unity among the four sections by numbering the longer verse maxims sequentially from beginning to end. The third part again contains a lengthy maxim in verse, but with a remarkable difference. Instead of being advanced by the narrator, the maxim, numbered VI to follow the previous ones, is offered by one of the characters. The male protagonist, Givry, lost the letters of his lover, Mme de Maugiron, in battle. When they are returned to him, they have undergone what the narrator terms "une censure judicieuse" (a discreet criticism) (126; 76). Someone has added maxims to each letter, and these maxims continue the narrator's creative reflections on love of the previous parts. The maxims make Givry reconsider Mme de Maugiron's sentiments: "Mais à mésure qu'il examinait le sens des vers, et celui de la lettre, il ne trouvait pas cette dernière [Mme de Maugiron] si exempte de blâme qu'il l'avait crue" (126) (But as he examined the meaning of the verses and the contents of the letter, he did not find her (Mme de Maugiron) as blameless as he had first thought) (76). Just as Villedieu's maxims inspire the reader to reconsider historical events, so too do these maxims prompt Givry to reinterpret a written text. The author of the maxims inserted into the letters, who turns out to be an illustrious princess, Mlle de Guise, mirrors Villedieu herself, valorizing female creativity on many levels.[90] In addition, she continues to emphasize the value of collaborative interpretation in the quest for knowledge. As the identity of the maxims' author is initially a mystery to Givry, he needs the help of his friend, the Grand Ecuyer, who recognizes the handwriting, to discover Mlle de Guise's role (129; Flannigan 78). His friend also helps him interpret their meaning, as does another character, the Baron de Vins (130, 136; Flannigan 71; 81–2). When Givry is left to his own interpretive devices, he proves to be incapable of correctly reading the princess and her actions.

Givry is not the only one to need the help of collaborative interpretation. Even the narrator appears momentarily perplexed. When Givry compliments the princess only to be rebuffed, the narrator remarks: "Ce compliment était honnête, et la manière dont Mlle de Guise avait vécu avec Givry pendant la trève aurait pu l'autoriser à faire des galanteries plus fortes ... On peut juger combien il fut surpris de cette réponse" (164) (The compliment was sincere, and the way Mlle de Guise had behaved during the truce could have justified Givry acting even more boldly ... One can well imagine how this response surprised him) (94–5). This seemingly surprised narrative perspective is an interesting departure from the dominating and knowledgeable narrator of the first two stories, and his/her new, less domineering role is reinforced by the provenance of the maxims in the third and fourth parts. We have already seen that the verse maxims are attributed to Mlle de Guise. In addition, throughout the final story, the internal maxims that guide the interpretation of the first two stories are for the most part replaced by maxims enunciated by the characters themselves.[91] For example, when asked by Givry "ce qu'il pensait du sens de ces vers, si on ne pouvait pas sans témerité les regarder comme une faveur, et en espérer d'heureuses suites" (130) (his thoughts about the meaning of these poems; [Givry] wanted to know if they might be considered, without temerity, as a sign of her interest in him) (78), Bellegarde responds with a maxim: "'qu'auraient-elles d'heureux pour vous? ... Un homme engagé doit plutôt craindre que désirer ces sortes de bonnes fortunes'" (130) (what flattering consequences could these verses have for you? ... A man already engaged in love should fear rather than welcome these kinds of flirtations) (78). The rejected Mme de Maugiron likewise responds to Givry with a maxim: "'Il ne faut avoir qu'un amour ordinaire ... pour aimer un amant qui vous aime'" (166) (It takes but an ordinary passion to love a lover who loves you) (96). Givry later responds with "'Mais, Madame, on n'aime point par choix; les caprices du coeur sont les tyrans de la raison'" (187) (But, Madame, love is involuntary ... the caprices of the heart rule our minds) (107).

In delegating most of her narrative authority in this section to the characters themselves, Villedieu underscores the collaborative nature of this composition. The maxims come from the characters. They could easily emanate from the readers themselves. In the first two stories, Villedieu endeavors to train her readers to look at history from a different perspective, to accept an alternative vision of what is *vraisemblable*. By the third and fourth parts, the characters, who reflect Villedieu's public, are capable of enunciating their own maxims. Villedieu has taught them, and her readers, to interpret events according to their own maxims based on worldly experience. By the end even the king becomes part of this collective interpretation of events and advances a maxim—"Les caprices d'une jeune personne dont le coeur n'est encore déterminé à rien ... sont aussi changeants que vaste" (194) (The heart of a young and immature person is boundless and forever changing) (113)—as Villedieu valorizes worldly experience and values to interpret the world in general and her literary creation in particular. Her novel conforms to the essential criterion of *vraisemblance* because it functions according to the worldly logic reflected by the maxims. Everyone has access to this creative process because it is founded on experience in society as opposed to learned scholarship. The public can determine the value of Villedieu's novel by employing its knowledge of society, a process that is outside of the control of traditional academic critics who judge according to pre-set academic standards, as opposed to the nebulous criterion of worldly experience.

Villedieu's novels reflect an exciting literary milieu in which the tastes and standards of a newly influential public authorized a new genre and changed the literary landscape for centuries. Even as late as the eighteenth century, Villedieu remained one of France's most popular writers, ranking first among all seventeenth-century authors in the inventories of private libraries.[92] According to one critic, this should teach us a valuable lesson. Bruce Morrissette concludes that Villedieu's popularity "should put us on our guard against the common opinion that the entire literary public under Louis XIV had exquisite and infallible taste, or that it demanded only the best."[93] But Villedieu's popularity contains a more positive and far-reaching lesson. Her adherence to the taste and standards of a newly influential public reveals the processes involved in the creation of a new genre. More important, Villedieu's status and her relationship to the worldly public compel us to analyze this public's position and function in our assessment of the seventeenth-century literary scene. Villedieu's status in the seventeenth and eighteenth centuries, and her precipitous fall into oblivion by the twentieth raise questions concerning what literary taste has been canonized, when this process occurred, according to what criteria and to what ends, questions that will be the focus of our study in the following chapters.

Notes

1   As cited by Nicole Aronson, *Mademoiselle de Scudéry*, p. 354. It should be remembered that Scudéry was inducted into the celebrated Académie des Ricovrati de Padoue, as Rambouillet had been, and also received the prize for eloquence from the French Academy.

2   Hélène Merlin in particular has studied both these quarrels in depth in *Public et Littérature*. In her analysis she reads the debates in terms of a general notion of the public.

3   The first version of this poem, in Latin, dates from 1633. When it was published in French in February 1637, one month after the premier of *Le Cid*, the public naturally interpreted it in light of the play's success.

4   Hélène Merlin, *Public et Littérature*.

5   Christian Jouhaud, *Les Pouvoirs de la littérature: Histoire d'un paradoxe* (Paris, 2000).
     See in particular Chapter 2.

6   Merlin states that the play itself did not cause the quarrel, the poem did. *Public et Littérature*,
     p. 239. However, the play did inspire the specific attacks. I will argue that Corneille
     provoked this attack, especially with the creation of Chimène.

7   "Excuse à Ariste," in *La Querelle du Cid: Pièces et Pamphlets*, ed. Armand Gasté (Paris,
     1899), p. 64. This edition contains all the contributions to the quarrel. All further references
     to the quarrel will be to this edition, with page numbers inserted parenthetically in the text.
     For a useful analysis of the quarrel in conjunction with the play, see Georges Forestier's
     edition of *Le Cid* in Magnard's series "Texte et Contextes."

8   Scudéry exclaims: "Mais faire arriver en 24 heures la mort d'un père, et la promesse de
     mariage de sa fille, avec celui qui l'a tué; ... c'est ... ce qui loin d'être bon dans les 24
     heures, ne serait pas supportable dans les 24 ans. Et par conséquent (je le redis encore
     une fois) la règle de la vraisemblance n'est point observée, quoi qu'elle soit absolument
     nécessaire" (To have occur a father's death and the engagement of his daughter to the one
     who killed him would not be acceptable in 24 years much less 24 hours. Thus, I say it
     again, the rule of *vraisemblance* is not observed in the least, even though it is absolutely
     necessary) (p. 77).

9   There have been numerous studies of both Lafayette's novel and the quarrel. For an
     overview of scholarship on *La Princesse de Clèves*, see my *Approaches to Teaching La
     Princesse de Clèves* (edited with Katharine Ann Jensen, New York, 1999). For discussions
     of the quarrel in particular, see Maurice Laugaa, *Lectures de Madame de Lafayette* (Paris,
     1971), Hélène Merlin, *Public et Littérature*, Elizabeth Goldsmith's essay in *Approaches
     to Teaching the Princesse de Clèves*, my *Revising Memory*, and Joan DeJean's *Tender
     Geographies*, among others. While the quarrel has elicited much critical commentary, no
     one as yet has examined it in light of the salons' influence on literary taste and criteria for
     literary evaluation.

10   This was my own reading of the quarrel in *Revising Memory*, where I focused on the
     critique of Lafayette's use of history in the novel and its relationship to *vraisemblance*.
     Here I will reorient my perspective and examine the inscription of the public in the rhetoric
     of the quarrel. As we have seen, the debate over *le Cid* shares this characteristic with the
     quarrel over *La Princesse de Clèves*. In both cases the female protagonist's behavior was
     condemned as *invraisemblable*. Critics have pointed this out in the case of Lafayette's
     novel, but have not identified Chimène as a kind of literary precedent, as I argue here.
     The debates both recognize women as important forces in the public, and seek to provide
     them with acceptable moral exempla by combatting the immoral ones supposedly present
     in these texts.

11   As we have seen, in the years separating the two debates, women established over sixty
     salons. Many turned to writing themselves, and there was already been a backlash against
     worldly, specifically female, influence, notably with the publication of Molière's two plays,
     Les Précieuses ridicules and *Les Femmes savantes*, as well as Boileau's satires on women
     who aspire to intellectual positions.

12   Jean-Baptiste Trousset de Valincour, *Lettres à Madame la Marquise *** au sujet de la
     Princesse de Clèves*, 1678, ed. Jacques Chupeau et al. (Tours.1972), p. 266. All further
     references will be to this edition, with page numbers inserted parenthetically in the text.

13   Jean-Antoine de Charnes, *Conversations sur la critique de la Princesse de Clèves*, 1679;
     (ed. François Weil et al. (Tours, 1973), p. 187. All further references to Charnes's text will
     be to this edition, with page numbers inserted parenthetically in the text.

14   *Conversations*, p. ii. Charnes's relationship to Lafayette has been the subject of speculation. For some critics, including myself, he was a part of Lafayette's inner circle and participated actively in her salon. Given this relationship, one could see him as the voice of Lafayette herself.

15   The twentieth-century editor, however, sees Valincour as reflecting worldly opinion: "Car le bon goût ne saurait aller contre le bon sens qui, plus que le plaisir, reste pour Valincour la grande règle de toutes les règles" (Good taste cannot contradict good sense which, even more than pleasure, remains for Valincour the rule of all rules) (p. VIII).

16   Thus Charnes, like Perrault after him, adopts a modernist stance according to which the critic is encouraged to think and reflect, as opposed to blindly applying rules to a work. As we have seen, Perrault characterizes his fictional "modern" voice in *La Parallèle* as "plus riche de ses propres pensées (more rich in his own thoughts).

17   For example, Charnes states that: "… on trouverait toujours que les digressions de la Princesse de Clèves sont bien plus du sujet, et beaucoup plus courtes à proportion, que les épisodes des poètes les plus exacts" (The digressions in *La Princesse de Clèves* will always be more pertinent and much shorter than those of the most exacting writers) (p. 50).

18   In discussing the various motivations of the princess, Charnes's fictional marquise, for example, comes to the conclusion that "tout cela devait arriver ainsi, et avoir les suites qu'on a lues" (everything happened as it should have, with the consequences that we read) (p. 177).

19   As is evident in the following passage: "Mais le Critique n'aurait pas fait un si grand crime de cette reflection à Madame de Clèves, s'il avait considéré cette princesse dans les deux états différents, où l'Auteur la montre dans toute son histoire" (But the critic wouldn't have made Mme de Clèves's reflection such a crime if he had recognized the two differing states of the princess, which the author showed all along) (p. 201).

20   In discussing the princess's feelings for Nemours, for example, Charnes's characters remark: "Mademoiselle de Chartres, à une première vue, se sent un penchant naturel pour Monsieur de Nemours: Elle n'y résiste que par une grande vertu. Tout ce qu'elle fait en faveur de Monsieur de Nemours ne doit plus nous surprendre après cela. C'est la nature qui l'instruit, et le coeur n'a pas besoin d'autre maître pour former ses mouvements" (At first sight Mlle de Chartres is naturally attracted to M. de Nemours. She only resists due to her great virtue. Everything she does in his favor after that shouldn't surprise us. Nature teaches her and the heart needs no other teacher to develop its movements) (p. 43). They spend much energy explaining the princess's marriage and the role her mother played in arranging it (pp. 158–62).

21   See for example, pages 199 and 249.

22   "Unreasonable" is often the attack leveled at Valincour, as when Charnes's critic states: "La seconde difficulté du Critique n'est pas plus raisonnable que la première" (The critic's second problem [with the text] is not more reasonable than the first) p. 218.

23   See my *Revising Memory* for an analysis of the tie between these values and social influence of these values, especially Chapter 4.

24   Huet's correspondence reveals that even 20 years after its publication, his treatise was discussed, especially by the worldly public. Fr example, Mme de Tille de Tergent writes "L'on fait aussi grand état de ce livre que vous fites, il y a environ vingt ans, de *L'origine des romans* … Je voudrais bien l'avoir ici, plusieurs personnes me le demandent" (People here talk very favorably about the book you wrote nearly twenty years ago, *De L'origine des romans*. I wish I had it here because many people ask me for it).

25 *Lettre-Traité de Pierre-Daniel Huet sur L'origine des romans,* 1669; ed. Fabienne Gégou (Paris, 1971), p. 147. All further references will be to this edition, with page numbers inserted parenthetically in the text.

26 In an interesting letter, the marquise de Lambert states: "Vous permettez les romans, et vous les autorisez par votre exemple" (You permit the existence of novels, and you authorize them by your own example).

27 As opposed to fables, for example, which he describes as "fictions de choses qui n'ont point été et qui n'ont pu être" (fictions about things that didn't happen and couldn't have been) (50). Later Huet specifies that the rules are those of epic poetry: "... j'appelle réguliers, ceux [novels] qui sont dans les règles du poème héroïque" (I call regular those [novels] that follow the rules of the heroic poem) (102).

28 As we saw in the quarrel over *Le Cid, vraisemblance* is defined not as "les choses comme elles sont" (things as they are) but rather "les choses comme elles doivent être" (things as they should be), a definition that underscores the quality of propriety contained in *vraisemblance.*

29 He states that while other nations may excel in epic poetry and history, "leurs plus beaux romans égalent à peine les moindres des nôtres." (Their best novels are barely the equals of our least good ones) *Lettre-Traité de Pierre-Daniel Huet,* p. 139.

30 See Joan DeJean's discussion of Huet's valorization of conversation in *Tender Geographies,* p. 174.

31 Huet explains: "Mais il ne suffit pas d'avoir découvert cette source des romans; il faut voir par quels chemins ils se sont répandus dans la Grèce, et dans l'Italie et s'ils ont passé de là jusqu'à nous ou si nous les tenons d'ailleurs" (But it is insufficient to have discovered this source of novels. We must see how they spread in Greece and in Italy, and see if they spread to us from there or if we got them from elsewhere) (69).

32 Huet often cites his sources in notes. Interestingly, when he talks about a single work, his rhetoric and style resemble that of the worldly critic. Of the *Pastorale* de Longus, for example, he says: "Son style d'ailleurs est simple, aisé, naturel et concis ... il produit avec esprit, il peint avec agrément" (His style is simple, easy, natural and concise ... He writes with wit, he describes pleasingly).

33 Huet explains: "Mais pour ne point confondre les choses, j'essaierai de rapporter selon l'ordre des temps ceux des écrivains grecs qui se sont signalés dans cet art" (In order to not confuse things, I will try to list chronologically the Greek authors who distinguished themselves in this art) (71).

34 For example he states: "C'est des Arabes, à mon avis, que nous tenons l'art de rimer"(In my opinion, we received the art of rhyming from the Arabs) (57).

35 For example, Huet writes: "L'erreur de Giraldi n'est pas supportable, quand il dit que la multiplicité d'actions est l'invention des Italiens" (Giraldi's error, when he states the the Italians invented the multiplicity of events, cannot be supported) (pp. 86–7).

36 The editor notes that Huet "fait passer la bienséance mondaine avant la moralité pure, alors que la littérature romanesque est attaquée non seulement par les moralistes, mais même par des lettrées comme Boileau ou Furetière" (places worldly propriety before pure morality, this when the novel was being attacked not only by moralists, but also by writers such as Boileau and Furetière) (p. 142, n. 9).

37 Huet remarks: "Mais au moins n'est-ce pas trop tard pour les romans, que de demander que, lorsqu'ils s'assujettiront aux lois de la modestie et de la pudeur, ils soient tolérés par les censeurs" (But at least it is not too late to ask that novels, when they adhere to laws of modesty and decency, be tolerated by censors) (144).

38 *Un Erudit: Homme du monde, homme d'église, homme de cour (1630–1721). Lettres inédites de Mme de Lafayette, de Mme Dacier, de Bossuet, de Fléchier, de Fénelon, etc. Extraits de la correspondance de Huet.* ed. C. Henry (Paris, 1879), note p. 14.

39 Pierre-Daniel Huet, *Mémoires* (1718) ed. Philippe-Joseph Salazar (Toulouse, 1993), pp. 99–100.

40 Consalve relates: "Ce fut par lui que j'appris toutes les choses que j'avais ignorées dans le temps qu'elles se passaient" (I learned everything that I had ignored when it happened from him). Mme de Lafayette, *Zaïde, Histoire espagnole,* 1670–71; ed. Alain Niderst (Paris, 1990), p. 88. All further references to *Zaïde* will be to this edition, with page numbers inserted parenthetically in the text.

41 John Lyons analyzes of the role of language and image in the search for knowledge in *Zaïde. Exemplum: The Rhetoric of Example in Early Modern French Literature* (Princeton, 1989), pp. 200–17.

42 Donna Kuizenga takes the opposite position to the one I am advancing here. In her view, male voices dominate in the novel, signifying the silencing of women's tales in men's romances. "Zaïde: Just another Love Story?", *Actes de Davis*, ed. Claude Abraham (Paris: Biblio 17, 1988), 26–7. I do not think that this interpretation accounts for Félime's strong influence. Dom Olmond relates her story, but it is inscribed in the text in Félime's first person voice.

43 John Lyons has discussed the themes of perception and communication in *Zaïde,* and the various forms of signification. He valorizes language as the only means to correct interpretations. "Speaking in Pictures, Speaking of Pictures: Problems of Representation in the Seventeenth Century," in *From Mirror to Method, Augustine to Descartes*, eds. John D. Lyons and Stephen G. Nichols (Hanover, NH, 1982), pp. 174–5. Commenting on Lyons's interpretation, Harriet Stone sees both verbal and visual means as inadequate to arrive at truth: "If then, we recognize the inability of painting to arrive at the truth through resemblances, we must accord some of this same inability to the narrative about the painting." "Reading the Orient: Lafayette's *Zaïde,*" *Romanic Review*, March 1990, 81 (2), 156. I would agree that language is often a necessary supplement to visual representation in the novel, but it is just as frequently problematized.

44 Stone, *Reading the Orient*, p. 151. See also her book *The Classical Model: Literature and Knowledge in Seventeenth-Century France* (Ithaca, 1996).

45 Michael Moriarty, *Taste and Ideology in Seventeenth-Century France* (Cambridge, 1988), p. 45.

46 Villedieu was eventually granted a royal pension in 1669, but it was not allocated until 1676, and then she received only half the amount. By the time she received the pension, she had stopped writing. *Les Désordres de l'amour*, considered to be her last novel, was published in 1675. Gabrielle Verdier underscores her literary personality, unique among women of her time, stating "Still, Mlle Desjardins is poor, of common birth, and must rely solely on her talent to succeed." In "Gender and Rhetoric in Some Seventeenth-Century Love Letters," in *French Dressing*, Nancy K. Miller remarks, "Mme de Villedieu supported herself by her writing and thus was dependent on public favor and royal pleasure. She had no other identity, precisely, on which to draw." "Tender Economies: Mme de Villedieu and the Costs of Indifference," p. 80, n. 1.

47 For an analysis of changes in the system of literary patronage during the period and the emergence of the concept of an author, see Alain Viala, *La Naissance de l'écrivain*. Drawing on Viala's work, Roger Chartier remarks that already in the seventeenth-century, authors were not forced to rely solely on a patron and could be recognized through other channels: "There were the salons and the academies ... there was the patronage system, which

substituted the recognition of talent for the obligations of the patron-client relationship; there was the emergence of a larger public that permitted notable successes without the support of the learned community or the court" (*The Cultural Origins of the French Revolution*, trans. Lydia G. Cochrane, Durham, North Carolina, 1991), p. 59. As we shall see, the latter of these developments was largely responsible for Villedieu's success.

48 For Villedieu's biography, consult Katharine A. Jensen, *French Women Writers: A Bio-bibliographical Source Book*, eds Eva Sartori and Dorothy Zimmerman (New York, 1991), pp. 503–12, and Micheline Cuénin, *Roman et société sous Louis XIV: Mme de Villedieu* (Paris, 1979); Donna Kuizenga, *The Dictionary of Literary Biography: Seventeenth-Century French Writers*, ed. Françoise Jaouên, New York, 2003.

49 See Bruce Morrissette, *The Life and Works of Marie-Catherine Desjardins* (St Louis, 1947), p. 6, and Cuénin, *Roman et société*, II, pp. 114–22.

50 Perry Gethner underscores the exceptional nature of this event: *Le Favory* was "the first play by a woman author to receive a command performance at the French court." "Love, Self-Love and the Court in *Le Favori*", in *Actes de Wakeforest*, eds Milorad R. Margitic and Byron R. Wells (Paris: Biblio 17, 1987), p. 407. See the introduction to his book, *Femmes dramaturges en France (1650–1750). Pièces choisies* (Paris and Seattle, 1993).

51 Morrissette gives an accurate picture of the literary milieu in which Villedieu found herself when he states: "Dedications and familiar references in the works of this first period of literary activity give evidence of an ever widening circle of social and literary relationships. She refers to Mlle de Montbazon, the Président Bellièvre, Gilles Boileau, Mlle Gaboury, Mme de Morangis, Saint-Aignan, the minister Hugues de Lionne, the duchesse de Montpensier, the chancelier Séguier, Mme de Montglas, Guillaume de Bautru, the abbé du Buisson, d'Aubignac, the Duc and Duchesse de Montausier, M. de Nanteuil, Colbert, and the comte de Séry." *The Life and Works*, p. 6. She was even proposed for admission to the French Academy, along with Mlle Deshoulières.

52 See Cuénin, *Roman et Société*, II, pp. 66–72.

53 And she seems to have succeeded. As Arthur Flannigan Saint-Aubin remarks "few writers enjoyed a popularity comparable to hers. This popularity—evident in part by the numerous editions of her individual and collective works—seems to have persisted well into the eighteenth century; and the nineteenth century witnessed the formation of a cult of her admirers." *The Disorders of Love* (Birmingham, 1995), p. 1. Tallemant des Réaux offers the following disparaging remark about Villedieu: "Ils [her contemporaries] l'ont mise au-dessus de Mlle de Scudéry et de tout le reste des femelles" (Her contemporaries put her above Mlle de Scudéry and all the rest of the females). *Historiettes*, ed. Antoine Adam (Paris, 1967), II: p. 900.

54 Cuénin, *Roman et société*, II, p. 66.

55 Ibid., II, p. 68.

56 Ibid., II, p. 72.

57 In an insightful article, Elizabeth Goldsmith analyzes Villedieu's dialogue with the public in terms of her desire to control her texts, especially the new genre of the *nouvelle galante* and how it should be read. She states: "Contemporary descriptions of Marie-Catherine Desjardins stress her concern with creating a public image ... we can see her preoccupation with creating a public identity that conformed to her professed ambition as a writer to invent new styles of feminine expression." "Publishing Passion: Mme de Villedieu's *Lettres et billets galants*," in *Actes de Wakeforest*, p. 440.

58 Montpensier was closely associated with literary endeavors. Her *Receuil des Portraits*, to which Villedieu contributed, appeared at approximately the same time as *Manlius*.

172   *Salons, History, and the Creation of Seventeenth-Century France*

Montpensier had recently published *Les Divertissements de la Princesse Aurélie*, composed with Segrais. In addition, she was writing her *Mémoires*, which most likely circulated in manuscript.

59 *Lisandre* (Paris, 1663).

60 Katharine Ann Jensen views Villedieu's choice of genres as imposed on her by Barbin, her publisher. "Barbin was interested in Desjardins de Villedieu's adaptability to the mercurial social literature of the day." *French Women Writers*, p. 506. While Villedieu was encouraged and even exploited by Barbin, her prefaces show her conscious choice to turn to novels, and her creation of an authorial persona dependent on this genre.

61 *Recueil de quelques lettres ou relations galantes* (Paris, 1668), Epître, n.p.

62 *Recueil de quelques lettres ou relations galantes*, Lettre VIII, 15 mai 1667), p. 68.

63 Goldsmith remarks that Villedieu's "innovative argument in the preface to the *Désordres de l'amour* that writers of fiction should speak from personal experience was doubly risky. For a woman writer to propose a new esthetic of self-exposure constituted a rejection ... of modesty, that most important of feminine virtues." "Publishing Passion," p. 440.

64 *Recueil de quelques lettres*, pp. 71–2.

65 *Cléonice, ou le roman galant*, in *Oeuvres* (Paris, 1720–21), Vol. I, p. 461.

66 *Les Amours des Grands Hommes*, in *Oeuvres* (Lyon, 1695), t. iv.

67 For in-depth analyses of Villedieu's use of history, see Arthur Flannigan, *Mme de Villedieu's Les Désordres de l'amour: History, Literature and the Nouvelle Historique* (Washington, DC,1982) and my *Revising Memory*.

68 For an analysis of this preface and Villedieu's relationship to history, see Domna C. Stanton, "The Demystification of History and Fiction in *Les Annales galantes*," *Actes de Wakeforest*, pp. 339–60 and my *Revising Memory*, pp. 66–7.

69 *Les Annales galantes,* preface, n.p.

70 Ibid., n.p.

71 Ibid., n.p.

72 Villedieu is, of course, not the only author producing this new genre of the *nouvelle historique*. But many of her contemporaries considered her to be the genre's primary practitioner, and in particular to be responsible for the careful mixing of history and fiction that characterizes the *nouvelle historique*. Witness Bayle's often cited remarks that Villedieu has "ouvert la porte à une licence, dont on abuse tous les jours de plus en plus; c'est celle de prêter ses inventions, et ses intrigues galantes, aux plus grands hommes des derniers siècles, et de les mêler avec des faits qui ont quelque fondement dans l'Histoire" (opened the door to a poetic licence that is more and more abused each day; that of attributing her inventions and her gallant intrigues to the greatest men of past centuries and combining them with facts that have some foundation in history). *Dictionnaire historique et critique* (Rotterdam, 1697), entry for Mlle Desjardins. Cuénin stresses Villedieu's responsibility for these new genres: "She founded or at least consecrated the *nouvelle historique*, definitively banished the long form of the genre, invented serial *nouvelles*, and created the autobiographical novel, the epistolary novel, and the worldly novel." *Roman et société*, p. 723.

73 Beasley, *Revising Memory*, p. 175.

74 *Les Annales galantes de Grèce,* in *Oeuvres* (Paris, 1720–21), t. VII, pp. 377–8, my emphasis.

75 In the introduction to her edition of *Les Désordres de l'amour*, Cuénin remarks upon Villedieu's innovative relationship with her public: "And curiously she already established a relationship with her readers, leaving behind novel conventions and addressing the public directly ... She introduced a note of familiarty unexpected for the period). (Paris,

1970," p. LIV. All further references to *Les Désordres* will be to this edition, with page numbers inserted parenthetically in the text. Flannigan has produced a translation of the *Désordres: The Disorders of Love* (Birmingham, 1995). I will be using this translation unless otherwise indicated, and will insert page numbers in parentheses in the text.

76   For an in-depth analysis of Villedieu's conception of history in relation to other women writers of the period, see my *Revising Memory*. Arthur Flannigan and Domna Stanton both focus on Villedieu's use of history.

77   Mary M. Rowan has analyzed Villedieu's relationship to previous literary models. In her view, "As [Villedieu's] unique narrative voice asserts itself, she bends traditional novelistic strategies to her own purposes." "Patterns of Enclosure and Escape in the Prose Fiction of Mme de Villedieu," *Actes de Wakeforest*, p. 302. She thus tries to "liberate a new genre of prose fiction from slavish imitation of models" (p. 382).

78   In *Mme de Villedieu's Les Désordres de l'amour*, Flannigan has examined in detail Villedieu's authorial interventions, in particular the maxims. He views Villedieu's authorial presence in her text as a key element of her transformation of history into a *nouvelle* (p. 55).

79   As Flannigan remarks, with the introductory maxim and others, Villedieu "provides the plan, the 'road map' with which her text is to be read; and, in so doing, she positions a 'voice' between the text ... and its recipient ... by channeling the reader's attention to certain aspects of the nouvelle, she prejudices him in effect by legislating and adjudicating 'how' the story is to be perceived; and in doing this she denies the recipient of the narrative any liberté de lecteur." *Mme de Villedieu's Les Désordres*, p. 57. While I agree that Villedieu's maxims are part of her effort to control the interpretation of her text, I view her relationship to her readers as more collaborative, as shall become apparent in what follows.

80   As Flannigan remarks, the maxims often justify what seems an infraction of the rules of *vraisemblance*. *Mme de Villedieu's Les Désordres*, p. 102. For a summary of the importance of *vraisemblance* to the *nouvelle historique*, see my *Revising Memory*, pp. 34–5 and 234–5.

81   Flannigan, *Mme de Villedieu's Les Désordres*, p. 102.

82   Flannigan, *Mme de Villedieu's Les Désordres*, p. 122. He stresses the difference between Villedieu and other novelists such as St. Real. Of St. Real he states: "His narrator, never personalized, is monotonously the objective historian detached at all times from the narrated event and the text ... In Mme de Villedieu's text, the narrator, as moralist, possesses a distinct personality." Ibid., p. 133.

83   Flannigan views this ending as reflecting Villedieu's control over her text. "The narrator seems confident that there is no leeway for a further elaboration or for a different interpretation of the events of history." *Mme de Villedieu's Les Désordres*, p. 69.

84   Elsewhere she refers to "nos Rois" (p. 43). When referring to the château de Saint Germain she brings the reader back to the present, stating that "on y voit encore" (that can still be seen) (p. 43) the element she is describing.

85   After explaining how she obtained a letter that she includes in the text she states, "c'est sans doute pourquoi elle est parvenue jusques à nous" (which is probably why the letter has come down to us) (p. 206), thus including the reader in the time of composition of the text.

86   Flannigan, *Mme de Villedieu's Les Désordres*, p. 75.

87   As I remark in *Revising Memory*, "Through the maxims and other narratorial interventions ... she creates a bond with the reader ... through honest complicity with the reader, [she] hopes to draw them into agreeing with this new perspective on history" (pp. 174–5).

88   Of many seventeenth-century women's texts in general Joan DeJean remarks that "their principal characters are shown to be obsessively concerned with telling their own or others' stories or with making others tell their stories. The goal of this obsession is the transformation of narrator and audience into a private academy, an interpreting assembly joined together for the purpose of analyzing the significance of even the smallest element of the narrated stories. This recurrent mise en abîme of the critical act, as Frank Kermode has recently shown 'works to create enigma rather than dissolve it'" ("The Female Tradition," *L'Esprit Créateur*, vol. XXIII, no. 2, summer 1983), p. 7. While characters are not constantly telling stories as they are in Lafayette's *Zaïde*, for example, the reader and the characters are constantly asked to interpret, as we shall see.

89   See Joan DeJean, *Tender Geographies*, pp. 22 and 43, and her "The Literary World at War."

90   It is intriguing to note that Villedieu chooses "judicieuse" (judicious) to describe her character's writing process. In the preface to *Les Annales galantes*, she states that "l'historien judicieux" (the judicious historian) would not compose history as she does. By using the same adjective, Villedieu is perhaps, through her character, valorizing her own literary creation, equating it with those of the judicious historians she uses as her sources.

91   As Flannigan remarks, "in the final nouvelle the historical characters appear no longer as mere literary objects manipulated by an omniscient narrator who analyses and condemns them from a distance, but they appear somewhat as [historical] 'subjects' capable of identifying and assessing their own passions." *Mme de Villedieu's Les Désordres*, p. 81.

92   Morrissette states "Mornet, in his noted article on the contents of private libraries in eighteenth-century France, gives a frequency table showing the occurrence of various works in some 392 private libraries of the period. According to this index of popularity, the *Oeuvres* of Mlle Desjardins rank twenty-sixth ... Mlle Desjardins, moreover, ranks first among the seventeenth-century French authors." *The Life and Works*, p. 194.

93   Ibid., p. 193.

Chapter 3

From Critics to Hostesses: Creating Classical France

L'empire des salons a passé avec celui des femmes ..."

Sophie Gay[1]

Sophie Gay's lamentation in the mid-nineteenth century of the parallel demise of salon sovereignty and women's power rings true when one examines the representation of the salons and female influence following the *Grand Siècle*. Subtly throughout the eighteenth century, and then more openly in the nineteenth, many literary critics, commentators and historians sought to sever the strong relationship between the salons and the classical literary field that we have seen in the preceding chapters. Concurrently, in the construction of France's literary legacy, a legacy that was a major component in France's conception of its nation's uniqueness and superiority, there was a move to bury what was arguably in the seventeenth century the most influential and important product of the salons, namely its unique female literary tradition and female influence on the literary field in general. From an admired space where critics and writers could shape and determine the taste of a large part of the literary public, the salons were reconfigured into loci that focused less on determining literary value than on civilizing a nation. This shift in the representation of one of seventeenth-century French culture's principal distinguishing characteristics had lasting ramifications for posterity's conception of one of France's premier historical moments, the classical France of the seventeenth century.

As we have seen, the seventeenth century acknowledged the specific functions of the salons in literary culture and women as major players in this movement. Indeed women's taste and reason became so influential that the *doctes* were compelled to reappropriate these terms and redefine them in the process. This backlash at the end of the century can be viewed as the beginning of an effort that gathered momentum over the course of the following two centuries to conceive of the seventeenth-century literary field in a way that reconfigured the relationship between the worldly arena and literary culture. The salons were viewed as having been one of the principal forces behind France's *sociabilité*, so it is only natural that this uniquely French institution attracted much attention as the nation tried to identify and create its sense of self. Similarly, France's cultural capital, namely its literary and philosophical heritage, were viewed as aspects of a culture unequaled by France's neighbors. But as shall become apparent, the image of classical France propogated by its nineteenth-century inheritors differs in significant respects from the way seventeenth-century contemporaries conceived of it.

This re-membering of the seventeenth-century literary field can be perceived when one examines some representative literary histories and anthologies that appeared beginning in the early eighteenth century and continuing into the nineteenth. These works, most of which were addressed to a worldly as opposed to an academic public, illuminate what I view as a gradual transformation of the memory of seventeenth-century salon and literary culture. Specifically, there is a move to redefine all salon culture and portray it as synonymous with its eighteenth-century manifestation, as opposed to the particular form it took in the seventeenth century. After having examined these literary histories I will turn to an analysis of the nineteenth-century's quasi obsession with the seventeenth, and in particular its female figures. During this period, which many cultural historians refer to as "the century of history," scholars worked to confirm the trends evident in the anthologies, and defined the perimeters of female participation in literary culture through their representation of the salons and their female participants. Sainte Beuve's portraits of seventeenth-century figures and Victor Cousin's voluminous biographies of seventeenth-century female luminaries are, as we shall see, representative of a generalized myth-making with respect to the salons and are intricately related to the broader process during the period of trying to define France as a unique nation. In the wake of the upheaval of the Revolution, nineteenth-century France found itself searching for self-definition and a vision of what greatness could be salvaged from the rubble of its recent past. Although the events of the revolution certainly did not attest to it, the image of France as a model of civilization was still ingrained in the nation's conscious and unconscious, and it is this image that would be revived and developed further in many of the histories of the period. The alternative representation of the seventeenth-century literary field is strikingly apparent in an analysis of the inscription of two of France's premier female "shadows" into the nation's memory. The histories of Madeleine de Scudéry and Catherine de Vivonne, marquise de Rambouillet crystallize the process of reformulation and mythologizing that began in the eighteenth century and reached its apogee in the nineteenth. The marquise de Rambouillet is consistently touted as the first *salonnière* and the premier representative and creator of polite society. Her younger counterpart, Madeleine de Scudéry, also remains alive in France's collective memory, but her existence as *salonnière* and in particular her literary influence is not nearly as universally celebrated. I conclude this chapter with an in-depth analysis of the processes that culminated in these very disparate views of Rambouillet and Scudéry. The fate of these two shadows illustrates to an exceptional degree the forces guiding the creation of France's literary past, and women's place in this national heritage.

The past ten years have witnessed the development of a vein of scholarship, both historical and literary, that attempts to analyze the uniquely French phenomena of *politesse* and *galanterie*. The works of Alain Viala, Emmanuel Bury, Myriam Maître, Delphine Denis, and Elena Russo, among others, take these terms that had become rather empty clichés and grant them much of the significance and complexity they had during the seventeenth and eighteenth centuries. In particular, recent scholars have illuminated how these categories of human interaction functioned in court and worldly society, and what influence they exerted on the development of the French literary field. The present study is designed to draw upon such work, complement it, and extend the field of inquiry by interrogating how and why the categories of *politesse* and *galanterie* came to be constituted and accepted as representative of French culture, particularly of the Old Regime. Many of these studies grant women a determining, often founding, role in the development of *politesse* and *galanterie*. It is not only acceptable to applaud women's contribution to France's culture in these domains, it has become cliché. I wish to trace the process by which women's influence, especially on the literary culture of seventeenth-century France, became associated almost uniquely with *politesse* and *galanterie*, to the exclusion of any other activity. As we have seen, the salons and the women who frequented and formed them used *politesse* and *galanterie* as powerful tools, but their influence on the literary field was not limited to these domains. Indeed, I would argue that limiting women to these categories sets them apart from the literary field as a whole, and allows for the vision that grants women little to no influence on the canon of classical France. Women's participation was not separate but emmeshed into the very fabric of the literary sphere as a whole. While some recognized this power and applauded it, others worked to counter and suppress it. To understand the whole one must take gender into account as one of the principal threads and not as a separate category of investigation. Seventeenth-century contemporaries, both foreign and French, viewed France as a nation that alloted a particular role to women in the literary sphere, a role not limited to that of hostess and lover/muse. It is the transformation and often erasure of this role from the annals of France's cultural history that I examine in this chapter.

The Changing Taste of Literary History

In *Le Siècle de Louis XIV*, Voltaire elevated the years of the Sun King as the culminating point of France's past, the one "qui approche le plus de la perfection" (that comes the closest to perfection).[2] Before the ascension of Louis XIV to the throne, France had not reached its true potential. Its "génie national" (national genius) had been suppressed by its government, and its language, the mirror of that "genius," was disorganized, not unified, and, worst of all, was "grossière" (crude) (289–91). The period of the Sun King corresponded to "une révolution générale" that pushed France in the direction of its almost preordained greatness. This "revolution," which one associates today more with Voltaire's own century than with the oppressive monarchy of Louis XIV, derived its power from its overwhelming nature. In Voltaire's estimation, this was a revolution that was not limited to government but extended its dominion to every aspect of human interaction: "Il s'est fait dans nos arts, dans nos esprits, dans nos moeurs, comme dans notre governement, une révolution générale qui doit servir de marque éternelle à la véritable gloire de notre patrie" (There occurred a general revolution in our art, our minds, our customs, as well as in our government that must serve as an eternal example of the true glory of our homeland) (288). The result of this upheaval benefited not just France but humanity in general: "la raison humaine en général s'est perfectionnée" (human reason in general was perfected) (287). France was able to export this civilizing influence to the rest of Europe, whose citizens in turn gratefully emulated France: "Cette heureuse influence ne s'est pas même arrêtée en France; elle s'est étendue en Angleterre; elle a excité l'émulation dont avait alors besoin cette nation spirituelle et hardie … L'Europe a du sa politesse et l'esprit de société à la cour de Louis XIV" (This beneficial influence did not limit itself to France; it spread to England; it inspired the emulation that this witty and bold nation needed … Europe owed its politeness and sociability to the court of Louis XIV) (288). While other countries may have attempted to copy France's culture, it remained constant that the source of "les grâces, la douceur, et une liberté décente … n'étaient qu'en France" (charm, sweetness, and proper freedom … were only in France) (278) because only France could boast such an exceptional monarch. Voltaire attributes the rise of France's cultural capital and prestige to Louis XIV and his court, a court where women's influence was not negligible. In his view, French women developed an art of *politesse* unique to France and this *politesse* and *sociabilité* were engrained upon Louis's court.

It is interesting to note that while Voltaire does grant women a prominent role in the civilizing process associated with the French nation, he locates this influence within the confines of the court, thus in a domain under the controlling rays of the monarch. It is the court and Louis that become identified as the principal catalysts of this "general revolution," to the exclusion of other arenas such as the salons. Voltaire's rendition of the rise of France's glorious period of perfection and and his canonization of certain characteristics as unique to France thus differs subtly but significantly from the association we have seen made previously by Huet, among others, between some aspects of culture unique to France and women's "freedom" and their roles in society in general, and in literary society in particular. Whereas Huet, for example, would grant women the power to influence or even exemplify "charm, sweetness, and proper freedom"—qualities that distinguish France from its neighbors—in arenas outside the court, Voltaire, while recognizing their influence, confines it to a court dominated by Louis XIV.[3]

At the beginning of the nineteenth century, Germaine de Staël reflected upon the historical processes that had established France as the exemplar of a refined European civilization. In her view and that of most Europeans during the period, French society prior to the Revolution both reflected and was the result of a national character specific to the hexagon. Staël's opening question at the beginning of Chapter 18 of her *De la littérature* identifies the principal traits of this exceptional nation: "Why was the French nation the one in Europe with the most charm, taste, (*goût*) and gaiety?" she queries.[4] In her detailed analysis of why "French gaiety, and French good taste were known throughout Europe," and how contemporaries attributed this exemplary taste to France's "national character," Staël focuses on the political institutions she considers to be at the heart of France's unique character, namely the absolute monarchy and the court society that accompanied it. Prefiguring Norbert Elias's well-known explanation of the workings of French court society, Staël explains that power, even that of the monarch himself, derived from one's ability to manage and to please others:

> People felt the need to please one another, and everyone multiplied the ways to succeed in this. One did not achieve power in France through work or study; a witty word, a certain charm were often the cause of the most rapid advancement ... When amusement is not only allowed but is often useful, a nation can reach perfection in this field ... the great perfection of taste and gaiety developed out of this universal desire to please.[5]

Sociability and pleasure thus become engrained in the nation's character due in large measure to its specific political structure.

From the seventeenth century until the Revolution, the monarch and his court profoundly influenced the image France projected to the world. Staël identifies a second, equally influential, feature of French society that functioned within the court and exerted its own unique influence: the place accorded to women. "Charm," "taste," and "gaiety" can be traced to the power women exerted not only at court, but in the institution they developed in France, the salon. Staël puts it succinctly when she states that "Women's influence is necessarily very great, when everything happens in salons and all character is expressed in words; in such a state of things, women are powerful, and people cultivate what pleases them."[6] Interestingly, from the past tense Staël used to describe the influence of court society, she passes to the present when she turns to the role of women, a role she does not view, or at least does not wish to view, as having been erased by the Revolution. In Staël's formulation of women's specific imprint on French culture, the power of women resides in their ability to inspire contemporaries to "cultivate" what the female sex would find pleasing. Principal among such activities is the art of conversation, which became highly developed during the seventeenth and eighteenth centuries. According to Staël, one can trace the development of what becomes a singular trait of French national character to the strong monarchy that provided the leisure time necessary for the "perfecting of the pleasure of *esprit* and conversation" (278). "Taste" "grace," "gaiety," and the art of conversation, which reflects these characteristics as it enhances them, were all intricately related to the specific role allotted to women in French society of the Ancien Régime.

Women thus were viewed as having left an indelible mark on French national character in particular through the salon activities that fostered the art of sociability. But Staël's remarks, as well as those of many other voices long before hers in the seventeenth century, imply a less obvious effect of women's specific status in French society. In a chapter of *De l'Allemagne* entitled "De l'esprit de conversation," another exploration of French character, Staël stresses that the art of conversation is responsible not only for the sociability so reputed in France, but also for the mindset of the nation: "The direction of French thought has been directed by conversation for a century."[7] Staël leaves her remark rather vague, preferring not to specify the exact nature of this "direction of French thought" generated by conversation. But it is clear that conversation has affected more than the nature of social interaction in France. In changing the course of ideas, conversation has changed the very fabric of the nation.

Staël's discussion of women's status in French society and their unique contribution to national character is reminiscent of similar reflections that we saw formulated by Daniel Huet one hundred and fifty years before her as well as Voltaire's. Like Voltaire, Staël attributes the rise of *gaieté* and *goût* to her country's political system, although she does not associate them with one particular monarch. And like Voltaire, Staël views France as having achieved a state of perfection in these arts, and she grants women a large role in the development of these national traits. In Staël's view, however, this female influence is not confined to the court setting. It infiltrates the entire society and emanates not only from the court but more specifically from the salons.

Voltaire's and Staël's explanations of the historical factors that resulted in a state of perfection particular to the French nation represent an attitude towards the Ancien Regime, and especially the seventeenth century, shared by many in the years following the reign of the Sun King. Voltaire and Staël were two among many who glorified aspects of a social system that, in Staël's opinion, had been destroyed by the Revolution. In their histories of French national character, this society in which women played a large role was responsible for unique qualities that continued to characterize France— sociability, conversation, love of pleasure, *gaieté*, *esprit*, among others—all traits associated in the seventeenth century with salon culture as well as with the court. But while Voltaire and Staël, among others, grant women a role in the development of a particularly French collective identity, their depictions of the salons, when they exist, identify their role as purely social, as opposed to the roles associated with them in the seventeenth century, namely as spaces for literary innovation and critique. It is interesting to note, for example, that when Staël elevates "good taste" as one of France's most recognizable traits, she understands it merely as an attribute of social intereaction, and not as a tool of the literary critic as Furetière had defined it.

Such a one-dimensional vision of the salons and the limitation of women's influence to objects to be pleased in a purely social sense are perhaps the result of the redefinition of the salon and women's participation in the intellectual realm that took place during the eighteenth century. From spaces that combined *politesse* and *galanterie* with literary expression, linguistic innovation, and literary critique, salons in the eighteenth century became gathering places for conversation and debate, but spaces in which women's roles were radically altered. As Elena Russo has argued in *La Cour et la ville: de la littérature classique aux Lumières*, *salonnières* in the eighteenth century take on the more effaced role of social facilitator than that of their seventeenth-century predecessors. Russo notes that, with the exception of Voltaire, who animated his own gatherings, eighteenth-century *philosophes* all frequented the salons of the period and used the institution to acquire readers, to test and circulate their ideas, and to gain public support.[8] But while the salons were recognized by the thinkers of the day as places of intellectual exchange, their nature, and especially their principal distinguishing characteristic of the previous century had changed dramatically. Instead of a social space established, defined and dominated by its female participants, who looked to the salons in many instances to circulate their own ideas concerning education for women and literary values, eighteenth-century women adopted the role of mediators and facilitators of male discourse. Russo explains:

> This return to antiquity and to classical taste brings about a radical transformation in the way women's roles were viewed in society, and in the salon in particular. The image of the salonnière and the way people conceived of her role in the community undergoes a clear change compared to preceding generations. From the goddess and inspiration of a fantasy cult, she becomes a maternal and nourishing figure, a simple mediator of a dialogue whose only protagonists are male, a figure who is voluntarily overshadowed. Whereas before she participated in the conversation like everyone else, now she remains on the sidelines and directs it without contributing [to it] directly.[9]

It can be argued that, just as seventeenth-century "taste" was eclipsed by a return to "le grand goût" (official taste), as defined by the French Academy and associated with Boileau, so too did the image founded upon the eighteenth-century *salonnière* usurp that of her seventeenth-century predecessor in France's national memory. While Russo's characterization of previous generations of *salonnières* as goddesses inspiring a fantasy view of reality is not the vision we have developed in previous chapters, her assessment of the striking shift that occurred in the conception of the *salonnière* in the eighteenth century is very accurate and attested to by numerous contemporaries. The female voice, both literary and conversational, in the literary and social fields of the seventeenth century *was* the *ruelle* under Louis XIV. Women created literary genres, determined taste, and even purified the language of the king, as witnessed to by the intense reaction against this influence. This defining and innovative female voice becomes muted, if not totally suppressed in the eighteenth century version of the salon, as women adopt the more traditionally acceptable social functions of listener and hostess as opposed to speaker and creator. Indeed the highest compliment one could pay to a *salonnière* in this latter phase of the movement during the Ancien Regime was that she knew how to retire, be modest, and listen—all qualities that one would not find in seventeenth-century descriptions of their female predecessors.[10] Eighteenth-century *salonnières* were still admired and even deified, but not for the same activities nor for the same qualities as those in the seventeenth century. Although public figures, they governed using a power that elicited less virulent reaction because it corresponded to more traditional views of the roles of women in public debate and intellectual culture. Women such as Geoffrin and Lespinasse were admired because they could inspire intellectual conversation among their male admirerers, while they themselves remained on the sidelines, intervening only to revive a lagging conversation, and to draw out the genius of their male guests. They rarely sought to exhibit any creativity or genius of their own, especially in literary matters.[11]

It is this conception of the salon, more acceptable because its power structure and the roles of its participants correspond to more traditional male and female roles, that colors both Voltaire's and Staël's descriptions of their influence, and will impact the vision of the seventeenth-century *ruelles* developed throughout the nineteenth and twentieth centuries.[12] Salons remain associated with *sociabilité* and *galanterie*, and valued as uniquely French institutions because of these associations, but their literary connections and influences, especially those identified with women, are redefined or effaced. In many ways the marquise de Lambert at the very beginning of the eighteenth century accurately predicted this transition to an alternative notion of the salon and the role women would play in them. As we have seen, in many of her writings, Lambert lamented the downfall of the salon milieu she had frequented in her youth, namely that associated with the marquise de Rambouillet, Madeleine de Scudéry, and Mme de Sablé, to name only those still recognized today.[13] She idealizes the seventeenth-century manifestations of the institution and values their example precisely because of the active intellectual role played by the *salonnières*. Lambert attributes the demise of this form of female cultural power, in which women actively participated in the literary and intellectual arenas on an equal footing with male counterparts, directly to Molière and his theatrical satires of women who were not content to occupy the traditional, specifically silent, roles to which they had usually been condemned. Thus already at the beginning of the eighteenth century Lambert identifies the change in the conception of the *salonnière* from intellectual figure to social hostess that will become critical coin in the eighteenth century and beyond. Lambert contends that women such as the seventeenth-century *salonnières* she so admires could not find a place in her own century. They would only find ridicule. In her own salon, the marquise tried to revive the intellectual role of the *salonnière*, but she would be one of the very last to do so in a manner consistent with that of her seventeenth-century counterparts.

As the role of the *salonnière* changed, so too did the memory of her seventeenth-century predecessors. The years following "le grand siècle" witnessed a plethora of literary anthologies and histories designed to commemorate what was immediately considered to be an exceptional moment in literary culture, and even the apogee of French culture, that would be difficult, if not impossible, to replicate. Even outside the hexagon, women's influence on French letters was acknowledged. In the nineteenth century, for example, George Eliot remarked that "in France alone woman has had a vital influence on the development of literature ... in France alone, if the writings of women were swept away, a serious gap would be made in the national history."[14] From anthologies that lauded the taste, specifically literary, exemplified by the salons and their female literary participants, and eulogized the positive effect it had had on the literary field in general, the historicization of the seventeenth-century literary scene gradually entailed a divorce of women from the classical literary scene. From illustrating one ray of the Sun King's fame and influence, worldly literary culture, in particular the women who shaped it and the salons they created and dominated, moved into the shadows.[15] An analysis of a few representative anthologies and literary histories will allow us to trace the gradual and subtle move from literary critic and intellectual figure to social hostess that comes to characterize France's seventeenth-century salons.

Tillet's Monument to Memory

In 1732, Evrard Titon du Tillet (1677–1762) published a detailed and comprehensive work dedicated to the memory of France's seventeenth-century literary culture. In *Le Parnasse français*, Tillet inscribes the writers and the works that constitute what he hails as this exceptional period of French cultural dominance.[16] Throughout his text, Tillet is keenly aware that he is shaping the memory of his country's literary past. In fact, the word "mémoire" (memory) appears frequently and is a governing force guiding his choice of the figures and works for his *Parnasse*. As he states in his opening "Discours sur le dessein de cet ouvrage" (Disourse regarding the purpose of this work), just as France must erect "un champ de Mars et un Temple de Victoire" to commemorate Louis XIV's military prowess and that of his captains and heros, so too

> la France doit former des Temples de mémoire, construire des bibliothèques
> et d'autres édifices publics, pour y placer les portraits et les statues du grand

nombre de personnes qui ont excellé pendant le règne de ce Prince dans toutes les Sciences et dans tous les beaux arts, et qui les ont portés à leur plus haut degré de perfection. (4)

(France must create temples of memory, construct libraries and other public edifices, in which to place the portraits and statues of a great number of people who excelled during the reign of this Prince in all the sciences and all the arts, and carried them to their highest degree of perfection.)

He conceives of this work less as a text addressed to his own generation than as a monument for posterity. This monument to exceptional cultural achievement is designed to preserve and promote the memory of the inimitable king who made it all possible, Louis XIV.

Le Parnasse français is less an anthology than a comprehensive portrait of the entire literary milieu under Louis XIV. What immediately strikes the reader is Tillet's effort to be all-inclusive. Male and female figures whom today are considered relatively minor merit a place alongside those now recognized as the canonical masters of France's illustrious "Grand Siècle." While one can see the pantheon of Corneille, Racine, Molière, and Boileau taking shape in this work, they do not yet completely overshadow their contemporaries, in particular those associated with the worldly milieu of the salons. Tillet does elevate nine male authors to the level of "muse," but his list does not correspond entirely to the rigid canon of later years.[17] And on the opening page these "muses" are preceded by Louis le Grand and "the three graces:" Henriette de la Suze, Antoinette Deshoulières, and Madeleine de Scudéry.[18] The list that follows of all the illustrious "geniuses" of Louis XIV's reign includes more than thirty-four women, most of whom would be unrecognizable to today's public. Tillet's focus is less on the lives of individual writers than on their works.[19] He thus gives descriptions of texts in order to describe a writer through his/her literary production, and ends each piece with a bibliography of the author's works, thus inspiring the reader to delve into this literary world. *Le Parnasse français* resurrects the entire literary world of seventeenth-century France. Tillet places each writer in his/her entourage. The worldly milieu and the verses and novels it especially prized and cultivated are presented with the same respect and in the same manner as the classical dramatic works that have come to dominate present-day conceptions of France's classical literary world.

Much of the innovation of Tillet's work can be attributed to the author's astute sense of the changing nature of literary taste. While Boileau's taste tends to act as a sort of touchstone throughout the work, it does not totally overshadow the taste and associated literary values of the worldly public.

Tillet acknowledges Boileau's presence when he describes his inscription of the judgments of "la plupart des Critiques" (the majority of critics) on the authors he includes: "Il est vrai," (It is true) he states, "que je n'ai pas toujours suivi exactement celui de Despréaux, parce que c'est un censeur trop sévère, et quelquefois un peu prévenu" (that I have not always followed Despréaux's judgment exactly, because he is a censor who is too severe, and sometimes a bit prejudiced) (7). The worldly taste associated with the public determines the shape of this work as much as that of the erudite Ancients embodied by Boileau. As a result, Tillet's portrait of the literary period he elevates as the most exceptional differs significantly from the majority of those that will follow *Le Parnasse français*.[20]

In Tillet's portrayal of the seventeenth-century literary world, women figure prominantly and are often characterized by their "discernement" (judgment) and the "justesse" (accuracy) of their taste. Ninon de Lenclos, for example "brilla aussi dans ce même temps par la délicatesse de son esprit et la justesse de son discernement, et par l'agrément de sa conversation"[21] (also shone during this time with the subtly of her mind, the accuracy of her judgment, and the pleasure of her conversation). Women are esteemed as literary judges. Tillet describes Mlle Louise-Anastasie de Serment as "une des personnes de son sexe des plus savantes, et du discernement le plus juste pour tout ce qui regarde les belles lettres: aussi plusieurs beaux esprits la consultaient-ils sur leurs ouvrages, et surtout M. Quinault, qui la consideroit comme sa muse choisie" (one of the most learned people of her sex, [possessing] the most accurate judgment with respect to literature: thus many excellent minds consulted her about their works, and especially M. Quinault, who considered her his chosen muse) (446). Anne le Fevre Dacier is admired for her critical acumen. She is "la femme la plus savante de son siècle" (the most learned woman of her century) and holds "un rang distingué entre nos meilleurs critiques et entre nos traducteurs" (a distinguished rank among our best critics and translators) (570). The worldly public is not only present, it constitutes a major component of the literary world, and its taste and judgment merit inscription for posterity.[22] Madeleine de Scudéry figures in a list of "bon critiques" (good critics). [23] Tillet seems to be aware that this worldly taste may no longer correspond to that of his own century, but because his goal is to give a sense of the entire literary milieu under Louis XIV, and not to judge or censure, he focuses on painting a complete, accurate portrait. This inscription of worldly taste is especially evident in Tillet's valorization of poetry. The majority of the voices he includes have been lost to posterity, inspite of this conscious effort to deny them such a fate. One example is Madame Deshoulières, a celebrated member of the Académie d'Arles and of Ricovrati de Padoue, whom Tillet praises for her poetry. In his words: "il y a peu de personnes qui aient porté l'excellence de la poésie française aussi loin que Madame Deshoulières, surtout pour l'Idylle ... Personne n'a mieux parlé de l'amour et de la noble galanterie qu'elle. Personne n'a mieux aussi parlé de la morale and fait des reflexions plus justes sur l'esprit humain, quand elle a voulu traiter des sujets aussi graves" (There are few people who have carried the excellence of French poetry as far as Mme Deshoulières, especially the Idylle, ... no one spoke better about love or galantry than she. No one spoke better about morality and made more accurate reflections about the human spirit, when she wanted to treat such serious subjects) (458). Deshoulières deserves to be remembered not only among the women of her time, but as an exemplary figure in the world of letters at large. Tillet accentuates her worthiness of inclusion into his Parnassus of memory by including the verses that the editor of her works inscribed under her portrait:

> Si Corinne en beauté fut célèbre autrefois,
> Si des vers de Pindare elle effaça la gloire,
> Quel rang doivent tenir au Temple de Mémoire,
> Les Vers que tu vas lire, et les traits que tu vois?

> (If Corinne used to be celebrated for her beauty,
> If she erased the glory from Pindare's verse,
> What rank in the temple of memory must hold
> The verses you will read and the traits that you see?)

Like Buffet before him, Tillet places many of the women authors he includes on a par with those of Antiquity in order to grant them greater legitimacy in the eyes of his public. But Tillet goes farther than Buffet by meticulously inserting each figure into the general literary milieu. He inscribes each writer's social and literary entourage for posterity. Of Deshoulières, for example, he states that

> elle était amie et en commence de Lettres avec plusieurs beaux esprits du royaume, et des plus distingués par une politesse aimable; entr'autres, messieurs des Ducs de la Rochefoucauld, de Saint Aignan, de Montausier, de Nevers, de Vivonne, Maréchal de France; Charpentier, Doyen de l'Académie Française, et Fléchier, Evêque de Nimes. Mademoiselle Chéron, illustre par ses talents pour la peinture et pour la poésie, était amie de Madame Deshoulières (458–9).

(She was a friend and in the literary circles of many of the best minds of the kingdom, and among the most distinguished because of an agreeable politeness; among others, the ducs of La Rochefoucauld, de Saint Aignan, de Montausier, de Nevers, de Vivonne, Maréchal de France; Charpentier, the head of the French Academy, and Fléchier, the bishop of Nimes. Mlle Chéron, famous for her talent in painting and poetry, was Mme Deshoulière's friend.)

One thus has a sense not of isolated female luminaries, exceptions to the literary world, but rather of a world peopled by both sexes, a world of mutual admiration where writers joined together in the search for perfect artistic expression. Tillet attempts to include all the influential actors on the century's literary stage.[24] A La Fontaine achieved his potential because certain colleagues were able to draw him out of what Tillet describes as a state of artistic reverie:

> Cependant trois personnes illustres dans des états différents, qui étaient aussi des plus aimables, avaient trouvé le secret de tirer la Fontaine de son humeur reveuse et de ses distractions: sa conversation auprès d'elles devenait agréable et des plus vives: C'étaient Madame la duchesse de Bouillon, Madame de La Sablière, et Mlle de Chanmes. (462)

> (Yet three people famous for different reasons, who were also among the most likable, had found the secret to pulling La Fontaine out of his dreamy state and away from his distractions: his conversation when he was with them became more pleasurable and animated. They were Mme the duchesse de Bouillon, Mme de La Sablière, and Mlle de Chanmeslé.)

Tillet goes on to clarify that "Madame de la Sablière, dame de beaucoup d'esprit et de savoir, qui aimait la poésie, lui servit de Mécène, et le retira chez elle pendant près de vingt ans jusqu'à sa mort, [et] Madame d'Hervart lui donne un appartement dans son hôtel et sa table" (Mme de la Sablière, a woman of a lot of *esprit* and knowledge, who loved literature, was his patron, gave him a home for almost twenty years, until her death, [and] Mme d'Hervart gave him an apartment in her mansion and a place at her table) (462). Thus one of the authors that Tillet designates a "muse" in his work was aided by his worldly entourage, whose support was not limited to providing for his physical comforts. These female protectors' *esprit* and conversation contributed to the creation of his literary works. Scudéry's entourage included some of the most recognizable names of the academic and literary world. According to Tillet,

Les talents que Mlle de Scudéry possédait pour l'éloquence et pour la poésie la firent surnommer Sapho par les savants et par les plus beaux esprits de son siècle; elle entretenait avec eux un agréable commerce de littérature, leur écrivait et leur répondait en prose et en vers. Scarron, Conrart, Péllisson, Ménage, le Père Bouhours, Huet et plusieurs autres personnes illustres dans la République des Lettres ont fait de grands éloges de cette demoiselle. (485)

(Because of the talents that Mlle de Scudéry possessed for eloquence and for literature she was called Sapho by the learned people and by the greatest minds of her century; she maintained a pleasant literary relationship with them, wrote to them, and responded to them in prose and in verse. Scarron, Conrart, Pellisson, Ménage, Père Bouhours, Huet and many other famous people in the republic of letters wrote important praises of this demoiselle.)

Like the other women Tillet includes, Scudéry was thus part of the Republic of Letters and her works shaped it as much as those of her male counterparts. In an effort to elevate her memory to a level consistent to the one he perceives her as achieving in the seventeenth century, Tillet concludes his entry on Sapho by reiterating her inclusion in the most admired company of the day:

... elle entretiendra toujours avec soin une aimable liaison et commerce avec plusieurs illustres amis qu'elle avait, au nombre desquels étaient Messieurs le Duc de Montausier, Conrart, Pellisson; les Demoiselles de la Vigne, de Serment, de Razilly, Descartes, et quelques autres personnes distinguées par leur merite et par leur savoir. (486)

(... she always carefully maintained a pleasant relationship and active engagement with the many famous friends she had, among whom were the duc de Montausier, Conrart, Pellisson; the young women de la Vigne, de Serment, de Razilly, Descartes, and other people known for their merit and knowledge.)

In Tillet's view, in order to comprehend what made the seventeenth-century cultural scene so exceptional, it is necessary to see the complete context, not individual geniuses working in isolation.[25] His *Parnasse* thus both reflects and celebrates one of the most important characteristics of the worldly salon milieu that we saw in the preceding chapters: its collaborative nature.

Tillet either begins or concludes many of his individual entries by justifying his inclusion of a particular figure. He does this by referring not to the place an author has achieved among later generations of readers, but by emphasizing how his/her own literary arena viewed the author's contribution to the culture of the time. Phrases such as "Mademoiselle de la Vigne était en grande estime parmi les plus beaux esprits de son temps" (Mlle de la Vigne was held in great esteem by the best minds of her time) (369) abound. Tillet is thus encouraging posterity to construct its literary memory based on how an entire period viewed itself collectively, with no one voice dominating, rather than on the assessments of a few voices chosen by succeeding generations. Sometimes Tillet goes even farther and compliments a particular figure for having risen to the level of genius of the nation. For example, in his opinion "Pellisson est sans contredit un des plus beaux esprits que la France ait produit" (Pellisson is without question one of the best minds France has produced) (448). Occasionally one can detect the effects of the censoring voice attributable to Boileau's taste, as when Tillet includes the critic's negative assessment of Chapelain.[26] But in order to mitigate Boileau's dismissive attitude, Tillet counters Boileau's critique with a vaguely attributed but nonetheless effective defense: "Les critiques judicieux ont trouvé que Despréaux avait été un peu trop outré dans le jugement qu'il a porté sur les ouvrages de Chapelain, qui n'ont pas laissé de trouver des approbateurs parmi les connaisseurs du premier ordre, tels que ceux qu'on vient de citer, qui en ont approuvé la plus grande partie" (Judicious critics found that Despréaux had been a bit too excessive in the judgment he made of Chapelain's works, which did not fail to find people who approved among the connoisseurs of the first order, such as those just cited, who approved of most of [his works]) (338). And in a conscious effort to balance negative depictions of influential salon figures and those such as Chapelain known because they were ridiculed by Boileau, Tillet depicts the complexity of the century's literary field and intersperses well-known respected names with their lesser-known counterparts. In addition, he attempts to underscore the fact that seventeenth-century France under Louis XIV had its own taste, one that succeeding generations might not share, but that was recognized and valued by this exceptional period, a taste that was as much worldly as erudite. In his portrait of Voiture, who will be characterized as the salon poet par excellence by succeeding generations, Tillet refers to Voiture's ability to reflect this "taste of his century."

> Voiture ... a beaucoup contribué à perfectionner notre langue, en y joignant la noblesse avec l'agrément. Il est considéré en France comme le père et l'auteur d'un nouveau genre de poésie ... Quoiqu'il ait eu un grand nombre d'admirateurs, il n'a pas été sans avoir trouvée quelques censeurs, qui en lui reprochant quelques défauts, comme d'être un peu précieux, conviennent cependant qu'il avait de l'esprit, de la politesse, et qu'il était selon le goût de son siècle. (228)

(Voiture contributed a lot to perfecting our language, by combining nobility with charm. In France he is considered to be the father and the author of a new literary genre ... even though he had a great number of admirers, he also had some critics, who criticized him for some faults, such as being a bit precious, yet they agree that he was witty, polite, and that he reflected the taste of his century.)

Tillet's use of the possessive adjective to characterize "century" distinguishes this taste from that of his own time period. More important, by associating Voiture's worldly taste with his "century," Tillet legitimizes this taste as one essential characteristic of the entire period he is describing.

In *Le Parnasse français*, Tillet describes a literary world inhabited by women as well as men and influenced by worldly as well as more traditional erudite taste. The "memory" he strives to propogate is that of a lively literary community that fostered many different genres of literature and was inclusive as opposed to exclusive. In the years that follow Tillet's enterprise, the worldly taste that permeates his conception of the seventeenth-century literary world will be written out of portraits of "le Grand Siècle." Tillet's *Parnasse* provides the evidence that women writers and female intellectuals figured prominently in the literary history of France's premier century. The dynamic literary milieu he portrays will be gradually reshaped to reflect another conception of literary taste, one that did not include the worldly values that animated Tillet's exceptional literary space.

Gendering Greatness: Reconfiguring the Old Régime

Tillet's *Parnasse français* reflects to an exceptional degree the acknowledgment that existed at least throughout much of the first half of the eighteenth century that the exceptional literary heritage bequeathed to them by the seventeenth was peopled by women as well as men, and that it was indeed this mingling of genders that was responsible at least in part for creating a culture, especially a literary one, that was unsurpassed in Europe and was the envy of France's neighbors. Alongside anthologies and literary histories such as Tillet's that included men and women together and dispensed in many ways with hierarchy, and certainly with any sense that women artists were somehow inferior cultural players, there arose a number of works that, while often complimentary to woman artists, intellectuals, and *salonnières*, nevertheless sought to isolate them from the general literary and cultural milieu. For example, in the introduction to his study of Voiture published in 1853, Halphen summarized his contemporaries' general assessment of seventeenth-century literary culture and the role of the salons in its formation. In his opinion, the salon de Rambouillet, although justly satirized by Molière and Boileau, nonetheless served an important function in the early years of "le Grand Siècle." Its members perfected the French language and their games "contribuaient à la fusion des classes" (contributed to the fusion of classes).[27] But the glorious canon of French literature would owe little to such gatherings:

> La révolution littéraire allait s'accomplir; du salon de Conrart était sortie l'Académie Française. Les chefs-d'oeuvres de Corneille, de Racine, de Molière, de Boileau, de La Fontaine, de Fénelon, de Bossuet, allaient illustrer à jamais le plus grand siècle de notre histoire. Louis XIV prenait en main les rênes de l'Etat. Toutes les gloires se groupaient autour de la plus glorieuse des Majestés, l'hôtel de Rambouillet pouvait se fermer.[28]

> (The literary revolution was coming to an end. The French Academy came out of Conrart's salon. The masterpieces of Corneille, Racine, Molière, Boileau, la Fontaine, Fénelon, Bossuet would illustrate forever the greatest century of our history. Louis XIV took the reins of the state. All glory surrounded the most glorious of majesties, the hôtel de Rambouillet could close.)

In this vision, the doors of the hôtel de Rambouillet, the only salon of note, close as Louis XIV rises to power. There is no sense whatsoever that "the greatest century of our history," actually limited to half of the seventeenth century, bore any imprint of worldly culture. As Louis XIV "took the reins of the state," he also reined in culture and the glorious names of Corneille, Racine, Molière, Boileau, La Fontaine, Fénelon, and Bossuet surrounded him, to the exclusion of any others or of any other influence.

In 1768, Pons-Augustin Alletz produced an anthology of seventeenth and eighteenth-century women writers entitled *L'Esprit des femmes célèbres du siècle de Louis XIV et de celui de Louis XV, jusqu'à présent*. Alletz composed a lengthy preface to his volume in which he identifies France's glorious position with women's participation in society, while at the same time delineating the place women could and should occupy in the literary field. The sheer number of famous women during the reigns of Louis XIV and Louis XV "est un de ces avantages qui honorent le plus notre nation" (is one of the advantages that honors our nation the most).[29] These illustrious women have composed in every genre and excelled in every field, including "les sciences." But while their contributions equal those of their male colleagues in diversity, Alletz is careful to point out the differences that naturally separate the two sexes:

Il est vrai qu'elles n'ont pas ordinairement cette force d'esprit qui invente et qui crée, et ce jugement ferme qui ne permet pas de s'égarer. Mais en récompense elles ont une extrême facilité pour concevoir les choses les plus difficiles, une netteté d'esprit qui leur fait apercevoir les objets dans leur ordre naturel, un goût délicat, une finesse que nous leur contesterions en vain, une aisance dans l'expression, et des grâces que nous n'imitons jamais parfaitement ... pour les recherches laborieuses ... pour la solidité du raisonnement, pour la profondeur il ne faut que des hommes. Pour une élégance naïve, pour une simplicité fine et délicate, pour le sentiment exquis des convenances, pour une certaine fleur d'esprit, il faut des hommes polis par le commerce des femmes. Il y en a plus en France que partout ailleurs, grâce à la forme de notre société. (I, iv–vii)

(It is true that they [women] do not ordinarily have the force of mind that invents and creates, and that strong judgment that does not allow one to go astray. But to compensate they have an extreme facility to conceive of the most difficult things, a clarity of mind that allows them to see objects in their natural order, a subtle taste, a sharpness with which we won't compete, an ease of expression, and charms that we never imitate perfectly ... for laborious research ... for solid reasoning, for depth only men are necessary. For a naïve elegance, a sharp and delicate simplicity, for the exquisite feeling of propriety, for a certain *esprit*, it is necessary to have men polished by interaction with women. There are more [such men] in France than anywhere else, thanks to the form of our society.)

Women such as those he includes in his anthology are responsible for the "a certain kind of *esprit*" that distinguishes France, in particular its men, from other countries. Alletz includes most of the recognizable literary figures from the seventeenth century, composing a brief biography and including an exemplary extract from their works. In many instances, his description of a particular work illustrates the premise enunciated in his preface. His carefully composed descriptions, such as "sa poésie est tendre, délicate, remplie d'esprit: le tour de ses vers est simple, naturel; on voit qu'elle composait avec facilité" (her poetry is tender, delicate, filled with *esprit*; her verse is simple, natural; it is evident she composed easily) as he describes the poetry of the comtesse de la Suze, for example, reinforce his conception of the differences between the male and female mind (I, 69–70). The works of Mme Deshoulières whom, as we have seen, Huet and Tillet both choose as one of the most intelligent women of the seventeenth century, are cited as a "modèle de la poésie naturelle et tendre" (model of natural and tender poetry) (I, 183). She is also admirable because she fits the female mold Alletz extolled in his preface: "A ces talents de l'esprit, elle joignait les qualités du coeur: elle était une amie généreuse, une épouse attachée à ses devoirs, et la plus tendre des mères" (To these talents of the mind, she joined qualities of the heart. She was a generous friend, a wife attached to her duties, and the most loving of mothers) (I, 183). Similarly, Sévigné's letters are "naturel, vif, plein de grâce" (natural, lively, full of charm) (I, 219). The example he chooses to include is designed to illustrate "sa tendresse pour sa fille" (her affection for her daughter) (I, 222). And although Scudéry became famous for "la beauté de son esprit et la grande réputation de ses romans et de ses autres écrits" (the beauty of her mind and the great renown of her novels and her other works), Alletz neglects her novels and chooses to include only an exerpt from one of her conversations (I, 322–3). Women writers might be what lend France that certain "je ne sais quoi," but their literary domain, in Alletz's portrait, must be made to coincide with the age-old stereotypes concerning their intellectual capacities. When Alletz finds it impossible to deny someone such as Graffigny "son jugement solide" (solid judgment) he resorts to separating her entirely from her sex. She has an "esprit mâle" (a male esprit).[30]

Thus while Alletz can be commended for inscribing such names into memory, his work is also an example of the effort to shape women's participation in the literary realm into a mold that traditionalists would find acceptable. His work stands in marked contrast with Buffet's earlier descriptions of France's illustrious women as well as with Tillet's *Parnasse*. It reflects the growing trend of the period according to which, while France could boast of more women participants in its literary and cultural field than any other country, they must be granted a certain, separate place due to their gender, especially when one is considering the great century of Louis XIV.

There were numerous anthologies and literary histories devoted to the age of Louis XIV in general, or to French female luminaries specifically. It is as though the age of Louis XIV, marked as it was by the exceptional role of women, inspired historians and literary critics to inscribe this unique French quality into the written historical record. Frequently, like Alletz, authors used the occasion to underscore just how exceptional the role of women in French society, particularly under Louis XIV, was when compared to that of its neighbors. In 1769, the abbé Joseph de La Porte penned his *Histoire littéraire des femmes fançaises* in which the majority of his entries were drawn from the century of the Sun King. Like Alletz, La Porte uses his preface to underscore the exceptional nature of French society with respect to women:

> C'est précisément en France, que les femmes peuvent profiter de ces avantages. L'usage du monde qu'elles voient de bonne heure, la liberté dont elles jouissent, le commerce qui règne entr'elles et les hommes, la nécessité

où elles sont de plaire; tout contribue à mettre dans leur esprit cette vivacité qui nous charme.[31]

(It is precisely in France that women can profit from these advantages. The ways of the world that they see at an early age, the freedom that they enjoy, the interaction between them and men, the need for them to please; all [this] contributes to the vivacity of their mind that charms us.)

And this "vivacity" is then incarnated in an impressive number and array of literary and intellectual enterprises. Like his contemporaries Alletz and La Porte, the Abbé Claude François Lambert composed a lengthy and detailed literary history of the reign of Louis XIV. Instead of overtly separating women contributors from men, however, he included them as a separate section of his *Histoire littéraire du règne de Louis XIV*.[32] In his introduction, Lambert explains that after having examined the century's theologians, scolastics, mystics, orators, historians, philosophers, physicians, mathematicians, astronomers, poets, musicians, critics, grammarians, bibliographers' translators, and all others "qui ont excellé dans quelque genre particulier de littérature" (excelled in a particular literary genre) he will turn to "les dames illustres, qui par leur esprit et leur science ont fait la gloire de leur sexe et de leur siècle" (famous women, who by their mind and knowledge were the glory of their sex and of their century). While such women may have been "the glory of their century," they do not merit being integrated into the principal literary field of the day consisting of anyone who had touched pen to paper, as long as they were male. In a similar move, when Lambert describes "les progrès de la poésie sous le règne de Louis XIV" (the literary advances under Louis XIV's reign), he discusses language, poetry, and the theatre, but never mentions the century's newest genre, the novel. Apparently he does not consider this particular innovation, associated with women, as progress. In the seventeenth century, women were often acknowledged as the novel's most illustrious practitioners. In his treatment of the male members of the literary field, an occasional reference to the opposite sex does arise. For example, when discussing Voiture Lambert refers to the poet's success at the *chambre bleue*, calling it "le rendez-vous des plus beaux esprits de la cour ... cette espèce d'Académie" (the meeting place of the best minds of the court ... that type of academy) (II, 293). Segrais's name evokes that of Lafayette, depicted as his protector, who also used him to her own advantage:

Mme la comtesse de Lafayette fut charmée de lui donner un appartement chez elle, dans l'espérance qu'elle pourrait en tirer de grandes lumières pour la composition de ses ouvrages. M. de Segrais eu en effet beaucoup de part à la belle histoire de *Zaïde*, aussi bien de celle de la princesse de Clèves, à laquelle M. de La Rochefoucauld contribua aussi, surtout pour les maximes qui sont répandues dans le livre (II, 447).

(Mme la comtesse de Lafayette was happy to give him an apartment in her home, in the hope that she could receive great insight [from him] for the composition of her works. M de Segrais did indeed contribute a lot to the beautiful story of *Zaïde*, as well as to *La Princesse de Clèves*, to which M. de La Rochefoucauld also contributed, especially the maxims that are strewn throughout the book.)

Women are thus a presence in Lambert's depiction of the republic of letters frequented by male authors, but their presence is subservient to the dominant male literary voice.

An analysis of Lambert's separate section entitled "Eloges historiques des dames savantes," however, yields an alternative vision of the seventeenth-century literary field, one that seems to correspond more closely to that advanced by many of his seventeenth-century predecessors and echoes Tillet. Lambert includes women who marked the field from the beginning of the century until the end.[33] In reading the individual portraits, one is struck by Lambert's admiration for this body of female work, as well as by the diversity of their contributions. Lambert's list is quite extensive. He provides detailed descriptions of the life and works of Marie de Gournay, Charlotte de Caumont de la Force, Marie Dupré, Henriette de Coligny, comtesse de la Suze, Marie Eleonore de Rohan, Marie Catherine de Villedieu, Françoise Bertaut de Motteville, Louise Anastasie de Serment, Anne de la Vigne, Charlotte Saumaise de Chazan, comtesse de Bregy, the comtesse de Lafayette, Marie l'Heritier de Villandon, Antoinette Deshouilleres, the marquise de Sévigné, Madeleine de Scudéry, Camus de Meslons, Marie de Razilly, Catherine Descartes, Elizabeth Sophie Cheron, Catherine Bernard, Marie de Louvencour, Louise Genevieve Gillot de Sainctonge, Thérèse Deshouilleres, Anne Lefevre Dacier, Antoinette de Salvan de Salies, Louise Marie Bois de la Pierre, and Anne Thérèse de Lambert. Some of these names have survived the centuries, but many belong to what has become the shadowy world that was obviously not so obscure when Lambert was writing. Scudéry merits the longest entry. Lambert includes women celebrated for their knowledge, their poetry, and their literary acumen. In many instances he revives the term "illustre savante" that we first saw used by Marguerite Buffet. And while Lambert felt the need to treat women separately from men, his portraits clearly exude great admiration for women's accomplishments. He never openly states that such works surpass those of their male contemporaries, but in many instances Lambert does hold up a particular woman or her work as a model to be followed. The works of Charlotte de la Force, for example, exhibit "mille traits d'une imagination vive et brillante, un génie, un feu, une élévation, une force, et généralement toutes les parties qui caractérisent les ouvrages des grands poètes" (a thousand traits of a lively and brilliant imagination, a genius, a fire, a grandeur, a force, and generally all the characteristics that compose the works of great poets) (II, 7). Antoinette Deshouillleres "porta l'excellence de la poésie française au plus haut degré de perfection; et l'on ne peut nier que parmi les plus grands poètes de l'un et de l'autre sexe, il n'y en a aucun qui ait mieux réussi qu'elle, surtout pour l'Idylle" (carried the excellence of French poetry to the highest degree of perfection; and it cannot be denied that among the great poets of both sexes, there is no one who succeeded better than she, especially for the Idylle) (II, 37). As a result, Lambert incorrectly predicts, the memory of "cette illustre dame ... durera autant qu'il y aura des amateurs de la poésie" (this illustrous woman ... will endure as long as there are poetry lovers) (II, 39). Sévigné's style is "le modèle du genre épistolaire" (the model of the epistolary genre) (II, 42). And Anne Lefevre Dacier "[a] surpassé les plus célèbres critiques de son temps" (surpassed the most famous critics of her time) (II, 78).

In the world Lambert evokes, many women devoted themselves to reading, learning, and writing. The critic does not portray these activities as unnatural. In fact, he never evokes these women's many critics. They are simply part of this exceptional seventeenth-century literary world. Lafayette, famous for her writings as well as for "la beauté de son esprit," (the beauty of her *esprit*) is depicted as a "généreuse protectrice des gens de lettres" (a generous benefactor of writers) because of "l'amour qu'elle avait pour les beaux arts qu'elle cultivait elle-même avec soin, et dans lesquels elle réussit parfaitement" (the love she had for the arts, which she herself carefully cultivated and in which she perfectly succeeded) (II, 32). A Marie Dupré, for example, could learn Latin as easily as her own maternal language, and then attack Greek with equal facility (II, 11). Louise de Serment actually composed in Latin, which she spoke as well as she spoke English. Women can be commended for literary innovation. Thus Mme de Villedieu is directly responsible for the change of literary taste from the *roman héroïque* to the shorter *nouvelle historique*.[34] Lambert frequently highlights their literary judgment, precisely the trait that will all but disappear in representation of the seventeenth-century literary field in the following century. Louise Anastasie de Serment, for example "se fit un grand nom dans la République des lettres par son érudition, et par la solidité d'un jugement exquis, qui lui procura la gloire d'être souvent consultée par les plus grands poètes de son temps, et en particulier par le célèbre Quinault" (made a name for herself in the republic of letters by her erudition and by the solidity of her exquisite judgment that brought her the glory of being consulted often by the greatest writers of her time, and in particular by the famous Quinault) (II, 26). Proof of Scudéry's exceptional qualities is to be found in the literary society that surrounded her:

> Rien ne prouve mieux le mérite de cette illustre savante, que le commerce de littérature que les plus beaux esprits de son siècle se sont empressés de lier avec elle et les grands éloges qu'ils ont faits de son savoir et de ses ouvrages (II, 46).

> (Nothing proves better the merit of this illustrous, wise woman than the literary interaction that the greatest minds of her century eagerly sought to have with her, and the great praise they gave her knowledge and her works.)

Similarly, Antoinette de Salvan de Salies, known for her "jugement exquis" (exquisite judgment) united "les personnes de l'un et de l'autre sexe, qui avaient quelque littérature" (people of both sexes who had some interest in literature) in her gatherings (II, 82). Another "illustre savante," now shadow, Louise Marie Bois de la Pierre, was renowned for her literary acumen and ability to judge all works of literature. In Lambert's words, "ce qui prouve l'étendue de ses lumières et l'estime générale que l'on en faisait, c'est que les auteurs les plus célèbres de son siècle, avec qui elle était en relation, s'en rapportaient communément à ses décisions sur le prix de leurs ouvrages" (what proves the extent of her insights and the general esteem that she obtained is [the fact that] the most famous authors of her century, whom she knew, all agreed with her decisions regarding the merit of their works) (II, 85).

In his meticulous description of the seventeenth-century literary realm, Lambert thus clearly allots an influential and highly-developed place to women participants. Lambert may categorize their efforts separately, but his descriptions actually bely this categorization, for he describes these "illustres savantes" as integrated into the general literary milieu, and admired and emulated by their contemporaries. While not as comprehensive a portrait as that found in Tillet, Lambert's nonetheless echoes his. Such representations of the literary field of "le Grand Siècle," in which women were fully integrated as writers, critics, and intellectuals, are replaced by the end of the eighteenth century and particularly in the nineteenth by a portrait according to which, if women writers and critics did influence the great century of Louis XIV, it was only marginally. According to this reconstructed vision, the "real" writers who constitute what came to be designated as the "classics" of French literature did not derive from a milieu that was created by both genders.

A Defensive Historian: Stéphanie de Genlis

One women writer at the beginning of the nineteenth century, Stephanie Félicité de Genlis, sought to revive the role she viewed women as having played in the literary field of the previous century. In 1811, she turned literary and social historian for her sex and produced *De L'influence des femmes sur la littérature française, comme protectrices des lettres et comme auteurs; ou Précis de l'Histoire des femmes françaises les plus célèbres* in an effort to celebrate what she hailed as one of the distinguishing characteristics of her country, namely women's participation in and specifically influence upon the literary world. Her work merits close examination, for it attests to the dramatic changes that had occurred from the seventeenth to the end of the eighteenth century with respect to women's roles in literary culture. According to Genlis's history, from participants in the full sense of the term—as writers, critics, and patrons—women and the milieu associated with them, the salons, became divorced from literary culture and production and redefined as patrons but not participants, their activities marginalized and limited to the support of "great" male writers. Genlis's literary history is an attempt to refute this relegation of women to the margins of literary history, as well as an effort to resurrect these female voices and hail them as one of France's most glorious and unique achievements.

   In *De L'Influence*, Genlis revives a vision of the literary scene in which women are collaborators in and contributors to the Republic of Letters. The literary milieu she depicts, particularly in the seventeenth century, emphasizes collaboration among all writers, male and female, as Genlis reveals how women's influence extended to the literary field in general, and not just to a few minor writers. In her opinion, women particularly during the age of Louis XIV worked with men to produce France's "génie national." France is unique among nations due to the generalized and highly developed participation of women in culture, as both patrons and as writers. Genlis opens her history by eliciting praise for her nation's uninterrupted continuum of female support of literary culture:

> In researching the life of protectors of learned and literary people, one discovers
> what cannot be found in any other nation, [that is] an uninterrupted line, from
> the beginning of the monarchy until today, of queens and princesses who
> encouraged, protected all talents, and even successfully wrote literature; thus
> the influence of women in this field had to be more evident and successful in
> France than anywhere else.[35]

Although she begins with the well-known names of France's queens and
princesses, as her portrait of literary France advances, Genlis includes
illustrious women, such as Scudéry and Lafayette, whose principal ties to
literature were their own salons and writings, as opposed to the more traditional
role of royal patron. In her portraits of these illustrious women Genlis places
less emphasis on their patronage than on their actual literary production.
She carefully enumerates all the works penned by her female compatriots as
she establishes an intricate web of literary relationships among the men and
women of the past.

One particular period is allotted the place of honor in Genlis's depiction
of French literary culture. Of the three hundred and seventy-three pages of
De L'Influence des femmes, two hundred and twenty-four are consecrated to
women of the seventeenth century. The strong tie between women and the
literary field that Genlis posits as unique to France reached its apogee during
the celebrated century of Louis XIV:

> During the century of Louis XIV, during which there were so many men of
> outstanding talent, when all these sublime geniuses who forever illustrate
> French literature shone, in that century whose ways were infinitely more serious
> than our own, there was a multitude of women writers in all genres and in all
> classes; and not only did people of letters not rail against these women writers,
> they took pleasure in valorizing them and in giving them all the honor and
> esteem of gallantry. (xxxiv)

Genlis constructs a detailed, often idealized, portrait of this particular time
period when, in her view, women and men worked together to produce a
literary climate unparalleled and unsurpassed in French history or in that of
any other nation. She is especially careful to note the interaction between
the women writers she inscribes for posterity and what in the nineteenth
century was becoming the celebrated canon of French literature. The salon of
Richelieu's niece, the duchesse d'Aiguillon, received "all people of letters ...
all the academicians and all those who, because of their talent, could aspire to
become [one]" regardless of class, creating "that social equality that has since

made the French so likeable" (46). Women's literary sphere, embodied by the *ruelles*, was not separate from the more officially sanctioned arena represented by the French Academy. Genlis's depiction is in accordance with that of her seventeenth-century predecessors, as well as with Tillet's at the beginning of the eighteenth century, who, as we have seen, viewed the *ruelles* as working in tandem with what would later be recognized and considered as official literary culture. The *ruelles* were an additional space, not a separate one, for the formation of France's literary excellence. "The immortal century of Louis XIV" (72) achieved its immortality in large part through the literary culture created and nutured by men and women alike. Throughout her history, Genlis disparagingly remarks upon the differences between the eighteenth century, which she considers her own time period, and this "immortal century." She carefully depicts the qualities and atmosphere of the seventeenth century, to the detriment of any time period that followed. In this idealized ambiance, novels could be celebrated, and even prefaced by the century's most religious men. An archbishop such as Huet did not hesitate to add a preface on novels to the work of a woman writer. Scudéry's novels, the epitome of the genre, were edifying and moralizing, unlike those that would constitute the genre in the eighteenth century. Genlis in fact uses the example of Scudéry's works to emphasize just how the world has changed: "the prodigious success of Mlle de Scudéry's novels is what illustrates the best how much, since that time, the customs and the mindset of worldly people have changed" (95). Reason, clarity of language, good taste, lack of pedantry, "veritable esprit" (true *esprit*), "solidité de jugement" (firmness of judgment) are all qualities that Genlis views as characterizing the seventeenth century but lacking in her own time period. And these ideals were developed through the conversations of the worldly gatherings frequented by men and women, but dominated by the latter:

> At that time people enjoyed clever and sound conversations, not only at the hôtel de Rambouillet, but also at court, at Madame's, at Mlle de Montpensier's, at the duchesse de Longueville's, Mme de Lafayette's, Mme de Sévigné's, Mme de Coulanges's, Mme de La Sablière's, at the duc de La Rochefoucauld's, and in all the houses where *gens d'esprit* gathered. (96)

This "taste," innovative and solid, emanated from these "houses" that created the unique social and literary fabric under the Sun King. Under Genlis's pen, the seventeenth century becomes the ideal foyer for artistic liberty: "[people] never wrote with more freedom than during this reign" (102). The existence of such large numbers of women writers and participants in the literary field attests to this unprecedented freedom that Genlis views as having evaporated from the realm of eloquence and innovation embodied by seventeenth-century France.

Throughout her text, Genlis remains cognizant of the voices of dissent that would not adhere to the vision of the feminized literary field she so convincingly offers. She subtly responds to those who would dismiss an author such as Scudéry, for example, as antiquated, outdated, and of minor influence and importance. Central to her strategy of reintegrating female participation, literary and other, into a representation of France's literary past is her effort to make her readers judge the seventeenth century on its own terms and not according to the subjective criteria developed subsequently. One is reminded of Tillet's sensitivity to the changing nature of literary taste. One thread that reappears in Genlis's text with regular frequency is the reminder of the subjective and constructed nature of literary consecration. Thus, for example, to those who would dismiss Scudéry as a minor figure whose style does not merit recognition, Genlis responds by urging her readers to acknowledge the subjectivity inherent in such judgments:

> Mlle de Scudéry wrote less carelessly than many authors of that time who today are more highly regarded than she; and her works, like those of all her contemporaries, do not have that gibberish that has become so common in our day. (102)

Genlis argues that literary history, like literary taste, is fickle and variable, and must be understood and appreciated in its own historical context. Succeeding centuries must be aware and wary of the fact that they subjectively construct their own pantheon of "great writers" often based on criteria divorced from the century they are representing. The next step in Genlis's argument is thus obvious: if we no longer remember or acknowledge the achievements of most women writers or view women as a literary force, it is not because they are inherently inferior to their male counterparts. The choices made may or may not correspond to the literary taste of the time period studied, and thus may or may not be justifiable on the grounds of pure literary merit. The pantheon of great writers from the past is thus forcibly a constructed vision that reflects the subjective criteria that are always an inherent part of any literary history.

Genlis goes to great lengths not only to inscribe women's participation, but also to isolate and emphasize the indelible mark their works have had on France's literary field. These women have not only distinguished themselves and their sex, they have had a profound effect on their male cohorts and thus on the literary field in general. Of Lafayette's contribution to France's literary canon, for example, Genlis remarks:

> *La Princesse de Clèves* was at that time a work with no precedent and completely original. It is the first French novel containing emotions that are always natural and true depictions. This distinguished merit will always elevate Mme de Lafyaette above all the novelists of her nation, male and female. Mme de Lafayette opened a new path for authors who wrote in the genre, and she knew how to forge this path with such originality and truth, that no one has ever been able to surpass her except in writing style and moral intentions.[36] (116–17)

According to Genlis, not content to simply follow trends, authors like Lafayette and Scudéry forged new paths in the literary field, paths that would forever alter the French literary landscape. Some of their works are universally deemed exemplary. In this respect, Sévigné's letters merit a special place, according to Genlis, in the world of French letters: "There is only one work in French that has never been criticized and that, without inspiring envy, has at all times met with universal approval, and this work was written by a woman. Mme de Sévigné's letters will forever offer a perfect model of epistolary style, a unique model" (134). And whereas literary history even today, traditionally limits Sévigné's exemplarity to her maternal devotion, Genlis stresses that the letters to her daughter are only one facet of this remarkable work. Equally if not more valuable is the fact that Sévigné's letters, with inimitable style and grace, resurrect her own time period: "No work contains as many interesting anecdotes, and transports [the reader] better to the time period that Mme de Sévigné's narratives relate: it is as if one has heard or seen everything she recounts, as if one knows what she describes" (139).

Throughout *De L'Influence des femmes*, Genlis thus portrays women as producers of literary culture as opposed to simple patrons of the arts. They exercise a profound influence on the literary field, a force that will be more and more suppressed as literary historians rewrite the history of what would become France's classical canon. As we shall see, the nineteenth century will elevate the salon model of the literary woman as defined by the eighteenth century over that of the seventeenth so carefully portrayed and explained in Genlis's text. The seventeenth century constitutes for Genlis the apogee of women's active participation in all aspects of literary production: creation, critique, and patronage. After enumerating even more female voices at the end of her dissertation on the seventeenth century, Genlis states simply that such activity went downhill after the century of Scudéry and Lafayette:

> A multitude of women writers could be added to this list; but it is enough to prove that, without counting those who have truly influenced French literature, the women of Louis XIV's century more generally cultivated literature than during the century that just ended, especially women of the upper classes. (161)

These women left their mark on a literary culture that had become a hallmark of Frenchness.

Brunetière: Same Question, Different Answer

The tone throughout *De L'Influence des femmes sur la littérature* is adversarial and defensive. Genlis felt the need to defend women's participation in the literary realm in reaction to a historical context that was less and less willing to allot women any serious cultural influence on France's *Grand Siècle*. This context would only worsen throughout the nineteenth century. It is perhaps because seventeenth-century literary culture became more and more hailed as a highpoint illustrating France's innate qualities of greatness that authors felt increasingly compelled to map out its parameters and identify the players who had contributed to this unparalleled greatness. Genlis's text can be viewed as responding to the growing penchant among critics and historians to relegate women's participation to the margins, separate it from mainstream literary culture, redefine it, or obfuscate it altogether. In the late nineteenth century, another critical voice was attracted to the question of women's influence on France's literary past. Ferdinand Brunetière (1849–1906) is of particular interest, especially when placed in dialogue with Stéphanie de Genlis. In 1889, Brunetière published *Questions de Critiques* in which he devoted almost forty pages to the same question that had attracted Genlis at the beginning of the century: "L'influence des femmes dans la littérature française."[37] He opens his investigation into this influence in much the same way as Genlis, by extolling the roles women have occupied as unique to France:

> If other literatures indeed had women writers, the succession was not as continuous, the tradition not as constant as in our country; and a literary history of French women would follow almost year by year the history of our national literature. (25–6)

Whereas other nations may have women writers, in France they are so much a part of the literary scene that they can represent the entire history of France's national literature. Brunetière's goal, however, differs from Genlis's in that he does not intend to trace this literary history author by author. Rather, he wishes to examine how "notre littérature nationale" has been influenced by the fact that women were so much a part of its history, not only as writers, but especially as participants in the world of letters. In this reconstruction of their influence, the salons figure prominently.

Brunetière dates the beginning of women's influence from the beginning of the seventeenth century, a period he identifies as the origin of "polite society." The early years of the seventeenth century mark, for Brunetière, the beginning of "real" French literature, "real" because it was adopting the more "feminine" qualities associated with polite society. In Brunetière's words

> Our French literature of the sixteenth century is still completely viril, without any sprinkling of feminine qualities, [it is] not only devoid of modesty and taste, and even shameless and, as such, barely French, but in compensation, truly gaulois and truly latin at the same time. (28–9)

Brunetière limits his pantheon of sixteenth-century writers to Rabelais, Calvin, and Montaigne, eliminating women such as Labé and Marguerite de Navarre who did perhaps add a more "French" influence, using his definition, to that literary corpus. But individual writers do not constitute the primary influence Brunetière is identifying and analyzing as unique to French literary culture. It is the alliance between women as actors in literary society, not necessarily as writers, that attracts this critic to his subject. His approach is in sharp contrast to Genlis's, whose focus was precisely the influence that Brunetière would seem to elide in favor of a more vague, civilizing influence managed through social interaction. Where Genlis highlights the women who actually composed works, Brunetière, while mentioning some of them, identifies women's influence as part of the civilizing process. He works to resurrect this influence, which he associates with the salons and the *précieuses*, and rid it of the ridicule heaped upon it by Molière. He urges readers to consider Molière as a dramatist, not as an historian, and his fellow critics to aid in this new approach "by not accepting a satire as the lasting expression of history's judgment" (30).

The *précieuses* and other women associated with seventeenth-century salons merit recognition in Brunetière's view for having inspired writers to try to please and not just slavishly follow the dicates of the Ancients. They are thus in large measure responsible for forcing their compatriots to find their own voice and their own uses for knowledge and ways of expressing that knowledge. In his words, women's maxims stressed the relationship between literature and life: "… one must learn in order to live and not live in order to learn. It is good to know what Plato thought, but his thoughts can no longer be ours" (33). This reorienting of the writer's vision was accompanied by a purification of their means of expression, again inspired by women:

> By imposing qualities of order and clarity on writers, [qualities] by the way, that they [women] do not always have when they write but that they value, women guaranteed the perfection of French prose and its dominance that for a long time was universal. (34)

In Brunetière's estimation, women are responsible for the qualities the French language embodies and illustrates to the greatest degree of perfection, qualities such as elegance, precision, "la perfection dans la mesure" (perfect moderation) and "la lucidité dans la profondeur" (lucidity among depth) (36).

But while acknowledging women's positive influences, Brunetière nonetheless takes the occasion to concur with Molière that this linguistic influence in particular went too far. Women's desire to dominate through the *ruelles* and enforce their own rules of "taste" and acceptability, while laudatory at the beginning of the "true" French literary tradition, soon became excessive. In Brunetière's representation of French literary history, women are responsible for the praiseworthy qualities of the French language, but also for rarifying it, creating a literary language with few ties to "popular language" and forcing writers into a class mold defined by elitist, aristocratic experience.[38]

> As writers, influenced by salons and women, moved away from everyday language usage and the observation of life, they also moved away from what is natural and from truth … most women will always prefer an elegant lie to unpleasant or even indifferent truth; and there would be no salons if we each were only ourselves there. (39)

Whereas in the seventeenth century, as we have seen, commentators such as Bouhours extolled women's "natural" linguistic talents, here Brunetière, while acknowledging women's civilizing influence on language, also follows Molière's judgment, even though he had cautioned against doing so. The salons are above all associated with *politesse*, not literary critique or creation, and this *politesse* creates an artificial environment that is detrimental to true literary genius. Women can thus perhaps be relied upon to sow the seeds of literary and linguistic excellence, but their control cannot go too far. Brunetière congratulates the great writers of the seventeenth century from having escaped the emprisoning hold of the *ruelles*. Echoing the refrain frequently heard throughout the nineteenth century, only second rate authors fell into the trap of the salons, accompanied by a public easily duped into following the false tastes of the *ruelles*.

> In fact, all writers of the second order bow down to them [the *salonnières*] and even one or two of the first ... Balzac and Voiture, Ménage and Chapelain, Conrart and Vaugelas ... Pellisson and Patru ... even Corneille and La Fontaine ... public approbation encourages [the *salonnières*] ... they have *esprit* and courage, good sense and taste for the exceptional and for what is great or rather grandiose, the art of understanding everything, and that of saying everything, everything except precisely what the Pascals, the Bossuets, the Molières, and the Racines, the Boileaus, and the La Bruyères would need to tell them and make them understand. (40–41)

The figures of the canon of seventeenth-century French literature, all the "the's" owe their genius to the fact that they were able to escape the influence of the salons and the "*précieuses*."

> That is why all of them each in his own way, and without conferring with each other, rise up against the domination of the *rheteurs* and the *précieuses*. That is also why—look in the memoirs and in the correspondence of the time—you won't find a single one of them who frequented the popular salons. And how would they have frequented them if that is where their adversaries and enemies were, if it was in the salons that Molière was criticized for the crudeness of his depictions and Racine [was reproached] for the truth of his. (40)

In this version of literary history, what makes a writer worthy of greatness is his ability to withstand the influence of the salons. Brunetière confirms this influence, but then erases it from the works his century has canonized as those best representing the French classics. He extends his condemnation of the salons to those of the eighteenth century, in which women were again "truly queens, masters and arbiters of taste and of opinion" (43), but luckily only influenced the minor writers "whose works perished almost entirely with them, and that can be eliminated from the history of the century almost without it showing" (45). The great French literary and philosophical tradition thus remains separate from a female influence that consisted primarily of a effort to view, treat, and discuss all subjects "pleasantly and superficially" (47). If indeed the salons exerted any influence on great works, it was a negative influence: "Such that the salons are responsible, without saying anything about

208 *Salons, History, and the Creation of Seventeenth-Century France*

anything else, for everything in *l'Esprit des lois* or in the *Essay on customs* that is artificial and superficial" (48). Any positive influence must be limited to minor genres. Brunetière echoes his predecessors in praising women for their epistolary prowess:

> ... salons were able to compensate in some measure for what they took away from us ... in no other literature, since the beginning of literature, is there anything that can compare with Voltaire's or with Mme de Sévigné's correspondence, nothing comparable to that of Mme du Deffand or to Mlle de Lespinasse's. (50)

Again French literature is exemplary due to women's influence, but this influence has been limited to one particular genre and does not extend to the full French literary corpus. Like so many of his contemporaries, Brunetière, while seeming to acknowledge a female influence specific to France, works to keep it in check so as to not identify true French literary greatness with women, as either *salonnières*, critics, or writers. He carefully boxes them into the acceptable role of letter-writer, a genre that is directly related to the "esprit de sociabilité" (sense of sociability) developed in the salons:

> In liberating women, society permitted them to be themselves; but they are without doubt not themselves except in how they differ from men; and it is in the epistolary genre, because it is more in their reach, that [they] placed their difference and thus their originality. (50)

To conclude his analysis of women's influence on French literature, Brunetière, as almost an afterthought, turns to the genre most associated with women, at least as readers: the novel. He almost begrudingly acknowledges some influence: "... I believe that one would commit an inexcusable oversight if one did not at least grant a role to the influence of women and the salons on the origins of drama and modern novels" (54). Consistent with his general view of women's limited incursion into the literary realm, Brunetière identifies their influence on the novel to their ability to make love one of the premier interests of society:

> By purifying love, by spiritualizing it, by mixing literature with emotions ... in making it a part of all conversation, women in France made it [love] an affair of the nation ... our modern literature has revolved around passions of the heart, like the conversations in Mme de Lambert's or Mme de Rambouillet's salons did. (54–5)

Conspicuously absent is any reference to the women novelists of the seventeenth century so praised by their contemporaries. Whereas in the seventeenth century such women were seen as one of the glorious distinguishing characteristics of the nation, in Brunetière's nineteenth-century treatment of female literary influence they are completely absent. Women's influence is narrowly defined to correspond to the stereotypical roles they were expected to play in the nineteenth century. Women could inspire love, raise the subject to an unprecedented level of importance, but not write about it. Or if they did, they would certainly not be part of a written record of France's literary pantheon. Brunetière grants women influence on the development of his nation, but not as the writers and critics so admired in the seventeenth century and inscribed into memory in many works of the eighteenth. This tangible evidence that left its mark on France's literary corpus as texts and criticism, in great and minor writers, and on the literary field as a whole, vanishes and is transformed by Brunetière into the vague entity of "esprit:" "If now we try to characterize in one word the nature of [women's] influence, one could say that women gave French *esprit* its form" (57). This *esprit* has a profound effect on literary expression. It affects the laws of composition, laws that in French:

> exist before the ideas to be expressed. Thus have women decided it. They did not want a writer to be permitted to remake language in his image ... They also wanted ... for no one to ever ignore the laws of pleasure ... women always followed the plan they had developed: to submit sooner or later innovators themselves to their [women's] need for clarity, precision, and order. (58)

This *esprit* thus results in a certain form of national expression that only those who are truly French can evaluate correctly. The *esprit* shared by the French leads to

> the mistakes, sometimes strange, that Germans or the English make regarding our writers. We [French] alone, in fact, thanks to this uniformity of custom and after much study, are capable of distinguishing what is mediocre from what is excellent, the vulgar from the innovative, and the talented *rhéteur* from a great writer. (58)

Literary taste is once again married to "study" associated with a Boileau rather than with the worldly public. Women have served the nation by inspiring authors to reflect the "the genius of the race" and to transmit "dans le monde l'empire de l'esprit national" (in the world the empire of national *esprit*) (60).

But this influence consists of rather vague inspiration, an ingrained sense of *politesse* and *sociabilité*, not of the critical ability to formulate criteria of taste or, even more important, influence literary culture with works of their own.

Cousin and Sainte-Beuve: Portraits of the Past

Brunetière's text represents a culmination of the general trends present throughout the nineteenth century to erase active female literary activity, and to transform the salons into foyers of politeness and sociability. These tendencies are evident in the works of many of the most recognized literary historians and critics of the nineteenth century. Joan DeJean has convincingly shown how in a process that began in the eighteenth century, what she terms the worldly anthologies destined for adults are eventually overshadowed and ultimately replaced by a pedagogical canon designed to instill "the ideals and standards of Frenchness" and "produce educated French male Christians."[39] Concurrent to this substitution of a pedagogical canon for a worldly one, is a shift, I have tried to show here, in the composition of the worldly anthologies themselves. In many instances,women writers of the seventeenth and eighteenth centuries were celebrated in such anthologies throughout the eighteenth century, but editors frequently used their authority to mold the vision of women's literary enterprises in the minds of their readers.[40] Although usually separated from his predecessors, the influential scholar and critic Lanson followed the trend that viewed women's works, when treated at all, as direct reflections of their life story.[41] In 1895, for example, Lanson is compelled to refer to Sévigné's *Correspondance* as a life in and of itself, thus denying it the literarity reserved for "true" literary efforts: "But Mme de Sévigné's correspondence, isn't it also a life?" he queries.[42] Such a remark underscores how history and literary history often worked in tandem during this period. In some ways, this symbiotic relationship between literature and history can explain why literature was called into service when historians began to strive not only to describe the past but to define a nation.

Two influential figures of the nineteenth century had a particularly powerful role in creating a lasting representation of the seventeenth century: Victor Cousin (1792–1867) and Sainte-Beuve are representative of the trend in the nineteenth century to acknowledge certain women and the female milieu of the salons as distinguishing characteristics of French history, and redefine this participation and channel it into acceptable gender roles. Cousin's and Sainte-Beuve's works contributed substantially to the creation of the particular vision of the seventeenth century that Genlis's text was designed to combat. One of the century's premier thinkers, Cousin's works made an indelible mark on the fields of philosophy, history, and literary studies. As a celebrated professor and later minister of education, Cousin had the power and influence to shape the nation's memory of the past in very significant ways. Sainte-Beuve's contributions to memory, like Cousin's, seemingly stem from his admiration and even love for the elegant figures of a society he would like to resurrect. Using a process founded upon idealization and praise, Cousin and Sainte-Beuve solidified the transformation of seventeenth-century salon women from literary critic to hostess whose thread we have followed in anthologies and literary histories.

Victor Cousin: Women Worthies

Cousin's early works reflect his interest and training in philosophy. His courses on the history of modern philosophy and moral philosophy were widely distributed. The long list of his publications attests to his expertise on Plato and Aristotle, but also to his interest in the philosophers of his own country, notably Pascal and the eighteenth-century *philosophes*. Many of his works are pedagogical in nature and reflect his conviction that the ways knowledge is transmitted and disseminated are as important as how it is created and developed. This philosophy of education is perhaps what attracted Cousin to a particular field of inquiry that at first glance would not seem to be a readily apparent choice for any philosopher, nor for a scholar to make his mark on his profession. In the middle of his career, Cousin made the decision to delve into the history of seventeeth-century French women. The numerous volumes he produced on this subject, many of which he reedited and revised until his death, attest to his passion for this area of France's national history. But Cousin's infatuation with women's history of France's classical age is perhaps more than simply a desire to add to the history of a period that fascinated his contemporaries. In reading these works, one has the sense that Cousin considered himself to be on a mission to shape the memory of his nation, particularly that of a century he regarded as a highpoint of French culture. His choice to focus on the century's women is not accidental. Given the silences surrounding these figures, the field of women's history afforded Cousin the perfect opportunity to fashion a specific vision of the past that could shape the entire way one saw the seventeenth century. His creation of this historical building-block of the nation was less likely to encounter resistance given its foundation in a relatively obscure past. Indeed his vision will become engrained in the fabric of national memory, consecrated as more officially true than portraits such as Genlis's or Tillet's. In Cousin's representation of the past, certain aspects of culture will be valorized, while others will be systematicallly forgotten, namely those related to women's influence on the mainstream empire of letters.

The titles of Cousin's magnum opus devoted to seventeenth-century women are indicative of his particular vision of what merits historical inscription. He begins his investigation with a work devoted to Jacqueline Pascal, although the complete title reveals his intention to go far beyond one particular figure: *Jacqueline Pascal, premières études sur les femmes illustres et la société du XVIIe siècle* (1845). Much more than a biography, Cousin's *Jacqueline Pascal* is designed to give a particular vision of the entire seventeeth century. This work proved to be so popular that by 1877 it was already in its eighth edition. From Jacqueline Pascal Cousin turned his attention to Mme de Longueville in a study of her youth (1853).[43] Interest in Longueville proved to be as great as that for Pascal and this work quickly achieved five editions by 1864. In 1854 he dedicated his considerable research skills to Mme de Sablé. He then composed a combined study of Mme de Chevreuse et Mme de Hautefort, which appeared in 1856. These works were subsequently published separately in numerous editions. The subtitle of this volume was designed to attract readers and heighten interest in Cousin's studies of women. "Nouvelles études" replaces "études" in the subtitle of the Chevreuse and Hautefort volume. Cousin almost immediately produced a second edition of Hautefort, advertised as having been "revue et augmentée par l'auteur" (revised and augmented by the author), indicating Cousin's careful management of the women's history he was creating for posterity. In 1859 he produced another volume on Mme de Longueville subtitled *Mme de Longueville pendant la Fronde 1651–53*. Cousin then had the good fortune to find a "key" to Scudéry's *Le Grand Cyrus* at the Arsenal. Considering Scudéry's novel to be simply a thinly veiled portrait of her own time period, he used *Le Grand Cyrus* to interpret and describe the seventeenth century and published *La Société française au XVIIe siècle d'après le Grand Cyrus" de Mlle de Scudéry* (1858). Cousin's works, and thus his particular representation of the seventeenth century as viewed through some of its principal female figures, were widely circulated, republished, and even translated into English. The English titles, such as *Secret History of the French Court under Richelieu and Mazarin; or the Life and Times of Madame de Chevreuse*, and *The Youth of Madame de Longueville, or New Revelations of Court and Convent in the Seventeenth Century*, attest to the at times novelistic tone of his history.

Cousin's intentions go far beyond a desire to provide light reading about interesting figures from a provocative past. The scholar uses his female subjects to constuct a particular vision of France's heritage and of women's place in that literary and social *patrimoine*. Each work contains a preface in which Cousin clearly states his intentions, the parameters of his study, and unveils his vision of women, their relationship to literary culture, and his conception of France's "Grand Siècle." Cousin's portrait will prove to be emblematic of the general tenor of scholarship that shaped and created the French classical canon and our modern-day vision of its literary context. Cousin creates an idealized image of the century according to which *politesse* becomes the governing principle of social interaction. Rambouillet is identified as the motor of this civilizing process. He glorifies almost the entire seventeenth century, not just the years corresponding to Louis XIV's reign, annointing this period "la plus belle époque de la société française" (the best period of French society) (vi).[44] Cousin states his purpose as follows:

> ... we are looking in France's history for the time when we feel France's grandeur rise, and its national genius unfurl in all its originality and force ... This is what draws us to this period ... that begins with the arrival of Henri IV and extends through three-quarters of Louis XIV's reign.[45]

For Cousin, this period illustrates "the very genius of France during the period of its true grandeur."[46]

What place does Cousin accord women in this period of true French greatness? He chose to inaugurate his project with a biography on Jacqueline Pascal, whom he admires specifically because she did not aspire to be a writer.[47] His first chapter, entitled "Introduction aux femmes illustres du XVII siècle," details his conception of the society he plans to examine, through the lens of women's biographies:

> Women who distinguished themselves by their writings will also have their place in the gallery, but there will be a great difference between a *femme d'esprit* and the woman writer. We infinitely honor one and we have little taste for the other. (*Jacqueline Pascal*, 3)

Cousin then goes into a long tirade against women writers who, in his opinion, violate the laws of their sex when they put pen to paper. Cousin acknowledges some women writers of the period, but only to lament their decision to tread upon the literary landscape. His diatribe merits quoting at length, given that it serves as a preface to his entire historical enterprise.

... it is not unimportant that the greatest writers were not professional authors. Are Descartes, Pascal, and Bossuet men of letters? Not at all. They do not write to show their *esprit*, but to defend a noble cause given to their courage and their genius. If we speak thus of the literary man, what will we say of the woman writer? What! The woman who, thanks to God, has no public cause to defend, who throws herself into the public space, and whose modesty is not appalled at the idea of revealing to every eye, of selling to the highest bidder, of exposing to examination of the bookseller, reader and the journalist, her most secret attributes, her most mysterious and most touching charms, her soul, her emotions, her suffering, her interior struggles! This is what we see everyday and in the most decent women, and that will be eternally impossible to understand. If someone said and claimed to prove that Mme de Sévigné destined her letters in which she expresses in a thousand ways the waves of her maternal tenderness and her unquenchable spirit, for the public and to be included in journals, we would respond without hesitation, you are spoiling Mme de Sévigné; She was a passionate mother and full of genius, you are turning her into a *bel esprit* ... Every woman who writes of her emotions for the public is attempting to deceive it; she plays a role and she does it badly; she writes with some superficial ferveur and animation, but without soul, because if it were inspiring her, it would also hold her back ... thus when a woman writes in prose, she is calm, and if she writes about herself, in our opinion, she makes a mistake. We only know two excuses for a woman to become an author, a great talent or poverty, and we respect the latter much more than the former. Whatever our admiration for *La Princesse de Clèves*, and even though we rank it barely below *Bérénice*, the profession of woman writer that Mme de Lafayette did without needing to reminds us in spite of ourselves that she gave her last affections to a very sad character, a scheming nobleman, a sullen *bel esprit*, who dared to inscribe his life in maxims, a lover without a heart, the ungrateful lover of the unfortunate duchesse de Longueville [M. de La Rochefoucauld]. After Mme de Lafayette, we only see in the seventeenth century three distinguished women of letters, if we can use this expression: Mlle de Scudéry, Mme Deshoulières, and Mlle Lefevre, since Mme Dacier; and in truth, if we had to choose a sister or a mother from among these three women, we would choose Mme Deshoulières, an excellent woman, learned, who spoke little about herself and barely wrote anything but translations, which will last much longer than supposedly original works. (*Jacqueline Pascal*, 11)

Women can be heard but not read, and above all should not have the bad taste to enter the public literary stage. A figure such as Sévigné is acceptable to Cousin because he views her letters as solely private maternal musings addressed to her daughter. Any insinuation that she actually circulated them publicly elicits Cousin's outrage. Cousin's portrayel of "le Grand Siecle" will thus accord the places of honor to "those distinguished women who exhibited intelligence or an elevated soul without having written anything, or at least without having written anything for the public, which is the true destiny and the greatest use of female genius" (13). Women's literary "génie" is thus completely severed from France's "génie national" embodied by the *grand siècle*.

Cousin uses his choice of seventeenth-century female figures to create a model for the women of his century to follow.[48] By glorifying the period as the apogee of French *génie* and civilization, he inspires his readers to seek to emulate its principal actors. But in order to use the example of some of these women as ideal models, Cousin had to eliminate any serious and intentional link between women and the literary field. As Cousin states in the lengthy introduction to his historical enterprise placed at the beginning of his biography of Jacqueline Pascal, women can be allowed to cultivate their mind, but only if they do so in private. The public stage of the literary world is not their space: "Let us allow her to cultivate her mind and her soul with all sorts of laudable knowledge and noble studies, as long as she upholds the supreme law of her sex, modesty which gives charm."[49] Cousin congratulates himself for being notably more liberal than Molière. Yet, for Cousin, "woman is a domestic being, just as man is a public figure" a sentiment with which Molière most likely would have been in accord.[50]

Cousin's ideological bias thus colors his portrait of seventeenth-century France. While this renowned scholar of philosophy clearly admires the women he chooses to inscribe for posterity, even referring at one point to his research as a personal and inexplicable passion, he nonetheless creates a vision of his idealized period of French history that, while very detailed and complete in many respects, is also an attempt to make women's roles in society correspond to his own ideals of female behavior.[51] If this period is representative of "le génie national," it is partly because, in Cousin's account, women may have played exceptional roles, but they also knew their place and only occasionally had the bad judgment to wander from it.

Cousin's inaugural biography on Jacqueline Pascal is indicative of the general tenor of his scholarship on seventeenth-century society. Cousin refers to Pascal's penchant for verse, for which she was celebrated in her youth, but he depicts this activity as the pastime of a young Pascal, one that she was willing to abandon for more serious, namely religious, pursuits. In his history, Cousin stresses her devotion to her father and her free choice of convent life. He includes a large selection of letters from her personal correspondence, most of which address religious questions. While this is not a negative portrait, what is important for our purposes here is what is elided or missing. Even though Pascal had important ties with the worldly literary milieu, and an obvious connection to her own brother, she is not depicted as someone who had either the inclination or the power to inscribe herself or her ideas into posterity through writing. Cousin recounts how, even once she had entered the convent, she was drawn to writing in verse. But he then goes on to praise her decision to abandon the pen, at the demand of her superior, except to compose her edifying letters to her family and friends. The world of verse was seemingly unimportant to her, and thus, in Cousin's portrait, she was able to abandon it without a second thought.

This subtle severing of women from serious literary pursuits and from the mainstream literary realm of their era continues in the biography Cousin states will afford the greatest insight into the workings of salon society, his biography of Mme de Sablé. For our purposes here, the Sablé biography illuminates especially well Cousin's subtle reworking of the worldly literary scene. In his introduction, Cousin continues to refine his historical project. He explains that this work:

> will represent on its own the whole seventeenth century, in all its apsects, religion, politics, war, literature, gallantry: our other studies express particular, diverse facettes. Jacqueline Pascal allows us to penetrate Port-Royal, ... with Mme de Chevreuse one sees the spectacle of political intrigue combined with gallant advantures ... Mme de Hautefort is a very different type. Just as beautiful and courageous, and at the same time with a stainless purity, understanding nothing about politics, but inflexibly attached to honor ... she is the model of a great lady ... it seemed to us that these studies of seventeenth-century French society and illustrious women could inspire in present generations the feeling and the taste of more noble customs, make them know, honor, and love France during the most glorious time of its history ... A France in which women were, it seems, fairly beautiful and inspired ardent love.[52]

In this "cortège," Mme de Sablé merits a place because of her ability to inspire others: "If she didn't do much herself, she had the fortunate gift for inspiring more forceful and stronger minds than hers: she gave the impetus for a new literary genre, the *pensées* and maxims. Thus Mme de Sablé could serve as a model today for some nice woman ... who ... would find her happiness in a moderate religion ... and would be proud to exert a useful and noble influence [on those] around her" (*Mme de Sablé*, V–VI). Throughout this volume, the operative word is indeed "influence," as opposed to, for example, Sablé's personal literary accomplishments or ambitions. He does occasionally give the impression that Sablé receives requests from her friends to judge literary works, as when the comtesse de Maure writes to her regarding Mlle de Montpensier's *Relation de l'Isle imaginaire* (*Mme de Sablé*, 82–3). But this epistolary form of collective critique is presented more as a pastime among female friends than as a serious activity of worldly society. Sablé is the quintessential salon hostess:

> She possessed everything necessary for that: a great name, a taste for influence, a calm heart, an active and likeable mind, little or no originality, which is the essential condition for this kind of success. In effect, the *esprit* of Mme de Sablé consisted above all of a perfect politeness. She barely rose above that happy mediocrity, sustained by *bon ton* and good taste, which are so important for a woman who aspires to hold a salon. Nothing outstanding or very rare in her and also nothing common [crude]. (*Mme de Sablé*, 98)

As we saw previously in the anthologies and literary histories, the principal quality of the *salonnière* again resides not in her creativity or originality, but in her *politesse*.

Given, however, Sablé's ties to La Rochefoucauld, Cousin cannot avoid addressing the relationship between Sablé and this uniquely French literary genre that originated in the salons. Indeed, Cousin spends a great deal of time detailing the genesis of La Rochefoucauld's maxims, but he is careful to delineate Sablé's role, and especially to attribute the genre to La Rochefoucauld as opposed to Sablé. Cousin recognizes that Sablé composed maxims herself, but he refuses them the literary qualities that he will identify with La Rochefoucauld's masterpieces:

> This genre derived naturally from [Mme de Sablé's] frame of mind, from her position, from her habits ... Her entire genius was taste and *politesse* ... We are even inclined to believe that the supposed writings of Mme de Sablé are nothing but maxims and reflections somewhat more developed, but that only her flatterers would call [literary] works. (*Mme de Sablé*, 111)

Sablé is thus salvaged from the dreaded category of "femme auteur," and the new, worldly genre can be safely attributed to its primary male practitioner.[53] Cousin does recognize the importance of conversation as well as the written portrait genre which he associates with Mlle de Montpensier on the elaboration of maxims, and in so doing allows a link between *mondain* culture and the world of French letters, but there is little sense throughout his work that worldly salon culture was an influence on mainstream literary culture of the period.[54] A woman like Sablé can set a certain tone, but her influence does not go

beyond this elusive quality. She is neither critic nor author. Cousin concludes
his analysis of the maxims by defining Sablé's role as marginal:

> All the maxims and thoughts [*pensées*] came out of the salon of a pleasant
> woman, withdrawn to the corner of a convent, who, having no other pleasure
> than to think about herself, about what she had seen and felt, was able to
> transmit her tastes to her society, in which by chance there was a man with a
> lot of *esprit*, who had in himself the fabric of a great writer ... And she always
> plays the same role: She provokes, she inspires, she supports; but she does
> more through others than she does herself. Her greatest literary merit is not
> to have written some maxims that are perfectly polite, but that will never be
> more than mediocre, it is to have turned La Rochefoucauld's ambition and
> talent to this subject [composing maxims].[55]

Sablé can be offered as a model because she is, in Cousin's formulation, the
quintessential female muse who worked her magic in a "modest" salon situated
in a convent. "Her role was to stimulate and to highlight other people's *esprit*"
Cousin concludes (*Mme de Sablé*, 363).

Interestingly, Cousin attaches a very lengthy appendix to his biography of
Sablé, one composed of primary texts such as letters, portraits, and various
other references to Sablé by her contemporaries, as well as works penned by
Sablé herself. This appendix is more than one-fourth of the entire work. The
portrait of this exceptional woman that emanates from these contemporary
voices, relegated to the margins of the book, has a very different slant than the
image Cousin provides in his biography. Sablé primarily emerges from these
pages as a respected critic and important author in her own right. It is as though
Cousin saved all these references that did not quite fit into the image he wished
to impart to posterity, and, in his role as dedicated historian, included them
only for the most "passionate" reader of the past.[56] In the appendix Sablé is a
respected intellectual figure, not merely the passive polite hostess. No longer
solely a specialist of worldly maxims due to her own experience, she is called
upon by her contemporaries to judge all sorts of literary works as a member
of the mainstream, learned, literary culture. For example, Cousin includes the
dedication to Sablé of *De la traduction, ou règles pour apprendre à traduire
la langue latine en la langue française* (1660) composed by Gaspard, comte
de Tende, in which the author praises Sablé's knowledge of language:

> I know the masters of our language consult you when they're in doubt, have
> made you the arbiter of their differences of opinion, and submit to your
> decisions. In fact, you are the person in the world who knows all the laws and

all the rules of speech the best, who knows best how to express your feelings and thoughts with elegance and clarity, who knows best how to use ways of speaking that are so ingenious, so charming, and so naturally French and finally who knows best all the subtleties and mysteries of style that M. de Vaugelas speaks about. (*Mme de Sablé*, 366)

Sablé is praised by her contemporaries for her critical taste and intellectual depth. Her editor included a detailed portrait of her when he published her maxims in 1678, the year of her death, in which he explained her contemporaries' admiration for this extraordinary woman:

> Her mind was filled with knowledge that could both instruct and polish reason ... She wrote perfectly well ... a natural and inimitable eloquence. Her feelings were so correct and so reasonable that for everything concerning good sense and good taste, they [her feelings] were like supreme decrees that decided the worth and the merit of everything that was submitted to her to be judged. (*Mme de Sablé*, 368)

Cousin explains in the appendix that Sablé was valued for this critical acumen by some of the most respected intellectual figures of her time. La Chambre, Saint-Evremond, and Arnauld, among others, sought her opinion on their most serious philosophical works (*Mme de Sablé*, 370–71). The portrait that emerges from this appendix is considerably different from the one Cousin constructs from these same sources for his biography destined to illuminate "le Grand Siècle." One is left to hypothesize as to why Cousin did not feel compelled to include this other dimension of Sablé into his main portrait of the age.

Cousin's impressive and careful research on these exceptional women is designed to honor them and their accomplishments, but only in certain fields and in particular ways. It is acceptable for Sablé to inspire La Rochefoucauld, but Sablé goes beyond the traditional limits of acceptable intellectual behavior for women when she accepts to critique a philosophical work. More important, intellectual luminaries such as Arnauld present a confusing portrait of their genius if they feel compelled to call upon a worldly woman's taste to arbitrate their written production. Such behavior can be included in the margins of history, but not foregrounded, for to do so would change the image being carefully crafted of seventeenth-century French society, its influences, and its actors.

In a similar reformulation of the seventeenth-century literary and intellectual realm, Cousin reduces one of the most celebrated literary works of the period, Scudéry's *Le Grand Cyrus*, to an anecdotal portrait of worldly society. He in fact calls the novel "that seventeenth-century portrait gallery."[57] In his introduction, Cousin explains why he feels justified in using Scudéry's novel in this manner, even though he acknowledges that the "key" he has found to the novel was not written by Scudéry herself but most likely by "someone who frequented those gatherings that were somewhat inferior where Mlle de Scudéry reigned supreme" (*La Société française*, 20). According to Cousin, no one was reading *Le Grand Cyrus* even at the end of the seventeenth century, when Scudéry herself was still alive, because it had become "unintelligible" (*La Société française*, 2). In his formulation, the work only enjoyed success previously because contemporaries liked to identify themselves in the novel. Cousin thus denies the work any literary quality whatsoever, and transforms one of the century's premier authors into someone who amused her contemporaries by making them players in a novel.

To emphasize his view of the novel as a ten-volume long portrait gallery, Cousin organizes his work, which is designed to reflect "a century dear to our sense of patriotism" into chapters dedicated to one particular, usually immediately recognizable, character or aspect of society such as the hôtel de Rambouillet (*La Société française*, 23). It is interesting to note that Cousin does not rely entirely on Scudéry's novel to paint his own historical portrait, but supplements it with reflections by other contemporaries, most frequently Tallement des Réaux. It should be remembered that Tallemant's *Historiettes* were not published until the mid-nineteenth century, and were enjoying much acclaim at precisely the time that Cousin was writing his history of the seventeenth century. Cousin's work in *La Société française* can be viewed as a pendant to the *Historiettes*. Both works confine any influence women had on the literary and cultural stage to forms of *politesse*, as opposed to the writing and critiquing of literature. Although Cousin finds Tallemant's observations often too negative or critical, he nonetheless reduces Scudéry's novel to the same level of literarity as Tallemant's reflections. But it can be argued that *Le Grand Cyrus* and Scudéry's other novels, as well as those of other novelists of the period, were not enjoyed by contemporaries solely because they might be able to recognize themselves or their friends in the characters. Scudéry's novels were immediately translated into other languages whose practitioners presumably would not have been able to appreciate à clé portraits, and thus found the works pleasurable for entirely different reasons. As we have seen with Villedieu, such works were very popular at least through the end of the eighteenth century. They corresponded to the literary tastes of worldly readers, tastes that continued well into the eighteenth century and beyond, to judge by the number of libraries that possessed novels.[58] The refusal to view

Le Grand Cyrus and other novels as actual works of literature, as opposed to cryptic historical documents, thus illustrates the elimination of worldly literary taste as a player in the seventeenth-century literary scene. As we shall see in the next chapter, only one novel from the period is granted any literary status whatsoever: Lafayette's *La Princesse de Clèves*. The other numerous examples of the genre that was the ultimate product of the worldly salon milieu will be eliminated in future portrayals of the seventeenth-century literary field. Cousin's constructed image of the place of women in the seventeenth-century literary scene will have a lasting effect. No longer valued as a novel, Scudéry's credibility as an arbiter of literary works, the literary merits of her salon—often touted as the most "literary" of all the salons of the period—as well as her status as an author are all confined to the shadows of the dominant image of seventeenth-century France being constructed by Cousin and his contemporaries.

Sainte-Beuve: Redefining the Literary Woman

Cousin's views concerning women who dared trespass the traditional boundaries governing female comportment in the intellectual realm, while extreme to the eyes of a modern-day public, reflect the general ambiance surrounding women's literary activity prevalent in post-revolutionary France. Apparently the revolution did not entail liberation for all segments of society. Indeed, women's roles became even more deeply entrenched in the stereotypical concepts that relegated women's activity to a very restrictive private sphere comprised of home and family. Literary interests and even composition could exist, but were safe from criticism only if they conformed to a strictly defined and limited concept of "feminine" behavior. Critics and literary historians such as Cousin viewed their own roles as part of an effort to ensure that women remained "feminine" and did not tread upon the serious domain of "real" literature, even if that meant rewriting the past or silencing it altogether. Most important, the conception of the seventeenth century, considered by many as the apogee of French intellectual and literary power, was made to adhere to these strict ideals concerning the roles women could and should play in defining a nation's culture.

Victor Cousin's history of the seventeenth-century literary scene is indicative of a general effort throughout the nineteenth century to devalorize women who dared to fashion themselves into serious players in the literary field. Accompanying this reassessment of the roles women could play with respect to writing was a reconceptualization of the salon, one of their principal spheres of activity, especially with respect to the relationship between salons and literary critique and production. As is apparent in Cousin's works, seventeenth-century salons could be valued as places where women played the role of hostess and purveyors of politeness, but the literary creation and critique that so defined them in their own century were either ridiculed or marginalized as having little effect on real literature. In a similar move, Cousin's contemporary, Sainte-Beuve, became fascinated with France's past female literary figures and their salons. But while Cousin focuses on the seventeenth century, Sainte-Beuve locates his social and literary ideals primarily in the eighteenth. Even when he turns to the seventeenth century, he does not remove his eighteenth-century spectacles. This critic, as shall become apparent, takes a less direct approach to putting literary women in their place than does Cousin, but achieves the same results.

In *Les "salons" de Sainte-Beuve: Le critique et ses muses*, Roxana Verona details the complex relationship Sainte-Beuve established between himself as literary critic and historian, and the numerous women who inspired his reflections, his concept of literary value, his view of literary history, and his own style of writing.[59] Her analysis of Sainte-Beuve is especially relevant to our purposes because it reveals how the present time of composition can determine and sometimes even radically alter the historical past one is trying to portray. In the case of Sainte-Beuve, his century's preoccupation with determining roles for women that would deny them true legitimacy and authority in the literary world had a profound effect on the way he viewed his female subjects and their literary enterprises.

An analysis of the nineteenth-century's general perception of women writers is beyond the scope of this study, and has been carefully and insightfully treated by scholars such as C. Planté and Mona Ozouf, to cite only two from a long list.[60] Of particular interest for our purposes here is how nineteenth-century attitudes concerning women's place infiltrated critics' and historians' depictions of the literary field of the classical age. In the case of Sainte-Beuve it can be argued that, while the forms of his criticism, namely portraits and conversations, were directly inspired by the women writers of classical France who perfected these genres, his portrayal of women writers and the salons was colored by his century's view of women as well as by what the institution of the salon had become in the eighteenth century. It is interesting to note that relatively few seventeenth-century female literary figures people Sainte-Beuve's immense critical and literary corpus.[61] Three who appear the most prominently—Mme de Maintenon, Ninon de Lenclos, and Mme

de Sévigné—are certainly interesting and curious choices to represent the
entire century. Maintenon is elevated for her "talent as an excellent writer,"
a superiority Sainte-Beuve attributes to the fact, based upon her letters, that
she writes concisely, a trait only Lafayette among all the other women of the
period shares with her.[62] He did publish one volume that united the portraits of
women he composed between 1828 and 1848. His choices from the seventeenth
century were Sévigné, Lafayette, Longueville, and Deshoulières. He was also
attracted to Motteville, as an author of memoirs. But Sainte-Beuve's tastes in
creative women lie primarily in the major salon figures of eighteenth-century
France, women who, while influential on the social scene, did not leave
much written record of their intellectual involvement. Like Cousin he values
women who did not trespass the boundaries imposed on their sex.[63] If the
women Sainte-Beuve inscribes into memory—figures such as Lespinasse, Du
Deffand, Boigne, de Verdelin, de Souza, de Rémusat, de Tracy—did write,
they chose genres such as personal memoirs or the epistolary form to express
themselves, genres deemed acceptable by male contemporaries because they
did not impinge on the domains of "true" literature.[64] Sainte-Beuve adopts
the position of defender of the women he portrays, and of their literary
endeavors. He valorizes "these somewhat secondary genres" such as memoirs
and correspondences, because they enable the reader to penetrate society in
ways other genres do not.[65]

But while Sainte-Beuve's valorization of such genres, and the women
who perfected them, is in itself laudatory, it becomes more problematic when
considered in light of all female literary production. Sainte-Beuve correctly
points out that most of the women who interest him excelled in these genres.[66]
But he neglects the many female literary luminaries renowned for their work
in the more traditionally masculine genres of theatre, poetry, and essays, as
well as the numerous novelists who actually published their works and even
signed many of them. As is the case for Cousin, professional women writers
are another story in Sainte-Beuve's pantheon of illustrous women. In fact,
he is quite disparaging when he does occasionally treat a woman writer who
dared to go beyond acceptable genres such as memoirs, or women who openly
declared themselves writers. Genlis, for example, attracts Sainte-Beuve's
wrath because she represents the type of woman writer he would prefer never
exist, that is, as he characterizes them, "those galant or loose women who
became the Menors and the Minervas, and write moral treatises on education
during the short periods of respite that their lovers give them."[67] "No one has
ever been more decidedly a scribbler than Mme de Genlis" he disparagingly
remarks.[68] Such women were incapable of reconciling femininity with literary

pursuits, that is, they could not stay in the place Sainte-Beuve believes to be women's destiny. Small wonder that Sainte-Beuve's vision, one that will gain much currency in both literary history and history itself, clouds any serious investigation into women's literary influence in the *Grand Siècle*. When he does treat "established" women writers, Sainte-Beuve prefers to dwell on their minor works, limits their literary production to the margins of literature, or carefully explains that they never wanted to be "real" writers.[69] Even Sévigné's letters, which he clearly admires more than any other woman's work, owe their existence to a mother's love, not to any literary pretentions: "Mme de Sévigné sought consolation from her problems in a constant correspondence that lasted until her death ... before [being separated from her daughter] in 1671, we only have a small number of letters from Mme de Sévigné addressed to her cousin Bussy, and to M. de Pomponne about Fouquet's trial."[70]

Yet at the same time Sainte-Beuve occasionally makes reference to how women such as Ninon de Lenclos and Lafayette were viewed by their own century, thus creating a subtle and implicit contrast with his own portrayals. For example, he relates that Lafayette's and Ninon's contemporaries viewed them as "oracles du goût" (oracles of taste), although he leaves the notion of taste undefined. His portrait of Scudéry contains this same contrast. Sainte-Beuve recounts how many in her own century praised her and her novels, an attitude he is incapable of sharing. He in fact makes excuses for Maintenon's and Sévigné's praise of Scudéry, as he tries to rehabilitate their taste.[71] He rejects those contemporaries who considered Scudéry to be a writer or intellectual force:

> And as for all those other names that are cited (I don't exempt any of them, neither Fléchier, Mascaron, nor Bouhours), they do not shine because of sound and judicious good taste (*le bon goût sain et judicieux*); they all retained to some extent a pronounced tint of the hôtel de Rambouillet, and they lagged behind their century in some respects. Admiration for Mlle de Scudéry is a touchstone that puts them to the test and judges them.[72]

Like Cousin, Sainte-Beuve works to eradicate worldly taste from his depiction of the seventeenth-century literary milieu. He also tries to erase Scudéry's novels from the literary production of the time. Sainte-Beuve's entire portrait is colored from the beginning by his categorical statement that "Mlle de Scudéry's books are no longer read."[73] Later he is even more disparaging: "To speak today about Mlle de Scudéry's novels and to analyze them would be impossible to do without slandering her, they seem so ridiculous."[74] Like

Cousin, Sainte-Beuve identifies any pleasure to be gained by opening one of her novels as its value as a historical document: "... when we know the true names, we skim the pages with some curiosity."[75] Without creating any affiliation between his own *Causeries* and the works of the illustrious Sappho, Sainte-Beuve does compliment Scudéry for the conversations she inscribes in her novels, conversations "for which she had a singular talent, a true vocation."[76] Like memoirs and letters, conversations can constitute an acceptable literary pursuit for women.

If Sainte-Beuve is drawn to the women who composed the more personal genres of memoirs and correspondences, it is in part because these works allow him access to information to compose his portraits. As Verona notes, Sainte-Beuve, like many of his contemporaries, is incapable of examining a work penned by a woman without recourse to her biography.[77] Even novels must contain glimpses into the life of a woman writer. This critical approach to women's works, developed and legitimated by critics such as Sainte-Beuve and Cousin, has a long life, and helps to explain why novels such as those by Scudéry are valued much more as "keys" to their author's society rather than as actual works of literature. Sainte-Beuve openly states that he is drawn to women of the past because of their ability to provide details that can illuminate "l'esprit français en particulier" (particularly French *esprit*) or even "l'esprit humain en général" (humanity's *esprit* in general), citing Goethe.[78]

As Verona rightly argues, Sainte-Beuve resurrects many of France's forgotten literary women and inscribes them into literary history. But at what price? In selecting and valorizing women who remained in a "traditional" place corresponding to nineteenth-century ideals of femininity, that is, those who animated salons, but facilitated discussion without entering into it, much less dictating its content, Sainte-Beuve propagated a revised and carefully delineated conception of the salon and women's roles in that arena, especially with respect to literature.[79] A figure such as Mme Récamier becomes exemplary in the *Causeries*, for example, not for her own literary initiatives, but for her support of Chateaubriand's monumental memoirs. In his description of her salon which he had personally frequented, Sainte-Beuve links the celebrated *salonnière* with a seventeenth-century predecessor, Mme de Sablé, whom he praises for having supported La Rochefoucauld and his *Maximes* and for having lived a quiet, retired life surrounded by her friends.[80] Sainte-Beuve thus joins Cousin in redefining Sablé primarily as a muse for her male friend. He does not even grant Sablé her own portrait, instead inserting her into his description of La Rochefoucauld.[81] In this view of the salon milieu and its literary occupations, women serve as muses and facilitators for their male guests, who are in turn able to compose great masterpieces. Sainte-Beuve dismisses Sablé's own *Maximes*, published in the seventeenth century, and separates them entirely from La Rochefoucauld's masterpiece.

> I'll only say a word about her *Maximes*, because they are published; they can serve to evaluate and to determine what is hers in those of her illustrious friend. She was an advisor but nothing else: La Rochefoucauld remains the sole author of his work.[82]

Were Sainte-Beuve to depict Sablé's salon as the place of collaborative literary creativity attested to by her own contemporaries, the parallel he wishes to establish between Sablé and Récamier would no longer be valid. Unlike Récamier, Sablé would not have been portrayed stretched out on a *lit de repos*, content to watch as her male guests composed literature. And unlike Récamier, Sablé's salon was peopled by women and men equally. Récamier reigned alone, with only the occasional female guest intruding on a primarily male assembly.[83] Récamier is admired because she does not write. Sablé, as the literary precursor chosen for her by Sainte-Beuve, does not, or rather should not, attempt to produce literature either. By allying the eighteenth-century salon with a revised representation of its seventeenth-century predecessor, and by conflating the two, Sainte-Beuve effectively rewrites literary history and makes seventeenth-century women's actions adhere to the much more strict and traditional social mores of the nineteenth.

Just as Sainte-Beuve's image of the salon illustrates a re-working of the representation of the seventeenth century, so too does his conception of the woman writer constitute a redefinition of women's literary sphere and competency. By limiting his literary history to those women who chose the acceptable "feminine" genres of letters or personal memoirs, and stressing that they had no intention of rendering them public, Sainte-Beuve effectively depicts a female literary tradition that is separate from the "real" male one, safe because it could have little effect on the great works of literature. Many seventeenth-century female literary luminaries such as Villedieu and Bernard, renown as novelists and playwrights, are not admitted to Sainte-Beuve's world. When he deigns to include someone like Germaine de Staël, it is not to extoll her virtues as a novelist or essayist, but rather to compliment her for her art of conversation, an art that informed all her writing in the opinion of Sainte-Beuve. While seeming to elevate a quality identified as specific to women, in reality Sainte-Beuve diminishes the literary quality of Staël's impressive corpus by rendering it a form of "bavardage."[84] And while he admires *La Princesse de Clèves*, Sainte-Beuve is more interested in Lafayette's relationship with La Rochefoucauld and her own personality than in her literary accomplishments. He does suggest that Lafayette was a kind of critic for La Rochefoucauld's maxims, but only "in her heart."[85] One of the principal threads that runs through his portrait of Lafayette is that she was not a writer in the true sense of the word: "This person only writes a little, in her free time, for amusement and with a kind of negligence that had nothing professional about it."[86] Her masterpiece is reduced to the story of her love for La Rochefoucauld: "Mme de Clèves, in a word, sickly, somewhat depressed, at the side of M de Nemours, old and the author of the *Maximes*: such is Mme de Lafayette's life and the exact relationship between her and her novel."[87]

It is interesting to note that what is considered "natural" for women in the nineteenth century is much more limited than their roles in the seventeenth, especially with respect to literary evaluation, critique, and production. As we have seen, women were often valued, and even feared, for their "natural" sense of correct language and their "natural" good taste. In the seventeenth century, reason (*raison*) and *sentiments* such as innate good taste are conflated and are embodied by the female sex. Throughout the nineteenth century, as historians and critics sought to transcribe France's past, one sees a divorce between "raison" and "sentiments" in discussions of salon women and female-authored texts.[88] Women no longer reason, they can only feel. Granted, they are better at expressing these feelings, but the loss of "raison" is in large measure responsible for the reconstruction of the literary field of the seventeenth century. Without "raison," women are no longer eligible for full citizenship in the empire of letters.

Were Sainte-Beuve to show the interaction between the more female-dominated world of the salon and conventional literary history, he would have had to alter the very foundation of the literary history he was so carefully constructing, a foundation built upon women participating in the world of letters but only in the traditional roles of "muse," worldly, refined woman, or *dame d'esprit*, or as intermediary between the author and the legitimizing world of the French Academy, a woman who chose to express herself only through letters, conversation, or personal memoirs.[89] Like Cousin, Sainte-Beuve deemphasizes women as producers and critics of literature—he either omits them entirely or rewrites the history of their contribution—and highlights the worldly woman who refuses to write but silently admires and encourages her male guests who do, as she creates a polite, refined oasis of civilization.

Rambouillet and Scudéry: *Politesse* and *Préciosité*

The vision of the French literary world, especially the revered seventeenth century, that Sainte-Beuve constructs reflects not only this particular critic's view of the literary legacy of French women, but that of many of his compatriots, what Compagnon refers to as "la vieille vieille critique."[90] Sainte-Beuve exerted a powerful influence on the development of literary criticism, eventually becoming almost an institution himself. His vision thus necessarily infiltrated and influenced the views regarding literature and the composition of literary history, and most important for our purposes, the image of the literary woman and the seventeenth-century literary field.[91] By the end of the nineteenth century, numerous literary critics and historians, having felt the influence of such figures as Cousin and Sainte-Beuve, were composing literary histories to correspond to the new heightened sense of what French culture was in relation to that of the rest of the world. As we have seen, the seventeenth century was granted a place of honor in such histories and anthologies, although the worldly component was reconfigured or even erased from such representations.

In this re-membering of the seventeenth-century literary field, not only has the history of the salons and women's literary participation been rewritten, but also the various salons have not been inscribed into the nation's memory equally. An analysis of the representation of two of the most influential *salonnières* yields some surprising results. The historicization of Rambouillet and Scudéry can be viewed as a culminating example of the process we have been elaborating. While the name Rambouillet conjures up images of aristocratic elegance and the quintessentially French arts of *politesse* and *galanterie*, Scudéry, her *samedis*, and the "carte de Tendre" often evoke dismissive giggles and an uneasiness with these particular manifestations of salon history. Rambouillet represents an acceptable and lauded vision of the past. Scudéry, on the other hand, is usually held up as an example of excess, of a "ridiculous preciosity" that, while part of France's past, is considered as unworthy of true French culture, evoked only to be censored as an aberration.

Georges Mongrédien's twentieth-century assessment of these two particular *ruelles*, among the few that remain ingrained in French cultural memory, is representative of what has become the traditional, accepted view. He makes the following distinction between Rambouillet's and Scudéry's worlds: "In the first, a conversation that is pleasant, light, playful, witty, and galant; in the second a conversation that is oriented, a bit formal, stilted, about light and sometimes childish verse, among blue stockings infatuated with literature."[92] Mongrédien attributes the differences to class and to each salon's relationship to literature. Literature is only "secondary at the marquise's" whereas Scudéry's salon, to its detriment, is "specifically literary." In the *samedis*, habitués critique, and worse, compose, literature, whereas at the *chambre bleue* literature is merely a "diversion" and a "pleasure."[93] Those who frequent the *chambre bleue* are aristocrats, but "at Sapho's, it's a bourgeois society, which will always be missing that certain something ... which is nothing other than breeding (*la race*) an indefinable quality in which finesse, tact, taste, refinement, a sense of moderation are combined through successive generations."[94] In Mongrédien's portrayal, the salons evolved from granting women an acceptable, but limited, role in society, to "a feminine protest movement" exemplified by Scudéry and her "bourgeois" habitués.[95] Similarly but less radically, Roger Picard elevates Rambouillet but denigrates Scudéry's *samedis*. In his view, after the *chambre bleue*, two other types of salons appear. One continues the "good taste" and "decent customs (*bonnes moeurs*) associated with Rambouillet; in the other type, habitués are infatuated with novels such as *l'Astrée* and Scudéry's works: "After Rambouillet, two groups of salons appear: in one, the traditions of good taste, refinement, and elevated customs; in the other people are passionate about novels such as *l'Astrée* and Mlle de Scudéry's works."[96]

The historical processes that have resulted in such disparate visions of these two salons illustrate to an exceptional degree the creation and meticulous management of France's cultural heritage and its officially-sanctioned national identity that I have been examining. Each figure is intimately identified with the seventeenth century and used to characterize it, one positively, the other negatively. By the nineteenth century, the vision of France's "Grand Siècle" was already beginning to include many of the stereotypes we see reiterated in Mongrédien's and Picard's studies of the worldly milieu that have taken on the authority of reference works since their publication. Victor Cousin, as we have seen, creates an idealized image of the century, especially in the early years, in which *politesse* becomes the governing principle of social interaction. Rambouillet becomes identified as the motor of this civilizing process. He states: "*politesse* was necessary to lead the century to perfection. The hôtel de Rambouillet was particularly edifying."[97] An in-depth analysis of the specific representative case whereby Rambouillet becomes "French" and Scudéry and her *samedis* become objects of ridicule and Molière's inspiration for *Les Précieuses ridicules* will illuminate some of the guiding principles of the mythologizing of seventeenth-century French culture, and the stakes of this process.

If one returns to the seventeenth century and to contemporary depictions of the two women most remembered today (in fact the only salon names engrained in memory), one finds that the portraits of the two figures and the differences between them and their salons rarely conform entirely to our present day image.[98] As we have seen, the marquise de Rambouillet's contemporaries often depict her *chambre bleue* as much more than a foyer for politeness. For many intellectuals and writers, it was a place of serious literary and philosophical discussion and critique. Jean Chapelain's characterization of the *chambre bleue* as "un banquet philosophique" (a philosophical banquet) comes to mind.[99] At the end of the century, this association of the *chambre bleue* with intellectual pursuits is still prevalent. The marquise de Lambert, for example, echoes Chapelain, identifies Rambouillet with Plato, and praises the particular forms of worldly knowledge developed and advanced in the *ruelles*. She portrays the marquise's gatherings as serious efforts to create, discuss, debate, and arbitrate literary and philosophical productions.[100] And in Saint-Simon's estimation, Rambouillet's gatherings were a literary tribunal, "une sorte d'académie de beaux-esprits, de galanterie, de vertu et de science" (a kind of academy of *beaux-esprits*, of gallantry, of virtue, and of knowledge):

> ... le rendez-vous de tout ce qui était le plus distingué en condition et en mérite, un tribunal avec lequel il fallait compter et dont la décision avait un grand poids dans le monde sur la conduite et sur la réputation des personnes de la Cour et du grand monde, autant, pour le moins, que sur les ouvrages qui s'y portaient à l'examen.[101]

> (... the meeting place of everything that was the most distinguished in social condition and merit, a court that had to be reckoned with and whose decision carried great weight in the world on the conduct and the reputation of people at court and in high society, as much, at least, as on the literary works that were submitted for examination.)

Even as late as 1768 Pons-Augustin Alletz, when describing Mme de Tencin's salon, describes it as "un tribunal où elle présidait, et où l'on décidait sur tous les ouvrages qui paraissaient; en un mot, un second hôtel de Rambouillet" (a court where she presided, and where one pronounced upon all the literary works that appeared; in a word, a second hôtel de Rambouillet).[102]

But while many remark upon the marquise's propensity for reading and the literary activities of her gatherings, contemporaries often stress that she does not flaunt such occupations. As will become apparent, this trait will make it easier for succeeding centuries to refashion her image. In a letter to the marquise,

Balzac, for example, compliments her for conforming at least superficially to his traditional expectations for women: "on ne remarque rien en vous que de naturel et de français ... On voit votre canevas, votre soie et vos aiguilles, mais vos livres et vos papiers ne paraissent point" (people only see in you what is natural and French ... people see your canvas, your silk, your needles, but your books and your papers are never apparent).[103] Her "papers and books" exist, but only what is "natural" and "French,"—an interesting choice of adjectives—are apparent. Another contemporary and salon habitué, Segrais, advances a portrait that, like Balzac's, corresponds to today's more one-sided and stereotypical image of the woman identified as the founder of the salon movement in France: "Mme de Rambouillet était admirable ... C'est elle qui a corrigé les méchantes coutumes qu'il y avait avant elle. Elle s'est formé l'esprit dans la lecture des bons livres italiens et espagnols, et elle a enseigné la politesse à tous ceux de son temps qui l'ont fréquentée" (Mme de Rambouillet was admirable ... it was she who corrected the nasty customs that existed before her. She developed her mind by reading good Italian and Spanish books, and she taught *politesse* to everyone during her time who kept company with her).[104] Segrais identifies her contribution to society as primarily that of a professor of politeness. In contrast to Balzac and Segrais, Madeleine de Scudéry consistently underscores the marquise's abilities as a literary critic and depicts her salon as a type of literary academy. In the following frequently cited portrait of the marquise composed by Scudéry and inserted in *Le Grand Cyrus*, the novelist identifies one of the primary activities of the *ruelle* as literary arbitration:

> Il n'y a personne en toute la cour qui ait quelque esprit et quelque vertu qui n'aille chez elle: Rien n'est touvé beau si elle ne l'a approuvé. On ne croit point être du monde qu'on n'ait été connu d'elle. Il ne vient pas même un étranger qui ne veuille voir Cléomire et lui rendre hommage, et il n'est pas jusques aux excellents artisans qui ne veuillent que leurs ouvrages aient la gloire d'avoir son approbation.[105]

> (there is no one in the whole court who has some *esprit* and some virtue who doesn't visit her. Nothing is judged to be good if she hasn't approved of it. One doesn't feel part of society if one isn't known to her. Even foreigners want to see Cléomire and pay her hommage, and excellent artists want their works to have the glory of her approbation.)

A "foyer for politeness" or a "banquet philosophique" devoted to literary pursuits? One portrait will be granted more truth-value, and be considered more representative of French culture.

Whether polite or literary, the mythology of the *chambre bleue* identifies its *habitués* as belonging primarily to the nobility. But as Nicole Aronson, among others, has shown, it is clear that the salon consisted of a much less homogeneous group than that imagined by succeeding centuries. The nobility mixed with the bourgeoisie, and writers and academicians with politicians and *dames d'esprit*.[106] And according to the correspondence of contemporaries, the banquet continued until the marquise's death in 1665, far beyond the period of the Fronde traditionally cited as the end of the *chambre bleue*.[107]

A brief survey of contemporary reactions to Rambouillet's counterpart, Scudéry, adds a few surprising elements to the portrait we have inherited. References to Scudéry and her *samedis* are often laudatory and deferential, a far cry from Molière's and Boileau's canonized portrayals. *Mondains* and *érudits* alike applaud her *esprit*, literary talent, and taste. While she was not of the *haute noblesse*, like Rambouillet, Scudéry was from a noble family in Rouen. When she was introduced at the *chambre bleue*, one contemporary praised her for fitting in so easily into this recognized bastion of quality:

> Tout l'hôtel de Rambouillet, ce tribunal où l'on décidait souverainement du mérite et de l'esprit, et dont les jugements étaient si équitables et si respectés, se hata de prononcer en sa faveur. On ne trouva rien à reprendre en elle, rien qui sentit la province; on la regarda comme si elle eut été née à la cour où qu'elle y eut passé toute sa vie.[108]

> (The entire hôtel de Rambouillet, that court where people determined surpemely merit and *esprit* and whose judgments were so fair and so respected, hastened to pronounce in her favor. They found nothing to reproach her for, nothing that revealed the provinces; they considered her as if she had been born at court and had spent her whole life there.)

In his memoirs, Daniel Huet expresses the pleasure he took in gaining access to Scudéry, and names her as one of the three most learned women of the century, along with Christine de Suède and Anna Maria Van Schurmann.[109] The illustrious Frenchwoman of Huet's list surpasses the others, in the author's opinion, "par l'étendue et la vigueur inépuisable de son imagination" (by the extent and the inexhaustable force of her imagination). Charles Sorel baptises her "une des plus excellentes filles qui aient jamais écrit" (one of the most excellent women who has ever written).[110] Sévigné refers to Scudéry's ability to enlighten others in literary matters when she instructs her daughter to read Petrarque: "Vos lectures sont bonnes. Petrarque vous doit divertir avec le commentaire que vous avez; celui que nous avait fait Mlle de Scudéry, sur certains sonnets, les rendait agréables à lire" (Your readings are good. Petrarque should amuse you with the commentary you have; the one Mlle de Scudéry did for us of some sonnets made them pleasurable to read).[111] She later records how "cette merveilleuse Muse" (this marvelous muse), as she calls Scudéry, was received at court by Louis XIV and granted a royal pension. "Tout le Parnasse est en émotion pour remercier et le heros et l'héroine" (All Parnassus is in awe to thank the hero and the heroine) she writes.[112] Her prose overflows with admiration in a letter she wrote to Sapho:

> En cent mille paroles je ne pourrais vous dire qu'une vérité, qui se réduit à vous assurer, Mlle, que je vous aimerai et vous adorerai toute ma vie; il n'y a que ce mot qui puisse remplir l'idée que j'ai de votre extraordinaire mérite. J'en fais souvent le sujet de mes admirations, et du bonheur que j'ai d'avoir quelque part à l'amitié et à l'estime d'une telle personne ... J'ose me vanter que je ne serai jamais assez abandonnée de Dieu pour n'être pas toujours tout à vous ... Je porte à mon fils vos Conversations; je veux qu'il en soit charmé après en avoir été charmée.[113]

> (In 100,000 words I could tell you only one truth, that can be reduced to assuring you, Mlle, that I will love and adore you all my life; there is no other word that can express how I feel about your extraordinary merit. I often express my admiration and the happiness that I have to have some part in the friendship and esteem of such a person ... I dare to boast that I will never be so abandoned by God that I won't always be completely yours ... I'm taking your Conversations to my son; I want him to be charmed after having been charmed [myself].)

Like the marquise de Rambouillet, Scudéry is often cited for her literary taste and arbitrage. Both salons were frequented by many of the same people.

The primary difference between the two in the seventeenth century is that Scudéry achieved great renown as a professional writer. It should be remembered that *Clélie* was the most successful novel of the century, and was almost immediately translated into English, German, Spanish, Italian, and even possibly Arabic.[114] And her literary accomplishments were not limited to novels. Scudéry's foray into the more classical, and thus male-dominated genre of the heroic *harangue* achieved acclaim. Her harangues of illustrious women was reprinted numerous times. We have already seen how Sévigné, among many others, values her *Conversations* and *Conversations morales*. According to Mongrédien, the first two volumes had five editions and the following two were reprinted four times each. As late as 1692 the

Journal des Savants praised Scudéry and these works produced near the end of a very illustrious career: "On reconnaît d'abord Mlle de Scudéry, dont le génie, loin de s'épuiser, semble prendre une nouvelle vigueur et de nouveaux agréments à force de travailler, comme un fleuve qui devient plus abondant, plus majestueux et plus utile à force de couler" (We recognize Mlle de Scudéry, whose genius, far from running out, seems to take on new vigor and new charms as she continues to work, like a river that becomes more abundant, more majestic and more useful, as it flows).[115] Critics have often referred to Scudéry's novels as "des romans-fleuves" due to their length. It is clear here that the river metaphor is not always used negatively! And Scudéry's "Discours de la gloire" was the first recipient of the French Academy's prize for eloquence in 1671. Scudéry's reputation extended far beyond the borders of France. She was responsible for creating and exporting a positive image of the intellectual woman and writer to the rest of Europe. The currency of this image, that went a long way in characterizing France as a country that could produce such a figure and others like her, is evident in the praise heaped upon Scudéry by an English translator of her *Conversations* in 1683. He describes Scudéry as a woman

> qui fait les délices de la cour de France, cette personne de qualité, d'une éducation si parfaite, si célèbre par toute l'Europe par la chasteté de son style, l'innocence de sa conversation, la pureté de son imagination, la solidité de son jugement en ses écrits élégants qui, depuis bien des années, excitent l'envie des plus grands esprits du siècle.[116]

> (who is the delight of the French court, this person of quality with such a perfect education, so famous all over Europe for the chastity of her style, the innocence of her conversation, the purity of her imagination, the solidity of her judgment in her elegant writings that for many years, have aroused the envie of the best minds of the century.)

In the opinion of many of Scudéry's compatriots, this exceptional woman brings honor to France. One of her portraits carries the following inscription:

> Si la Grèce autrefois fertile en beaux esprits
> S'applaudissait de voir sa Sapho sans pareille,
> La France en Scudéry produit une merveille
> Qui ne lui fait pas moins d'honneur par ses écrits.[117]

> (If Greece which was so fertile in *beaux esprits* in the past
> Applauded to see its Sapho without equal

In Scudéry France produces a marvel
Who gives it no less honor through her writings.)

Even Madeleine's brother Georges acknowledges her elevated status among her compatriots.[118] In a sonnet addressed to his sister, Georges gushes poignantly "Vous que toute la France estime avec raison, Unique et chère soeur, que j'honore et que j'aime" (You whom all of France rightly holds in high esteem, unique and dear sister, whom I honor and love).[119] As we have seen, Scudéry's female contemporary, Marguerite Buffet, composed a similar portrait of this "illustre savante" that extols her elevated status within France and throughout Europe. In Buffet's opinion, Scudéry in fact represents France and its superior literary culture, a culture created and influenced in large measure by the position it accords women.

> ... la France n'est pas plus au dessus des autres nations par la gloire de ses héros, que par la science et la vertu de ses héroïnes. Que la Suède admire son illustre Reine, la Hollande sa docte Schurman; nous trouverons en la Sapho de nos jours, l'incomparable Mademoiselle Scudéry, plus de science, de doctrine, et d'esprit que dans la Sapho des Grecs tant vantée dans l'Antiquité ... Aussi voyons-nous que tous ceux qui savent parler et écrire en français lui [Scudéry] ont donné une estime si universelle, qu'ils la prennent pour un modèle achevé de bien parler et de bien écrire ... elle ne peut être inconnue ou méprisée que par des pédants ou des babares, ... la cour trouverait plus à se plaindre dans le silence de cette éloquente fille, que dans le retranchement d'une des académies du royaume. (243–8)[120]

> (... France is not just above other nations because of the glory of its heroes, but also because of the knowledge and virtue of its heroines. Let Sweden admire its illustrious Queen, Holland its learned Schurman; we will find in the Sapho of our times, the incomparable Mlle Scudéry, more knowledge, more doctrine, and *esprit* than in the Greek Sapho so touted in Antiquity ... Therefore we see that all those who speak and write in French so universally esteem her [Scudéry] that they take her as a perfect model of good speech and writing ... she can only be unknown to or scorned by pedants or barbarians ... the court would find more to lament in the silence of this eloquent woman than in the elimination of one of the academies of the kingdom.)

Seventeenth-century portraits of Rambouillet and Scudéry, representative of the salon movement as a whole, include some similarities between the two—their salons are both foyers for literary critique and innovation, many of the same people frequented them, both women are seen as embodying many of the qualities being touted as exemplary of France's character, that is, France as a place that accords women an influential position in the cultural field, and characteristics such as literary innovation, conversation, and civility. Differences seem to be on the order of degree—the marquise de Rambouillet was of a higher nobility than Madeleine, and Scudéry's salon had more associations with actual literary production. But it is these differences that will become engrained and reshaped in the later historicization of the salon movement.

As we have seen, the nineteenth century in particular becomes almost obsessed with seventeenth-century France—its women, as well as the institution that best embodies their cultural activity, the salon.[121] While both Rambouillet and Scudéry illustrate aspects of a culture that is considered unique to France, the nineteenth-century decides that one can be canonized and adopted as expressing an essence of Frenchness, if her image is carefully constructed and revised, but the other cannot. The trends that I will briefly evoke here in many ways mirror the portraits of the two women developed by Tallemant des Réaux in his *Historiettes*. Tallemant becomes validated as a respected source in particular for seventeenth-century women, due perhaps to the fact that his *Historiettes* were first published during the nineteenth century (around 1835) and correspond to the image historians and critics were developing about women's role in France's classical literary field.[122] Of particular interest is his rendition of the two key figures we are examining. In Tallemant's portrait of the marquise, the *chambre bleue* is the gathering place of polite society, but its ties to the literary realm are barely visible.[123] The marquise does read, but there is no mention of literary arbitrage: "Elle lit toute une journée sans la moindre incommodité, et c'est ce qui la divertit le plus" (She reads all day without the slightest problem, and this is what amuses her the most) (I, 455). Tallemant's choice of the verb "divertir" (to distract, amuse) is indicative of his view of the marquise's playful relationship to literary matters. For Tallemant, the tone of the marquise's gatherings is decidedly exuberant, fun, and light. He devotes a large part of his *historiette* to describing in detail the marquise's love of jokes and the various tricks she played on friends. While such a description may indeed be true, it is the absence of other salon activities that is striking. One has the impression that polite society only met at the *chambre bleue* for amusement and pleasure, certainly not for anything serious such as literature or the refinement of language. It is this portrait that will find currency throughout the century and even today.

Tallemant's account of Scudéry also contains many of the clichés that will remain associated with her. He underscores her vanity and pretension to nobility. While he compliments Scudéry for her novels, stating that "il y a de la belle morale dans ses romans, et les passions y sont bien touchées; je n'en vois pas même de mieux écrits, hors quelques affectations" (there is good morality in her novels, and the emotions are well expressed; I don't thnk there are any better written, except for some affection) (II, 689), he nonetheless attributes the popularity of her works primarily to women's taste and to their desire to be inscribed into literature: "Vous ne sauriez croire combien les Dames sont aises d'être dans ses romans, ou, pour mieux dire, qu'on y voit leurs portraits" (You wouldn't believe how much women are pleased to be in her novels, or more precisely, that people see their portraits [in her novels]) (II, 689). Tallemant refers to Scudéry's less-than-appealing physical qualities, which the editor of the Pléiade edition of the *Historiettes* then feels obliged to reinforce with a note explaining that "Cette laideur était fameuse, et reconnue par les amis de Madeleine de Scudéry. Chapelain écrivait: 'Enfin ce serait une personne accomplie si elle n'était un peu beaucoup laide. Mais vous savez que nous autres philosophes ne connaissons de vraie beauté que celle de l'âme'" (That ugliness was famous, and acknowledged by Madeleine de Scudéry's friends. Chapelain wrote: "She would be perfect if she weren't very ugly. But you know we philosophers only know beauty of the soul as true beauty") (II, 1453, n. 4). And although Tallemant inscribes the popularity of the novels and compliments Madeleine for her *esprit*, the Pléiade editor identifies not Madeleine but her sister-in-law as the true author of talent in the family, this despite the fact that Tallemant refers to Georges's marriage as "mettre un rien avec un autre rien" (unite a nothing with another nothing) (II, 695). Regarding Madeleine's sister-in-law, the editor writes: "Les nombreuses lettres de Mme de Scudéry à Bussy-Rabutin sont excellentes d'esprit et de style. Sauf le très grand respect que l'on doit à Madeleine de Scudéry, on ose penser que sa belle-soeur était née écrivain bien plus qu'elle. Mais elle se borna à être femme d'esprit" (Mme de Scudéry's numerous letters to Bussy-Rabutin have excellent *esprit* and style. If it weren't for the great respect due to Madeleine de Scudéry, one could dare think that her sister-in-law was more of a born writer than she. But she [Mme de Scudéry] limited herself to being a *femme d'esprit*).[124] Such remarks echo the comments we have seen by Cousin more than a century previously.

An analysis of the dominant depictions of Rambouillet and Scudéry throughout the nineteenth century reveals an effort to construct a past of these two women that echoes and expands upon the particular vision offered by Tallemant. Interestingly, the nineteenth century seems to have rediscovered the *chambre bleue*, which Aronson asserts was all but forgotten in the eighteenth. Roederer, among others, elevated the *chambre bleue* above all other salons of the *siècle classique*.[125] The marquise de Rambouillet is consistently portrayed as representing the highest rank of society. Her name becomes synonymous with politeness, gentility, refinement, beauty, *sociabilité*, civility, and elegant conversation. Victor Cousin, for example, characterizes the salon de Rambouillet as fun as opposed to intellectual. It is a place of "perpetual amusement" imbued with "Voiture's often farcical inventions" where "all the *esprit* ... was spent in all sorts of amusement" and "everything was done jokingly."[126] He associates Rambouillet uniquely with politeness.[127] He particularly admires the marquise because she does not write: "... she passionately loved *gens d'esprit* without having any personal ambition: one could barely find a few notes and two quatrains by her."[128] As Aronson has remarked, writers in the nineteenth century worked hard to recreate the marquise in the image of the "perfect women" according to their own standards.[129] Rambouillet becomes the quintessential worldly woman and her salon a gathering place for "amusement." As we have seen, these qualities were identified in the seventeenth century, but what is important here is what is missing, specifically any relationship to literary creation and critique. According to the common nineteenth-century narrative, the *chambre bleue* ended before the Fronde.[130] The rash of women writers that followed the civil disruption did not taint it. More important, by ending the salon's influence before Molière's triumphant entry onto the theatrical scene with his *Précieuses Ridicules*, this constructed image of Rambouillet remains intact. She could not have been a target of the playwright's satire, so Molière's reputation, and his validity as a social historian, are also enhanced. He was not wrongly satirizing a French institution of merit, but only a deformation deserving of such venom.

When one compares references to the *chambre bleue* in the seventeenth century to the majority of such portraits in the nineteenth, one is particularly struck by the fact that any reference to the *chambre bleue* as a space of literary critique is virtually absent. One exception is Genlis, who in her *De L'influence des femmes sur la littérature* provides a response to these revisionist protraits that were already present at the beginning of the century, to judge by Genlis's effort to counter them. Genlis opens her description of the marquise de Rambouillet, for example, by rebutting those who would seek to dismiss or ignore women's contribution to French literature. She stresses that Rambouillet perfected the art of conversation. She describes the *chambre bleue* as "une petite académie" (a small academy) composed of "la société entière" (all of society), engaged in "la critique littéraire" (literary criticism).

She then defends the *bon goût* of the marquise and her habitués, and stresses that this taste must be understood in its cultural and historical context.[131] Genlis takes the approach of a cultural historian, placing the marquise in her own literary and cultural context. She urges her readers to try to understand seventeenth-century taste as opposed to judging the activities of the *chambre bleue* by nineteenth-century standards. In particular she defends the marquise's own *goût* in an effort reminiscent of the marquise de Lambert over a century previously.

Even though Genlis's portrait conforms to the vision of many of Rambouillet's own contemporaries, her assessment does not reflect the dominant trend of scholarship concerning the marquise in the nineteenth century. Those who advance *politesse* and *gaieté* as the principal traits of the *chambre bleue* win out, and this image becomes the authoritative vision in the twentieth.[132] In his study of the *chambre bleue* in 1927, for example, Louis Batiffol privileges this vein of scholarship. His principal source, like that of many historians and literary specialists, is Tallemant. He goes to great lengths to separate the *chambre bleue* and the marquise from any true influence on what has been canonized as the classics of French literature:

> For *hommes d'esprit*, it was the writers who provided them ... they came in crowds, members of the nascent French Academy first, and many others, but unfortunately also those who would be denounced by Boileau's satirical pen ... in sum, the men of letters who frequented the hôtel de Rambouillet in the seventeenth century were almost all, as we have seen, with the exception of Malherbe, authors of a second or third degree order. Molière didn't know the hôtel de Rambouillet, which had disappeared before his beginnings. Corneille went for an instant and had no success ... Bossuet made a short appearance ... With the exception of these ... names, no great writer of the seventeenth century came near these famous meetings. Thus what influence could they [the meetings] have exerted on them [famous writers]?[133]

The classical canon remains intact, its authors devoid of any female literary influence in critique or creation. Perhaps not surprisingly, Scudery's salon is not even included in this particular collection of essays dedicated to "les grands salons littéraires."[134] Batiffol continues to dig the chasm that critics were creating to separate Rambouillet from a negative Scudéry, and identifes Scudéry as the sole culprit in the spread of preciosity:

> It isn't correct ... to criticize Mme de Rambouillet for the affectation and preciosity that were the effects of the movement we are discussing. She wasn't

the cause ... the mansion closed, the Godeaus, the Chapelains, the Conrarts took refuge at Mlle de Scudéry's and it is there, as well as in similar places, that these precious women that Molière so rightly mocked, proliferated.[135]

Twentieth-century descriptions of the *chambre bleue* follow many of the same lines as those dictated by the nineteenth-century myth-makers. In his influential work on the salons, Roger Picard, for example, does refer to Rambouillet's salon as "the temple of taste and the court of literary reputations."[136] He glorifies it as "a milieu both serious and pleasant, of good education but without banality, literary without being pedantic, with easy and polite customs."[137] As Picard views its most influential period as being 1624–48—although he acknowledges that the salon continued until 1665—he can safely assert that "it is certain that the ridiculous *précieuses* were found more in the less important salons."[138] While the marquise was in his view "at the top of these arbiters of literary glory" Picard details a *chambre bleue* in which women "embellished the house," "animated its receptions," and served as "the ornament of the hôtel" allowing the male *habitués* to judge and especially to compose literature. Such a conception of the *chambre bleue* allies it more with eighteenth-century manifestations of salon life than with those that populated Louis XIV's century.[139]

Most recently critics spend more time trying to refute any effect the marquise and her entourage may have had on the celebrated canon of seventeenth-century French literature than in trying to determine what its influence might have been. Rambouillet's most recent biographer, Nicole Aronson, for example, struggles with an alternative vision that grants Rambouillet a role in literary critique and creation. She acknowledges those in the seventeenth century who would endow the marquise with arbitrating power in the literary world, stating "the supreme court of the *beaux esprits*, as Mesnardière defined the hôtel de Rambouillet," and he adds: "and the great Arthénice having given her pronouncement, wise people lost their freedom of choice," which would seem to confirm the theory that Mme de Rambouillet and her friends were "the arbiters of Parnassus."[140] But in the end, Aronson concludes that, while writers may have gathered at her salon, any serious literary activities were reserved for different venues: "These authors saw each other at the hôtel de Rambouillet, but ... they needed a different meeting in order to tend to literature in a serious way ... her salon was not the literary one that it is too often described to be."[141] In Aronson's final assessment, "Despite the great renown it acquired, Arthénice's salon was simply a place of amusement for the guest and for its hostess."[142]

Rambouillet is glorified in French memory, and accepted, but for certain traits. Madeleine de Scudéry is another story. Throughout the eighteenth century, a fairly positive image of Scudéry seems to have remained intact. In 1751, for example, the Abbé Lambert celebrated her in his *Histoire littéraire du règne de Louis XIV*, associating her first with the hôtel de Rambouillet, where Scudéry had "l'entrée libre" (free entry) and thus could "se faire connaître des savants qui s'y assemblaient, et qui ne purent lui refuser leur admiration" (become known to the learned people who gathered there, and who could not refuse her their admiration).[143] He recognizes her exceptional reputation: "Mais rien ne prouve mieux le mérite de cette illustre savante, que le commerce de littérature que les plus beaux esprits de son siècle se sont empressés de lier avec elle et les grands éloges qu'ils ont faits de son savoir et de ses ouvrages" (But nothing proves better the worth of this famous learned woman than the literary dealings that the best *beaux esprits* of her century were anxious to have with her and the great praise they had for her knowledge and for her works).[144] In the early nineteenth century, Genlis celebrates Scudéry as a great novelist "entourée par les meilleurs écrivains de son temps"[145] (surrounded by the best writers of her time). Other depictions, however, are much less flattering. Victor Cousin refashions Scudéry and her gatherings into something he can accept. In early studies he qualifies Scudéry as "the most extravagant of the *précieuses*, driven crazy by grandeur ... a drivelling old fool."[146] He later becomes more positive, a move that can be attributed to the fact that he found the key to *Le Grand Cyrus* at the Arsenal, and thus viewed this "drivelling old fool" as a key to his own scholarly success. Of her *samedis* he writes:

> Mlle de Scudéry was the queen of the arena. The charms of her *esprit*, the nobility and sweetness of her character, the reliability and pleasure of her relationships, made her adored, and she remained constantly in the public's esteem by the perfect innocence of her behavior. In fact, even though people only spoke of gallant subjects at her home, she was never known to have any suspicious relationship.[147]

Gone is any reference to literary creation, to arbitrating literary debates, or to her *génie*, although, as we have seen, Cousin does attribute Georges de Scudéry's election to the Académie française to the fact that his sister had so many admirerers and friends there. Echoing Tallemant, the popularity of her novels is due solely to their relationship to society, a group Cousin characterizes as "bourgeois and inferior."[148]

Scudéry becomes almost a metaphor for *préciosité* and particularly for every negative connotation associated with the word after Molière's dramatic attack. Picard identifies the origin of *préciosité* as Scudéry's literary works: "her works contributed to the spread of that deformation of *esprit* that is preciosity."[149] Such a vision is reiterated in a recent study of European salons entitled *Salons européeans: les beaux moments d'une culture féminine disparue*. The author, Verena von der Heyden-Rynsch, characterizes Scudéry as representative of those women who "forbid the natural to such an extent that they refuse any burst of tenderness, and to assure independence, choose celibacy."[150] Having stripped Madeleine of any "natural" qualities, it becomes easy to transform her into a symbol of unnatural language and literary pursuits. For von der Heyden-Rynsch, among others, Scudéry is more a symbol than human: "In the context of preciosity, which spread like a plague in the seventeenth century, let us briefly discribe a character who represents a symbolic figure in this play form of linguistic mania, both literary and social, and who also established a salon, Madeleine de Scudéry."[151] This portrait yields no new insights and simply repeats all the clichés we have already seen associated with the most celebrated novelist of her time. Yet again the success of Scudéry's novels is attributed to their sociological references. *Le Grand Cyrus* "owes its success only to the identification of the heros with the important personalities of the period."[152] And Molière's direct satire of Madeleine in *Les Précieuses* was done "in an amusing way" since the playwright's target obviously deserved such derision. Von der Heyden-Rynsch's description confirms Molière's consecrated version of the past, but ends with a paradox that this author, like most of her nineteenth and twentieth-century predessors, does not try to resolve: "A ridiculous *précieuse* certainly, but her Saturday meetings were attended by all the dominant figures of the court and of the city of Paris."[153] Instead of trying to explain this enigma, the author lets it stand, for to try to resolve it would entail first recognizing the existence of the mythology created around Scudéry and then questioning it as well as the myth of the entire seventeenth-century literary landscape according to which Scudéry was an aberration and the salons mere foyers for pleasure.

Politesse and genteel conversation are thus elevated, through the consecration of reformulated image of the marquise de Rambouillet, as national traits, and the marquise is identified as the source for the quintessentially French version of these attributes. Scudéry, who became a national icon during her own time, is symbolic of the effort to dismiss all women's artistic production and influence on literary culture, especially on the period deemed to have produced the purest "classics" of French literature. In the effort to consecrate the seventeenth century as a reflection of France's *génie*, the woman most associated with writing and influencing literature, Scudéry, is relegated to the realm of ridicule. Her detractors and critics, such as Molière and Boileau, achieve immortality and more important, the status of social historians.[154]

* * * * *

Echoing Antoine Compagnon, Roxana Verona points out that "the nineteenth century seems to freeze on the side of positivism, historicism and the biographical from which 'old, old criticism' is born, represented by Sainte-Beuve, Taine and Brunetière and the old criticism of Lanson."[155] She congratulates the twentieth century for having thrown off the shackles and prejudices of this "old criticism" in the name of "creative autonomy and literarity."[156] While this may be true of critics' evaluation of literature in general, I would argue that many of the trends present in this "old criticism" remain deeply engrained in the attitudes of literary critics as well as historians when they are confronted with women writers of France's *grand siècle* and the salon milieu. Sainte-Beuve's portraits and "causeries," like those of his fellow literary historians and critics, have had a profound and enduring effect on how the salon was conceived of and perceived by following generations. The supposedly more enlightened twentieth and twenty-first centuries have difficulty grappling with women's past, and especially with including women's literary activity in the larger context of France's exceptional literary history. While a separate history or critique may be acceptable, a national history that places women's activities and spaces on equal footing and seeks to unveil how women's history is a part of national history proves to be much less prevalent and even acceptable. A few more representative voices can serve to illustrate the malaise within the hexagon inherent in taking women out of the shadows and margins of classical France.

In 1927, a conference series entitled *Les Grands salons littéraires (XVIIe et XVIIIe siècles)* was organized at Sévigné's former *hôtel particulier*, the Musée Carnavalet. Published in 1928, these lectures reveal the lasting legacy of the nineteenth-century rewriting of seventeenth-century literary culture. The introduction to the volume by Louis Gillet sets the tone and creates a specific vision of the salon that will be carried through in the individual lectures. Gillet invites the public to enter an idealized world, to spend "a few moments in this society, the most polite there ever was, to hear a du Deffand, a Lespinasse, an Aïssé, and to live for an hour surrounded by charming *shadows (ombres)* [my emphasis], two centuries of that thing we will never see again, that refined thing called salon life."[157] Gillet's image corresponds to the common vision of politeness and sociability, separate from any real influence on France's glorious past. To emphasize this marginalization of the salons, in particular those of the seventeenth century, from any real influence, Gillet goes on to separate the salon milieu even further from the great century of Louis XIV:

> Without a doubt, here we do not have the profusion of treasure, the almost overwhelming richness of the century of Louis XIV that triumphed almost at the same time in the Galerie Mazarine. The exhibit at Carnavalet is naturally more discreet; the object here is no longer the state, it's about private life. This is no longer Opera, it's chamber music.[158]

Following the vision inherited from the nineteenth century, Gillet creates a historiographical hierarchy according to which seventeenth-century salons and their "shadows" discreetly occupy a separate and unequal place in French history. There is no attempt to view these gatherings as an integral part of "the overwhelming richness" of Louis XIV's reign, because in his view, like Opera and chambre music, the two separate entities never mixed. In fact, Gillet reserves any possible influence beyond the confines of a salon's walls for the eighteenth-century manifestations of "this refined thing." While he acknowledges that the salons began in the seventeenth century with the "*précieuses* and the hôtel de Rambouillet" he categorically states that the "great service" such gatherings rendered to society at large was to teach manners. Seventeenth-century salons were merely "a school for delicacy" that then "lose ... all importance during the great period of Louis XIV's reign."[159] Only at the end of the eighteenth century, with Geoffrin's salon, does "salon life really become an institution."[160] Gillet's history, like the volume for which it serves as the preface, thus functions to rid the seventeenth century of any real female influence, while at the same time consecrating a completely different manifestation of the salon as the truly influential institution that merits admiration.

Although the title of the volume is *Les Grands salons littéraires*, there is little effort to detail the relationship between "salon" and "literature." Only two seventeenth-century salons merit inclusion in this particular pantheon: Rambouillet's and Mme de La Sablière's. The rest of the volume is devoted to the eighteenth-century salons of Tencin, Geoffrin, and du Deffand. The author of the lecture on Rambouillet, Louis Batiffol, goes to great length to stress that the marquise is not a writer: "She does not pride herself on any literary claims."[161] Similarly, André Hallays depicts Mme de La Sablière as "a pretty woman, witty and knowledgeable, without the shadow of pedantry" but focuses on her relationship with La Fontaine. She received many of the major women writers of the time—Lafayette, Sévigné, Lambert, for example—as well as male intellectuals and writers, but there is no sense of any literary activity actually occurring in her gatherings, and no references to her own compositions. The portrait in fact ends with a renunciation of the one work that Hallays associates with the salon. He recounts how La Fontaine, in order to be accepted into the French Academy, had to distance himself from his *Fables*:

> Not until a few weeks after Mme de La Sablière's death did he agree to confess the errors of his life ... but also to publicly disavow his fables – which must have been very hard for him, because he honestly believed they were innocent, and they were the children of his muse.[162]

The image of the *salonnière* as muse and professor of politeness remains dominant and intact. Any literary product from the worldly milieu is in fact rejected as a false note in literary history's great opera.

Many modern scholars have been drawn to the salons not because of their interest in women writers but because of the perception that the salon is a uniquely French phenemenon. Thus to study the salon is to engage in trying to understand what precisely makes France the country that it is. The very title of Roger Picard's frequently cited study, *Les Salons littéraires et la société française, 1610–1789*, underscores the symbiotic relationship between this female-dominated institution and French society.[163] But while Picard, like Gillet, states that he will be treating "literary" salons, it is clear from the opening pages that it is the salons' social qualities, the famous *sociabilité* so celebrated by the nineteenth century, that will attract most of his attention. When he turns to the salons during France's classical age, he again underscores the relationship between national character and the salons:

> By the end of the seventeenth century, these literary gatherings in Parisian salons had become an integral part of intellectual and social life in France. They respond to a need in national character. Cultivated French people, so inclined towards sociability, passionate about things of the mind [*esprit*], loving both the pleasure of criticism and the joy of disseminating their opinions and their tastes, found in the atmosphere of the salons all the necessary conditions to develop these unselfish tendencies.[164]

Picard relies primarily on Sainte-Beuve, Tallement des Réaux, and Maurice Magendie's *La Politesse mondaine* to construct his history of this uniquely

French institution. As we have seen in his treatment of Rambouillet's *chambre bleue*, while Picard begrudingly grants the marquise some influence on literary reputations, calling her salon "the court of literary reputations" and "the temple of taste," his conception of the *ruelle* is highly imbued with characteristics that belong more to the eighteeenth century salons. The male habitués figure prominently, with women serving as "embellishments" (adornments) and "hôtesses littéraires" (literary hostesses), an intriging choice of qualifying adjective that he leaves unexplained. After listing all the men who frequented the *chambre bleue*, for example, Picard turns to the women, in what seems to be more of an afterthought: "Among the women who embellished Mme de Rambouillet's home and who animated her memorable receptions, we will only cite a few."[165]

As we have seen, eighteenth-century salons were often dominated by one woman who effaced her opinions in order to encourage those of her primarily male guests. Picard adheres to this conception of the salon, as opposed to the more collaborative version we have seen as prevalent throughout the seventeenth century. In his opinion, echoing his nineteenth-century predecessors, the "literary hostess" is most successful when she is relatively silent. Picard's perspective on the ideal role for women in a salon reflects one of the principal threads that runs through depictions of the seventeenth-century salon milieu. Women may receive guests and direct conversation, but the system works best if she encourages her male guests rather than exercising her own critical judgment or, worse yet, writing herself. Picard, in a move that is atypical, does grant the seventeenth-century salon a role in the critique of literature.[166] But he also emphasizes that it is primarily minor writers who submitted their works to such female-dominated literary tribunals.[167] Other critics do not hesitate to point out the greatest danger, that is, combining literary occupations with the supposedly primary function of social hostess. In particular, to be a woman writer and *salonnière* at the same time is to go against the very essense of the *ruelle*. We have seen how Scudéry's *samedis* are eliminated as unrepresentative of the true French salon. Other critics extend this rejection to the entire seventeenth-century salon milieu, stressing that to write is to risk ruining one's salon. In this vein of scholarship, von der Heyden-Rynsch's commentary is exemplary. Commenting on the relationship between women writers and their salons in the seventeenth century, she states

> ... as Mme de Sablé illustrates, another general phenomenon appears clearly: the difficulty of combining personal literary creativity with the role of *salonnière*. The composition of her maxims and portraits which even inspired

La Rochefoucauld, absorbed Mme de Sablé so much internally and externally that little by little her salon was transformed into a closed literary circle, and soon after, was dispersed.[168]

Instead of viewing the salon as the locus for female literary activity, existing in large measure to promote female creativity as well as men's such as La Rochfoucauld's, this historian, like many others, views literature when practiced by women as detrimental to the salon milieu, and indeed responsible for destroying one of the "beaux moments d'une culture féminine" (great moments of a feminine culture), to cite von der Heyden-Rynsch's own title.

Recently André Burguière and Jacques Revel initiated a series entitled *Histoire de la France: Choix culturels et mémoire*, for which they invited the participation of some of the century's best known historians. Roger Chartier was solicited for an essay on the Ancien Régime, which he entitled "Trajectoires et tensions culturelles de l'Ancien Régime" (Trajectories and cultural tension in the Old Régime). Chartier acknowledges the sociological effect on the salons, but, surprisingly, depicts worldly culture's influence on the literary field as completely separate from "mainstream" literary culture and marginal:

> … salon society of the first part of the seventeenth century combines the cultural promotion of women with the fusion of elites. This created, outside of academic canons, a critical and creative authority that elevated the genres the most closely tied to the practices of worldly sociability: the poem, the letter, the maxim. On the margins of the important forms regulated by patented literary rules, the literary game, galant conversation and the taste for the portrait guaranteed the success of a literature that satisfied the taste of a chosen public, wary of the decrees of scholars.[169]

From this description one gets no sense that authors such as Corneille sought the approbation of the salons, or that academicians like Chapelain were part of both the salon world and the one that created the "academic canons." "Outside" and "on the margins" come to characterize the literary production associated with the salons. Although less overtly than their nineteenth-century predecessors, many present-day historians often replicate the vision they have inherited, and preserve a vision of the seventeenth century divorced from female literary influence. Such a move allows critics to extoll the virtues of the salon, and hail it as uniquely French, without acknowledging what the seventeenth-century viewed as equally unique to its culture, that is the alliance between the salons and women's impressive participation as writers and critics in the literary world at large.

* * * * *

Historians have become increasingly attracted to questions regarding the subjective nature of the historical enterprise. Nineteenth-century France has been recognized as both a defining period of historiography as well as a time when, as Jacques Le Goff, for example, describes it, "national sentiment contributes powerfully to disseminating the sense of history."[170] Le Goff advocates analyzing historical texts as products of their particular time period, and states strongly that "one must interrogate the silences" inherent in historical narratives as well as the elements that are included in a given text. A nation's historical narrative, as well as its collective memory, are products of various active forces, not simply undistorted mirrors of the past:

> Collective memory is an important game in the struggle for power of social forces. To become the master of memory and forgetting is one of the great preoccupations of the classes, the groups, and the individuals that have dominated and dominate historical societies. What is forgotten, the silences of history are revelatory of the mechanisms of manipulation and collective memory.[171]

The case of the historization and the representation of the literary field of seventeenth-century France is a particularly illuminating example of these "mecanisms of manipulation" in the creation of a nation's collective memory. In the case of France, the "silences" and shadows were enhanced and created by a particularly powerful "mechanism," namely the French educational system. As we have seen, the representation of France's classical literary arena was gradually reshaped to eliminate or at least overshadow women's contributions to the mainstream literary world, revise the conception of one of their major spheres of influence, the salon, and to eliminate worldly taste as an important force in the construction of the memory of the period identified as a highpoint in France's literary past. For this revised memory of a collective past to become so ingrained in the national psyche, a force besides history itself had to be employed.[172] Teaching memory proves to be even more important than creating it. It is to the power of pedagogy that we now turn.[173]

Notes

1 Sophie Gay, *Salons célèbres*, 1837 (Paris, 1864).
2 *Le Siècle de Louis XIV*, p. 287. Voltaire began this work around 1732 for Mme de Chatelet. It was first published in 1751. All further references will be to this edition, with page numbers inserted parenthetically in the text.
3 The court is not synonymous with the salons. As Elena Russo has shown, while there were similarities, these were two very different arenas of social influence and interaction. One has only to think of Richelieu's opposition to the salon de Rambouillet and his establishment of the French Academy in the wake of the *chambre bleue*'s popularity to appreciate the significant differences between them. See Russo, *La Cour et la ville* (Paris, 2002), epecially pp. 18–21.
4 Germaine de Staël, *De la littérature* 1800 (Paris, 1991), p. 271. All further references will be to this edition, with page numbers inserted parenthetically in the text.
5 *De la Littérature*, pp. 274, 278. Staël explains: "Thus only in France where the authority of kings was consolidated by the complicity of the nobility, the monarch had a power without limits in fact, and yet uncertain by law. This situation obliged him to manage his courtisans" (p. 273).
6 Staël, *De la littérature*, p. 278.
7 Staël, *De l'esprit de conversation*, p. 102 in *De l'Allemagne*, 1810 (Paris, 1968).
8 Russo, *La cour et la ville*, pp. 107–8.
9 Ibid., p. 109. Dena Goodman's comprehensive and innovative study of the eighteenth-century salons reveals their central importance to the ideas of the Enlightenment. I wish to underscore here, however, the ways in which the seventeenth-century salon differed from its later counterpart, regarding in particular the relationship between women and literature, its production and critique, as I analyze how it has been represented.
10 Russo succinctly underscores this change, stating that "Isolated from the exchange [the salon woman] controls the mechanism from above; her guests profess to her a gratitude without limit, an extreme respect for her modesty and her retiring and unassuming role" (p. 109). Russo goes on to cite Morellet's praise of Mme Geoffrin as an example of the reevaluation of the qualities of the perfect *salonnière*: "… [Mme Geoffrin] had above all the art and the obliging attention to bring up for those with whom she engaged subjects that could interest them, and to let them talk without interrupting them … In a larger group she did not add regularly to the conversation; most often she was content to listen with interest" (p. 109).
11 Russo, following Dena Goodman's analysis, advances that "the authority of the [*salonnière*] is benevolent and invisible; she reigns by love" (p. 109).
12 David Bell describes in detail the discussions of French national character in the eighteenth-century. As he states "For most French authors, the civilized traits of sociability, *légèreté*, and politeness reflected the extraordinary influence of women … Many observers considered the position of women the main difference between France and nations which restricted women to what Rivarol called 'the domestic tribunal.'" *The Cult of the Nation*, p. 149.
13 I agree with Russo views who Lambert's salon as straddling the seventeenth and eighteenth centuries. See her *La Cour et la ville*, pp. 90–98.
14 George Eliot, *Essays of George Eliot.* ed. Thomas Pinney, (New York, 1963), p. 54. As cited by Eva Martin Sartori and Dorothy Wynne Zimmerman, *French Women Writers: A Bio-bibliographical Source Book* (Westport, CT, 1991), p. xv.

15　At the same time that women's historical roles were being revised, France also witnessed the creation of the "cult of great men." I would argue that the two movements are not unrelated. David Bell has analyzed this "cult" in the eighteenth century, a movement that used ancient Greece as its model. In Bell's words, "Collectively, the attempts to realize this vision in France amounted to nothing less than a conscious reshaping of national memory" (p. 107). See Chapter 4 in his *The Cult of the Nation*, pp. 107–39. Bell points out the gender bias of this movement, stating that "… while women could perform glorious and heroic actions, as Joan of Arc and innumerable saints had done, they did not, according to the architects of the cult, have the qualities requisite for republican citizenship" (p. 127).

16　Tillet exudes great enthusiasm when he discusses the exceptional nature of Louis XIV's seventeenth-century, as when he states "Qu'on compterait peu de ces grands hommes depuis le règne de César et d'Auguste! On croirait que la nature se serait reposée plus de dix-sept cents ans pour faire un pareil prodige, et rendre le règne de Louis le Grand l'admiration de tous les siècles" (One can count few of these great men since the reign of Caesar and Augustus! It seems as though nature rested more than seventeen hundred years in order to create a similar wonder and make the reign of Louis the Great the admiration of all centuries). Evrard Titon du Tillet, *Le Parnasse français* 1732 (Geneva, 1971), p. 9. All further references will be to this edition, with page numbers inserted parenthetically in the text.

17　The nine geniuses he chooses are: Corneille, Molière, Racine, Racan, Segrais, La Fontaine, Despréaux, Chapelle, and Lulli (p. 20).

18　It is interesting to note that Tillet uses the three graces to distinguish his French *Parnasse* from its Greek predecessor: "Les trois graces dont il est rarement parlé sur le Parnasse de la Grèce, brillent avec raison sur le Parnasse Français; on n'ignore pas que ces trois déesses n'aient le don d'embellir tous les lieux où elles paraissent, et que rien ne peut plaire sans leur présence" (The three graces who are rarely mentioned in the Greek Parnassus, shine with reason on the French Parnassus; no one ignores the fact that these three goddesses have the gift of embellishing all the places where they appear, and nothing can be pleasing without their presence) (p. 81).

19　Tillet states: "… je veux tâcher de suivre le projet que je me suis proposé, et de parler plutôt des ouvrages de nos poètes, que de m'étendre sur le cours ordinaire de leur vie" (I want to try to follow the project that I proposed and to speak about the work of our poets, rather than to elaborate on their lives) (p. 463).

20　While Tillet grants Louis XIV's France exceptional status, he nonetheless views his own period as possessing a superior taste, "notre langue [est] devenue plus pure et plus élegante, notre esprit plus éclairé et plus juste, et notre goût plus délicat et plus difficile" (Our language has become more pure and more elegant, our *esprit* clearer and more exact, and our taste more subtle and discerning) (p. 8).

21　Ibid., p. 327. See also p. 446.

22　Throughout his work Tillet refuses to qualify the public as either erudite or worldly, opting instead for ambiguity in order to include both possibilities. He inscribes works "selon le mérite des ouvrages qu'un auteur a donnés, et selon qu'ils ont été reçus du public" (according to the worth of the works that an author gave, and how they were received by the public) (p. 12).

23　In his entry on Ménage, Tillet states that Ménage's works were praised by "plusieurs savants du Royaume, et même de ceux des pays étrangers. Parmi les Français on doit compter Balzac, Antoine Halley, Monmor, le Père Mambrun, Chapelain, Godeau, Sarasin, Colletet, Costar, Charpentier, Petit, Commire, Santeuil, la Monnoye, Mlle de Scudéry et plusieurs autre bons critiques" (many learned people of the realm, and even those of foreign countries. Among the French are Balzac, Antoine Halley, Monmor, le Père Mambrun, Chapelain, Godeau, Sarasin, Colletet, Costar, Charpentier, Petit, Commire, Santeuil, la Monnoye, Mlle de Scudéry and many other good critics) (pp. 438–9). It is interesting that Tillet does not include Georges de Scudéry, who exercised his critical pen, notably against *Le Cid*.

24   When describing la comtesse de la Suze, for example, he lists other women who excelled in letters: "Du temps de Madame la comtesse de la Suze, il parut plusieurs dames, qui se distinguèrent par le bel esprit et par quelques ouvrages de leur composition; telles furent les Dames des Loges, de Bregy, de Sévigné, de La Fayette, et quelques autres, dont on trouvera occasion de parler dans la suite de cet ordre chronologique" (During the time of Mme la comtesse de la Suze, there were many women who distinguished themselves by their *bel esprit* and the works they composed; such as the Dames des Loges, de Bregy, de Sévigné, de La Fayette, and others that we will discuss in chronological order (p. 327).

25   In his portrait of Segrais, Tillet refers to his collaboration with Montpensier and especially with Lafayette (p. 478).

26   Tillet clearly admires Boileau's works. He recounts that he actually knew Boileau during the last years of his life, and states with pride that Depréaux's bust "fait présentement un des ornements de mon cabinet" (is presently one of the decorations in my study) (p. 537). Anne le Fevre Dacier is also admired for her critical acumen. She is "la femme la plus savante de son siècle" (the most learned woman of her century) and holds "un rang distingué entre nos meilleurs critiques et entre nos traducteurs" (a distinguished rank among our best critics and translators) (p. 570).

27   Halphen, *Etude sur Voiture et la société de son temps. Lettres et poésies inédites* (Versailles, 1853), p. 37.

28   Ibid., p. 40.

29   Pons-Augustin Alletz, *L'Esprit des femmes célèbres du siècle de Louis XIV et de celui de Louis XV, jusqu'à présent*, 2 vols (Paris, 1768), p. iii. All further references will be to this edition with page numbers inserted parenthetically in the text.

30   Ibid., II, p. 295. Similarly, Mme du Bocage, who composed epic poetry, has "un style mâle" (a male style) (II, p. 317). Interestingly, the passage he includes is not one of these male epic poems, but letters she wrote from England.

31   Abbé Joseph de La Porte, *Histoire littéraire des femmes françaises* (Paris, 1769), vol. I, avertissement, n.p. All further references will be to this edition with page numbers inserted parenthetically in the text.

32   Abbé Claude François Lambert, *Histoire littéraire du règne de Louis XIV* (Paris, 1751). All further references will be to this edition with page numbers inserted parenthetically in the text.

33   In many ways, he is trying to be complete, in the tradition of the worldly anthologies analyzed by DeJean in "Classical Reeducation."

34   Lambert notes that: "L'on ne peut cependant nier que la République des lettres n'ait à cette dame une obligation essentielle, car c'est elle qui a fait perdre le goût de ces longs et volumineux romans, qui n'avaient point de fin" (Yet one can't deny that the republic of letters owes an essential obligation to this woman, because it is she who made [readers] lose taste for those long and voluminous novels that were endless) (ibid., II, p. 22).

35   Stephanie Féicité de Genlis, *De L'Influence des femmes sur la littérature* (Paris, 1811), pp. 1–2. All further references will be to this edition with page numbers inserted parenthetically in the text.

36   It is important to note that while Genlis praises the contributions of her female literary predecessors, she does not praise them indiscriminately nor does she idealize them. Here, for example, she criticizes Lafayette for producing a work that, while exemplary in many respects, is "far from being moral" and is even "very dangerous for young people" because in Genlis's view, the princess gives in, albeit privately, to her passion instead of resisting it entirely. Women writers, like male ones, can be innovative but are not more perfect than they are.

37   Ferdinand Brunetière, *Questions et Critiques* (Paris, 1897). 3ième édition. All further references will be to this edition, with page numbers inserted parenthetically in the text.

38   Brunetière states: "The *précieuses* must be criticized, in constituting the language of *honnêtes gens*, for having aggravated the difference that separates everywhere literary language from popular language. In France we no long have popular literature ... and every writer worthy of that name is really an aristocrat" (p. 38).

39   Joan DeJean, "Classical Reeducation," p. 29.

40   DeJean differentiates between the worldly anthologies and the overtly pedagogical ones, stating that the editors of worldly anthologies were not guided by the same ideological principals as their pedagogically-oriented colleagues. Editors such as the one who composed the 1692 *Recueil des plus belles pièces des poètes français* do set themselves up as arbiters of literary taste. They simply include works that have achieved a certain reputation. DeJean, ibid., p. 23. While I agree with this assessment, I believe that many of these worldly anthologies in the eighteenth century do reflect a trend to analyze and judge literature according to stereotypes based on gender, as the following analysis will show.

41   Compagnon, for example, categorizes Lanson as part of "la vieille critique" as opposed to the "vieille, vieille critique" represented by Brunetière and Sainte-Beuve. For an in-depth analysis of the development of literary history and criticism in the late nineteenth century, see his *La Troisième République des lettres: De Flaubert à Proust*, especially pp. 21–113 and 134–47.

42   As cited by Roxana Verona, *Les "salons" de Sainte-Beuve: Le critique et ses muses* (Paris, 1999), p. 208.

43   Victor Cousin, *La Jeunesse de Mme de Longueville, études sur les femmes illustres et la société du XVIIe siècle* (Paris, 1853).

44   *La Société française au XVIIieme siècle d'après le Grand Cyrus de Mlle de Scudéry* (Paris, 1866), p. 43.

45   *La Société Française*, I, pp. 21–2.

46   *La Jeunesse de Mme de Longueville* (Paris, 1869), p. xii.

47   In the Avant-Propos of Jacqueline Pascal, he explains his enormous enterprise and justifies his choice of Pascal: "First, she represents for us the women of the first half of the century, the contemporaries of Richelieu, Descartes and Corneille, who were not women writers, but who had an infinite amount of *esprit*, with strength and grandeur spread throughout; who, without knowing how to write and without ever learning it like those who followed them, when by necessity they took up the pen, found in their mind and heart admirable traits and often entire pages that the greatest writers would envy" (p. iv). Pascal is thus especially valued for not being one of those detestable "femmes-auteurs." In reality, however, she did produce a number of works that were translated and published by the University of Chicago Press in 2003.

48   Mme de Chevreuse is an exception: "We do not offer Mme de Chevreuse as a model to follow" he specifies. But Cousin is not worried that his biography will inspire unwanted

behavior among his female readers because in his opinion, no one could follow in her shoes in the nineteenth century even if they aspired to. (*Mme de Chevreuse*, Paris, 1856), p. viii.

49 *Jacqueline Pascal*, (Paris, 1856), p. 4.

50 *Jacqueline Pascal*, pp. 4–5.

51 In his introduction to *La Jeunesse de Mme de Longueville*, Cousin states that he conducted his research "with the perseverence born of passion" (Paris, 1869), p. v.

52 Victor Cousin, *Mme de Sablé* (Paris, 1859), pp. x–xii, xiv.

53 Some of Sablé's maxims are included in editions of La Rochefoucauld's. Arthur Chandler provides Sablé's corpus of eighty-one maxims and their English translation on-line, thus taking them out of the shadow of La Rochefoucauld's works.

54 Cousin cites La Rochefoucauld's self-portrait where the author of the maxims himself extolls the benefits of reading and critiquing in the context of worldly society: "'I like reading in general, and above all I find extreme satisfaction in reading with a *personne d'esprit*, because this way one thinks at all times about what one is reading, and from the reflections one makes the most likable and useful conversation develops ... The conversation of *honnêtes* people is one of the pleasures that touches me the most'" (p. 145). He does not, however, develop La Rochefoucauld's remarks.
    Cousin does attribute the move from Roman and Greek history to the use of French history in French narrative to Montpensier and her collaboration with Segrais on *Les Nouvelles françaises*: "This was already a step towards a literature that is truer and more national; it is these short stories that prepared and led to *Mlle de Montpensier* and *La Princesse de Clèves* a few years later" (*Sablé*, p. 74). But Cousin undermines Montpensier as a writer, stating that "Mlle, having nothing better to do, busied herself with literature" while she was exiled at St Fargeau after the Fronde. Segrais is given the principal responsibility for transforming what Cousin portrays as a simple game among women into a work of literature (*Mme de Sablé*, pp. 72–3).

55 Ibid., pp. 188–90.

56 In the body of the biography, he does recount a moment when M. d'Andilly called upon Sablé to judge his translation, stating that "he sent a copy to the [woman] who was known as the best judge of literary works" (*Sablé*, p. 230). Such a statement does not correspond to the dominant portrait Cousin paints throughout the biography, and would be confusing were the reader not to delve into the tiny print of the appendices.

57 Victor Cousin, *La Société française d'après le Grand Cyrus* (Paris), p. 25.

58 Joan DeJean discusses the continued popularity of Scudéry's novels in "Classical Reeducation." As I noted in the previous chapter, Villedieu's popularity extended well into the nineteenth century.

59 Verona, *Les "salons" de Sainte-Beuve*. I will have much occasion to draw upon Verona's insights in the following analysis of Sainte-Beuve.

60 C. Planté, *La petite soeur de Balzac: Essai sur la femme auteur* (Paris, 1989), Mona Ozouf, *Les mots de Femmes* (Paris, 1995).

61 Verona notes that "his eight hundred articles with three hundred characters offer a sampling of the best *esprits* of French society as it appeared in the nineteenth century." *Les Salons de Sainte-Beuve*, p. 29.

62 *Causeries du lundi*, "Mme de Maintenon" (Paris, 1955), vol. 4, pp. 386–7.

63 As Verona remarks: "The critic's preference leans less towards women of genius than to those women writers who don't see themselves as such, such as Mme de Rémusat, Mme de Guizot, Mme de Duras or who speak, but don't write such as Mme de Récamier, or

who write little, as a pastime, such as the princess Mathilde, the protector of artists and writers" (*Le Critique et ses muses*, p. 36).

Verona cites Charles de Rémusat's succinctly expressed opinion of women and their destined place: "'The life of a woman, and especially of a happy woman, is always short to recount. Society, in accord with nature, did not separate women's happiness from their peace of mind, and their destiny is almost always determined in the shadows of obligations, affections, domestic interests.'" From *Introduction à M. et Mme Guizot*, le Temps passé (Paris, 1887), p. 5, as cited by Verona, p. 120.

64   And as Verona points out, the majority of these "private" musings entered the literary field through the efforts of the male literary establishment or male relatives. Such effacement of women's active participation in literary creation simply enhanced the woman writer's reputation in the eyes of male critics. She could be valued because her intention was never to publish but only to remain in the shadows, conforming to the true "destiny" of a woman, to return to Cousin's formulation.

65   In his "Lettres de Madame de Graffigny à Voltaire à Cirey," he states, "French literature is very rich if you follow it in these genres a bit secondary (journals, correspondences, memoirs) which are related to society and to the rhythm of life. This is the way, by coming back to it often, to penetrate it and to traverse it in many directions." As cited by Verona, p. 184.

66   As Verona remarks, "His preference is for those who remain feminine while writing, and who write the way they speak" (p. 191).

67   "Mémoires et correspondance de Madame d'Einay," as cited by Verona, p. 199.

68   Verona, p. 199.

69   As he does with Graffigny, for example. See Verona, pp. 201–2.

70   "Madame de Sévigné" in *Portraits de femmes* (Paris,1845), p. 8.

71   According to Sainte-Beuve, they were simply showing Scudéry the respect due to an older woman. *Causeries du lundi*, "Mademoiselle de Scudéry" (Paris: 1855), vol. 4, p. 139.

72   Ibid., pp. 139–40.

73   Ibid., p. 121.

74   Ibid., p. 132.

75   Ibid., p. 133.

76   Ibid., p. 134.

77   Verona, p. 189. She also remarks that Sainte-Beuve "dares to often ask this 'very French' question: Was she pretty? Question that provokes an incursion into the woman's love life or an analysis of the emotional literature that represents her work" (pp. 189–90). The "French" question will prove to be particularly problematic with respect to Madeleine de Scudéry, as we shall see.

78   *Causeries du lundi*, "Saint-Evremond et Ninon" (Paris, 1855), vol. 4, p. 174.

79   Even when he does treat a woman whose salon was associated with literary production, Sainte-Beuve's tendency is to elide this conception of the salon as literary or philosophical laboratory in favor of a portrait that depicts rivalries among salon figures, or focuses on the love letters that emanated from such gatherings, in sum, "la petite histoire" of salon life. One certainly does not have the impression that any serious discussions took place in salons such as those of Mme Geoffrin or Mlle de Lespinasse, or that these gatherings influenced the course of French thought, as Dena Goodman has convincingly shown that they have. See Verona, p. 204 and Dena Goodman.

80   Verona remarks that "… Sainte-Beuve looks for models, especially in the seventeenth century, and finds one in the small and popular salon of Mme de Sablé, La Rochefoucauld's

friend, also withdrawn from the world and surrounded by her faithful acquaintences" (Verona, p. 118).

81 It is interesting to note that "M. de la Rochefoucauld" appears in *Portraits de femmes* (Paris, 1845), pp. 288–321.

82 Ibid., p. 309.

83 Verona, p. 123. Many salons in the eighteenth century actually discouraged female participation, something that would have been impossible to imagine in the seventeenth century. Verona cites in this regard the salon of the duchesse de Rauzan, from which women were excluded from 4–6 when only "hommes de qualité" could join in "serious discussions." In the evening, "la more frivolous company gathered" (p. 123). The same could be said of the princesse Mathilde's salon, where most women were considered intellectual inferiors, and thus unwelcome in the salon (Verona, p. 139).

84 As Verona remarks, "Conversation surrupticiously became a criterion of sexual difference since women's works could not escape the accusation of being chatter" (p. 160).

85 "She sets about correcting them in her heart." Sainte-Beuve, "M. de la Rochefoucauld," in *Portraits de femmes*, p. 310.

86 "Madame de Lafayette," in *Portraits de femmes*, p. 249.

87 Ibid., p. 251. He also asserts that La Rochefoucauld and Lafayette composed the novel together (p. 274).

88 Critics such as Sainte-Beuve value women's writing, but only if it can be conflated with their life story and if it expresses the "natural" sentiments so unique to women. Sainte-Beuve, for example, admires Mme Valmore precisely because "she doesn't reason, she follows her emotions" (as cited by Verona p. 208). Verona astutely concludes that "the 'cry from the heart' is for him the proof of a woman's natural talent" (Verona, p. 208).

89 As Verona remarks, Sainte-Beuve shared his century's opinion of the "natural" place for women: "confined to the private sphere, her true sphere, which she abandons if she becomes an author, thus a public figure: 'Everything a woman gives to the public, she takes away from respect and true happiness'" p. 127.

90 Antoine Compagnon, *La Troisième République des lettres* (Paris, 1983), p. 8.

91 Verona states that Sainte-Beuve "lays the foundation for nineteenth-century criticism." She goes on to cite G. Delfau and A. Roche who remarked in 1977 that by 1860, Sainte-Beuve was acknowledged as a literary "institution" (p. 24). Verona elaborates on Sainte-Beuve's role as consecrated by the following century: "Sainte-Beuve the institution, the one who makes and breaks literary careers, who decides the hierarchies of literary history to be used by succeeding centuries; this is the image that the twentieth century takes up and replicates" (p. 24).

92 Georges Mongrédien, *Madeleine de Scudéry et son salon* (Paris, 1946), p. 148.

93 As Mongrédien states, "if literature occupies a large place in the activities of the participants of the hôtel de Rambouillet, it is above all in function of the pleasure literature can give and the amusement it can produce." *La vie de société au XVIIe et XVIIIe siècles* (Paris, 1950), p. 49.

94 Mongrédien, *Madeleine de Scudéry*, p. 145–6. Such qualities are often associated with France as a nation. In *Citizens of Sovereignty*, Daniel Gordon interprets Montgrédien's use of the term bourgeois differently. Of Scudéry's salon he remarks that "the mixing of ranks appears as one of its salient features ... Scudéry herself was a noble, yet she never lived at court. George Mongrédien called her salon 'bourgeois' meaning not that its membership was entirely middle-class, but that it contributed to the rise of a fashionable urban milieu separate from the court at Versailles" (p. 108). Gordon thus places a positive

slant on Mongrédien's very negative assessment, which certainly does not seem to be referring to the rise of a different milieu but rather to innate personal qualities attributable to class differences. As we shall see, Gordon's analysis here illustrate the lasting power of the myths created around Scudéry and Rambouillet. Rambouillet's salon, according to those who frequented it, also mixed ranks and Scudéry, as we shall see, was actually as much a part of court society as Rambouillet.

95   Mongrédien states: "Thus in the exaltation of this feminine ideal born at the hôtel de Rambouillet, Mlle de Scudéry's salon's bid even higher. Worldly life at the beginning of the century had contributed to women's liberation ... They had access to social life. This freeedom of women, sketched out in aristocratic society, became an emancipation among our bourgeoisie. With them preciosity took on the characteristics of a feminine protest movement." *Madeleine de Scudéry*, p. 149.

96   Roger Picard, p. 62.

97   Cousin, *La Jeunesse de Mme de Longueville*, 7th edition (Paris, 1869), p. 124.

98   Aronson, *Rambouillet*, p. 30. According to Georges Mongrédien, the seventeenth century had at least sixty-two important salons but the only ones we remember are Rambouillet and Scudéry.

99   *Correspondance de Chapelain*, from *Documents Inedits sur l'histoire de France*, ed. Ph. Tamizey de Larroque (Paris: Imprimerie nationale, MDCCLXXXIII), vol. 222, pp. 148–9. See my discussion of Chapelain's portrayals of the *ruelles* in Chapter 1.

100   Lambert, *Réflections sur les femmes*, p. 43.

101   As cited by Roger Picard, *Les salons littéraires*, p. 62. Picard goes on to cite Boileau as recognizing the function of literary arbitration in the *chambre bleue*, although he associates it primarily with a male *habitué*, Montausier, the marquise's son-in-law.

102   Pons-Augustin Alletz, *L'Esprit des femmes célèbres du siècle de Louis XIV et de celui de Louis XV, jusquà présent* (Paris, 1768), II, p. 93.

103   Cited by Aronson, *La Marquise de Rambouillet*, p. 32.

104   As cited by Aronson, ibid., p. 35.

105   As cited by Aronson, ibid., p. 37. It is interesting to note that this portrait of the *chambre bleue* and its relationship to literature does not become the dominant one, due perhaps to the fact that the person who advances this vision is Madeleine de Scudéry.

106   Aronson states that the marquise opened her salon around 1613 and received "a rather hetereogenous company" from the beginning (ibid., p. 99). She goes on to specify that "foreign writers received a warm welcome in this house where their works were read and understood" (p. 100). There were just as many women as men: "This anecdote proves that Arthénice, from the beginning, received not only the chosen society that one would expect, but a fairly mixed group, princes and the bourgeoisie, or writers as different as Malherbe and Neufgermain. With Julie's arrival, those from court became more numerous, without making the gatherings more homogenous or more elevated" (p. 118).

In *Salons européens: Les beaux moments d'une culture féminine disparue*, Verena von der Heyden-Rynsch remarks that the salon de Rambouillet was not just frequented by the nobility: "It was there, at the hôtel de Rambouillet, that representatives from diverse social classes met, old nobility and petite noblesse, men of letters and financiers, government officials and clerics, scholars and artists, this is where society was democratized" (p. 37).

107   Aronson, *La Marquise de Rambouillet*, p. 206. She offers an explanation for the tendency to say the salon had already stopped functioning as of the early 1650s, remarking that the purpose of stating its early demise is to disassociate the salon de Rambouillet from the

composition of *Les Précieuses ridicules*. If the marquise had stopped receiving before *Les Précieuses*, then Molière probably did not satirize it. Aronson thus points to a desire to keep the marquise pure. Contemporaries, however, negate such an effort. Aronson points out that Loret, for example, writes about the Dauphin going to the salon in 1662. In his *Mémoires*, Huet speaks of the "éclat de l'hôtel de Rambouillet à son arrivée à Paris, après la mort du marquis" (the influence of the hôtel de Rambouillet as soon as he arrived in Paris, after the marquis's death), and in 1660 he was received by the marquise herself (p. 211). In 1664 "elle invita Molière à représenter l'Ecole des maris et L'impromptu de Versailles" (she invited Molière to present l'Ecole des maris and l'Impromptu de Versailles at the hôtel) (p. 212).

Roger Picard identifies the "most brilliant period" of the *chambre bleue* as 1624–48. (*Les Salons littéraires*, p. 26).

108 As cited by Aronson, *Mademoiselle de Scudéry*, pp. 88–9.
109 Huet describes her as "cette dame qui joignait à des vertus admirables, à l'esprit le plus heureux une modestie singulière" (this woman who joined a singular modesty to admirable virtue and the most fortunate mind). Pierre-Daniel Huet, *Mémoires* (Toulouse, 1993), pp. 86–7.
110 Charles Sorel, *La Bibliothèque française* (Paris: 1664), p. 161.
111 Sévigné (Paris: Pléaide), I, p. 280, 28 June 1671.
112 Sévigné, III, pp. 104–5.
113 Sévigné, 11 September 1684, III, pp. 134–5. Cousin attributes such hyberbolic discourse to Sévigné's impressionable age when she first met Scudéry. One finds it difficult, however, to believe that this first impression would have lasted over a lifetime, given that this letter was composed near the end of Sévigné's life.
114 Aronson, *Mademoiselle de Scudéry*, p. 47. Cousin, however, dismisses *Clélie* as inferior to *Le Grand Cyrus* because supposedly *Clélie* represents Scudéry's own society, which Cousin characterizes as "inférieure et bourgeoise." The novel is thus impossible to read because one could hardly be interested in a world so different from the aristocratic one reflected in *Le Grand Cyrus*. Of course, the fact that Cousin did not find a key to *Clélie* and could not use such a key to further his career might also have hindered his enjoyment.
115 As cited by Aronson, *Mademoiselle de Scudéry*, p. 298.
116 As cited by Aronson, ibid., p. 47 from the introduction to the English translation of *Conversations sur divers sujets*, ed. Ferrant Spence, 1683.
117 Aronson, ibid., p. 69. As Aronson remarks, to judge by this portrait, Madeleine was not nearly as unattractive as future generations portrayed her to be.
118 Cousin states that Georges was eventually admitted to the French Academy in 1650, replacing Vaugelas, not because of his own literary genius, but because of his sister's many powerful friends at the Academy. *La Société française au dix-septième siècle*, p. 114.
119 Aronson, *Mademoiselle de Scudéry*, p. 74.
120 Buffet, *Eloge des illustres savantes*, p. 213. Buffet praises France stating: "Notre florissant royaume, le premier de l'Europe capable de satisfaire les désirs et la curiosité de toutes les nations qui se rencontrent depuis la naissance de cette monarchie, combien d'augustes, d'habiles et de savantes princesses ont donné des marques de la beauté de leur esprit" (Our thriving realm, the first in Europe capable of satisfyng the desire and the curiosity of all the nations ... how many august, clever, and knowledgeable princesses have displayed the beauty of their mind). In 1647, Conrart wrote to Rivet, stating: "quoique la plupart des dames de condition fassent aujourd'hui profession de n'être pas ignorantes et de bien parler et de bien écrire, je ne pense pas qu'il y en ait aucune qui la surpasse" (Even though most

women of a certain station today profess not to be ignorant and to write and speak well, I don't think there is a single one who surpasses her). Cited in the Kerviler and Barthelémy edition of Conrart's correspondence, p. 86.

121 Aronson notes that from the mid-nineteenth-century there was a flurry of activity, citing the first edition, albeit censored, of the *Historiettes*, Monmerque's important edition of Sévigné's letters, and the discovery of texts at the Arsenal, Conrart's works, and Livet's edition of the *Dictionnaire des Précieuses*. An edition of the Gazette de Tendre was under preparation, but the manuscript disappeared at the beginning of the twentieth century without having been published; *Mademoiselle de Scudéry*, p. 64.

122 Tallemant in fact attributes the truth value of the *Historiettes* to the marquise de Rambouillet, whom he cites as his principal source: "c'est d'elle que je tiens la plus grande et la meilleure partie de ce que j'ai écrit et que j'écrirai dans ce livre" (It is from her that I received the greatest and best part of what I have written and that I will write in this book). *Historiettes*, I, p. 455.

123 Tallemant states: "L'hôtel de Rambouillet était, pour ainsi dire, le théâtre de tous leurs divertissements, et c'était le rendez-vous de ce qu'il y avait de plus galant à la Cour, et de plus poli parmi les beaux esprits du siècle" (The hôtel de Rambouillet was ... the theatre of all their amusements, and it was the rendez-vous of everything that was the most gallant at court, and the most polite among the *beaux esprits*). *Historiettes* (Paris: Pléiade), p. 443.

124 *Historiettes*, vol. 2 p. 1465 n. 5.

125 Aronson advances that the nineteenth century elevated the *chambre bleue* over all its contemporary, especially bourgeois salons which Mlle de Scudéry's *samedis* were seen to epitomize. *La Marquise de Rambouillet*, pp. 37–8. The split between Scudéry and Rambouillet dates primarily from the nineteenth century, when the elevation of the canon of seventeenth-century literature began in earnest.

126 Cousin, *La Société française au dix-septième siècle*, vol. I, p. 259.

127 Cousin states: "Civility was necessary to lead the century to perfection. The hôtel de Rambouillet was the leader." *La jeunesse de Mme de Longueville* (Paris, 1869), p. 124.

128 Cousin, ibid., pp. 126–7.

129 In this refashioning of Rambouillet's image, Aronson remarks that certain characteristics had to be eliminated, notably those that did not conform to nineteenth-century formulations of the perfect woman. *Rambouillet*, p. 13.

130 Georges Mongrédien continues to support this myth in the twentieth century. He identifies the decline of the hôtel de Rambouillet as the period of the Fronde, due to the war but also to the death of Voiture, the marriage of Julie, the marquise's daughter, and the death of Mlle Paulet. *Madeleine de Scudéry et son salon*, p. 64. In her study of the salons, Marie Gougy-François echoes Mongrédien and Batiffol, among others, and states that the *chambre bleue* functioned primarily from 1638–45. *Les Grande Salons féminins* (Paris, 1965), p. 13.

131 Genlis, *De L'influence des femmes*, pp. 61–3.

132 Another perspective occasionally surfaces especially in scholarly works, but does not represent the general public opinion. Timmermans cites Alain Viala who describes the salon de Rambouillet in the following manner: "... all well-known writers in the first half of the century, either by frequent visits or by less direct contact, tried to obtain recognition of their literary merit from this group." *Rambouillet*, p. 77.

133 Louis Batiffol, "Le Salon de la marquise de Rambouillet au XVIIe siècle," in *Les Grands Salons Littéraires*, pp. 36; 44–5.

134 The five salons that merit study are: Rambouillet and the salon de Mme de la Sablière in the seventeenth, and the gatherings of Tencin, Geoffrin, and du Deffand in the eighteenth. One wonders how the editor interprets "littéraire ...."
135 Louis Batiffol, "Le Salon de la Marquise de Rambouillet," pp. 45–6.
136 Picard, *Les Salons littéraires*, p. 27.
137 Ibid., p. 53.
138 Ibid., pp. 26 and 53.
139 Ibid., pp. 40 and 52.
140 Aronson, *Rambouillet*, p. 225.
141 Aronson, ibid., p. 218.
142 Aronson, ibid., p. 231.
143 Lambert, *Histoire littéraire du règne de Louis XIV*, vol. 9, p. 46.
144 Ibid., vol. 9, p. 46.
145 Genlis, *De l'influence des femmes*, p. 91.
146 As cited by Aronson, *Scudéry*, p. 64.
147 *La Société française au dix-septième siècle*, vol. II, pp. 121–2.
148 As cited by Aronson, *Scudéry*, p. 64. As we have seen, in his preface to his works, Cousin openly states that he has no respect for women who write.
149 Picard, *Les Salons littéraires*, p. 72.
150 Verena von der Heyden-Rynsch, *Salons européeans*, p. 42.
151 Ibid., p. 43.
152 Ibid. p. 43.
153 Ibid., p. 45.
154 It should be remembered that during his own lifetime Boileau did not possess the status he currently enjoys. As Aronson remarks, Scudéry's downfall can be attributed in many ways to the elevation of Boileau to canonical status. Aronson, *Scudéry*, p. 54. Aronson states that Boileau's contemporaries "did not accord Boileau the place that posterity has made for him). *Scudéry*, p. 56.
155 Roxana Verona, *Sainte-Beuve et ses muses*, p. 17.
156 Ibid., p. 17.
157 Louis Gillet, *Les Grands Salons littéraires*, p. 9.
158 Ibid. p. 9.
159 Ibid., p.11.
160 Ibid., p. 12.
161 Batiffol, "Le salon de la marquise de Rambouillet," p. 28. We will return to his description of the marquise later.
162 Ibid., pp. 77–8.
163 Roger Picard's work is very frequently cited by those interested in the salons. Elena Russo, for example, frequently refers to Picard in her discussion of the seventeenth-century salons. The exception to this general trend in literary and historical scholarship is the work produced by American scholars such as Joan DeJean, Nancy K. Miller, Elizabeth Goldsmith, and Gabrielle Verdier, to name only a few. Recently French scholars such as Myriam Maître, Linda Timmermans, and Delphine Denis, to name the most prominent, have followed the lead of the American-based scholarship, in conjunction with British scholarship, and have been working to revise the scholarship bequeathed them by such voices as Picard and Montgrédien.
164 Picard, *Les salons littéraires*, p. 135.
165 Ibid., p. 27.

166 Of the seventeenth-century salons he states: "from simple gatherings of cultivated people
    ... they were imperceptibly transformed into veritable small literary academies, where
    authors came to try their creations and from which emanated critical judgments on literary
    works." Ibid., p. 101.

167 Paradoxically, Picard notes that Corneille read *Pulchérie* at Mme de Lafayette's salon and
    Molière read *Les Femmes Savantes*, although he does not give a source for this information.
    This would seem to contradict his affirmation that only lesser talents frequented the salons.
    Picard distinguishes the eighteenth-century salons from their predecessors by the quality
    of their participants: "On the contrary in the eighteenth century, the foremost authors
    frequent the salons." Ibid., p. 139.

168 von der Heyden-Rynsch, *Salons européens*, p. 42.

169 André Burguière and Jacques Revel, eds, *Histoire de la France: Choix culturels et mémoire
    1993* (Paris, 2000), p. 112.

170 In *Histoire et Mémoire*, Le Goff analyzes the influence of nationalism during the period
    on historiography. See in particular pp. 254–7.

171 Ibid., p. 109.

172 David Bell traces the relationship between education and nationalism back to the
    Revolution. He states that "particularly under the Terror, in 1793–94, plans proliferated
    for reeducating the French, providing them with what we would now call a common
    national culture ... With the fall of the Jacobins in 1794, the programs were in large
    measure abandoned. Nonetheless, they prefigured the extensive and ambitious nation-
    building programs undertaken by later French regimes, particularly the Third Repubic
    of 1871–1940" (*The Cult of the Nation*, p. 15). Bell convincingly shows throughout his
    book how "the early nationalists sought to create a new form of civic harmony and ...
    concluded that the solution lay in giving a large and disparate community what we would
    call a shared culture-common language, customs, beliefs, traditions" (p. 21). I would add
    "a shared history," and "literary history" to his list.

173 Bell attributes the difference between the processes that formed national consciousness
    in France and other countries to education: "... French republican nationalism owed its
    peculiar character and extraordinary vigor, from the late eighteenth century to the mid-
    twentieth, precisely to the extraordinary sense of mission and purpose that animated its
    principal agents: adminstrators, soldiers, and above all educators. In this sense, France's
    experience has differed greatly from that of its neighbors. Generations of teachers formed
    in the *écoles normales* were trained to see themselves not merely as instructors, but as the
    "black hussars of the Republic" sent out to convert the young and to form them into good
    republican French citizens." *The Cult of the Nation in France*, p. 207.

Chapter 4

Disseminating a National Past: Teaching *Le Grand Siècle*

Nos classiques, ce sont les écrivains du XVIIe siècle; et non pas tous, on le pense bien, mais seulement les meilleurs.

L. Petit de Julleville, 1900[1]

"La Patrie, c'est la France dans le passé, la France dans le présent, la France dans l'avenir. La Patrie je l'aime de tout mon coeur" (The homeland is France of the past, France of the present, France of the future. I love the homeland with all my heart).[2] These powerful words, inscribed by Ernest Lavisse in his influential *Histoire de France*, attest to a shift in national consciousness that took place in nineteenth-century France.[3] The word "patrie" (homeland) evoked emotional connotations and national pride for historians such as Lavisse. In the seventeenth century, the word did not carry such resonnances.[4] Furetière, for example, simply defines it as "le pays où on est né; et il se dit tant du lieu particulier, que de la Province et de l'Empire ou de l'Etat où on a pris naissance. Un Français qui s'en retourne de l'Inde en Europe, dit qu'il s'en retourne à sa patrie" (the country where one was born; and it is used to refer to the specific place, such as the province, the empire, or the state where one was born. A Frenchman who returns from India to Europe says that he returns to his homeland).[5] "Europe," "l'Etat," "la Province," "le pays" all refer equally to "patrie." There is no effort to delineate the concept further, nor is there any emotional affiliation with this particular "patrie." In fact, Furetière explains that "patrie" can possess such strong emotions, but not in the context of the France of his day. The affiliation emotion/*patrie* is reserved in his definition for the past, specifically for those considered to be the Ancients by the seventeenth century: "Les Romains et les Grecs avaient grande amour pour la patrie, se dévouaient pour la patrie. Quintus Curtius Chevalier Romain se jetta dans un abîme pour le salut de sa patrie. On dit figurément que Rome est la patrie commune des Chrétiens" (The Romans and the Greeks had great love for the homeland, devoted themselves to the homeland. Quint threw himself into an abyss to save his homeland. Figuratively it is said that Rome is the common homeland of Christians). Furetière's use of the past tense for his classical example makes it clear that such sentiment is no longer part of the consciousness of his own time.

When Furetière's definition is contrasted with Lavisse's use of the term, the redefinition of "patrie" becomes strikingly clear. Lavisse resembles Furetière's Roman soldier, devoted to a "patrie" he envisions not only as his birthplace, but as his nation. The tinting of "patrie" with nationalist ideology is a phenomenon that developed out of the Revolution, but only crystallized in France in the nineteenth century.[6] The fact that one finds this formulation in one of the most important histories of the day, a history that would form the minds of generations of French citizens, reveals the strong alliance between historical narrative and national identity during this period.[7] In composing a historical narrative to imbue readers and students with a particular sense of "patrie," historians like Lavisse worked to shape the image of "France in the past," constructing a narrative that would conform to the "patrie" they were defining. This molding of the past to reflect a collective sense of "patrie" was meant to be long-lasting and determine "France in the future." The seventeenth century proved to be an essential building block of "patrie," but in need of revisionist shaping if it were to constitute the "patrie" someone like Lavisse could love so profoundly.

* * * * *

From its inception at the end of the eighteenth and primarily during the nineteenth century, France's centralized educational system has privileged one century's literature over all others: the seventeenth century's, or more specifically the period corresponding to the apogee of the reign of the Sun King, roughly 1661–80. Even today, the classics from the seventeenth century are the best known among French students.[8] From curricula in primary and secondary schools to preparation for national exams, the seventeenth century has been selected as the one century that must be transmitted to future generations as the nation's intellectual capital. While other centuries were added at the beginning of the twentieth century, "classique" (classic) still has particular affiliations with le Grand Siècle.[9] We have already seen the central place that continues to be accorded to Molière. Classical theatre in general is the most frequently taught genre, a fact that has the effect of identifying the seventeenth century primarily with this one genre in the minds of the French. The national *aggrégation* exam used to select the nation's top teachers and professors emphasizes the "classiques" and reduces the century's literary field to a few names. Similarly the pedagogical programs put in place from the beginning of the nineteenth century reserved the lion's share of study for the seventeenth century pantheon. As Martine Jey has shown, from 1803–80 authors from the seventeenth century constituted almost 70 per cent of official educational programs. The eighteenth century was next with about 20 per cent, with the rest devoted to the study of manuals of rhetoric. After 1880, with the reforms put into place beginning with Jules Ferry, other centuries were included, but the seventeenth century still constituted over half of the work on programs.[10] In the list of authors, Corneille, Racine, Molière and Boileau appear the most frequently, both before and after 1880.[11] Educational models are decisively associated with the great reign of Louis XIV. While others can potentially find a place, government officials at the end of the nineteenth century exhort great care when choosing these less-than-unanimous choices.[12] To stray from the accepted models of a very limited conception of classicism is to risk presenting students with less than acceptable morals and examples. Jey remarks that, as educators and administrators were revising the architecture of the national educational system at the end of the nineteenth century, debates as to whether or not to expand the literary curriculum beyond the seventeenth century elicited powerful sentiment and genuine worry. One report in 1895 portrays particularly well this anxiety associated with what influence other literary texts might have on a malleable public:

> If one goes too far in either direction, doesn't one risk appearing to invite professors and students to take too many seductive wanderings far from those classic centuries that remain the citadel and sanctuary for serious studies of French letters?[13]

The seventeenth century became a "citadel" and a "sanctuary" in which reposes the essence of Frenchness to be tranmitted. To permit "seductive wanderings" into other centuries might give students and professors alike an alternative version of France's "national genius." I would argue that the Parnassus of authors that constituted the teachable seventeenth century was a "fortress" and a "citadel" in another, equally important, way. As only a very select number of authors were considered worthy of inclusion, namely Corneille, Racine, Molière, Boileau, Bossuet, La Fontaine, and a few others, the rest of the literary field lay outside of the fortress. "Seductive wanderings" might encourage students to look beyond these models even within the confines of classicism and thus change the image of the Grand Siècle that had been so carefully shaped for the nation's memory. As we will see when we turn to specific manuals, the seventeenth century is constantly encased in the strict dictates of classicism. "Equilibre," (balance) "la maîtrise," (mastery) "la clarté," (clarity) "la mesure," (moderation) and "raison" (reason) (as defined by Boileau) are all touted as the qualities of *l'âge classique* as expressed by its best authors. To allow for other authors and the tendencies and values they expressed in their works is to lose the "mastery" over the composition of France's model period.

Implicit in the use of pedagogical manuals and anthologies is an effort to inculcate a shared sense of values and heritage. As Emmanuel Fraisse remarks, the choice of authors to include in classrooms as well as on the standardized programs for national exams, although often not explicitly expressed, reflects an effort to transmit a shared collective sense of *le patrimoine*.[14] In the case of France, one of the values that has been transmitted with particular success has been the exceptional nature of France's Grand Siècle and the pride associated with the authors who contributed to this highpoint of French cultural dominance. The seventeenth century literary field is the ultimate embodiment of France's *génie national*. It is frequently touted at the end of the nineteenth century as the period that is the most "French," when France developed a literature entirely on its own, as opposed to the eighteenth century, for example, which was too influenced by England to incarnate true "Frenchness."[15] Studying the selected seventeenth-century literary corpus provides a common *patrimoine*. As Jey has advanced, the prefaces of pedagogical manuals and official governmental instructions concerning education at the end of the nineteenth and beginning of the twentieth centuries constantly reaffirm the relationship between patriotism and the study of the seventeenth-century classics: "But even more than national literature, it is classic literature that is to be studied, because it best incarnates *l'esprit* of France."[16] The study of these French classical models will produce a "man of taste" and *l'honnête homme*, figures produced in the seventeenth century, but who become models for French citizens in the nineteenth.[17] Given these strong ties between patriotism, *francité*, and the literature of the seventeenth century that best expressed this and was best able to transmit it to future generations, any attempt to alter the context of the classics much less present alternative models, was, and in many instances still is, met with the utmost suspicion.

Scholars have recently been drawn to the question of how the "classics" of French literature came to be constituted and, in the United States in particular, how women were systematically eliminated from the corpus of seventeenth-century writers, considered to be the models of "Frenchness, particularly as French literature became an essential part of the pedagogical mission."[18] The elimination or at least marginalization of women writers is, however, part of a larger story of a reconceptualization of an entire period of French literary history. If the seventeenth century and its literature were to serve as a model literary milieu for the creation of a concept of "Frenchness," not only female literary production but female influence in any form needed to be eliminated, or reconfigured to conform to a more traditional, stereotypical, and gendered ideology. More important, perhaps, than eliminating women's actual literary works was the suppression of the female voices that had united with those of their male contemporaries to create what were consistently touted as the greatest works of French literature. Corneille, Racine, Molière, Boileau, and La Fontaine were separated from the unique literary milieu that had influenced the creation of their works, and made to represent the great century of Louis XIV, but without full acknowledgment of the myriad voices, male and female, that had combined to create this literary scene unique to France.[19] This process of re-membering the seventeenth century literary scene was thus much more than putting women's works in their separate, inferior place. It was about reconceptualizing a century to make its literature worthy of being the centerpiece of a French educational system and a model for Frenchness. The very quality often touted as unique to France, that is, the particular status of women in the cultural arena, was eliminated from this model for the nation.

In a process that began in the eighteenth century, but reached its apogee in the nineteenth, France composed its canon of "classics" designed to illustrate the hallmarks of a nation and the character of its people. As recent critics have pointed out, the seventeenth century would not have designated the literary products of its own time as "classics" in the modern sense of the term.[20] Such an appellation was reserved for the great writers of Antiquity. And in perusing the various literary compliations of the period, and listening to the many voices that weighed in on the writers of the day, it is clear that had the seventeenth century actually composed a list of the best writers of their illustrious century, it would bear little resemblance to the ones their eighteenth and particularly their nineteenth-century successors comprised, and to which most of today's public still adheres. For example, Scudéry would no doubt have figured on everyone's but Boileau's list, whereas Boileau himself might not have been chosen with such unanimous enthusiasm. Obviously every century has its own sense of literary taste. But in the case of the literature associated with seventeenth-century France, what is striking is the clear effort by succeeding centuries to mold a literary scene and accompanying list of "great works" that could be used to illustrate the genius of a nation. In this process, the literary opinions of future generations were forced upon a past and made to appear universal. In the historical and literary process I have been tracing, it is less important who becomes elevated as the deities of French literature and more what happens to the entire context in which they evolved. Specifically, when Molière, Boileau, and others become representative of the Grand Siècle, the entire image of the literary field of the seventeenth century undergoes a transformation. And in this transformation, not only were women's literary works dismissed as minor, outdated, and unworthy of readers, but more importantly their acts as agents in the literary field were ridiculed, neglected, and even negated.

As recent studies have shown, as early as the eighteenth century many literary works of "the century of Louis the Great" were already designated as "classics," although not in the original sense of the word. According to Furetière, "classique" in the seventeenth century was reserved only for those authors taught in classes, that is, authoritive models inherited from Antiquity:

> Classique: adj. qui ne se dit guère que des Auteurs qu'on lit dans les classes, dans les écoles, ou qui ont une grande autorité. St Thomas, le maître des sentences, sont des auteurs classiques qu'on cite dans les écoles de théologie. Aristote en philosophie, Ciceron et Virgile dans les Humanités. Ce sont des auteurs classiques … Ce nom appartient particulièrement aux auteurs qui ont vécu du temps de la République, et sur la fin d'Auguste où regnait la bonne Latinité, qui a commencé à se corrompre du temps des Antonins.

> (Classic: adj. Only refers to the authors read in classes, in schools, or who have great authority. St Thomas, the master of *sentences*, are classic authors read in theology schools. Aristotle in philosophy, Cicero and Virgil in the humanities. These are the classic authors … This name refers especially to authors who lived duirng the time of the republic, and at the end of Augustus's during which good Latinité reigned, which began to become corrupted in the time of the Antonins.)

Such authors were valued as much for their form of their works as the content. As we have seen, while some members of the salon public would have been imbued with such texts, especially those members such as Chapelain who straddled the academic and the worldly spheres, many others, especially women, would have had little occasion to read such authors, and no opportunity to be taught in classes to revere them.[21]

The term "classique," undergoes a transformation in the eighteenth century, however, and becomes less allied with the texts of Antiquity, as well as less associated with the classroom. According to the Robert's *Dictionnaire historique de la langue française,* under the influence of Voltaire and the *Encyclopédie,* the word "classique" becomes associated with French authors during the reign of Louis XIV.[22] Such texts were designated as "classics" not because they were taught in the classroom—French texts were just beginning to be viewed as worthy of inclusion in curricula—but because they illustrated "an art of moderation, of reason" and reflected and imitated the literary genius of the texts of Antiquity.[23] The seventeenth century eventually replaces Antiquity as the model in subsequent usage of the word. As the *Robert historique* remarks, "it is the notion of respect for tradition offered as a model that underlies later usage of the word. In the nineteenth century it applied to those who imitated antiquity, as opposed to the Romantics ... and, by extension, to an art that respects the aesthetic values of the seventeenth century." In these definitions, the seventeenth-century literary scene becomes unified under a general desire to conform to specific, supposedly universally accepted, aesthetic criteria. It reflects what will come to be known as the values of "classicism," which the *Robert historique* defines, following Stendhal's usage in 1817, as "a term in aesthetics, denoting the character of works that refer to the art of antiquity, then equally to that of the seventeenth century. It has come to denote what is harmonious, balanced, respectful of established aesthetic norms and those established in the intellectual and moral domains." A salon public, with the very different values of "good taste" among others, does not correspond to such a limited characterization of an entire literary scene. When historians subsumed seventeenth-century literary production under the rubric of "classicism," they also installed a false sense of order and unanimously accepted standards in "the intellectual and moral domain" of a period that, as we have seen, vigorously disputed notions of *vraisemblance,* literary taste, generic development, the question of truth and literature's role in expressing this truth, to name only a few contentious subjects in the empire of letters. Definitions of *classique* and "classicism" indicate a refashioning of the context of seventeenth-century literary production, a narrowing that corresponds chronologically to the efforts we have seen to reformulate women's roles during the classical period, as well as to the desire to ally the seventeenth century with particular concepts of Frenchness.

The formation of the cultural memory of a nation is evident in these simple but illuminating definitions. This process is long and complex, but it can be, and indeed was, in the case of France, accelerated by certain sociological phenomena. Allied as it was from the beginning with education, the concept of "classic" literature and its association with cultural memory was solidified during the nineteenth century by the French educational system. We have already seen in some of the representative anthologies and histories of the eighteenth and nineteenth centuries how the literary context of what would be designated as the French "classics" underwent a process of re-membering that effectively reduced or eliminated the influential role of the worldly public, women's literary production, and the salons that fostered both. Education consolidated this process and disseminated the new image of a "classicism" that was "harmonious, balanced, respectful of established aesthetic norms," but devoid of the rebellious novel, the worldly public that fostered it, and the women who contributed to the literary scene that gave birth to the genre and to new concepts of *goût* and even *bon sens*. And as of the early 1800s, the educational system in France became highly centralized, ensuring that the future guardians and purveyors of France's literary and cultural capital—young men, and much later, and to a lesser extent, young women—would all look reverently on the same canon of classical authors and view their literary context in the same manner.

In "Les Classiques Scolaires," an article that is part of Pierre Nora's monumental *Les Lieux de mémoire*, Daniel Milo traces the role of the educational system in the formulation and dissemination of France's artistic canon. One of the goals of *Les Lieux de mémoire* is to isolate phenomena that illustrate aspects of France's national character. As Milo convincingly shows, the centralization of France's educational system in the nineteenth century, and in particular its alliance with the state, worked to produce a well-determined literary canon that would determine French outlooks on its past and its culture for more than a century. In many ways, the creation and marketing of "les classiques scolaires" continues to have a strong impact on how the French view their past, in particular their literary culture and especially the period most associated with the "classics," the seventeenth-century France of Louis XIV. As Milo explains, "canonization correlates to the centralization of the school system. The more this system is centralized, the more the canon becomes stable and universal."[24] As this canon becomes more universal, the sense of classic author or text also expands to take on connotations of literary value. Thus an "auteur classique" becomes the equivalent of a "grand auteur" or great author. The more an author is taught, the greater he, and very occasionally she, becomes until no one questions why the author is taught nor the criteria according to which s/he is chosen. From the nineteenth century until very recently, the seventeenth century has been highly disproportionately represented in French educational programs. As Milo states, "the uncontestable models" are those belonging to the century of Louis XIV.[25] And the names of those dominating the educational system throughout the nineteenth century and into the twentieth? Corneille, Pascal, Racine, Molière, and Boileau.[26]

Historians such as Lavisse were in accord with the canon their literary colleagues were establishing. The two disciplines of history and literary history thus worked in tandem. Lavisse, for example, includes a section in his volume on Louis XIV entitled "Les Lettres" (literature). The authors he designates as exemplary are La Rochefoucauld, Retz, Sévigné, Bossuet, Molière, La Fontaine, Racine, and Boileau. The novel is conspicuously absent, as is the literary context that produced these models. As Milo points out, editors and anthologists then as well as today reflect and enhance this educational trend, for the more an author is studied, the more his works are rediscovered, reedited, and republished.[27] More important for our purposes, the establishment and diffusion of this very specific, and I would argue limited, canon of seventeenth-century authors inculcated French students with a certain vision of their country's literary past. Many of these chosen authors were openly critical, even hostile, to the worldly literary public and its authors. In anthologies as well as histories, authors such as Molière and Boileau are studied as isolated examples, not placed in the larger context of the literary field of their day. Even La Fontaine, who was an influential salon figure, is praised for coming to his senses and rejecting his *fables* produced in this worldly milieu in order to be accepted into the French Academy. By excluding all women, with the occasional exception of Sévigné—who, we must remember, is constantly hailed as someone who would have adamantly rejected being considered a writer—from the classical canon, the educational system, supported by the State, ensured the promotion of a monolithic vision of its classical, canonical past.[28]

Milo argues throughout "Les Classiques Scolaires" that the educational system does not create reputations but only disseminates them.[29] According to this view, the choice of Corneille, Racine, Molière and Boileau, among other seventeenth-century representative icons, is not a political one, but one founded upon some kind of intrinsic literary value inherent in these particular authors. At the same time, it is clear from his statistics, that once an author is chosen, his reputation is greatly enhanced as he becomes part of the necessary cultural baggage of a nation. The slippage is evident. If one admits that "auteur classique" (classic author) becomes the equivalent of "grand auteur" (great author), it is difficult to argue that teaching an author, especially in France's centralized educational system, does not create or enhance that author's reputation. In any case, the choice of certain authors as representative of a nation's cultural capital would have a profound effect on how its citizens viewed a particular period, specifically the seventeenth century.

Milo argues that after 1960, the role of the educational system in France changed from one that was designed to equip French citizens with their cultural baggage for a lifetime, to a role in which schools merely prepare students for further study. Thus "relieved of its heavy responsabilities, no longer the guarantor nor the manager of the cultural patrimony, school can be more open to the present."[30] No doubt many of the texts taught in French schools have changed, but not the "classics" of the seventeenth century. Corneille, Racine, and Molière are still cornerstones and consistently cited among France's great authors. The vision of the seventeenth-century literary scene taught in schools has changed little from what was presented in a nineteenth-century classroom, and as a result, the nation's collective memory of its classic past is particularly gendered.

The canon associated with France's highly nationalized system of higher education is indicative of the static vision of the seventeenth century as it is incorporated into the educational system. In an illuminating study, Anne-Marie Thiesse and Hélène Mathieu have traced the changes in the literary programs developed for the *agrégation* national exam, an exam used to assess the knowledge of France's future teachers for both the secondary school level and the college level.[31] They focus on the period 1890–1980, which witnessed changes in the preparation of future teachers and in the exam that prepared them for their missions, as well as the introduction of a new *agrégation* designed specifically for female candidates. If one focuses attention on the inclusion and fate of the seventeenth-century literary world in the general depiction of the *agrégation* depicted by Thiesse and Mathieu, it is clear that, while the exam may have undergone changes, the canon of seventeenth-century French authors has remained static. From the nineteenth century until today, the same "classic" authors are required over and over again for study in the *agrégation*. What has changed primarily is the percentage of these authors on the exam, not the actual authors. As Thiesse and Mathieu point out, until the end of the nineteenth century, the only French literary works deemed worthy of inclusion on this prestigious exam were those from the seventeenth century.[32] Racine, Corneille, Bossuet, Molière, La Fontaine, La Bruyère, Pascal and Boileau were the premier examples used to inculcate literary taste, and rhetoric into the minds of future professors, who, in turn, usually limited their teachings to this well-established and revered canon. Even when the *agrégation* was reformulated at the end of the nineteenth century, these same writers continued to be the primary ones proposed for study of the period that was advanced as "the great century" of French literature. While it is true that the percentage of seventeenth-century authors in the *agrégation* program dropped from a high of 80 per cent in 1890 to roughly 25 per cent in 1914, the prestige of such authors was already well established in the minds of France's pedagogical elite, as well as among the general public. More important than the percentage of seventeenth-century authors included for study is the corpus chosen as worthy of this official honor. Today's exam requires one author per century, and whereas the actual author chosen from the nineteenth and twentieth century can vary considerably, the same names from the seventeenth century appear with regularity, a fact that prompts Thiesse and Mathieu to remark that "time-honored tradition had canonized the classical authors of the classical century."[33]

The process of selection has also "masculinized" the classical canon and the canon of French literature as a whole. More important, the entire seventeenth-century literary scene is viewed through the lens of this limited selection. The list of authors figuring on the *agrégation* program as compiled by Thiesse and Mathieu lists only four women: Sévigné and Lafayette for the seventeenth century and Staël and Marguerite de Navarre for the rest of the female literary tradition, and even these four appeared very infrequently. One can have no sense of all that women were anything but marginal contributors to French literary culture, nor that they exerted any profound or lasting influence on those designated as the purveyors of France's literary heritage. Thiesse and Mathieu attribute Sévigné's inclusion to the fact that the epistolary genre was once considered a particularly useful pedagogical tool, which is no longer the case today. Lafayette is chosen because of the "exemplary character of her heroine, incarnation as she is of the values of the Eternal Feminine (depth of feeling, sacrifice of passion to duty!)."[34] Lafayette's novel can be taught, but only in a fashion that interprets her heroine as a self-sacrificing and subservient woman, an interpretation that many critics, particularly feminist, would reject.[35] Lafayette's inclusion is also perhaps due to the fact that in France her novel is still routinely attributed to the men who surrounded her, namely La Rochefoucauld and Segrais, because she opted not to sign the work.[36] The paupacy of women writers on the *agrégation* program has, in the words of Thiesse and Mathieu, "contributed to a situation in which women teachers are persuaded that great literature is written by men."[37] One can add, for our purposes here, that they are no doubt also persuaded that the "auteurs classiques/grands auteurs," to return to the analogy referred to by the *Robert historique*'s definition of "classique," were all male with the exception of a few women like Lafayette and Sévigné who amused themselves in their leisure by writing letters to a distant daughter and by helping men write novels. As the texts for the *agrégation* are usually taught out of context, and the context in any case for these masterpieces has been reconstructed over the years as male, there is little chance for any student to think otherwise.

The French educational system has thus worked to instill a strong sense of a shared literary past with its citizens, but a past that has been carefully constructed to erase the complex and gendered dynamics between society and writer, writer and public, and men and women in the Ancien Régime. The anthologies and literary histories of the previous chapter illustrate a gradual reworking of the image of France's classical literary scene. France's exceptionally strong and centralized educational system from the nineteenth-century on worked to inscribe a similar vision of the salons and women's contribution to national literary culture. While an examination of every aspect of this revisionist pedagogy is beyond the scope of the present study, an analysis of a few representative examples of how the salons and women's taste figure into the pedagogical scene will serve to reveal how a nation's memory of a key period of its past came to be mastered.

Consecrating the Voices of Dissent: Moliere's Lasting Legacy

The case of Molière provides a perfect illustration of the consecration of one voice and the deformation of the image of the context that surrounded his literary production. In what follows, I am not interested in determining Molière's "true" opinions of *précieuses* or learned women, were such a thing even possible. The focus of my investigation is instead the way Molière's representation of the salons and women's roles in the seventeenth-century literary milieu has been portrayed and has shaped the public's view of "le Grand Siècle." In a fascinating study, Ralph Albanese has traced the elevation of Molière to the status of national icon during the last third of the nineteenth century.[38] Albanese's research clearly illustrates the process whereby, in his words, "nineteenth-century France designated Molière as the accredited representative of the characteristic traits of its national identity."[39] This sacralization of Molière as France's Shakespeare, to use Sainte-Beuve's formulation, occurred at precisely the same time that Victor Cousin, Sainte-Beuve, Brunetière, and others were "re-membering" the seventeenth century. The sheer number of studies devoted to Molière from the mid nineteenth century on attests to the unanimous desire to designate Molière as the voice of his century. While the first half of the century saw the publication of only three hundred critical works on Molière, during the years 1850 to 1900 more than 1,500 studies flooded the market.[40] Significantly, *Les Femmes savantes* was performed more than twice as much in the nineteenth century as it was in the seventeenth and eighteenth, which can be explained by the fact that the nineteenth century worked particularly hard to create a specific image of the classical age in formulating its idea of nation.[41] Albanese convincingly shows how Molière became the model for French literature and for the French nation, a model that France exported throughout Europe, for Molière's popularity was not limited to the hexagon.[42] Molière incarnates French national genius and is the most "French" of all authors.[43] Most important for our purposes, one play in particular was heralded as the ultimate expression of Molière's art: *Les Femmes savantes*. In his *Essais de critique idéaliste* (1882), for example, Victor de Caprade extolled Molière's satire as "perhaps our most perfect literary work."[44] *Les Femmes savantes* did not, however, merit such distinction for its portrayal of intellectual women and the learned salon they created. Rather, critics hailed Henriette, the character who refuses her century's new learned model for women, as the ultimate example of the perfect woman.[45] Molière's *Les Femmes savantes* was useful not only as a social critique of a period long past, but also for its pedagogical value for the present day. In his encyclopedia article devoted to Molière, A. Gazier expresses the nineteenth century's view of Molière's pedagogical value:

> The Learned Ladies puts forward a model of femininity perfectly adapted to the needs of French youth. It is recognized that pedantry takes away from women the feeling of their duties as wives and mothers, and we promise ourselves, if we ever have a girl, to make a Henriette and not an Armande out of her.[46]

Albanese also points out that pedagogical manuals in the late nineteenth and early twentieth century not only designated Henriette as the model of femininity, but also as the incarnation of French *bon sens* and a national figure: "Accomplished female model, the heroine of the *Learned Ladies* comes to incarnate French good sense, even perfect moral health. 'She is a figure [who is] essentially nationalistic, and that is found in everyday life'."[47] In these formulations of Molière's value to the nation, literary satire is transformed into historical truth worthy of emulation. More important, the valorization of Henriette over Armande reflects the generalized effort during the nineteenth century to purge the seventeenth century of salon and female influence and construct a national literary history and canon devoid of this influence.

   Molière's canonization is indicative of more than a desire to create a national literary icon. In idealizing Molière and adopting him as France's quintessential playwright, critics and historians were also consecrating

Molière's particular, and very negative, portrayal of the salon milieu, women intellectuals, and the worldly public. Even today the vast majority of people, whether French or other, intellectual or other, associate the salons of seventeenth-century France specifically, and usually uniquely, with Moliere's "precious" and "learned" women. *Les Femmes savantes* joins Molière's *L'Avare* and *Tartuffe*, as the plays most frequently presented by France's national theatre, La Comédie Française. Concurrent with the coronation of Molière as the supreme social portraitist of his time is the consecration of the negative view of the salon milieu present in his satires as the legitimate vision of women's participation in the literary sphere. Moliere's theatrical versions of the salons commemorate this *mondain* environment more than anything else. *Les Précieuses ridicules* and *Les Femmes savantes* have been performed respectively 1,500 and 1,600 times apiece at the Comédie Française alone. Only *L'Avare* and *Tartuffe* have been staged there as much as *Les Femmes savantes*. The way Moliere's plays are presented in theatres as well as packaged for pedagogical consumption have had a determining effect on how we view the particularly French institution of the salon.

Just as the seventeenth-century canon of classical writers is disseminated by the educational system, so too is Molière's portrayal of the seventeenth-century intellectual field propagated by its inclusion in the classroom, as well as its constant production on stage. Easy to read, at first glance simple to teach, Molière's plays have enjoyed constant popularity in secondary schools as well as advanced education on both sides of the Atlantic. A recent survey of French elementary and secondary school students confirms Molière as the most taught and most recognized author of the French literary canon. As M.P. Schmitt remarks:

> The classics, and first of all Molière, today are identified and registered in a way that they constitute the stock of possible literary references, common to professors and to students, that permits educational discourse to function. Even more specifically Molière's plays are without a doubt the only literary object [that is] unanimously legitimated and on which teachers can found their remarks most surely, certain that everyone does the same. Molière the commonplace, true cultural commonplace.[48]

Moreover, of the fifteen works most frequently studied in France, nine are from the seventeenth century and the top five are, in order, *L'Avare, le Cid, Les Femmes savantes, Le Bourgeois gentilhomme*, and *Le Malade imaginaire*.[49] As a result of this pedagogical fame, Molière's works can be found in a number of editions designed specifically for a student public. Given the accessibility of these texts, many pedagogues are attracted to Molière's plays, and when one wants to explore women's roles in seventeenth-century France, especially the phenomenon of the salon, one naturally turns to plays including *Les Précieuses ridicules* and *Les Femmes savantes* on a syllabus.[50] For the non-specialist, the pedagogical editions of these works provide a detailed context in which to situate the comedies. But a brief analysis of the presentation of this context underscores how prevalent and pervasive the re-membering of the seventeenth century actually is. A theatrical audience today, given that it would have little or no context in which to place these plays, would come away feeling that women merely played at having an influence on literature, and that their literary production, which most do not know exists, would not be worthy of their attention. But presumably, if one is reading these plays, especially in an explicitly pedagogical edition such as those produced by Bordas or Classiques Larousse, one is given a context in order to place Molière's satires into perspective. Interestingly, it is primarily the voices that confirm Molière's negative vision—such as Boileau, Tallemant des Réaux, Somaize, and de Pure—that serve as references for the editors. In many ways the editors of these editions only confirm and legitimize Moliere's satire of the relationship between women and literary creation and criticism.

In his 1984 Bordas edition of *Les Précieuses*, Fernand Angué uses his introduction to evoke preciosity and briefly describe the salon milieu that supposedly inspired Moliere. He refers above all to René Bray's account of the movement and to Tallemant's description of the various salons. In a move that mirrors Molière's preface to the play, in which he instructs readers to interpret his satire as one directed against false, provincial *précieuses*, not the noteworthy "real" ones, this editor distinguishes between two types of salons and "precious" behavior embodied by the marquise de Rambouillet and Madeleine de Scudéry. He portrays Rambouillet's *chambre bleue* as the place where "the entire court" as well as writers—"everyone who had a title, everyone who had made a name for him/herself" united to listen to Voiture and play various "society games." Angué makes a point to say that Rambouillet's salon was anything but learned and pedantic: "However, there was no pedantry at all on the rue Saint-Thomas du Louvre." And he cites an excerpt from the letter we have already examined from Chapelain to Balzac: "People there don't speak with wisdom but with reason" (22). Like Batiffol before him, this editor attributes any negative connotations of preciosity to Scudéry, while preserving the laudable aspects of the French institution of the salon by placing them in Rambouillet's court, but in a *chambre bleue* devoid of any true literary or linguistic influence. Rambouillet thus certainly could not be the model for Molière. The editor goes on to chronicle the downfall of this polite society and its deformation by someone he portrays as the opposite of the marquise, Scudéry.

We have already seen how the images of the marquise de Rambouillet and Madeleine de Scudéry underwent profound changes during the course of the eighteenth and nineteenth centuries. The pedagogical editions of Molière's plays keep this revisionist legacy alive and transmit it to future generations, in France as well as in the United States. Angué's carefully constructed context contains myriad references to Madeleine de Scudéry, given that Molière himself overtly ties the novelist to his satire. Founding his description of Scudéry's *samedis* on the abbé d'Aubignac, Somaize, de Pure, and his nineteenth-century predecessors, Angué categorically states that Scudéry, not Catherine de Rambouillet, is responsible for the attacks against *préciosité*: "[Scudéry] and not Catherine de Rambouillet is responsible for the attacks flung at preciosity" (23). His description of the *samedis* and their animator make it difficult to believe that anyone would have wanted to attend:

> She made her worldly debut at the home of the widow of a financier, Mlle Aragonnais … In her forties, she created in her house on the rue de Beauce, a ceremonial room that one reached after having climbed an obscure staircase, and she was able to gather an active company there. There were a few representatives of the nobility … above all there were bourgeois, each of whom had his/her literary name … They took themselves seriously because Sapho, a famous novelist, glorified people in style … by including them under their pseudonyms in the ten volumes of her *Grand Cyrus*, and this saga [*roman fleuve*] finished, conceived of another of 7,316 pages, *Clélie*, that was said to be the modern manual of worldliness. Not a single provincial bumpkin [*pecque provinciale*) who didn't promise herself to read it … Galant at the home of the marquise de Rambouillet, *préciosité* was literary at the illustrious Sapho's home … thanks to Pellisson they imagined the Carte de Tendre. (23)

Here and elsewhere, there is an effort to divorce Scudéry from Rambouillet.[51] Scudéry supposedly started out in a bourgeois salon, whereas, as we have seen, her contemporaries recount what they characterize as her illustrious beginnings at the *chambre bleue*. The samedis are above all bourgeois—yet the same people who frequented the *chambre bleue* were often present at the *samedis*. In contrast to the glorified portraits of Rambouillet where everyone had fun, at Scudéry's "they took themselves seriously" and the ties between literature and the *samedis* were much greater, to the detriment of the salon.

There is an effort to deny any true legitimacy and influence to Scudéry's salon by emphasizing its supposedly bourgeois nature—as though anything bourgeois could not have or should not be an influence on *le grand siècle*—by ridiculing the "romans fleuves" Scudéry produced, and by transforming her writings into ridiculous ramblings. Angué, for example, refers to the epitaph written for Scudéry's dead chameleon as an example of the level of literary creativity in the *samedis*. Not only is Scudéry's literary production fit primarily for "country bumpkins"—Molière's term in *Les Précieuses ridicules*—she is, in this portrait, responsible for the ridiculous language satirized by Molière. Angué states that Tallemant des Réaux accused Scudéry of having "introduced as many unpleasant ways of speaking as anyone had in a long while" (29). Angué ends his description by citing La Bruyère's assessment of worldly control over language: "by everything they called *délicatesse*, sentiment, ways and refinement of expression, they finally finished by not being understood and by not understanding themselves" (29).

The mythology surrounding these two *salonnières*, which Angué resurrects to create his context, grants the marquise de Rambouillet eternal youth and beauty. Indeed she never seems to age. In contrast, Scudéry is never young. She is admonished for being a decrepit prude, a virgin, and a spinster.[52] Scudéry's popularity derives from the fact that her novels are "à clé"—her bourgeois habitués, infatuated with themselves, created the novelist's reputation, not true literary quality. *Galanterie* might be acceptable, but pretentions to influence Parnassus are not. And in Angué's version, like many others, Molière only mirrors his society's disgust for Scudéry: "Tired of worldly and literary mannerisms dictated by an ugly woman who had reached a venerable age, school children and *honnêtes gens* thus greeted the comedy with enthusiasm" (31).

Interestingly, Angué legitimizes Moliere's portrait by stating that "the entire hôtel de Rambouillet applauded it, the queen of Tendre and her court also did" (31). This seems at odds with the other facts he presents, particularly that the play was suspended because "a male salon figure of quality obtained a stop to the presentation ... a noble man without a doubt." The second time the marquise de Rambouillet's daughter had it suspended (31). Why, given the previous description, a "grand seigneur" would see fit to defend Scudéry is not easy to understand. The actual reception of the play is difficult to document. Perhaps *salonnières* did approve the production, but the written version would have had a different reception—witness Moliere's unease in his preface at having the play published without his permission. In this editor's pedagogical dossier, there is no sense of "true" salons as anything but polite aristocratic gatherings that played with minor literary genres. The editor thus works to confirm and legitimize Moliere's satirical vision of the salons, *préciosité*, Scudéry and all the literature associated with them and with her, and reflects the efforts of nineteenth-century historians and critics to reshape the seventeenth century into something they could accept.

Not surprisingly, one finds similar trends in the introductory material for *Les Femmes savantes* in the 1984 Bordas edition, given that it was edited by the same person. Again, Scudéry is held responsible for the negative aspects of learned women, but this time she is joined by one of the marquise de Rambouillet's daughters, Angélique d'Angennes. Angué states: "Not content to govern good manners, these animators of worldly life claimed to set the tone for literature. Having conquered the worldly empire, they also needed to govern Parnassus" (15). Later, in situating the play within the context of the *querelle des femmes*, he states "Long before 1672 there were pretentious women who believed themselves capable of renewing customs ... and who wanted to reign through means other than their natural charms" (17). Like Molière, the editor's remarks make it clear that while the "worldly empire" and "good manners" are perhaps acceptable occupations for women, determining "Parnassus" and "customs" are certainly not "natural" occupations.

In many respects, the notes throughout pedagogical editions such as Angué's mirror the vision of the salons and women's literary occupations as found in the introductions. For example, in Angué's edition of *Les Précieuses*, the editor critiques Scudéry's supposed pretentiousness (61) and often refers to Tallemant's description, as when he states that "Molière did not invent anything" since Tallemant remarked the same thing (67). He thus works to pass Molière off as historical truth, rather than as the satire it is. In his edition of *Les Femmes savantes*, he supplements the text with humorous examples of women's tyranny over language (75) but never gives the impression that anyone took their influence on literature or language seriously. Interestingly he affiliates Philaminte's salon's with Scudery's by stating that it has bourgeois undertones: "Philaminte obviously did not frequent the nobility like her husband did" (65).

The new Larousse edition of *Les Précieuses ridicules* edited by Brigitte Diaz in 1998 gives a somewhat less pejorative description of the salon scene, but still preserves the distinction between Rambouillet's and Scudéry's salons. Rambouillet's is the perfect salon, whereas Scudéry's is Molière's model. She portrays the *chambre bleue* as "the most brilliant" salon of the first half of the century, from 1620–45. Literature is merely "worldly amusement"

(15). In Diaz's history, following the end of the *chambre bleue* in 1645, "myriad rival salons where preciosity would prosper" took its place (16). Diaz paraphrases d'Aubignac's satirical description of these salons to illustrate how they functioned: "Women of the faubourg Saint-Germain or the Marais now receive in the *ruelles*: throned as idoles on their bed, they receive around them a small circle of close friends" (16).[53] She uses this description to introduce Scudéry:

> Of all the *ruelles*, the most popular one is that of Mlle de Scudéry, who had herself called "Sapho" ... theoretician of preciosity, she intends to purge language of all its slang, but she is also a militant feminist. She is the queen of the prudish *précieuses*. (16)

Scudéry is thus clearly Molière's model, especially given that Diaz says her salon flourished from 1652–59, thus dying out as soon as Molière's *précieuses* appear on the scene.[54] Diaz later states: "Exemplary of this precious verbosity, Mlle de Scudéry and her sagas [*romans fleuves*]" (136). Also striking in the introductory material is Diaz's echo of Molière's preface. She emphasizes that Molière is only mocking what *préciosité* had become in bourgeois salons such as Scudéry's and in the provinces: "One can already feel, that thanks to these two scenes, Molière's target is not so much preciosity, a cultural phenomenon that some great ladies such as the marquise de Rambouillet gave their stamp of approval, as it is its [preciosity's] imitation in bourgeois salons." Yet by all accounts, the same people frequented Rambouillet's and Scudery's salon. The only difference is that Scudéry was and is recognized as a writer. Diaz, like many other editors of these pedagogical editions, cites Sainte-Beuve's remark in 1844 to confirm the effect Molière's play had, seemingly justifiably, on Scudéry's *romans fleuves*: "'Molière balaya la queue des mauvais romans. La comédie des *Précieuses ridicules* tua le genre; Boileau, survenant, l'acheva par les coups précis'" (143) (Molière swept away the bad novels. The comedy *Les Précieuses ridicules* killed the genre; Boileau arrived and finished it off with precise blows). Molière is thus redeemed as having rectified the scene by exterminating Scudéry's bad literature.

The newest Larousse edition of *Les Femmes savantes* by Thanh-Vân Ton-That in 1998 gives more of a general overview of the status of learned women in France during the period and places Molière's play in the general context of the *querelle des femmes* rather than in a specific seventeenth-century context. This editor's focus is on the question of marriage, not Molière's presentation of the salon milieu. Still, Thanh-Vân Ton-That sets the tone to viewing the salon scenes by using as a frontispiece for the edition an engraving by Bosse depicting women around a table with instruments of astronomy, with one woman reading a book to the group while holding a musical instrument. Significantly, the engraving is entitled "Les Vierges folles" (the crazy virgins). When he does turn to describing the salon milieu, he maintains the same distinction between Rambouillet and Scudéry, Scudéry's salon being "more bourgeois" than Rambouillet's. Somaize is his primary reference. As in the nineteenth-century, this editor underscores that Henriette "incarnates good sense and a feminine ideal made of beauty, realism, and delicate nobility" (165). Armande does not fare well: "To a coldness of heart is added an absence of taste and judgment" (166). In the appendix, he cites Rapin who, like Sainte-Beuve after him, attributes the death of such folly to Molière:

> *Les Précieuses ridicules* and *Les Femmes savantes* made women who prided themselves too much on their *bel esprit* so ashamed that the whole nation of *précieuses* was extinguished in less than fifteen days, or, at least they disguised themselves so well that they were no longer found either at court or in town, and ever since that time, they have been more wary of the reputation of learned and precious than of gallant or mentally disturbed.[55]

For his "complementary readings on the image of women in literature, preciosity, the education of girls, and the salons" only Molière and La Bruyère are cited for the seventeenth century.

> Molière, *Les Précieuses ridicules, L'Ecole des femmes, Le Misanthrope*
> La Bruyère, *Les Caractères*
> George Sand, *Indiana, Valentine, Lélia*
> Honoré de Balzac, *Eugénie Grandet, Physiologie du mariage*
> Gustave Flaubert, *Mme Bovary*
> Edmond Rostand, *Cyrano de Bergerac*
> Marcel Proust, *A la recherche du temps perdu*
> Colette, série des Claudine et Gigi
> Simone de Beauvoir, *Le Deuxième Sexe*

Many earlier Classiques Larousse editions also pair *Les Femmes savantes* with *Madame Bovary*, presumably in an effort to show what a nefarious effect reading, especially novels, can have on the delicate minds of women.

These editions produced in the 1970s, 1980s, and 1990s are representative of the ways editors have presented the literary context for these plays over the past century.[56] Each subsequent editor has reproduced many of the same preoccupations of his/her predecessors. As we have seen in these representative examples, there is always an effort to elevate Henriette over Armande as the female model worthy of emulation.[57] In editions of *Les Précieuses ridicules*, editors try to define the elusive concept of *préciosité*. While many trace it to the marquise de Rambouillet, they unanimously absolve her of any negative qualities associated with the movement, and characterize preciosity at the *chambre bleue* as an effort to be more refined after the "gaulois" court of Henri IV.[58] While many editors openly state that Scudéry is the inspiration for *Les Précieuses*, some are less categorical and follow and elaborate upon Molière's own lead established in his preface, according to which he was only satirizing provincial versions of the salons. Some editors remark that Molière had more sense than to try to anger influential Parisian nobility and even Scudéry. Some even go to great lengths to try to prove that, in spite of the numerous references in the plays themselves to Scudéry and her novels, Molière was not attacking Sapho but only her influence. Most editors laud Molière's success with *Les Précieuses* and try to locate the marquise and Scudéry in the audience in order to confirm Molière's supposed intention of only portraying precious imitations.[59] This can be interpreted in part as an effort to show that "le Grand Siècle" should not be viewed as accepting of absurdities such as women's influence on language and literature. In this perspective, even Rambouillet and Scudéry would not endorse such a vision. Editors often attribute the lack of success of *Les Femmes savantes* to the more serious nature of the play, but not to any anger on the part of the worldly public, whom they portray as largely in agreement with Molière's satire.

While it is possible to justify and comprehend these efforts to contextualize the plays, what I find difficult to reconcile with my own teaching of the period is that such portraits are decidedly one-sided. These editors give voice to only part of the seventeenth century, a part associated with Boileau, La Bruyère, and Molière himself. The influence of women as writers and as critics is barely a shadow. But it is this vision of the salons that is commemorated each time the plays are presented today, or read in most classrooms. And it is also the portrait that was carefully created and perpetuated throughout the nineteenth century and even today in France. Molière's version of the seventeenth century and the salons is one that is constantly replayed because he advances a more acceptable vision of the classical canon, one in which, while women may have tried to exert influence, or have an effect on the intellectual and literary realm, they did so only in ridiculous ways.

Pedagogical Perspectives on the Seventeenth-Century Literary Field

In addition to specifically pedagogical editions of individual French classical texts, another genre, the pedagogical literary anthology or "manuel scolaire," has played and continues to play an important role in the dissemination of a particularly gendered conception of France's seventeenth-century literary heritage.[60] The past thirty years have witnessed the development of a new area of research in France dedicated to analyzing the content, ideology and historical context of the *manual scolaire* and related pedagogical texts.[61] Most recently sociologists, linguists, historians, and literary critics have all delved into questions of how France's very centralized educational system and the manuals and anthologies that are an integral part of that system have been used to forge a sense of collective identity. Each discipline has its own approach to these questions.[62] My goal here is not to provide an overview of this fascinating area of research, but rather to use some recent findings to shed light on the construction of literary history and the reasons behind the particular form this construction has taken in the case of seventeenth-century France.

To judge from the various manuals and pedagogical anthologies, the "génie national" best expressed by seventeenth-century literary texts, as well as the literary field that produced these models, is associated with both a specific gender and a genre. A brief survey of a few representative literary anthologies from the nineteenth and twentieth centuries reveals the prevailing images of a seventeenth-century literary scene devoid of any serious female influence, as well as the continued elevation of this period as representative of the essence of Frenchness. Not surprisingly, with few exceptions, from the late eighteenth century until today the same names figure prominently. More important for our purposes here, are the silences, shadows, and inscription, or lack thereof, of the overall literary field of the period. These pedagogical anthologies highlight the careful construction of France's classical literary heritage and the meticulous shaping of national memory.[63]

The Abbé Charles Batteux's *Les Beaux Arts réduits à un seul principe* and his *Cours de belles-lettres*, first published in 1746 and 1747 respectively, and later reissued as *Principes de Littérature*, is often considered to be the first attempt in France to systematically construct a literary program for the formation of the minds of French elite. According to Alain Choppin, Batteux's program was directed at the nation's twelve military schools, was very limited in scope, and was a commercial failure.[64] It nonetheless does indicate the direction pedagogical anthologies would eventually take with regard to the seventeenth century literary canon. As Joan DeJean has argued, Batteux's text is organized around the premise of taste and how it can best be inculcated through literature.[65] In Batteux's opinion, there is only one good taste, which can be learned through contact with certain works of literature that incarnate this natural taste. As DeJean describes Batteux's formulation, "good taste may be unique and innate, but it must also be taught, for only an educated public immediately understands great literature."[66] One is reminded of the French Academy's assertion that Boileau had restored taste to a nation that had forgotten what it should be. Batteux's conception of taste, like Boileau's, is the polar opposite of the worldly taste advanced by the salons. Whereas one must be learned, the other is inherent in women. Given the redefinition of literary taste at the heart of Batteux's pedagogical project, it is not surprising that the seventeenth-century literary field he creates is equally gendered. Batteux only includes two women writers as examples of his principles, Sévigné and Deshoulières, and even these two are not necessarily models to be followed.[67] Batteux states that Sévigné, for example, should be used with care, although he does leave it up to the reader to decide: "Mais elle [Sévigné] se montre partout si aimable, qu'on aime tout ce qu'elle dit, et qu'on ne peut pas s'empêcher de le trouver bien. C'est à chacun à lui dérober ce qui lui convient, et ce qu'il pourra" (But [Sévigné] shows herself to be so likeable, that people like everything she says, and they can't help but find it good. Everyone can take from her what they can and what suits them).[68] He mentions Mme de Maintenon's letters, but only in passing.[69] Most important, in a move that will become common practice, Batteux removes the novel as a genre from his seventeenth-century literary world. In his discussion of prose genres, he focuses on history, oratory genres, and pronunciation, including only the epistolary genre. As DeJean states succinctly: "Batteux's program is also a monument to the official exclusion from the pages of literary history of the novel, and therefore of the women writers who were until then its most illustrious practitioners."[70] The premier examples of Batteaux's taste become isolated from a literary world that, even if it contested women's influence and literary taste, at least recognized its existence and effect on the forms and values of the seventeenth-century literary field.

It is one thing to exclude women from the pedagogical canon. It is yet another to reformulate a period during which women were recognized for their critical acumen, writing, and formation of writers through the salons and turn it into one where women were no more present than during the Middle Ages. It is this silencing of female influence that characterizes the pedagogical projects and their depictions of the classical field, especially during the nineteenth century. The elimination of women writers was due less to a fear of the values or taste that their works might transmit, than to an anxiety of influence upon the authors chosen to represent the models of classical France. In this respect, while I agree with her assessment, I would interpret this phenomenon differently than DeJean, who attributes the relative erasure of the female literary tradition to a fear of their works: "Women writers were so threatening to the ideology of the developing pedagogical canon that their elimination had to be reimposed until the new curriculum was firmly established."[71] As becomes more and more clear as the preponderance of pedagogical anthologies grows, the writers chosen to illustrate "le Grand Siècle" are primarily those who were openly hostile to female influence, such as Molière and Boileau, or those whose worldly salon roots and influences could be most easily erased, namely Pascal, Racine, and La Bruyère, among others. The pedagogical revisions were just as much designed to reformulate the vision of "le Grand Siècle" as they were to promote certain notions of literary value. Given that the literary field under Louis XIV was consistently touted, especially during the pedagogical reforms of the nineteenth century, as representing the best France had ever offered the world, indeed a universal model as well as a reflection of France's national genius, this particular gendering of the past takes on new valences and implications.

J.F. La Harpe's *Lycée ou Cours de Littérature ancienne et moderne* of 1813 provides a particularly exemplary and effective revision of the classical era to which the author devotes three volumes. As La Harpe states in his preface, the *Lycée* is not addressed to either students or scholars, but rather is designed to serve as "le complément des études pour ceux qui peuvent pousser plus loin celles qu'ils ont faites: c'en est le supplément pour les gens du monde qui n'ont pas le temps d'en faire d'autres" (the complement to studies for those who can push [the studies] they have done farther: it is the supplement for worldly people who do not have time to study further).[72] This educational "supplement" provides its worldly reader with a portrait of the seventeenth-century literary scene devoid of serious female influence, not only as writers, but as participants. It is interesting to note that La Harpe's text appears the same time as Genlis's, which leads me to believe that many worldly readers still recognized women's influence on the classical world of letters. La Harpe's decision to address an adult public reflects his perception that it is just as important to correct adults' misperceptions of their literary heritage as it is to shape the malleable minds of young students. It is also more difficult, which is why La Harpe leaves little room for an alternative vision such as Genlis's. A few examples must suffice.

In the introduction to his first volume devoted to "le siècle de Louis XIV," La Harpe offers a description of the salon de Rambouillet that strips it of any legitimacy:

Une société qui depuis longtemps n'est guère citée qu'en ridicule, mais qui, par le rang et le mérite de ceux qui la composaient, devait avoir une grande influence, le fameux hôtel de Rambouillet, contribua plus que tout le reste à mettre en faveur ce langage obscur et affecté qu'on prenait pour l'exquise politesse, et qui n'était que le pédantisme de l'esprit remplaçant le pédantisme de l'érudition. Si l'on se rappelle que c'était un Richelieu, un Condé, un Montausier, qui fréquentaient cette maison célèbre, où l'amour et la poésie étaient soumise à l'analyse la plus sophistiqué, on concèdera également que ces hommes si grands, chacun dans leur classe, pouvaient n'être pas d'excellents maîtres en fait de goût. (IV, 50)

(A society that for a long time has hardly ever been cited except in ridicule, but which, by the rank and the merit of those who composed it, had a great influence, the famous hôtel de Rambouillet, contributed more than everything else to putting into favor that obscure and affected language, that people took for exquisite politeness, and that was only pedantry of *esprit* that replaced erudite pedantry. If we remember that Richelieu, Condé, Montausier frequented this famous house, where love and poetry were submitted to the most sophisticated analyses, then we will concede equally that these great men, each in his own class, were capable of not being great masters when it comes to taste.)

Clearly the definition of "taste" has changed dramatically, as well as the concept of "pedantry." One has only to recall Chapelain's letter to Balzac in which he praised the *chambre bleue* for its lack of pedantry, as well other contemporaries' assessment of Rambouillet as the "temple of good taste." La Harpe's teaching is more in line with Molière's later portrayal of salons, as he corrects the past, including Richelieu, in order to right a wayward seventeenth-century literary heritage. The latter half of the seventeenth century becomes worthy of emulation and of teaching, with Pascal the epitome of eloquence and Racine "le modèle éternel de la poésie française" (the eternal model of French poetry) (IV, 52). La Harpe focuses his pedagogy on Racine, going carefully through all his plays, as well as on Molière and even more revelatory, on Boileau, to whom he devotes over one hundred pages alone. La Harpe singles out *Les Précieuses ridicules* and *Les Femmes savantes* for praise. Thanks to Molière's satires, salon influence was eradicated:

Les Précieuses ridicules ... firent une véritable révolution: l'on vit pour la première fois sur la scène le tableau d'un ridicule réel et la critique de la société. Elles furent jouées quatre mois de suite avec le plus grand succès. Le jargon des mauvais romans, qui était devenu celui du beau monde, le galimatias sentimental, le phebus des conversations, les compliments en metaphores et en énigmes, la galanterie ampoulée, la recherche des jeux de mots, toute cette malheureuse dépense d'esprit, pour n'avoir pas le sens commun, fut foudroyée d'un seul coup ... Il fallut convenir que Molière avait raison ... Tout ce qu'il avait censuré disparut bientôt. (IV, 217)

(*Les Précieuses ridicules* created a veritable revolution: for the first time on stage we witnessed the picture of a realistic ridiculousness and the critique of society. [The play] was presented with the greatest success for four consecutive months. The jargon of bad novels, which had become that of worldly society, the sentimental gibberish, the Phoebus of conversations, compliments made in metaphors and enigmas, pompous gallantry, the search for word play, this entire sad expenditure of *esprit*, because it did not have common sense, was struck down with only one blow ... People had to agree that Molière was right ... everything he had censored quickly disappeared.)

Molière, qui l'avait [la prétention au bel esprit] déjà attaqué dans *Les Précieuses*, l'acheva dans *Les Femmes savantes* ... Si, d'un côté, Philaminte, Armande et Belise sont entichées du pédantisme que l'hôtel de Rambouillet avait introduit dans la littérature, et du platonisme de l'amour qu'on avait aussi essayé de mettre à la mode, de l'autre se présentent des contrastes multiples sous différentes formes: la jeune Henriette, qui n'a que de l'esprit naturel et de la sensibilité ... la bonne Martine .... (IV, 271–72)

(Molière, who had already attacked [the claim to *bel esprit*] in *Les Précieuses*, finished it in *Les Femmes savantes*. If, on the one hand, Philaminte, Armande and Belise are infatuated with pedantry which the hôtel de Rambouillet had introduced into literature, and with amorous Platonism, which people had also tried to promote, on the other hand multiple contrasts present themselves in different forms: the young Henriette, who only has natural *esprit* and sensibility ... good Martine ....)

La Harpe goes farther than other pedagogues and historians in his effort to destroy any legitimate influence of worldly culture. While others, as we have seen, at least grant Rambouillet a positive civilizing influence, La Harpe associates the *chambre bleue* directly with Molière's satires. He does not even mention other salons, most notably Scudéry's, who not suprisingly, barely figures in the *Lycée* as an author. In the three volumes devoted to the seventeenth century, La Harpe only dedicates twenty pages to the novels and "contes," the genres most associated with the salons and with women. Scudéry is evoked to illustrate Boileau's good taste. La Harpe states

Je n'ai pas lu non plus, du moins jusqu'au bout, la *Clélie* ni le *Cyrus*, dont Boileau s'est tant moqué et avec tant de raison, ni l'*Ariane* de Desmarets, qui vaut encore moins, et qui n'eut pas moins de réputation: ce n'est pas faute de bonne volonté; mais il m'est impossible de lire ce qui m'ennuie … Mademoiselle Scudéry [sic], avec ses grands romans, se fit une grande renommée, du moins jusqu'au moment où Despréaux les eut réduits à leur valeur. (VI, 345)

(Nor have I read, at least not entirely, *Clélie* or *Cyrus* that Boileau so mocked and so correctly, nor *l'Ariane* by Desmarets, which is worth even less, and had just as good a reputation; it's not because I haven't wanted to; but I can't read something that bores me … Mlle Scudéry (sic) with her long novels achieved great renown, at least until Despréaux reduced them to their true worth.)

Only Lafayette escapes La Harpe's censoring pen. La Harpe admires *La Princesse de Clèves* for its portrayal of love conquered by duty. Boileau is depicted as the shining knight who brings enlightenment and justice to a wayward literary field. Interestingly, La Harpe acknowledges that the public granted Rambouillet and Scudéry a "great renown," yet at the same time he also depicts Boileau as sharing in the public's adulation:

Tout son mérite a été dès lors généralement reconnu, tandis que celui de Molière, de Racine, de Quinault, de La Fontaine, n'ait été bien parfaitement senti qu'avec le temps. Corneille et Despréaux, parmi les grands poètes du dernier siècle, sont les seuls qui aient joui d'une réputation à laquelle les générations suivantes n'ont pu rien ajouter. (VI, 443)

(At the time his entire merit was generally recognized, whereas Molière's, Racine's, Quinault's and La Fontaine's were only correctly felt with the passage of time. Corneille and Despréaux, among the great poets of the last century, are the only ones who enjoyed a repuation to which following generations could add nothing.)

La Harpe's stance on Corneille can be supported by historical evidence, but his elevation of Boileau by his own contemporaries is more difficult to justify. Even La Fontaine was elected to the French Academy before Boileau was. La Harpe's assessment and lesson have the effect of consecrating Boileau's taste as representative of the "true" seventeenth century. While contemporaries may have admired Scudéry, they also admired and listened to Boileau. Seventeenth-century taste is thus shared between worldly and academic, but in the end the *doctes* represented by Boileau win out in this depiction of *le Grand Siècle* because novels and salon influence are no longer valued.

The tenets that guided the composition of La Harpe's *Cours de Littérature* and other similar pedagogical programs remain part of succeeding pedagogical initiatives, not only in the nineteenth century but even into the twentieth. The same depiction of the classical literary field becomes canonized. Ch.-M. Des Granges's *Histoire de la Littérature française: à l'usage des classes de lettres et des divers examens*, which first appeared at the beginning of the twentieth century and was already in its eleventh edition by 1913, is just one of many examples of the prevalence of the re-membered history of seventeenth-century literary culture. His *Morceaux choisis des auteurs français du Moyen Age à nos jours* appeared in 1910 and was republished and reedited forty-three times before 1948, proof of its popularity.[73] Des Granges does not totally eliminate the novel in his detailed history, and even recognizes that it was appreciated during the period, but he elevates Boileau's taste above worldly taste, and praises Boileau for creating the seventeenth century so admired by succeeding generations.[74] In his words, "the role of satirical Boileau, during his time, was double: on the one hand, to ruin the false reputations that encumbered the salons and the theatre, in order to pave the way for the great geniuses; on the other hand, to impose the Racines and the Molières."[75] Another of Des Granges's successful pedagogical works, *La Littérature française au brevet de capacité*, a brief manual to prepare students for national exams, illustrates the triumph of Boileau over the worldly taste of his contemporaries. Only Sévigné figures in the brevet. There are no novels or poetry included to illustrate the seventeenth century.[76] Another popular manual produced by Hachette, P. Castex's and P. Surer's *manual des études littéraires françaises* ressembles Des Granges's. There is little evidence of any women writers in the seventeenth century, with the exception of Sévigné and Lafayette, and no sense of worldly influence on the literary arena.[77] Perhaps the most well-known anthology edited since the mid-twentieth century by André Lagarde et Laurent Michard continues the trends established in the nineteenth century. Even in the most recent edition of 1985, only three women's works merit inclusion: Sévigné, Lafayette, and Scudéry. There is a one-page portrait of Cléomire, the marquise de Rambouillet, excerpted from Scudéry's *Le Grand Cyrus*, which the editors use to establish Rambouillet's credability, stating that "We are a long way from the ridiculous preciosity attacked by Scarron, Furetière and Molière."[78] Lagarde et Michard do recognize the influence exercised on society by Rambouillet, but they limit their description to *préciosité* and group the entire history of worldly influence into twenty pages of the four hundred and forty-eight pages of the volume devoted to the seventeenth century. In their view, *préciosité* did influence classical language and inspired authors to be more psychologically analytical, but for the most part this worldly culture existed alongside the truly tasteful one that represents the seventeenth century in the rest of the anthology, not intersecting and influencing the real classics.[79]

Anthologies and manuals continue to be produced at regular intervals, in addition to the reediting of classic texts. These supposedly new and revised compilations reveal how tenaciously scholars and editors adhere to a vision of the seventeenth century that has changed little since the late eighteenth. In 1988, for example, Hatier published a volume devoted to the seventeenth century in its "Itinéraires littéraires" (literary itineraries) series, which is designed to be "a useful and complete tool" for French students.[80] In the "Avant-Propos," the editor, Robert Horville, enumerates his various intentions: to provide the historical background for texts, to study authors with respect to each other, to give biographical background on the major figures and excerpts of their works, to give a few representative examples of the criticism associated with a particular work, and also to provide a questionnaire that conforms to the instructions of "le Bulletin Officiel de l'Education Nationale." To attract the potential student of literature, the volume is filled with engravings and paintings of the period that give students a visual as well as a textual sense of the seventeenth century. Of the sixty-two authors whose works merit inclusion, four—Christine de Suède, Sévigné, Lafayette, and Scudéry—are women. Christine de Suède and Sévigné are both illustrations of "l'esprit mondain," and the epistolary genre that, along with poetry, is depicted as best illustrating this worldly milieu. Scudéry is classified under the rubric "Preciosity and its Sparkles (chatoiements)" and Lafayette finds her place under "Romanesque fiction and reality." Horville does make an effort to briefly evoke salon culture, describing it as "a societal phenomenon that was organized around women ... around them a veritable ceremonial made of refinement and subtlety was elaborated" (75). Conforming to traditional assessments, the hôtel de Rambouillet is valorized over Scudéry's *samedis*, which attract the "upper-crust bourgeoisie and writers" and are at the origin of "l'esprit précieux."[81] Horville grants the institution considerable influence on "the evolution of ideas," and even states that salon habitués took pleasure in judging literary works. But he undercuts their importance by repeatedly using the adjectif "oisif" (leasurely, idle) to describe the milieu and its participants (75). There is no sense that authors took these literary critics seriously, nor that the gatherings had any lasting influence on the literature and the authors of the period. In this traditional portrait, literature is merely an amusement for a bored leisure class. In the descriptions of most of the writers, the worldly, salon public is rarely, if ever mentioned, thus confirming one's impression that "real" authors might frequent the salons, but the worldly milieu was extraneous to true genius. The one exception are the authors whose works clearly emanate from the worldly milieu, namely La Rochefoucauld, Méré, and Retz, whom he chooses to illustrate the genre of the aristocratic memoir.

The depictions of the four women included also follow well established interpretive lines. Scudéry, the essence of *préciosité*, is a successful author because her contemporaries delighted in trying to identify themselves in her works (77). Sévigné's merit lies in the maternal love that emanates from her correspondence, an enterprise which, according to the editor, did not really begin until Sévigné started writing to her daughter. Horville thus echoes Cousin and Sainte-Beuve, among many others, before him. Sévigné is recuperated as "this exclusive and passionate mother" (275). Lafayette receives praise for being "a *femme d'esprit* who avoided making too obvious a display of her knowledge" as opposed to one of those detestable "femmes savantes" (320). Her masterpiece is described as a conflict between desire and reason in which the heroine nobly sacrifices her happiness to her guilty memory of her husband: "she resists her passion, but her husband, ravaged by jealousy, perishes from languidness. Distraught, this young woman retires from the world and dies soon after" (323). The passages are chosen to highlight this submission of a woman to the memory of her husband, to the exclusion of any other interpretation. Each female literary figure is thus made to conform to acceptable roles, even though the editor does attempt to give an inkling of the "mouvement féministe" present in seventeenth-century France, a movement that, according to Horville, provoked Molière's satire, but only because of its excesses, for Molière could never be against women wanting to educate themselves.[82]

Another anthology, this one addressed primarily to English speaking students of French literature, follows many of the same principles of Horville's *XVIIe Siècle*. This editor is clearly conscious of the tradition of French women writers and explains in his preface that he eliminated Malraux, Robbe-Grillet, and Butor in order to make room for Colette, Beauvoir, and Sarraute. However, the seventeenth-century literary scene has not undergone much revision. Only Sévigné and Lafayette are included, and the usual canon of Malherbe, Descartes, Corneille, Racine, Molière, Pascal, La Rochefoucauld, La Bruyère, La Fontaine, and Boileau is well represented. Salons are part of the literary scene and in this history are responsible for the works of moralists, memoirs and correspondences, as well as the more negative *préciosité*. Boileau is elevated as the architect of classicism, the great writer who was able to determine the principles of "clarity, truth, good form, honor, with which the century is connected to the national genius of France."[83] In a departure from many other anthologies, Leggewie includes an excerpt from *La Princesse de Clèves*, but does not portray the princess as the self-sacrificing heroine we saw in Horville's anthology. Leggewie leaves the ending more open to interpretation: "Mme de Clèves, even though free, refuses to marry the duc de Nemours, and retires to a convent."[84] He does, however, eliminate the fact that the princess only spends half of the year in a convent, thus making the ending conform to more traditional romanesque conventions than Lafayette herself chose to do.

What conclusions can we draw from these representative examples designed to form the minds of French students as well as adults? I find two traits particularly striking: the representation of the novel and its context, specifically the salon and its worldly taste, and the canonization of Boileau, who becomes the premier example of classical taste. The novel is consistently eliminated as a serious genre in the seventeenth century. As we have seen, the century is associated primarily with the theatre, a genre practiced by few women during the period, and to judge by anthologies, by none of quality as none are even mentioned.[85] In the case of the novel, we have already amply documented Scudéry's elimination from consideration as a serious author. Lafayette's status proves to be more ambiguous. She is remembered, but usually behind the shadows of Segrais, Huet, and La Rochefoucauld. Even when a work appeared anonymously, as did *La Princesse de Clèves*, literary historians upon occasion state that it appeared under Segrais's name. Most praise the novel as a masterpiece, but are reluctant to attribute sole authorship to Lafayette, preferring at the very least to give credit to La Rochefoucauld for the maxims. This can be explained in part by the fact that the literary context that produced the novel as a genre is usually eliminated from the depiction of the seventeenth century. It is thus difficult to believe that a woman would have been inspired to write a novel, especially one of such high quality. As Sablé and her salon are rarely evoked in relation to La Rochefoucauld's maxims, it would seem not only that he invented the genre, but that he did so alone and was the only one who published them. Other women novelists, notably Marie-Catherine Desjardins, Mme de Villedieu, completely disappear from the scene. Female memorialists such as Motteville and Montpensier occasionally merit a reference, but only to say that their works pale in comparison with someone of Retz's talent. If Lafayette's masterpiece is to figure as an example of classical genius, then it must be severed from its salon roots and female literary tradition that produced it.

The consecration of Molière's portrayal of the salons as historical truth was compounded in the nineteenth century by the canonization of another seventeenth-century figure who was overtly opposed to women's actions in the literary realm. Whereas Molière's comedies can be attributed to a playwright's desire to satirize his own time period, Boileau's overt attacts against the novel as a genre, Scudéry in particular, the literary taste of the worldly milieu, and all those affiliated with the *mondains*, such as the academician Chapelain, can only be explained as products of his intense opposition to worldly influence in the empire of letters. As we have seen, Boileau focused his attacks on the worldly literary taste of the salon and in particular on women's literary production, primarily the new genre of the novel. But while Boileau during his own time was admired by some, he just as often was detested by leading intellectual figures such as Huet, and especially the defenders of the values of the worldly public.[86] The creation of the legend of Boileau entailed a radical silencing of these other worldly voices. His status begins to change by the late eighteenth century. René Bray has traced the development of the myth of Boileau. He cites Batteux, La Harpe and Daunou in their roles as regents for the French educational system as decisive players in the shaping of the classical literary and the elevation of Boileau within this field.

> A scholarly poetry was discovered in the *Art Poétique* and in the *Epîtres*, to which maxims and stylistic advice, moral and rhetoric give a great pedagogical value. Volumes that before would not have been put into everyone's hands became valuable books. They were read in classrooms; people learned them by heart; these were the first works in French, along with La Fontaine's fables, to figure in pedagogical programs next to the Ancients. The masters made Boileau another regent, the master of Parnassus, the pedagogue of French genius.[87]

Boileau's place at the top of the seventeenth-century Pantheon is consecrated by Batteux's and La Harpe's continuators in the nineteenth century.[88] Indeed, the nineteenth century hailed him a legitimate voice for his century, the ultimate arbiter of literary taste for the classical period.[89] As Bray notes, this period became even more fascinated by Boileau. Between 1711 and 1789 there were one hundred and fifteen editions of Boileau's collected works produced. The nineteenth century more than doubles that number.[90] It is hardly coincidental that this deification of Boileau occurs at precisely the same time that France is developing a pedagogical system devoted to creating students and citizens imbued with a strong sense of national heritage founded upon particular vision of France, especially its literary past. Boileau's reputation changes little following this pedagogical consecration. Bray refers to Lanson's remark that Boileau is in the blood of every Frenchman and another assessment that he is France's national poet.[91] Boileau remains at least through the 1960s an integral part of the French pedagogical project, a figure, according to Bray, "in the company of whom all our students must live for years."[92]

Thus, as Bray states, "For more than two centuries, Boileau's monumental statue erected by the masters rises up at the entry of the temple of good French taste."[93] This unambiguous portrayal of Boileau as the best representative of literary taste during the classical period has the effect of transforming the seventeenth-century literary scene into something much more stable and uniform than many contemporaries of Boileau would have accepted. Instead of a dynamic world in which different tastes combatted for recognition, Boileau's *Art poétique* becomes the reflection of the supposed true taste of his time. As Nicole Aronson has remarked, this consecration of Boileau had serious consequences for the images of Boileau's seventeenth-century adversaries and even those who simply did not adhere to his vision of the literary field. We have already seen the effect the choice of Boileau as a premier voice of the classicism had on the nineteenth-century's image of Scudéry. Equally important is the silencing of these other adversarial voices, notably those of Chapelain, Huet, and Perrault in favor of the single, ancient voice of the author of *l'Art poétique* and the *Dialogue des Héros de Romans*. As we have seen, Chapelain, Huet, and Perrault were all major players in worldly literary culture and admirers and defenders of women's participation in the *champs littéraire*, as well as being notable academicians. In singling out Boileau among such luminaries who were considered at least his equals during the seventeenth century, and privileging his vision of the seventeenth-century literary scene, literary historians and pedagogues were and still are making a clear decision to suppress a principal part of the seventeenth-century literary arena, the arena influenced and often dominated by female literary initiatives and taste. Perrault becomes known solely for his fairy tales. His *Parallèle des Anciens et des Moderns*, which so enraged Boileau, is rendered obscure and no longer considered as representing the views in the seventeenth century of a large, legitimate public with its "modern" taste.

Anthologies and literary histories stress the classical qualities of *clarté*, *raison*, order, and adherence to models, all of which Boileau advocated, in particular in his *Art poétique*. The elevation of Boileau as the primary critical representative of seventeenth-century France is thus simultaneous with the elimination of the salons and worldly influence from the century's literary past. Although various critics and commentators have remarked upon the creation of the myth of Boileau, no one has questioned or even hypothesized why this myth has been propagated. I would advance that Boileau's consecration as the "architect of classicism" and the arbiter of "true" literary taste is an effort to present a unified myth of the classical literary scene devoid of the worldly literary taste that is the opposite of Boileau's. Worldly taste, founded upon its vague, unwritten rules and determined by worldly society dominated by women, has no place a world represented by Boileau. The collective taste and process of criticism and literary production that we have seen associated with the salons thus gives way to the magisterial voice of the critic, a voice that reflects the singular voice of its all-powerful monarch. The rejection of worldly taste and of the salon culture that gave rise to it corresponds to a reinventing of an entire historical period, a refashioning that could make it correspond to the image of France's most powerful monarch. In remodeling and defining France's classical canon, worldly taste is equated with ridicule, epitomized by Armande's and Philaminte's ecstatic "Oh" when confronted with Trissotin's poetry. Boileau's literary taste is advanced as reasonable, and the true taste of France's *Grand Siècle*, the only taste worthy of association with the French nation.

Legitimate Taste and National Memory

What I have been tracing here is an alliance between a representation of the seventeenth-century literary field developed primarily in the nineteenth century as part of a grandiose project to create a national, collective memory, and the dissemination of that memory through a centralized educational system. Proof of the power of this pedagogy is can be found in the enduring images of a seventeenth-century literary scene in which women played only marginal roles founded upon *politesse* and *sociabilité*, roles that they indeed played during the period, but to which their activities were not limited exclusively. In the vast majority of French historical and literary works destined for the general public today, Yourcenar's shadows remain precisely that. A few final, particularly stunning examples, will suffice to illustrate the historical revisionism inherent in the creation of a nation's memory and identity.

To judge by these works, the seventeenth century continues to intrigue and inspire twenty-first century France, or at least is considered an essential part of any French person's cultural baggage. Anthologies dedicated to the "splendid century" continue to see the light of day. Every year new historical works devoted to Louis XIV and his architectural masterpiece, as well as anything surrounding the Sun King are granted often lavish editions and join the impressive array of similar works on bookstore shelves. France is far from desirous of forgetting this particular national past. But the image of "the Great Century" as contrived and propagated by the nineteenth century has been challenged little. Only very recently, for example, have French editors seen fit to publish a few seventeenth-century works by women, and even when they are published, it is often in abridged forms.[94] In general, the image the French public continues to have of a seventeenth-century salon is that of the marquise de Rambouillet enthroned on her bed politely discussing the intricacies of love with her chosen guests, and few, if any, can name any seventeenth-century woman writer except Sévigné or Lafayette. There are literally hundreds of anthologies of French literature destined for students of French inside and outside of the hexagon. Alongside this market for pedagogical manuals is another that could be likened in some respects to the tradition of the worldly anthologies of the late seventeenth and early eighteenth centuries that we have already examined briefly. These literary histories, collections of works, and commentaries on authors are addressed to an educated, but not necessarily scholarly French public. A foreigner to French culture could be somewhat surprised at the appeal of such works, which often resurrect centuries-old texts and figures, for consumption by a general as well as a scholarly public in the twenty-first century. An economically-minded foreigner would no doubt question the marketability of such works. But the fact that compilations such as Alain Niderst's *Le Siècle de Louis XIV: Anthologie des mémoralistes du siècle de Louis XIV* are in fact considered as meriting publication attests to France's continued preoccupation and love of its past, especially of seventeenth-century literary culture.[95] For his volume, Niderst attempts to piece together passages from memoirs of the period in order to give the reader a complete, insider's view of this great period. Interestingly, he takes many of his passages from the memoirs penned by women, although he does not acknowledge that they were indeed innovators of the genre of personal memoirs during the period.[96] In fact, he categorically relegates them to a marginal role when he states "The two most illustrious [memorialists] are assuredly Retz and St Simon."[97] Nonetheless, women's names are resurrected from the shadows given that figures such as Montpensier and Motteville often gave the most detailed descriptions of people and events, so Niderst is forced to include their remarks.

It would seem that reviving and revisiting certain moments of French history is as much a national trait as reflecting on past moments of cultural and literary supremacy. But actually revising the vision of these periods is less attractive to scholars or even to much of the French public. An exemplary case is Jean d'Ormesson's *Une autre histoire de la litterature française*. Readers are expected to be attracted to this supposedly new literary history because of the pedagree of its author as advertised on the cover: Jean d'Ormesson de l'Académie Française. The author of numerous novels and essays, d'Ormesson explains in his introduction that he was inspired to compose this new history because of his love of literature, his desire to figure out why he was drawn to the profession of author, and also because he wanted to transform the medium of television into print. As the host of a television show, "Histoire personnelle de la littérature," d'Ormesson compiled a number of notes that he then decided to put into a less ephemeral medium.

D'Ormesson places himself within the public he is addressing, refusing from the first paragraph to elevate himself to the level of expert. "Above all, do not be afraid, reader, you know almost as much as the author" he assures his reader.[98] D'Ormesson's stance appears a bit disingenuous given his stature in the world of letters, as both a member of the illustrious forty immortals and as director of *Le Figaro*. But such a stance works to identify d'Ormesson as a lover of his nation's literature above all other positions. Presumably by taking this position among his public D'Ormesson is also suggesting that his views are his fellow countrymen's views, or at least opinions that could be shared. His *Autre histoire* can thus be regarded not simply as the musings of an Academician, but as the reflections of a general public on its particularly rich literary history.

But is this history new? D'Ormesson states that his purpose is to inspire the public to revisit this literary past, or perhaps only to discover it, a purpose that has much in common with the original worldly anthologies produced through the eighteenth century.[99] There are, however, striking differences between such previous worldly anthologies and d'Ormesson's "new" addition to literary history. As we have seen, earlier worldly anthologies also sought to make authors known to a general public and to inspire them to read such works. But the seventeenth-century, the period that concerns us here, as portrayed in the previous century's literary portraits differs profoundly from d'Ormesson's depiction. Although he markets his history as "autre," d'Ormesson's literary history is the culmination and product of the forces that shaped the classical literary field. The general public will follow the tide of these forces, for the forty authors d'Ormesson has chosen for his new history have been filtered out by these forces as the "chefs-d'oeuvre" of French literary culture.[100] The early worldly anthologies allowed their readers the freedom to construct their own hierarchy of value. D'Ormesson opts on the other hand to confirm what traditional literary history has constructed, without acknowledging the processes that shaped the canon or questioning the result.

D'Ormesson identifies three exceptional periods: "l'âge classique" (the classical age), "le romantisme"(romanticism), and "notre entre-deux-guerres" (between the two wars). He portrays the classical period as the foundation of French genius:

> The first is the classical age. Let's say, to be precise, from Corneille, who opens it, to Voltaire, who closes it. Geniuses follow each other an an acccelerated rhythm. Descartes establishes modern philosophy. Pascal creates classical French prose. You could wander around the taverns to find the four friends drinking and laughing: La Fontaine, Molière, Boileau and Racine. Bossuet and Montesquieu chase chance from history and substitute providence or the nature of things for it. (I, 13)

These canonical names are not only the foundation of the classical age, they are at the heart of d'Ormesson's own literary enterprise. In reflecting on what guided him in his choice of authors, d'Ormesson allies himself with his illustrious predecessors:

> What has guided me? But pleasure ... I believe that literature, which is probably much more, is first a source of pleasure. I believe, like Corneille, Molière, Boileau, Racine, that it is about pleasing the reader and the public, who is the supreme judge. (I, 15)

As we have seen, pleasure was a subject of much discussion among seventeenth-century authors such as Corneille, Molière, Boileau, and Racine, but its relationship to literary production and taste was not nearly as direct and simple as d'Ormesson would have us believe. The public may have been the "supreme judge" for Corneille, but for Boileau and Racine that same public could only judge if it were educated and did so by the rules. In stating that Boileau's principal interest in writing was to please the reader and the public, without precisely delineating this public or specifying the ways advocated by Boileau to please it, d'Ormesson seeks to ally the classical canon with today's public, to remake it into something to which a twenty-first century reader can relate. At the same time he simplifies the literary field of seventeenth-century France.

D'Ormesson may attempt to render the classical canon less foreign to his own public, but the vision he offers of this classical past is the same as the one advanced and determined by his nineteenth-century predecessors, with the exception of his emphasis on what he views as a unanimous and unambiguous desire among classical authors to please the public. At the same time, he

298 Salons, History, and the Creation of Seventeenth-Century France

qualifies the classical period as a time that was dominated "by a certain idea of order, grandeur, harmony, and the necessity for fixed rules" all more traditional associations with le Grand Siècle (I, 41). The salons make a brief appearance into his reflections on the classical literary realm. In d'Ormesson's words, and to his own surprise, a woman actually had an influence on literature: "What paved the way, among many others, was a striking precursor and a salon animated by a worldly woman to whom—a rare moment—literature owes a lot," that is the marquise de Rambouillet (I, 45). According to d'Ormesson's new history, "from society games come the maxims of La Rochefoucauld" (I, 47). It should be remembered that La Rochefoucauld's maxims were elaborated in Mme de Sablé's salon, not in the *chambre bleue*. D'Ormesson's misattribution continues the process whereby the marquise de Rambouillet remains the only *salonnière* truly worthy of mention. Scudéry's salon is alluded to, but only as an example of the salons that were totally eclipsed as soon as Louis XIV came to power, and were dominated by the defenders of the Ancients, namely Boileau, Racine, La Fontaine, and La Bruyère.

In this first volume, the seventeenth-century authors who find a place are Corneille, Retz, La Rochefoucauld, Molière, Pascal, Bossuet, Boileau, Racine, and La Bruyère. Women appear in their descriptions, but usually as mistresses or as figures playing at literary games. D'Ormesson refers to Mme de Sablé, Mme de Lafayette, and Mme de Sévigné as players in La Rochefoucauld's game of maxims, for example. Molière is extolled as "one of the founding myths of our national identity" (I, 77). His "band of friends" are La Fontaine, Boileau, and Racine, a group d'Ormesson calls "the famous school of 1660 whose rules were nature, reason, truth, and the public's pleasure" (I, 101). Novels have no place in this depiction of the classical world. Indeed, d'Ormesson compliments Pascal for never having read a single one (I, 86). This is the period that saw the birth of the classic French language, but in this literary history, men alone are responsible for its existence: "Corneille is the creator of our classic verse. Pascal is the creator of our classic prose. These two together ... presided over the birth of ... classical French" (I, 92). Boileau is the "the master of taste and expression" (I, 103). D'Ormesson admires his "frondeur" (recalcitrant) personality that led him to abolish false literary taste: "And what he loves above all is to attack the powerful. Those powerful ones, today, are completely forgotten ... Boileau taunts the salons where literary reputations were made, and denounces with audacity, almost carelessly, writers who were consecrated and flattered by the public" (I, 103). In this description it is clear that pleasing a public was not the only criteria for literary creativity advocated by the classics, despite d'Ormesson's previous assertion.

When d'Ormesson turns to the eighteenth century, he grants the salons more influence because the philosophical ideas he admires were often generated within the confines of the salons. But the image of women remains static. According to d'Ormesson, the seventeenth century "with some exceptional women ... is a masculine century" whereas the eighteenth, peopled with women who are "exquisite, ravishing, and easy, [who] talk ... laugh ... dance and reason like men" is "a feminine century" (I, 126). Salons in the seventeenth had "grace," but in the eighteenth, they have "ideas," a characterization that leaves the seventeenth century canon free of female influence (I, 127). But it is clear from d'Ormesson's choice of writers that the ideas in the eighteenth century are generated not by the salons' hostesses, but by her male habitués.

In d'Ormesson's first volume the only woman included in his pantheon of forty is George Sand. When he composes his second volume, he is careful to specify that it is not peopled by minor figures and second choices. In his words, the two volumes constitute "a kind of introduction to one of the most accomplished masterpieces of man's mind since his birth: French literature" (II, 9). This time five women become part of this masterpiece of the mind of humankind: Sévigné, Lafayette, Desbordes-Valmore, Colette, and Yourcenar. Sévigné was able to contribute to the masterpiece because of her maternal love: "We owe one of the masterpieces of our literature to the sadness of a mother faced with separation from her adored daughter" (II, 55). Above all, d'Ormesson insists upon the fact that Sévigné was not a real writer. He speaks through her to deny any pretention to authorship:

> Mme de Sévigné was far from having any literary ambition at all. She would die of laughter at the idea of passing for a writer ... Mme de Sévigné's letters were not meant to be published; they were only meant for her daughter ... I imagine that, to her stupor and her delight, Mme de Sévigné entered posthumously into the circle of great writers. (II, 56–7)

Lafayette 'created the modern novel," but given this literary history, her feat seems incredible given that no other women were drawn to writing. In the absence of any detailing of French female literary tradition, or even women's serious involvement in the literary field, the assertation that Lafayette must have had help with *La Princesse de Clèves*, which d'Ormesson resurrects, gains credibility.[101] He resolves the dilemma by stating that the unique qualities of Lafayette and La Rochefoucauld "conspired to create the masterpiece *La Princesse de Clèves*" (II, 62). Yet again the seventeenth century remains devoid of worthy female literary figures and influence. Scudéry, not surprisingly, remains a shadow, mentioned only in relation to her brother's intervention in the quarrel over Corneille's *Le Cid* (I, 58).

Les Lieux de mémoire

D'Ormesson's reflections are representative of the vision of the seventeenth-century held by mainstream France. Another recent project, destined for an academic as well as a general public, also reflects, but in greater depth, the effort to keep the seventeenth century a monument to France's power and genius, but one that is "a masculine century," to use d'Ormesson's formulation. In 1984, Pierre Nora published the first part of his enormous collection of essays illustrating and studying what he coined France's "lieux de mémoire" (realms of memory). The second volume appeared in 1986, and the third in 1992. The project was inspired by Nora's sense that France's *mémoire nationale* was rapidly disappearing. He thus decided to encourage colleagues to create "an inventory of the places where [national memory] is incarnated and that have, by men's will or by the work of centuries, remained the most striking symbols: holidays, monuments and commemorations, but also eulogies, dictionaries, and museums."[102] This monumental work has attracted much commentary, adulation, and critique. I wish only to examine here the inscription, or lack thereof, of women's literary influence in seventeenth-century France into this monument to French national identity.

In *Les Lieux de mémoire*, literature and the seventeenth century both occupy central places in this examination of the elements that make up the French national psyche. In addition to various studies of historical monuments such as Notre-Dame or the Eiffel Tower, there are a number of essays devoted to the ways in which the written record of France's cultural superiority has become a part of the nation's sense of itself. Contributors composed in-depth analyses of dictionaries, the French language, historiography, pedagogical works, monuments to writers, and even a few on individual authors themselves, as the following partial list reveals: "Le Panthéon," "Le 'Grand Dictionnaire' de Pierre Larousse," "Lavisse, instituteur national" (national teacher), "Le Tour de France par deux enfants," "Les centenaires de Voltaire et de Rousseau," "Les funérailles de Victor Hugo," "Les 'Lettres sur l'histoire de France' d'Augustin Thierry," "'L'histoire de France' de Lavisse," "Les mémoires d'Etat," "les classiques scolaires," "la khâgne," "'L'Histoire de la langue française' de Ferdinand Brunot," "La 'Recherche du temps perdu' de Marcel Proust," and "Descartes," among others. This massive enterprise thus accords a great amount of importance to words and to the teaching of those verbal traces—historical, literary, and linguistic—as well as to the ways in which the nation's past as been transmitted to posterity. Indeed, there is one whole section devoted specifically to "Pedagogy," which is comprehensible given, as we have seen, France's overt use of pedagogy to shape collective identity.

Given my own interests, when I first perused *Les Lieux de mémoire* I was struck by the fact that there was no article devoted to a peculiarly French cultural institution that had played a role in the shaping of many of the literary and philosophical artifacts that merited inscription: the salon. Constantly referred to by various figures since the seventeenth century as an example of French sociability and an institution developed in France, especially during the old regime, its omission is puzzling. The seventeenth-century itself is very present throughout *Les Lieux de mémoire*, proof of its important status in any conception of France's memory and historical identity. There are two essays devoted to Versailles. In the essay devoted to "La Cour" (the Court), Jacques Revel, like many before him, identifies the court of Louis XIV as the quintessential court, the "global model:" "In this essay we will start with the Louis XIV stereotype because it has been constructed and still functions as the emblem of 'court' in the French imaginary."[103] Revel adopts the position that this court is not history, but national memory, and as such continues to exercise a powerful influence on France's institutions and conceptions of power.[104] Milo's "Les Classiques scolaires" (The School Classics) also places the seventeenth century at the heart of the nation's memory, and shows, as we have seen, how the literary texts of the seventeenth century came to serve as pedagogical models, thus forming the minds of the nation. While both these essays delve into seventeenth-century society, women are barely evoked. Marc Fumaroli's "La Coupole" explores the significance of the French Academy and the importance of language to France's collective identity. His "Le Génie de la langue française" also focuses much attention on the seventeenth century. "Descartes" is granted his own essay. Another contribution is devoted to a major player in religious, political, and cultural arenas of the seventeenth century, Port-Royal. Noémi Hepp's "La Galanterie" also focuses on the seventeenth century as the origin of the modern conception of this "trait spécifique de la civilisation française."[105] Tracing its roots back to the seventeenth century, Hepp refers to Vaugelas and Méré, but, conforming to the views of the *ancien régime*, she identifies women as the ultimate professors of this French art:

> Thus it is women who teach men that pinnacle of worldly comportment that is
> gallantry and even more, it is with the objective of pleasing them that a man seeks

to become galant. Because women want refined manners, brilliant and playful conversation, a pleasant and flattering attitude, that "je ne sais quoi" that is piquant and that ability to put them into play without embarassing them.[106]

A specialist of the seventeenth century, Hepp briefly discusses the expression of *galanterie* in the salons of the period, referring in particular to the art of poetry, with "La Guirlande de Julie" and the "Carte de Tendre" as ultimate expressions of *galanterie*. Women thus figure prominently in the description of this French trait, but their role is the traditional one of muse and professor of social graces. The salons appear not as places of literary invention but as loci of games, light verse, and gallant conversation.[107]

Given that there are no studies in *Les Lieux de mémoire* devoted specifically to women, with the exception of Jeanne d'Arc, in order to find evidence of women's participation in aspects of France's national memory, one has to look in less obvious places, and follow threads as opposed to reading an essay directly on the subject. The next logical place after the subject of salon would be the art of conversation, to which Nora does indeed devote an essay. Nora's choice of "Conversation" as one of the *lieux* to be treated reveals its consecration as a particularly French phenomenon. In the seventeenth century, conversation, as we have seen, was viewed as an art in which women were especially adept. Developed in the salons, women's "conversation is a school for the best minds ... people consult them like oracles" as we have seen. This late twentieth-century exploration of the art of conversation, however, follows the same lines as that developed by the nineteenth-century nation builders. While conversation, when analyzed in terms of France's identity, may still possess some female roots, it is no longer valorized as a particularly female arena of excellence, its ties to literary production are viewed as minor, and the salon as the locus of female influence is displaced in favor of a history in which women figure only marginally.

The placement of the subject of conversation within the multi-volume set underscores its tie to national identity. It is found in the second of the volumes grouped under the rubric "Les Frances," which is subtitled "Traditions." The volumes has three parts: Modèles, which includes subjects such as "le clocher" (the church tower), "la cathédrale," and "la cour," none of which are uniquely French, followed by "Enracinements" (roots), which includes "Proverbes, contes et chansons," and "Le manual de folklore français," a rather vague category seemingly devoted to popular culture, and finally "Singularités" (singularities), where we find first "La Conversation," followed by most of the stereotypical traits foreigners would identify as typically French: "La galanterie, la vigne et le vin, la gastronomie, le café, le tour de France, and, rather less obvious, *La Recherche du temps perdu*." Conversation's placement among such hallmarks of Frenchness consecrates it as a quality on equal footing with wine and food in the conception of France's national identity.

Marc Fumaroli's article provides us with a perfect illustration of the curious process of remembering the salons. He begins not with France, but with "les Anciens," not surprising perhaps for a renowned French seventeenth-century literary scholar and a revered member of Le Collège de France. Fumaroli locates the origin of conversation in Plato's and Socrates's dialogues. From there he turns to Kant, who in 1798 identified conversation with France: He includes Kant's well-known description of France: "'The French nation is characterized among all others by its taste for conversation; in this respect it is a model for other nations'."[108] Fumaroli goes on to cite Kant's association of the art of conversation with women:

> Since taste concerns interaction with worldly women, women's conversation became the common language of the people of this milieu; and a similar tendency, it can't be contested, must have its effect on the willingness to help, to come to the aid of someone, and little by little on universal philanthropy founded on principles: it makes a whole people likeable. (III, 3619)

Fumaroli's commentary on Kant elides the philosopher's references to female influence as the literary specialist concentrates on the relationship between France as a nation and the art of conversation: "Could France be chosen for this supreme form of happiness for free men, conversation, the banquet in good company?," he queries (III, 3619). He then does turn to a woman, Germaine de Staël, whose remarks he characterizes as "less profound, but more famous:" "'It seems to be known that Paris is the city in the world where *esprit* and the taste for conversation are the most generally widespread'" (III, 3619). Fumaroli then describes the ties between conversation and politics.

Fumaroli's history of France's conversational art form in this article destined more for the general French public than for scholars, is a subtle refutation of salon and women's influence on this French characteristic.[109] Much of his carefully crafted and detailed account seems to vacillate between the need to give the salon milieu its due, following the leads of Kant, Staël and others, and Fumaroli's own opinion that "Parisian conversation should not too hastily be limited to worldly society" (III, 3630). While he admits that for Europe, French conversation is identified with "its worldly version" Fumaroli underscores that "conversation among scholars" continued. If worldly conversation first comes to mind, it is only because the Moderns ultimately triumphed over the Ancients, in Fumaroli's opinion (III, 3632). When he rather reluctantly evokes the salon milieu that fostered the art of conversation, he portrays it as primarily mixed, certainly not as female dominated.

Fumaroli does attribute some literary influence to the salons, even on the great works of the classical era, portraying the salons as centers for collective writing:

> In this respect memoirs are collective works, as are the maxims of this society of conversation of Mme de Sablé and La Rochefoucauld, and the novels attributed to Mme de Lafayette. If we add to this already imposing library the volumes of poetry that were composed for conversational groups (La Fontaine's fables are the masterpiece [of this form]) plays, isolated poems that were first read, judged, and commented upon by "good society," then one must admit that this oral milieu was the place of invention as well as reception for entire chapters, and the most brilliant, of our literature. (III, 3626)

But even while he evokes this literary influence, he subtly undervalues or even erases women's own contributions that developed out of the salons. Fumaroli's disassocation of women and literary creativity is remarkably apparent in his "and the novels attributed to Mme de Lafayette." Throughout his discussion of conversation, one figure in particular remains a shadowy presence: Scudéry. The marquise de Rambouillet is recognized for her role as salon queen, but Scudéry is simply her lesser shadow: "Of her kind, Mme de Rambouillet thus exercised a kind of monarchy that Mme de Lambert will find again in 1690, but that Mme du Plessis-Guénégaud and Mlle de Scudéry, to a lesser degree, had already inherited from her during Fouquet's and Colbert's time" (III, 3632). In a move consistent with his erasure of the female literary works that evolved from the salon milieu, Fumaroli does refer to Scudéry's published conversations in a footnote, but never to her novels, from which the majority of the conversations were drawn. He inscribes the *précieuses*, but refuses Scudéry a place at the center of salon culture.[110] He mentions Gilles Ménage's *mercredis*, but not Scudéry's *samedis*. Lafayette is also missing, as well as her salon, although since works have apparently only been attributed to her, this omission is seemingly justifiable.The marquise de Rambouillet figures prominently among the women mentioned, but even she is not evoked in order to show female influence. Rambouillet is consistently partnered with men. Fumaroli's first mention of the marquise is to illustrate how worldly, salon conversation is replaced by political conversation: "Mme de Rambouillet (wife of one of Louis XIII's best diplomats, gives Retz his court, Mme du

Deffand and Mlle de Lespinasse leave the speaking to Mirabeau and Marat"
(III, 3623). These three principal *salonnières* are first mentioned only to show
how they were voluntarily eclipsed by their male contemporaries.[111] Fumaroli
does refer to the practice of literary critique in the *chambre bleue*, but what
Chapelain had referred to the "tribunal de bon goût" is primarily male, with
the marquise playing the role of eighteenth-century female salon muse:

> After Malherbe, Voilture sets the tone for the *chambre bleue*, in perfect harmony
> with Arthénice-Mme de Rambouillet. But this duo allows all kinds of variants
> and vocal harmonies: other literary people, with different temperaments and
> styles, rival Voiture: the Chapelains, the Racans, the Godeaus. (III, 3634)

When Fumaroli wants to describe aspects of salon culture, he most frequently
has recourse to men for his examples. In describing the mixing of classes
at the salon de Rambouillet, he cites the "men of letters" rather than any
examples of women who not only participated in the salons but founded
their own: "The man of letters, with no birthright, no rank, no fortune, such
as a Voiture, can mix as equals at least, in this circle of chosen people, with
a prince de Condé, on the condition that the prince properly maintains his
part [of the conversation]" (III, 3634). When Fumaroli describes the interest
in conversation and the salons in the nineteenth, we encounter two familiar
figures. He refers to Victor Cousin the "inexhaustible apologist of the muses of
conversation during the *grand siècle*: Mlle de Scudéry, Mme de Longueville,"
and especially to Sainte-Beuve (III, 3651).

Two other men figure prominently in this remembrance of a conversational
past, Plato and Socrates. Woven into Fumaroli's account are constant
references to the two ancient philosophers, as though they were the models
France necessarily followed. In order to reconstitute conversation as French,
as opposed to Greek or Latin, Fumaroli ultimately identifies a Frenchman as
the model, but one who imbued the art with the essence of the Ancients:

> … we will say out of the blue that the modern and French model of conversation
> is Montaigne's Essays: vaste improvisation, dictated or written, the Essays
> preserve the impulsive [character], the friendly tone, the unsuspected twists and
> turns of a personal and socratic conversation with the reader, who is already
> for Montaigne "my equal, my brother," but also with this excellent society
> of ancients, philosphers, poets, heros, who, thanks to Montaigne cease to be
> books and become interlocutors in a general and passionate conversation.
> (III, 3628)

Fumaroli's inscription of conversation as a national trait is thus decidedly male-oriented and dominated. His treatment of Scudéry is symbolic of the erasure of *femmes savantes*, women writers, and women's literary taste and critique during the seventeenth century. This vision is the culmination of the long process we have witnessed, a process by which a certain image of the classical age, and a reformulation of women's participation in its literary culture, achieved the status of national history. The "singularité" of France's history as emphasized by Nora eliminates one of the principal "singularités" of French literature and culture at least during the century touted as an integral part of France's national memory: the female literary tradition and the worldly taste that shaped the literature and the thoughts of the classical period.

Notes

1   "Our classics are those by seventeenth-century writers; and not all, of course, but only the best." L. Petit de Julleville, *Revue universitaire*, vol. I, 1900, p. 325, as cited by Martine Jey, "Les Classiques de l'ère Ferry," *Littératures classiques*, vol. 19, 1993, p. 246.

2   As cited by Pierre Nora in "Lavisse, instituteur national," *Les Lieux de mémoire*, I, p. 265.

3   Nora details the relationship between Lavisse's history, France's pedagogical mission, and nationalism explaining that, "No one sensed better the extent to which teaching was tied to the functioning of democracy." Thanks to Lavisse, "youth will associate the cult of the homeland with that of knowledge" (I, p. 248). Lavisse's history was so popular that it was already in its seventy-fifth edition in 1895 (I, p. 256).

4   In *The Cult of the Nation in France*, Bell traces the valences of the terms nation and *patrie*. See pp. 1–21 in particular.

5   Dictionnaire de Furetière, 1690.

6   The Robert's *Dictionnaire historique de la langue française* details this transformation in meaning: "The word evolves at the end of the 17th century: the modern sense was only spread after Vauban's reforming works ... and especially in the 18th, in relation to patriot, with nation, and with certain uses of republic, concepts that are joined during the Revolution. This political value then evolves; then in the 19th and 20th, it is colored by nationalist ideologies, taking on stronger connotations during wars."

7   As Niek van Sas points out: "In the nineteenth century the development of the historical discipline had gone hand in hand with the process of nation-building: historians were the henchmen of the nation." "Towards a New National History: *Lieux de Mémoire* and Other Theatres of Memory," in *Historians and Social Values*, ed. Joep Leerssen and Ann Rigney (Amsterdam, 2000), p. 170.

8   Drawing upon a survey the author did in 1986, M.P. Schmitt advances that "in all, it appears that the classics represent the literary space best consolidated by the State." "Les Classiques en classe," *Cahiers de littérature du XVIIe siècle*, vol. 10, 1988, p. 129. Students, for example, when asked to cite authors from the seventeenth century, made

the fewest errors. 161 students were able to name three seventeenth-century authors. In contrast, only 13 were able to cite three authors from the surrealist movement. Corneille, Racine, and Molière were the most frequently cited (p. 128).

9   Emmanuel Fraisse traces the evolution of the content of pedagogical anthologies in *Les Anthologies en France* (Paris, 1997), pp. 216–19.

10   Martine Jey, "Les classiques de l'ère Ferry," p. 238. After 1880 the percentages Jey gives are: seventeenth century: 54.45 per cent, eighteenth century 15.05 per cent, nineteenth century 15.05 per cent, sixteenth century 8.11 per cent, Middle Ages 7.34 per cent. Manuals of rhetoric are dropped from programs after 1880.

11   Ibid., p. 238.

12   Jey cites the official instructions issued in 1885 for "la classe de cinquième" as an example: "The commission ... decided that the word 'classics' should not be understand as only the works of seventeenth-century authors, but also the great writers of the 18th and 19th centuries. Nevertheless, teachers should only admit [the later writers] very prudently." Ibid., p. 240.

13   Ibid., p. 241.

14   Fraisse states: "... they have as a goal to contribute to the formation of educated minds and of citizens who, sharing common references that constitute the collective patrimony, express the same values." Ibid., p. 216.

15   Jey explains that "compared to the literature of the 17th century, those of the 18th and of the romantic period are distanced from France; they had been subjected to foreign influences. The cosmopolitanism of the 18th century appears suspicious." Ibid., p. 245

16   Ibid., p. 245.

17   Ibid., p. 245.

18   See in particular Joan DeJean, "Classical Reeducation" and Anne-Marie Thiesse and Hélène Mathieu's "The Decline of the Classical Age and the Birth of the Classics," in *Displacements: Women, Tradition, Literatures in French* (Baltimore, 1991), pp. 74–96.

19   In "Men's Reading, Women's Writing: Gender and the Rise of the Novel," Nancy K. Miller details the erasure of women's fiction from the register of the eighteenth-century novel and advances that one must read women's and men's literature side-by-side, as it was originally produced, in order to truly understand male literary production, as well as to perceive how the very categories we use to judge literature and canonize it are gender-based categories and constructions. *Displacements*, pp. 37–54. We will have occasion to return to her provocative study later.

20   DeJean, "Classical Reeducation," as well as Milo's "Les Classiques Scolaires" in *Les Lieux de mémoire*.

21   For a history of women's education, see *Histoire des Femmes XVI–XVIII siècles*, ed. Natalie Zemon Davis and Michèle Perrot (Paris, 1991), vol. 3.

22   "Under Voltaire's pen and the *Encyclopedie*, the word qualifies French authors from the century of Louis XIV who, as opposed to baroque authors (named such much later) elaborated an art of balance and reason, by advocating the respect and imitation of the Ancients." *Dictionnaire historique de la langue française.*

23   According to Milo, French texts began to be incorporated into the classroom between 1720 and 1770. But, he specifies, such texts were included for their linguistic, as opposed to their literary, value: "It was not about texts with aesthetic function, but those that allowed one to uncover the linguistic rules for the students." "Les Classiques Scolaires," in *Les Lieux de mémoire*, Ii, p. 2084.

24   Ibid., p. 2085.

25   Gustave Merlet, *Etudes sur les français classiques*, as cited by Milo, p. 2108.

26   Ibid., p. 52103.

27   Milo uses the example of Balzac to illustrate this point: "It is from around 1895, when Balzac became an author taught in classes, that his translation became massive, with dozens of titles [produced] annually." Ibid., p. 2088.

28   Alain Viala has recently analyzed Sévigné's status. See "Un jeu d'images: Amateur, mondaine, écrivain?" in *Europe: revue littéraire mensuelle*, pp. 57–68.

29   According to Milo, the school's role "is not the creation of reputations but their diffusion." "Les Classiques Scolaires," II, p. 2087.

30   Ibid., p. 2123.

31   Anne-Marie Thiesse and Hélène Mathieu, "The Decline of the Classical Age and the Birth of the Classics," in *Displacements*, pp. 74–96.

32   Ibid., p. 75.

33   Ibid., p. 83.

34   Ibid., p. 84.

35   I will return briefly later to the divergent interpretations of Lafayette's masterpiece. It can be argued, I believe, that scholarship on Lafayette's novel in France continues to follow the trajectory alluded to by Thiesse and Mathieu.

36   French scholars seem particularly desirous of finding the man behind the masterpiece in the case of *La Princesse de Clèves*. As we shall see, even Marc Fumaroli, Academician and revered seventeenth-century scholar, doubts Lafayette's authorship, echoing Cousin of one hundred and fifty years previously. The most developed of these attacks is Geneviève Moulineaux's two-volume opus *Mme de Lafayette romancière?* and *Mme de Lafayette historienne?* in which she works to deny Lafayette any authorial position whatsoever.

37   Thiesse and Mathieu, "The Decline of the Classical Age," p. 86.

38   Ralph Albanese, *Molière à l'école républicaine* (Saratoga, CA, 1992).

39   Ibid., p. 56.

40   Ibid., p. 60.

41   Milagros Palma, Preface to Anne-Thérèse de Lambert, *Réflections nouvelles sur les femmes* (Paris, Côté-femmes, 1989), p. 20. In his edition of *Les Femmes savantes*, Jean Lecomte explains that *Les Femmes savantes* was not particularly popular in the seventeenth century. In the eighteenth, many philosophers took issue with the premise of the play, which they viewed as an attack on the intellectual emancipation of women. Thus the play was only performed three hundred and fifty-three times during the eighteenth century, and only eleven times between 1741 and 1750. In contrast, in the nineteenth century *Les Femmes savantes* was presented seven hundred and forty-three times. *Les Femmes savantes* (Classiques Larousse, 1971), p. 12.

42   Albanese, *Molière à l'école républicaine*, p. 102. See Albanese for an in-depth analysis of the Molière's elevated status during the second half of the nineteenth century.

43   Albanese cites one author at the beginning of the twentieth century who states that "'Molière's comedy is both humanist and to a great degree a French work above all, in which one can see the characteristic traits of national genius.'" Another Molière specialist elevates the playwright as "'the most complete incarnation of French genius.'" Lanson also emphasizes his "Frenchness," calling Molière the author "'the most completely French.'" Albanese, "Le Discours scolaire au XIXe siècle," in *Continuum* (New York, AMS Press, 1989), vol. 1, p. 43.

44   As cited by Albanese, *Molière à l'école républicaine*, p. 108.

45 Albanese cites Saint-Marc Giradin's *Cours de littérature dramatique 1843–1863* as an example of this idealization of the character of Henriette, whom Giradin touted as "'the highest feminine ideal in Molière's works.'" Ibid., p. 85.

46 A. Gazier, *La Grande Encyclopédie* (Paris, 1886–1902), p. 25. As cited by Albanese, ibid., pp. 112–13.

47 Ralph Albanese, "Le Discours scolaire au XIXème siècle," p. 39. Albanese is citing a speech given by M. Dugard at the beginning of the twentieth century.'

48 M.P. Schmitt, "Les classiques en classe," *Cahiers de littérature du XVIIe siècle*, vol. 10, 1988, p. 127.

49 Ibid., p. 131. Schmitt also points out that when questioned as to what plays students had actually seen on stage, 60 per cent of the plays were from the seventeenth century, and Molière represented nine-tenths of the 60 per cent. Not surprisingly, the plays most often seen were the same as the ones studied in class, thus making *Les Femmes savantes* one of the most frequently read as well as seen plays among French students. "Les classiques en classe," p. 131.

50 James Gaines and Michael Koppish have edited a volume on Molière for the MLA's Approaches to Teaching Series. This volume provides a number of less traditional ways of teaching Molière, including my own essay on teaching *Les Femmes savantes* and *Les Précieuses ridicules*.

51 The newest Larousse edition of *Les Précieuses* edited by Brigitte Diaz in 1998 also preserves the distinction between Rambouillet's and Scudéry's salons. Rambouillet is the perfect salon, whereas Scudéry's salon is Molière's model: "Exemplary of this precious verbosity, Mlle de Scudéry and her sagas" (p. 136).

52 Aronson refers to Sainte-Beuve who reproaches Scudéry "to have remained a virgin and an old maid until the age of 94." *Mademoiselle de Scudéry*, p. 14.

53 It should be remarked that, while the marquise de Rambouillet was known for receiving her *habitués* in bed, most *salonnières* did not, and Scudéry was never portrayed in this position by her contemporaries.

54 But, as we have seen in the preceding chapter, Scudéry continued to animate her salon well into the 1680s and probably beyond.

55 Père Rapin, *Lettres*, 1673, p. 186.

56 The format for the 1970s Classiques Larousse editions of the plays varies somewhat from the most recent ones. These editions contain lengthy "documentation thématique" consisting of excerpts of texts from the seventeenth to the early twentieth century. There is not much commentary included, giving the reader more leeway to interpret the context on his/her own than one finds in subsequent editions. Of course, the choice of texts is still a determining factor. In general there is little effort to present the relationship between women and literature during the period. Scudéry is consistently presented negatively. This "documentation" is very dense. One has a hard time imagining the typical student plugging through it. The most recent editions have drawn upon this documentation for their own introductions and notes, without reproducing the actual texts. There is thus more of an effort on the part of editors to guide the reader's view of the plays, especially in the editions produced in the 1990s.

57 Brigitte Diaz in her edition of *Les Précieuses ridicules* states that "Henriette portrays the reasonable ideal of a balanced femininity, in which the concern for education and knowledge does not take precedence over the blossoming of emotions and love" (p. 111). One wonders where in *Les Femmes savantes* one can sense Henriette's "concern for education and knowledge."

58   Thus Isabelle Ducos-Filippi in her 1995 Bordas edition of *Les Précieuses ridicules* has the *chambre bleue* die out before the Fronde, and designates Scudéry her unworthy, bourgeois successor (p. 86).

59   It is interesting that in many cases, editors say that Mlle de Rambouillet was there, not Mme or the marquise. There is confusion as to who was actually there. Yet they use this reference to advance that neither the marquise nor Julie d'Angennes, her daughter, felt attacked. Most editors refer to Ménage's remark in his *Menagiana*. Brigitte Diaz is typical in this instance. She states that "Ménage attended the opening with Mme de Rambouillet" and then cites Ménage himself: "'I was at the opening of the *Precieuses ridicules* by Molière at the Petit-Bourbon. Mlle de Rambouillet was also there, Mme de Grignan, and the *cabinet* of the hôtel de Rambouillet'" (*Les Précieuses ridicules*, p. 29). We do not have the marquise's reactions, nor Scudéry's, so it is possible to create a mythology according to which the principal representatives of the worldly milieu applauded Molière's satire. Such an interpretation does not leave open the possibility that they sensed the growing critique over women's influence on the literary scene that had started a few years before Molière's play.

60   I am aware that I am conflating what could be viewed as two separate genres, the "manuel scolaire" being the more generic term for French school books of any discipline. My term "pedagogical literary anthology" would not exist in France, where a work such as Lagarde et Michard would simply be categorized under the rubric of "manuel scolaire." In order to be more specific as to the type of text that interests me, I thus prefer to use anthology, knowing that it also takes forms that are not specifically pedagogical.

61   See, for example, Alain Choppin, *Les manuals Scolaires: Histoire et actualité* (Paris, 1992); Emmanuel Fraisse, *Les Anthologies en France* (Paris, 1997) and Fraisse's extensive bibliography, Antoine Compagnon, *La Troisième république des lettres* (Paris, 1983), and A. Prost, *L'enseignement en France, 1800–1967* (Paris, 1968), to cite only a few of a vast scholarly corpus devoted to this subject. In a review essay entitled "Histoire de l'enseignement du français: La République, l'école et les 'textes français'," Eric Walter gives a good overview of the field (in *Le Français aujourd'hui: revue de l'association française des enseignants de français*, vol. 52, December, 1980, pp. 97–105). Thiesse and Mathieu's influential article "The Decline of the Classics" is also very enlightening.

62   There has been little to no interdisciplinary research on these questions in France due to the autonomy each discipline still tends to seek.

63   Fraisse provides an overview of the relationship of various anthologies and pedagogy in *Les Anthologies en France*, pp. 213–57. The author focuses on how the composition of these anthologies has changed in the past 100 years. Like many scholars, Fraisse notes the preponderant presence of the seventeenth century, but does not delve into why this is the case or question the presentation of the classical literary field.

64   Alain Choppin, *Les manuals scolaires*, p. 24.

65   See her discussion of Batteux's and other early pedagogical anthologies in "Classical Reeducation," especially pp. 28–34.

66   DeJean, ibid., p. 29.

67   See DeJean, ibid., pp. 31–2.

68   Batteux, *Principes de littérature*, p. 355.

69   Batteux actually admired Maintenon's style because it is succinct: "Mme de Maintenon is an excellent model … she only says what has to be said, says it well, and says only that" (p. 351).

70 DeJean, "Classical Reeducation," p. 31.
71 "Classical Reeduction," p. 33.
72 J.F. La Harpe, *Lycée ou Cours de littérature ancienne et moderne* (Paris, 1816), p. vi. All further references will be to this edition, with page numbers inserted parenthetically in the text.
73 See Fraisse's discussion in *Les Anthologies en France*, pp. 225–8.
74 Des Granges states: "And the 17th century, if it didn't leave any classical masterpiece in this genre [the novel], did produce a great number of novels. Their success shows us, better perhaps than a tragedy by Racine or a sermon by Bossuet, the dominant taste in the 17th century." Ch.-M. Des Granges, *Histoire de la Littérature française: à l'usage des classes de lettres et des divers examens* (Paris, 1913), p. 448.
75 Des Granges, ibid., p. 529. Des Granges reminds readers of the misguided taste of seventeenth-century France, a taste that fortunately has been eradicated. He explains that the writers admired by the worldly public, such as Scudéry, Chapelain, Saint-Amand, and Colletet have become des "grotesques" today thanks to Boileau's courageous imposition of true classical taste over worldly taste. Ibid., p. 528.
76 Des Granges does explain the hôtel de Rambouillet and mentions Voiture, but does not include any works to be studied. Scudéry does not figure at all, and Rambouillet is cited as the source for Molière's satires. *La Littérature expliquée*, ed. Ch.-M. Des Granges and Ch. Chartier (Paris, not dated), pp. 71–2,
77 There are numerous editions of Castex's and Surer's various histories and manuals. By the mid-twentieth century Hachette was producing volumes dedicated to individual centuries, such as one I consulted published in 1947, produced with the collaboration of G. Becker.
78 André Lagarde and Laurent Michard, *XVIIe siècle: Les Grands auteurs français du programme, anthology et histoire littéraire* (Paris), p. 73.
79 The authors state, for example, that "next to the great genres dominated by classical taste there exists the minor worldly genres in which *esprit précieux* reigns." Lagarde et Michard, ibid., p. 75.
80 *XVIIe Siècle*, ed. Robert Horville (Paris, 1988).
81 Ibid., p. 75. Horville's description of the salon phenomenon is limited to one page.
82 Ibid., p. 215. Horville remarks "Molière, in fact, is not critiquing the desire to learn, but, as he often does, the excesses that accompany it. How could he deny the positive role that women play in French cultural life?" (p. 215).
83 *Anthologie de la litérature française*, ed. Robert Leggewie (New York, 1990), vol. 1, p. 108.
84 Ibid., p. 219.
85 Perry Gethner has devoted much of his scholarly work to rediscovering these female playwrites. As his work shows, writers such as Villedieu and Catherine Bernard were actually very successful during their day.
86 René Bray describes Boileau's reception during his own time period, stating that while today Boileau's works are hailed as models of good sense, for many of his contemporaries he symbolized "unreasonableness, bad taste, and incorrect expression" (Bray, *Boileau: L'Homme et l'oeuvre* (Paris, 1962), p. 159.
87 Ibid., p. 154.
88 I did a very unsystematic and informal survey of the number of editions of Boileau's works listed in the catalog of France's National Library by century. The results confirm the nineteenth century's obsession with Boileau. For the seventeenth century there were

fifty-six entries, the eighteenth had eighty, the twentieth had nine and the nineteenth had four hundred and eighty-seven entries.

89   Joan DeJean details Boileau's efforts to dismiss all female literary production from the literary arena. She states that as early as 1711, he "was already accepted as 'the arbiter of literary taste.'" *Fictions of Sappho 1546–1937* (Chicago, 1989), p. 111. This status became etched in stone by the nineteenth century.

90   Bray states that there were fifty-seven editions of Boileau's works published between 1789 and 1815, one hundred and thirty between 1815 and 1850, and one hundred and twenty-two between 1850 and 1929.

91   Ibid., p. 156.

92   Bray, ibid., p. 5. Bernard Beugnon and Zuber have also examined in detail Boileau's reception in *Boileau: Visages Anciens, Visages Nouveaux* (Montreal, 1973).

93   Bray, ibid., p. 156.

94   A recent example is Madeleine de Scudery's *Promenade de Versailles*, which was republished in a tiny boxed set along with Felibien's *Relation des Fêtes* to commemorate Versailles. By contrast, in the United States, the Publications of the Modern Language Association as well as University of Chicago Press have made many seventeenth-century women's texts available, in the original French as well as in translation, a few representative examples being Scudéry's "Histoire de Sapho" from *Le Grand Cyrus*, Jacqueline Pascal's works, Maintenon's pedagogical treatises and letters to her teachers at Sainte Cyr, and Villedieu's *Mémoires de la vie de Henriette-Sylvie de Molière*, among others.

95   Alain Niderst, *Le Siècle de Louis XIV: Anthologie des mémoralites du siècle de Louis XIV* (Paris, 1997). This work is over nine hundred pages long.

96   For an analysis of the development of the memoir genre during the period, and women's contribution to the form of the genre, see my *Revising Memory*.

97   Niderst, *Le Siècle de Louis XIV*, p. xiv.

98   Jean d'Ormesson, *Une autre histoire de la littérature française* (Paris, 1997), vol. I, p. 11. All references will be to this edition with page numbers inserted parenthetically in the text.

99   For a description of such anthologies, see Joan DeJean, "Classical Reeducation."

100 D'Ormesson, vol. I, p. 14.

101 He states: "that Mme de Lafayette is the author of *La Princesse de Clèves* is not at all in doubt. The true, the only question is that of the part played by La Rochefoucauld in the composition of the work" (II, p. 61).

102 Pierre Nora, "Présentation," *Les Lieux de mémoire*, 1984; (Paris, 1997), vol. I, p. 15. Nora further explains his concept of "lieux de mémoire" in his essay "Comment écrire l'histoire de France," vol. 2, pp. 2219–34.

103 Jacques Revel, "La Cour," in *Les Lieux de mémoire*," vol. III, pp. 3146–7.

104 Ibid., pp. 3144–6.

105 Noémi Hepp, "La Galanterie," in *Les Lieux de mémoire*, vol. III, p. 3677.

106 Ibid., pp. 368–81. Hepp cites Méré's definition of *galanterie* here.

107 Ibid., p. 3689.

108 Marc Fumaroli, "La Conversation," in *Les Lieux de Memoire*, ed. Pierre Nora (Paris, 1992), vol. 2, p. 682. All references will be to this edition, with page numbers inserted parenthetically in the text.

109 It is interesting that Fumaroli does accord women more influence on language and conversation in some of his scholarly works, in particular in *L'Age de l'éloquence*.

110 The only time Scudéry is actually cited is in his discussion of the nineteenth century: "Mlle de Scudéry had even found the expression '*esprit de joie*' to define the climate and the ultimate object of aristocratic leisure occupied by the conversations" (p. 717), a remark that portrays her as a *mondain*, not as a writer.

111 It is interesting to note that Fumaroli does mention the architectural changes that salon culture brought to France, but he does not identify the marquise de Rambouillet, as most historians do, as the source of this change (p. 687).

Afterword

Christine de Pizan: C'est pourquoi je vous saurais gré, ma Dame, de bien vouloir me dire si l'esprit féminin est capable de jugement et de discernement...

Raison...Mais tu dois savoir que le jugement auquel tu fais allusion est un don que Nature fait aux hommes et aux femmes, à certains plus qu'à d'autres. Il ne vient absolument pas du savoir, qui pourtant le couronne chez chex qui naturellement en sont doués. Car tu sais que deux forces réunies sont plus puissantes et plus efficaces que ne le serait individuellement chacune d'elles. C'est pourquoi j'ose affirmer que si une personne a naturellement ce discernement que l'on appelle le bon sens, et en plus le savoir, alors elle mérite véritablement la palme de l'excellence.

La Cité des Dames[1]

In 1882, Ernest Renan posed a central question that continues to inspire and haunt scholars today, perhaps even more so than in the philosopher's own lifetime. In *Qu'est-ce qu'une nation?* (*What is a Nation?*) Renan interrogates the essence of nationhood and passes in review many of the characteristics usually identified as the reasons why people band together to form a country: ethnicity, linguistic similarities, religious affinities, and geographical considerations, to name only the most obvious. While such attributes may indeed influence the composition of a nation, Renan comes to the conclusion that they are not the true essence of nationhood. Language, religion, and geography are insufficient to unite individuals and inspire them to define, defend, and feel the essence of a nation. Far more powerful and influential in Renan's view is history, the sharing of a common past. For Renan, a nation is "a soul, a spiritual principle" that is constituted above all of the shared memories of its countrymen. It is "the collective possession of a rich inheritance of memories ... the cult of the ancestors is the most legitimate; ancestors have made us what we are. A heroic past, great men, glory (by which I understand genuine glory), this is the social capital upon which one bases a national idea." [2] The memories of this past need not be uniquely positive to serve their unifying function. Renan stresses that a people must have suffered together as well as reveled in triumph. It is in the acceptance of this shared past, the decision to acknowledge it as shared, that Renan locates the national solidarity essential for the soul of a nation to exist.

Renan acknowledges the subjectivity inherent in the creation of this shared past. Those who are united by this "spiritual principle" born out of the past must not only remember, they must forget: "Forgetting, and I will even say historical error, are an essential factor in the formation of a nation ... the essence of a nation is that all individuals have a lot of things in common, and also that all have forgotten a lot of things."[3] Renan is referring to the less-than-glorious moments in French history such as the brutal way the north and south of France were united. As Renan remarks, few Frenchmen know the "continual terror" this union created at the time. The "cult of the ancestors" that unites a nation often eliminates such reprehensible actions, or relegates them to the deep recesses of the national unconscious. But as we have seen, what is forgotten in the creation of a shared national past is not always something that could be universally identified as ignominious or negative. Sometimes a decision is made to forget aspects of the past in an effort to forge a certain identity for a nation.

Renan's remarks are particularly applicable to the case of seventeenth-century France. Women's participation in the literary field of this formative and formidable period was "forgotten" or revised in order to advance a particular "spiritual principle" of the French nation. The "element of forgetting" is especially apparent when one examines France's literary ancestors during the classical period, arguably the time that provides France with its most identifiable and stable collective sense of literary identity. While the mid-seventeenth century in particular recognized the influence women had on the development of French literature and culture, the backlash beginning in the eighteenth century and developed in the nineteenth seems designed to ensure that the "soul of France," composed of the "rich legacy of memories" would be of a particular gender.[4] Not all "ancestors" are acknowledged. Critics and historians worked to erase the influence of women on France's "social capital," and ensure that France could claim "a heroic past, great men" as its "national idea." In the preceding pages I have offered an analysis of the place attributed to Yourcenar's "shadows" in France's "rich legacy of memories," and tried to show how and suggest why they became shadows in the first place. When the French literary canon became identified primarily with the seventeenth century, certain authors, social structures, and an entire distinctive characteristic of the literary field was forgotten or redefined, namely the works and literary influences created by and associated with women. The case of the seventeenth century salons and their literary influence is a powerful illustration of the subjective nature of historical memory and of the symbiotic relationship between this memory and power.

Renan's observations of over one hundred years ago were not only applicable to his own time period, but even more surprising, especially prescient of what would happen in the succeeding century. In speaking of the necessity of national forgetfulness, Renan points to the danger of historical scholarship: because forgetting is essential to nationhood, "progress in historical studies is often a danger for a sense of nationality. Historical investigation, in fact, reminds people of the violence that occurs at the origin of any political formation."[5] The proliferation of histories of French activities during World War II over the past thirty years in particular have presented a challenge to the country's sense of unity as a nation. On a different level, historical and literary scholarship has challenged the sense of collective nationhood associated with France's literary history and heritage, especially its revered seventeenth century. Debates between American scholars and their counterparts in the hexagon, for example, have illustrated to an exceptional degree that literature, especially the "classics," and the historical setting from which they emanated, remain an integral part of France's cultural values and a means by which the nation defines itself as exceptional. Some of these debates have revolved around scholarship, but the most virulent have involved pedagogical issues, proof that teaching is still viewed in France in particular as an essential tool in the creation of a shared, collective sense of nation. In particular, there has been resistance to the widening of the French literary canon.[6] French critics have referred to American curricula in French departments as "irresponsible," citing in particular the inclusion of women writers and francophone texts to the exclusion of the "real" representatives of the French literary "patrimoine."[7] The emotion accompanying these attacks on America's presentation of French literature indicates that the fear is not that American professors might teach the wrong texts. Rather, it is that they might teach the wrong France, or at least a different past from that consecrated by the French as a nation.

In this study, I have offered a series of close readings designed to resurrect the salon movement from a history that has not recognized its full importance and revitalize its image. Instead of a canonized portrait of a Rambouillet enforcing rules of social comportment and a Scudéry dabbling in literary games and genres that no one would deign to read, I have shown how the salons and the worldly public they created and fostered were major players in the literary sphere, defining taste, creating new genres with important social messages and implications, and, as Buffet's text strikingly illustrates, polishing and molding a language that was a monarch's unifying tool. Literary quarrels such as those surrounding *Le Cid* and *La Princesse de Clèves* attest to the fact that the seventeenth-century worldly public, in particular its female constituents, is ingrained in the seventeenth-century literary field. The satirical pens of the

Molières and Boileaus belie the unease with which this female influence was met. Had salon and worldly literary influence been considered ineffectual or inconsequential, there would have been no need for such prominent voices to attempt to rectify a "monde à l'envers." Tracing the threads of influence and resistance leads to the conclusion that France's seventeenth-century women were a force to be reckoned with, and the literary realm was arguably the sphere they chose to assert their influence on the century's political and social structures.

In characterizing seventeenth-century France in the shadow of the Sun King, Orest Ranum has remarked that Louis XIV sought to channel *esprit* and creative impulses into "established channels and institutions."[8] In many ways his methods of encouraging literary and cultural creativity were at exact odds with those advanced by the worldly milieu of the salons. In an effort to impose stability and uniformity upon the cultural realm, Louis XIV espoused a singular vision, not the collaborative methods that characterized the critical and literary approaches of the *mondains*. As we have seen in the quarrels and in the analyses of the works of two of the major participants in salon culture, Lafayette and Villedieu, the collaborative methods of the salons resulted in the development of new genres, primarily the novel, and new methods for judging, neither of which could be easily controlled and classified. The resulting literary field with its worldly influence offered alternative models for behavior, such as the Princesse de Clèves and Chimène, new ways of achieving knowledge, as played out in *Zaïde*, and ultimately a new literary culture at a time when literature played a political role in the shaping of an image of France. The danger of worldly influence is thus more than a weakening of scholastic values and an elevation of a new public. These new literary values and genres, as products of the worldly milieu, offered a vision of a new society and a new literary culture that found itself frequently at odds with that reflected in the politics of Louis XIV. The image of *le Grand Siècle* that will eventually be transmitted to posterity is also an image of France offered to its people as well as to the world. The history of the control and creation of this image, and the fate of worldly influence in this process, reveals the complex shaping of a nation's collective identity.

History has found it easier to associate any salon influence with the inheritors of the seventeenth-century salon tradition.[9] But this recognition and acceptance of eighteenth-century salon influence was made possible through a redefinition of women's roles within their favored institution. Most eighteenth-century *salonnières* did not resemble their seventeenth-century ancestors. And the price to pay for this acknowledgement was high. The concept of the eighteenth-century salon has overshadowed that of its predecessor, indeed replaced it almost all together, leaving the uniqueness and originality of the early salons unrecognized, and more important, the standard male-dominated history of France's canon unchallenged. In *Mastering Memory* I have traced a process by which the conception of seventeenth-century salons evolved over a period of two hundred years. Recognized and lauded by their seventeenth-century contemporaries as a unique trait of French society, the earlier manifestation of this female-dominated institution was eventually erased from the history of the period it had so shaped, and was reformulated to advance a more acceptable image of female influence, one that the eighteenth-century salon more easily embodied.[10] The salon milieu was eliminated as a serious influence from the depiction of one of the most celebrated and revered periods of France's past, especially its literary history. And whereas many French scholars, historians, and publishers today are drawn to this period of French literary history, the image of the seventeenth-century literary field and of women's roles in that field has not changed significantly from those propagated by the nineteenth-century nation builders. It remains difficult for scholars to challenge the images of seventeenth-century salons similar to those that have developed outside of the hexagon because the stakes are very different. To revise the memory of the seventeenth-century salon in France entails placing into question one of the building blocks of French national identity. As we have seen, the same seventeenth-century texts continue to be reedited in France and the context to explain the various plays in particular has undergone little to no revision. Similarly the same texts appear on the programs of national exams. As a result, the view of women's participation in *le Grand Siècle* held by the vast majority of the French, scholars as well as the mainstream public, remains largely the same as it was in the nineteenth and early twentieth century. D'Ormesson's literary history is just one example of the common conception of France's illustrious literary past. And while some scholars have recently focused on the salons, and on specific women writers such as Scudéry and Villedieu, for the most part women continue to be treated as separate entities. It remains much more difficult to integrate their participation and influence into discussions of the classical literary field at large.

The history of one genre in particular illustrates to an exceptional degree the effect a reevaluation of the salons and their influence on the classical literary field can have. Perhaps the most recognizable contribution of France's seventeenth-century salons is the development of the genre that would come to dominate France's literary scene, the novel. The fate of the seventeenth-century novel in standard literary histories is another indication of the effort to divorce the salon milieu from any serious literary innovation and creation, and to preserve a classical period devoid of serious female influence. As we have seen, Scudéry's contributions are condemned as unreadable and as illusive mirrors of an equally unfathomable worldly society. Villedieu remains largely a shadow, her works reedited in France only in expensive scholarly editions.[11] Lafayette's universally acclaimed masterpiece, *La Princesse de Clèves*, is the only seventeenth-century novel to merit publication in mainstream paperback collections in France. It also now exists in more than four English translations. The interpretations of this particular novel illustrate the different views of classical France determined in large measure by how scholars perceive the context to which *La Princesse de Clèves* belongs. Many scholars, following the lead of feminist scholars such as Nancy K. Miller, view the heroine as a positive figure who succeeds in forging a new direction for herself and offers an alternative model to her contemporaries. Advocates of this more positive interpretation often rely on Joan DeJean's analysis of the avowal or "confession" scene according to which *aveu* is used by Lafayette in the sense of an oath of loyalty, rather than as "confession" or admonition of guilt. Following these readings, the princess does not retreat from love and society but rather rejects what she considers inevitable unhappiness were she to marry a duke known for his inability to remain faithful. Convinced that Nemours could never be faithful to her, the princess prefers to keep her idea of love alive by not acting upon it. She does not simply retire to a convent, as would other heroines of the period. Nor does she die immediately, the other frequent fate for female characters. Rather, she chooses to divide her time between her country estate and the convent, determines her own fate, and keeps alive an ideal love that does not risk destruction from jealousy and infidelity. Her own "repos" or peace of mind is at the heart of these actions, not guilt or weakness.[12]

As we have seen in the various anthologies evoked here, the above interpretation is not the dominant one, especially in France. Concurrent with the effort to advance Lafayette as an exception to her time rather than as a particularly outstanding example is the canonization of a particular interpretation of her novel. A favorite passage to anthologize is the princess's withdrawal from society at the end of the novel. Many literary historians praise the heroine for her renunciation of love in favor of duty. The princess is hailed as a model because she is able to withstand passion and remain faithful to the memory of her husband. She is often portrayed as being the cause of her husband's death. None of the anthologies or histories we examined underscores the fact that the princess only spends half the year in the convent, and the rest at home. There are no other reasons aside from guilt over her husband's death given for her rejection of Nemours. Lafayette's atypical ending is thus reconfigured in order for the princess to be advanced as an acceptable classical model. These very different interpretations of the century's best-known and most controversial novel are directly related to how one views the context that produced it. The interpretation that advances the princess as a powerful heroine as opposed to a dejected victim is in large part a product of a new vision of the seventeenth century in general advanced by many scholars, especially in the United States. Instead of teaching *La Princesse de Clèves* as the first modern French novel, many scholars consider it and teach it within the larger context of the salons and the female literary tradition in France.[13] When female influence is restored to the seventeenth-century literary scene, new, provocative interpretations are possible. For example it becomes possible to argue that Lafayette uses the novel as a social tool in order to advance an alternative notion of *vraisemblance* or plausibility. As scholars have delved into the works of Lafayette's friends and contemporaries, such as Villedieu and Scudéry, many have argued that women writers often actively chose the novel and used it to engage in the debates of the day, from what was history, to the questions of marriage and women's education.[14] This use of the genre would make little sense in the framework traditionally presented in France and to French students, whose sense of women, the salons, and female authorship during *le Grand Siècle* are derived largely from Molière's satires and from anthologies with little female presence.[15]

The increased emphasis on women's and gender studies and on cultural studies has led to a proliferation of works that enable scholars to teach texts such as *La Princesse de Clèves* in this wider context in which women are given a role. Some recent literary histories have also adopted this perspective. One well-known example is *A New History of French Literature* edited by Denis Hollier in 1989, and composed by some of the most well known scholars of French literature.[16] This "new history" is remarkable in many ways. First, it is organized according to specific dates instead of the traditional organizational principles of centuries, literary movements and genres. Thus, for example, for the seventeenth century, 1654 is chosen for the essay entitled "The Salons and 'Preciosity,'" 1661 for one devoted to "From *Roi Soleil* to *Louis le Grand*" and 1677 for "Historiography in the Age of Absolutism." Many of the topics, as well as the contributors, hail from different disciplines, including history, literature, and comparative literature. The project is clearly interdisciplinary in nature. Within a single essay, many works are analyzed and discussed, as is the context that produced the work. This history thus corresponds to pedagogical trends that cut across traditional disciplinary boundaries, trends that have been further developed in the years following the publication of this volume. As Hollier explains, it presents French literature "as a historical and cultural field viewed from a wide array of contemporary critical perspectives." In addition to this cross-disciplinary approach to the literary context, publishers, in particular the Modern Language Association and the University of Chicago Press, have made many women's texts available to teach alongside this "masterpiece." When one teaches *La Princesse de Clèves* with Scudéry's *Histoire de Sapho* from *Le Grand Cyrus*, for example, or in conjunction with Montpensier's correspondence with Motteville on the subject of marriage, it becomes easier and indeed logical to view her as a strong heroine who reflects the preoccupations of her time.[17]

France's seventeenth-century literary *patrimoine* is thus undergoing revision, especially outside the hexagon, but increasingly within it as well. The resistance in France to incorporating the salons and women's influence into considerations of the seventeenth-century literary realm, relative to outside its borders, is due to the strong relationship between the classical period and France's long-standing concept of itself and its identification of its exemplary literary heritage with the seventeenth century in particular.[18] As Timothy Reiss remarks, to exclude women from cultural influence is "an action as much political as cultural" as literature more and more "adopted the masculine job of founding rational public society."[19] To propose a revised vision of this past is to alter France's sense of itself, its past, its ideology, and its values. Scholars outside the hexagon have perhaps found themselves in a more liberating position than that of their French colleagues. With little cultural baggage to influence our perspectives, we have been able to pursue various avenues in our analysis of a period that is particularly rich for the study of women's history and a female literary tradition.

The refound *patrimoine* that restores women to the exceptional position they enjoyed in seventeenth-century culture presents a defiance of the past and a challenge for the future. Raising women from the shadows is a first, essential step. A next, and perhaps more important, step is to integrate this women's history more fully into all considerations of the seventeenth century. As Nancy K. Miller argues in a discussion of scholarship devoted to the history of the novel, men's and women's texts need to be read together:

> To understand the history of the French novel ... it is crucial to perform two gestures: first to restore feminist writing to the body of fiction that becomes the novel; the second, to reread the texts retained by literary history through this supplemented and redoubled vision.[20]

In the case of seventeenth-century France, adopting a "redoubled vision" changes the way one interprets the male-authored texts that have served not only as models for literature but for an entire culture. To restore women's texts and especially women's influence on the development of the literary public alters the very fabric of the nation's cultural past in a way that simply studying women writers as separate entities and the salons as isolated institutions cannot. As Miller explains, it is insufficient to resurrect women's texts and advance them as a "parallel history":

> ... the establishment of such a parallel history (or curriculum) runs the risk of generating, and perhaps guarantees, an even greater indifference to the question of women's writing itself on the part of those authorizers and disseminators of cultural value, who ... are happy enough to have a women's chapter that leaves their story intact ... It may ... be that to produce a literary history that articulates the complexities of the cultural record, it is important to conceive a pedagogy that leaves less already in place. This would mean among other things a commitment to the practice of a gendered poetics that rereads men's texts in the weave of women's.[21]

This is an audacious proposition when one is dealing with seventeenth-century France and its all-male classical canon, yet this is precisely what I am suggesting should be done. In *Mastering Memory* I have shown how Molière's use of the term "taste," for example, takes on very different valences when read in light of women's relationship to *bon goût* and taste's role in literary culture. A rereading of other authors such as Pascal, for example, in relationship to an expanded conception of the seventeenth-century literary context that gives serious consideration to the salons and the worldly public would not only be illuminating, but could possibly change the way we view the whole field of this dynamic century. But it is also not enough to reread men's texts with those penned by women. One must resurrect an entire literary context influenced by women and reread this classical canon in all its complexity, and in so doing, not only reintegrate women's participation, but enrich the interpretations of such well known classics as Molière's dramatic corpus. And the next step in the effort to revise society's memory of this building block of French culture would be to teach it the same way we do our scholarship. Only then will Renan's "spiritual principle" truly include all its ancestors and memories.[22]

In a similar vein, but from a different disciplinary perspective from Miller's, Michèle Perrot reiterates the position enunciated by Miller. In "Women and the Silences of History," Perrot explains the development of the field of women's history in France, and the particular difficulties the discipline, derived primarily from an American context, has faced when confronted with France's impressive and powerful national historical narrative. According to Perrot, "the place of history in the national French culture and its connection with politics gave it a "virile" status, which was not necessarily to be found elsewhere."[23] She defends the discipline of women's history and argues that it not only changes the way one looks upon women's participation in the past, but also raises more far-reaching questions central to the discipline of history as a whole.[24] It is not enough to study women and simply add their stories as a kind of subset to the existing narrative that has excluded them for hundreds of years. Perrot rightly argues that integrating female experience and taking gender into account in all historical investigations leads to an inquiry into the very relationship between representation and reality, the foundation of historical scholarship.[25] Thus like literary studies, historical studies undergo a radical transformation when women and their texts are incorporated into the picture, and not just studied as appendages to mainstream culture and history.

Perrot astutely points out that collective memory is the result of a selection process steered by power relations and value systems.[26] The relationship between representation and reality, and the shaping of collective memory are brought to the forefront in the examination of the historical inscription of the salons of France's classical age. The treatment of the salons and their inscription into collective memory illustrates to an exceptional degree how France's memory of its past was determined by the values ingrained in its society and by the pens of the powerful shapers of France's identity. The development of the seventeenth-century classical literary canon in France was concomitant with the rejection of female taste as defined by the salons and female influence on the literary field. The ultimate erasure of the links between salons, literary criticism, women's literary production, and the classical cultural field reveals the power of critical myth-making. If Corneille's sister's literary influence, representative of general salon taste, and Scudéry's novels provoked such critical fire and historiographical backlash, it is because of the power they exerted during a premier moment in the formation of France's national culture and identity. In this process, products of the salons, forms and approaches to literary evaluation, as well as the novel were eliminated because of their association with the wrong gender. Recuperating women as influential actors in the literary field by unearthing a past that has been carefully and deliberately buried changes not only the way we look at women, but also literary criticism, our methods of establishing literary value, and a celebrated period of French literary history. A collective, worldly voice shaped the literary territory of

France's classical age. To incorporate women's active participation, to change our view of this influence from that of a shadowy parallel subculture into influential rays of light that rivaled the Sun King's own rays, is to change the way we read the period and the works that represent it.

Notes

1   Christine de Pizan, *La Cité des Dames*, 1405 (Paris, 2000), p. 115.
2   Ernest Renan, *Qu'est-ce qu'une nation?* (Paris, 1882), p. 26.
3   Ibid., pp. 7 and 9.
4   Who are France's founding literary critics? Whose taste prevailed? In traditional literary histories and historical accounts, as we have seen, the answer would have to be Renan's "great men."
5   Ibid., pp. 7–8.
6   These discussions have even reached the mainstream media, appearing in *Le Monde*, for example, proof that the subject represents much more to the French than simply differences in pedagogy.
7   In his article on "Les Classiques scolaires" for *Les Lieux de mémoire*, Milo states: "The key word is responsibility: the French educational system is neither the guarantor nor the manager of English cultural patrimony; it thus can be mistaken, or even ridiculous (the French programs in the United States are a perfect example of this irresponsibility)" (II, p. 2113). Yet it has also been shown that seventeenth-century classics remain very much alive on American campuses … proof that the threat has been exaggerated.
8   *Creating French Culture* catalogue (New Haven, 1995), p. 251.
9   Dena Goodman's accounting of the role of the eighteenth-century salon during the enlightenment is a particularly striking example.
10   Of course I recognize that the eighteenth-century salon has undergone its own process of historicization which may have entailed many of the same revisions we have seen associated with the seventeenth. Still, women in the seventeenth century had more direct and active roles in literary culture of the salons than they did in the eighteenth.
11   In contrast, in the United States, the University of Chicago has published a translation of Villedieu's *Mémoires de la vie de Henriette-Sylvie de Molière*, edited by Donna Kuizenga and is in the process of producing Lafayette's *Zaïde*. These inexpensive volumes, available in both hardcover and paperback, are part of their impressive series entitled "The Other Voice in Early Modern Europe," that allows the works to be taught in a variety of contexts. These texts join works by Montpensier, Maintenon, Jacqueline Pascal, and Scudéry for the French seventeenth century alone.
12   The Princess states to Nemours "Croyez que les sentiments que j'ai pour vous seront éternels" (Believe that the feelings that I have for you will last forever).
13   An example of the various approaches adopted by American scholars for teaching the novel can be found in the *Approaches to Teaching La Princesse de Clèves* volume that I co-edited with Katharine Ann Jensen for the Modern Language Association.
14   This is the position I took, for example, in *Revising Memory*.
15   In addition to different interpretations of the novel itself, although Lafayette is acknowledged as the novel's author, she is usually paired in many French anthologies

and by French scholars with male contemporaries, especially La Rochefoucauld and Segrais. American scholars explain her anonymity differently. Joan DeJean, for example, sees her refusal to sign as an act of power. See "Lafayette's Ellipses and the Privileges of Anonymity."

16   Cambridge, 1989. Significantly, perhaps, the vast majority of the participants in this project were from outside France or were French scholars working in the United States.

17   Both these texts are now available in translation from the University of Chicago. It should be remembered that Valincour himself suggested the parallel between Lafayette's heroine and Scudéry's Sapho when he complained that both women were equally *invraisemblable* (implausible).

18   It is striking that the majority of the scholarship in France devoted to women's history and women's literary achievements deals with France after the Revolution. Michèle Perrot and Mona Ozouf, for example, have both produced a considerable body of work on these subjects, but they are not specialists of the seventeenth century.

19   Timothy Reiss, *The Meaning of Literature*, pp. 199 and 196.

20   Nancy K. Miller, "Men's Reading, Women's Writing: Gender and the Rise of the Novel," p. 42.

21   Ibid., pp. 50–51.

22   This is precisely the emphasis of a forthcoming MLA Options for Teaching volume devoted to French seventeenth- and eighteenth-century women writers which I am editing. Instead of focusing on the works of these women, contributors are concerned with incorporating the study of these writers into the general curriculum.

23   Michèle Perrot, "Women and the Silences of History," in *Historians and Social Values*, ed. Joep Leerssen and Ann Rigney (Amsterdam, 2000), p. 163.

24   Perrot states that, because women's history has been identified by the French with American influences, it has frequently been ridiculed. Ibid., p. 166.

25   Ibid., p. 167.

26   Ibid., p. 160.

Bibliography

Académies et sociétés savantes en Europe (1650–1800). Ed. Daniel-Odon Hurel and Gérard Laudin. Paris: Champion, 2000.

Antoine Adam, *Histoire de la litterature francaise au XVIIe siècle*. 5 vols. Paris: Editions Domat Montchrestien, 1948–56.

Albanese, Ralph. *Molière à l'Ecole Républicaine: de la critique universitaire aux manuels scolaires*. Saratoga, CA: Anma Libri, 1992.

———. "Le Discours scolaire au XIXe siècle, le cas de Molière," *Continuum*, Vol. 1. New York: AMS Press, 1989.

Albistur, Maïté, and Daniel Armogathe, eds. *Histoire du féminisme français du moyen âge à nos jours*. Paris: Des Femmes, 1977.

Alletz, Pons-Augustin. *L'Esprit des femmes célèbres du siècle de Louis XIV et de celui de Louis XV, jusquà présent*. 2 vols. Paris: Pissot, 1768.

Annales. "Littérature et histoire." 49, No. 2, March–April 1994.

Apostalidès, Jean-Marie. *Le Roi-machine*. Paris: Minuit, 1981.

Aronson, Nicole. *Madame de Rambouillet ou la magicienne de la Chambre Bleue*. Paris: Fayard, 1988.

———. *Mademoiselle de Scudéry ou le voyage au pays de Tendre*. Paris: Fayard, 1986.

Backer, Dorothy. *Precious Women*. New York: Basic Books, 1974.

Balzac, Guez de. *Lettres familières de M. de Balzac à M. Chapelain*. Paris: Courbé, 1656.

Batteux, Abbé Charles. *Principes de littérature*. 5 vols. Paris: Saillant et Nyon, 1774.

Beasley, Faith E. *Revising Memory: Women's Fiction and Memoirs in Seventeenth-Century France*. New Brunswick: Rutgers University Press, 1990.

———. *Approaches to Teaching La Princesse de Clèves*. Ed. with Katharine Ann Jensen. New York: Modern Languages Association, 1999.

Barthélemy, Eduard de. *Sapho, le mage de Sidon Zénocrate: étude sur la société précieuse*. Paris: Didier, 1880.

Batiffol, Louis. "Le Salon de la Marquise de Rambouillet au XVIIe siècle," *Les Grands salons littéraires (XVIIe et XVIIIe siècles): conférences du Musée Carnavalet (1927)*. Paris: Payot, 1928.

Bayle, Pierre. *Dictionnaire historique et critique*. Rotterdam: R. Leers, 1697.

Beik, William. *Absolutism and Society in Seventeenth-Century France: State Power and Provincial Aristocracy in Languedoc*. Cambridge: Cambridge University Press, 1985.

Bell, David, *The Cult of the Nation in France: Inventing Nationalism 1680–1800*. Boston: Harvard University Press, 2001.

Beugnon, Bernard and Zuber. *Boileau: Visages Anciens, Visages Nouveaux*. Montreal: University of Montreal Press, 1973.

Boileau, Despréaux Nicolas. *Oeuvres complètes*. Paris: Gallimard, 1966.

Bouhours, Dominique. *De la manière de bien penser dans les ouvrages d'esprit*. Paris: Mabre-Cramoisy, 1687.

——. *Entretiens d'Ariste et d'Eugène*. Ed. René Raouant. Paris: Bossard, 1920.

——. *Les Entretiens d'Ariste et d'Eugène*. Paris: Mabre-Cramoisy, 1673.

——. *Remarques nouvelles sur la langue française*. Paris: Mabre-Cramoisy, 1675.

Bray, René. *Boileau: L'Homme et l'oeuvre*. Paris: Nizet, 1962.

——. *Formation de la Doctrine Classique*. Paris: Nizet, 1945.

——. *La Préciosité et le précieux de Thibaut de Champagne à Jean Giraudoux*. Paris: Nizet, 1946.

Brunetière, Ferdinand. *Questions et critique*. Paris: Calmann Lévy, 1897.

Buffet, Marguerite. *Nouvelles Observations sur la langue française*. Paris: Cusson, 1668.

Bury, Emmanuel. *Littérature et politesse: l'invention de l'honnête homme 1580–1750*. Paris: PUF, 1996.

Chappuzeau, Samuel. *L'Académie des femmes*. Paris: Courbé, 1661.

——. *Le Cercle des femmes*. Lyon, 1656.

Charlier, Gustave. "La fin de l'hôtel de Rambouillet," *Revue belge de philologie et d'histoire*, Vol. 18, 1939, pp. 409–26.

Charnes, Jean-Antoine, Abbé de. *Conversations sur la critique de la Princesse de Clèves*. 1679. Ed. François Weil et al. Tours: Université de Tours, 1973.

Cholakian, Patricia Francis. *Women and the Politics of Self-Representation in Seventeenth-Century France*. Newark: University of Delaware Press, 2000.

Compagnon, Antoine. *La Troisième République des lettres, de Flaubert à Proust*. Paris: Seuil, 1983.

——. "The Diminishing Canon of French Literature in America," *Stanford French Review*, Vol. 15, nos 1–2, 1991, pp. 103–16.

Corneille, Pierre. "Excuse à Ariste," in *La querelle du Cid: Pièces et Pamphlets*. Ed. Armand Gasté. Paris: H. Welter, 1899.

——. *Le Cid*. Ed. Georges Forestier. Paris: Magnard, 1988.

Chartier, Roger. *The Cultural Origins of the French Revolution*. Trans. Lydia G. Cochrane. Durham, NC: Duke University Press, 1991.

Correspondance de Chapelain from documents Inedits sur l'Histoire de France. Ed. Ph. Tamizey de Larroque. Paris: Imprimerie nationale, MDCCLXXXIII, Vol. 222.

Choppin, Alain. *Les Manuels Scolaires: Histoire et actualité*. Paris: Hachette, 1992.

Cousin, Victor. *La Jeunesse de Madame de Longueville*. Paris: Didier, 1867.

——. *La Société française au XVIIe siècle d'après le Grand Cyrus de Mlle de Scudéry*. Paris: Didier, 1866.

——. *Mme de Chevreuse*. Paris: Didier, 1856.

——. *Mme de Sablé*. Paris: Didier, 1859.

——. *Jacqueline Pascal*. Paris: Didier, 1856.

Creating French Culture catalogue. Yale University Press, 1995.

Cuénin, Micheline. *Roman et société sous Louis XIV: Mme de Villedieu*, 2 vols. Paris: Champion, 1979.

Davis, Natalie Zemon. "Women's History in Transition: The European Case," *Feminist Studies*, Vol. 3, Nos 3/4, 1976, pp. 83–103.

DeJean, Joan. *Ancients Against Moderns: Culture Wars and the Making of a Fin de Siècle*. Chicago: The University of Chicago Press, 1997.

———. "Classical Reeducation: Decanonizing the Feminine," in *Displacements: Women, Tradition, Litteratures in French*. Ed. Joan DeJean and Nancy K. Miller. Baltimore: Johns Hopkins University Press, 1991.

———. "The Female Tradition," *L'Esprit Créateur*, Vol. XXIII, No. 2, summer 1983.

———. *Fictions of Sappho 1546–1937*. Chicago: Chicago University Press, 1989.

———. "Lafayette's Ellipses: The Privileges of Anonymity," *PMLA* 99, No. 5, 1984, pp. 884–900.

———. *Tender Geographies*. New York: Columbia University Press, 1992.

Denis, Delphine. *La muse galante: Poétique de la conversation dans l'oeuvre de Madeleine de Scudéry*. Paris: Champion, 1997.

———. *Le Parnasse galant: Institution d'une catégorie littéraire au XVIIe siècle*. Paris: Champion, 2001.

Dens, Jean-Pierre. *L'Honnête homme et la critique du goût: Esthétique et société au XVIIe siècle*. Lexington: French Forum, 1981.

Des Granges, Ch.-M. *Histoire de la littérature française: à l'usage des classes de lettres et des divers examens*. Paris: Hatier, 1913.

———. *La Littérature expliquée*. Ed. Ch.-M. Des Granges and Ch. Chartier. Paris: Hatier, n.d.

Dewald, Jonathan. *Aristocratic Experience and the Origins of Modern Culture, France, 1570–1715*. Berkeley: University of California Press, 1993.

Dictionnaire des lettres françaises: Le XVIIe siècle. 1951. Ed. Patrick Dandrey. Paris: Fayard, 1996.

Dictionnaire des littératures de langue françaises. Ed. Jean-Pierre de Beaumarchais, Daniel Couty and Alain Rey. Paris: Bordas, 1994.

Dix-Septième siècle. "Les Pouvoirs féminins au XVIIe siècle," July–September, Vol. 144, No. 3, 1984.

Duchene, Roger. *Les Précieuses ou comment l'esprit vint aux femmes*. Paris: Fayard, 2001.

Elias, Norbert. *La Société de cour*. 1969. Paris: Calmann-Levy, 1974.

Fabre, abbé de. *Chapelain et nos deux premières académies*. Paris: Didier-Perrin, 1890.

The Female Autographe. Ed. Domna C. Stanton. 1984. Chicago: University of Chicago Press, 1987.

Femmes savantes, savoirs des femmes: du crépuscule de la Renaissance à l'aube des Lumières. Ed. Colette Nativel. Geneva: Droz, 1999.

Flannigan, Arthur. *Mme de Villedieu's Les Désordres de l'amour: History, Literature and the Nouvelle Historique.* Washington, DC: University Press of America, 1982.

Fraisse, Emmanuel. *Les Anthologies en France.* Paris: PUF, 1997.

France, Peter, ed. *The New Oxford Companion to Literature in French.* New York: Oxford University Press, 1995.

Fukui, Y. *Raffinement précieux dans la poésie française du XVIIe siècle.* Paris: Nizet, 1964.

Fumaroli, Marc. *La Diplomatie de l'esprit.* Paris: Hermann, 1994.

———. "Génie de la langue française," in *Les Lieux de Memoire.* Ed. Pierre Nora. Paris: Gallimard, 1992.

———. "La Coupole," in *Les Lieux de Memoire.* Ed. Pierre Nora. Paris: Gallimard, 1992.

———. "La Conversation," in *Les Lieux de Memoire*, Vol. 2. Ed. Pierre Nora. Paris: Gallimard, 1992.

———. *Quand L'Europe parlait français.* Paris: Editions de Fallois, 2001.

Furetière, Antoine. *Dictionnaire universel contenant généralement tous les mots français tant vieux que modernes, et les termes de toutes les sciences et des arts.* Rotterdam: Ausgaben den Haag, 1690.

Gaines, James and Michael Koppish, eds. *Approaches to Teaching Molière.* New York: Modern Language Association, 1995.

Gay, Sophie. *Salons célèbres, 1837.* Paris: Lévy, 1864.

Genlis, Stéphanie Félicité, de. *De L'influence des femmes sur la littérature française, comme protectrices des lettres et comme auteurs (ou Précis de l'histoire des femmes françaises les plus célèbres).* Paris: Maradan, 1811.

Gethner, Perry. "Love, Self-love and the Court in *Le Favori*," in *Actes de Wakeforest.* Eds Milorad R. Margitic and Byron R. Wells. Paris: Biblio 17, 1987, pp. 407–20.

Gillet, Louis. "Introduction," in *Les Grands Salons littéraires: Conférences du Musée Carnavalet.* Paris: Payot, 1928.

Gillot, Hubert. *La Querelle des Anciens et des Modernes en France.* Paris: Champion, 1914.

Glotz, Marguerite and Madeleine Marie. *Salons du XVIIIe siècle.* Paris: Nouvelles éditions latines, 1949.

Goldsmith, Elizabeth. *Exclusive Conversations: The Art of Interaction in Seventeenth-Century France.* Philadelphia: University of Pennsylvania Press, 1988.

———. *Publishing Women's Life Stories in France, 1647–1720: From Voice to Print.* Aldershot: Ashgate Publishing Company, 2001.

———. "The Quarrel over La Princesse de Clèves," in *Approaches to Teaching La Princess de Clèves.* Eds Faith E. Beasley and Katharine Ann Jensen. New York: Modern Language Association, 1999.

———. "Publishing Passion: Mme de Villedieu's *Lettres et billets galants*," in *Actes de Wakeforest.* Eds Milorad R. Margitic and Byron R. Wells. Tuëbingen: Biblio 17, 1987, pp. 439–49.

Goodman, Dena. "L'ortografe des dames: Gender and Language in the Old Régime," *French Historical Studies*, Vol. 25, No. 2, Spring 2002, pp. 191–223.

———. *The Republic of Letters: A Cultural History of the French Enlightenment.* Ithaca: Cornell University Press, 1994.

Gordon, Daniel. *Citizens Without Sovereignty: Equality and Sociability in French Thought, 1670–1789.* Princeton: Princeton University Press, 1994.

Gougy-François, Marie. *Les Grands salons féminins.* Paris: Debresse, 1965.

La Grande encyclopédie, inventaire raisonné des sciences, des lettres, et des arts, par une société de savants et de gens de lettres. Paris: Lamirault, 1886–1902.

Gabriel Guéret, *La Guerre des Auteurs anciens et modernes*, 1671. Amsterdam: L'Honoré et Chatelain, 1723.

Guillaume, Jacquette. *Les Dames illustres.* Paris: 1665.

Haechler, Jean. *Le règne des femmes 1715–1793.* Paris: Grasset, 2001.

Halbwachs, Maurice. *On Collective Memory.* Ed. and trans. Lewis A. Coser. Chicago: University of Chicago Press, 1992.

Halphen. "Etude sur Voiture et la société de son temps," in *Lettres et poésies inédits.* Versailles: Montalant-Bougleux, 1853.

Hampton, Timothy. *Literature and Nation in the Sixteenth Century: Inventing Renaissance France.* Ithaca: Cornell University Press, 2001.

Harth, Erica. *Cartesian Women: Versions and Subversions of Rational Discourse in the Old Régime.* Ithaca: Cornell University Press, 1992.

Ideology and Culture in Seventeenth-Century France. Ithaca: Cornell University Press, 1983.

Hazard, Paul. *La Crise de la conscience européenne.* 1935. Paris: Fayard, 1961.

Henry, C. *Un Erudit: Homme du monde, homme d'église, homme de cour (1630–1721). Lettres inédites de Mme de Lafayette, de Mme Dacier, de Bossuet, de Fléchier, de Fénelon, etc. Extraits de la correspondance de Huet.* ed. C. Henry.

Hepp, Noémi. "La Galanterie," in *Les Lieux de mémoire.* Paris: Quarto Gallimard, vol. 3, pp. 3677–710.

Hervier, Marcil. *Les Ecrivains français jugés par leurs contemporains.* Paris: Delaplaine, 1922.

Heyden-Rynsch, Verena von der. *Salons européens: les beaux moments d'une culture féminine disparue.* Trans. Gilberte Lamrichs. Paris: Gallimard, 1993.

L'Histoire, No. 100, May 1987.

Histoire de la France: Choix culturels et mémoire. Ed. André Burguière and Jacques Revel, 1993; Paris: Seuil, 2000.

A History of Women's Writing in France from the Middle Ages to the Present. Ed. Sonya Stephens. Cambridge: Cambridge University Press, 2000.

Historia, No. 9710, Sept. 1997.

Horville, Robert, ed. *XVIIe Siècle.* Paris: Hatier, 1988.

Huet, Pierre-Daniel. *Huetiana.* Paris: J. Estienne, 1722.

———. *Traité de Pierre-Daniel Huet sur l'Origine des romans.* 1669. Ed. Fabienne Gégou. Paris: Nizet, 1971.

———. *Mémoires* (1718). Ed. Philippe-Joseph Salazar. Toulouse: Société de littératures classiques, 1993.

———. *Mémoires*. Paris: Hachette, 1853.

Jensen, Katharine Ann. "Madame de Villedieu," in *French Women Writers: A Bio-bibliographical Source Book*. Eds Eva Sartori and Dorothy Zimmerman. New York: Greenwood Press, 1991.

———. *Writing Love: Letters, Women, and the Novel (1605–1776)*. Carbondale: Southern Illinois University Press, 1994.

Jey, Martine. "Les Classiques de l'ère Ferry," *Littératures classiques*, Vol. 19, 1993.

Jouhaud, Christian. *Les Pouvoirs de la littérature: Histoire d'un paradoxe*. Paris: Gallimard, 2000.

Kelly, Joan. *Women, History and Theory*. Chicago: University of Chicago Press, 1984.

Kuizenga, Donna. "Zaïde: Just Another Love Story?," in *Actes de Davis*. Ed. Claude Abraham. Paris: Biblio 17, 1988.

Lafayette, Marie Madeleine Pioche de la Vergne, comtesse de. *Correspondance*. Ed. André Beaunier. Paris: Gallimard, 1942.

———. *Zaïde, Histoire espagnole*. 1670–71. Ed. Alain Niderst. Paris: Classiques Garnier, 1990.

Lagarde, André and Laurent Michard. *XVIIe siècle: Les Grands auteurs français du programme, anthologie et histoire littéraire*. Paris: Bordas.

La Harpe, J.F. *Lycée ou Cours de littérature ancienne et moderne*. Paris: Crapelet, 1816.

Lambert, Anne Thérèse de Marguenat de Courcelles, marquise de. "Réflexions sur le goût," in *Oeuvres*. Paris: Veuve Ganeau, 1748.

———. *Réflexions nouvelles sur les femmes*. 1727. Paris: Côté-femmes, 1989.

Lambert, Claude François, abbé de. *Histoire littéraire du règne de Louis XIV*. Paris: Prault, 1751.

La Mothe le Vayer, François. *Observations diverses sur la composition et sur la lecture des livres*. Paris: Billaine, 1668.

Lanson, Gustave. *Histoire de la littérature française*. Paris: Hachette, 1898.

La Porte, Joseph, abbé de. *Histoire littéraire des femmes françaises; ou Lettres historiques et critiques, contentant un précis de la vie et une analyse raisonnée des ouvrages des femmes qui se sont distinguées dans la littérature française, par une société de gens de lettres*. 5 vols. Paris: Lacombe, 1769.

La Rochefoucauld, François de. *Maximes*. Paris: Flammarion, 1967.

Lathuillère, Roger. *La Préciosité: Etude historique et linguistique*. Geneva: Droz, 1969.

Laugaa, Maurice. *Lectures de Mme de Lafayette*. Paris: Armand Colin, 1971.

Leggewie, Robert ed. *Anthologie de la littérature française*. New York: Oxford University Press, 1990.

Livet, Charles-Louis. *Précieux et précieuses: Caractères et mœurs littéraires du XVIIe siècle.* Paris: Didier, 1860.

Le Goff, Jacques. *Histoire et Mémoire.* 1977. Paris: Gallimard, 1988.

Loret, Jean. *La Muse historique.* 4 vols. Paris: Daffis, 1857–78.

Loucif, Sabine. *A la recherche du canon perdu: L'enseignement de la littérature française dans les universités américaines.* New Orleans: Presses universitaires du nouveau monde, 2001.

Lougee, Carolyn C. *Le Paradis des femmes: Women, Salons and Social Stratification in Seventeenth-Century France.* Princeton: Princeton University Press, 1976.

Lyons, John. *Exemplum: The Rhetoric of Example in Early Modern French Literature.* Princeton: Princeton University Press, 1989.

———. "Speaking in Pictures, Speaking of Pictures: Problems of Representation in the Seventeenth Century," in *From Mirror to Method, Augustine to Descartes.* Eds John D. Lyons and Stephen G. Nichols. Hanover, NH: University Press of New England, 1982.

Maclean, Ian. *Woman Triumphant (1610–52).* Oxford: Oxford University Press, 1977.

Magendie, Maurice. *La politesse mondaine et les gens d'honnêteté.* 2 vols. Paris: Alcan, 1925.

Magne, Emile. *Voiture et les origines de l'Hôtel de Rambouillet 1597–1635.* Paris: Mercure de France, 1911.

Maître, Myriam. *Les Précieuses.* Paris: Champion, 1999.

Marin, Louis. *Le Portrait du roi.* Paris: Minuit, 1981.

Mathieu, Hélène and Anne-Marie Thiesse. "The Decline of the Classical Age and the Birth of the Classics," in *Displacements: Women, Tradition, Litteratures in French.* Eds Joan DeJean and Nancy K. Miller. Baltimore: Johns Hopkins University Press, 1991.

Merlin-Kajman, Hélène. *L'absolutisme dans les lettres et la théorie des deux corps: Passions et politique.* Paris: Champion, 2000.

———. *L'Excentricité académique: Littérature, institution, société.* Paris: Les Belles Lettres, 2001.

———. *Public et Littérature en France au XVIIe Siècle.* Paris: Les Belles Lettres, 1994.

Miller, Nancy K. "Men's Reading, Women's Writing: Gender and the Rise of the Novel," *Yale French Studies 75.* 1998.

———. "Emphasis Added: Plots and Plausabilities in Women's Fictions," *PMLA* 96, No. 1, 1981, pp. 36–48.

———. *Subject to Change.* New York: Columbia University Press, 1988.

———. "Tender Economies: Mme de Villedieu and the Costs of Indifference," *L'Esprit Créateur,* Vol. XXIII, No. 2, summer 1983.

———. *French Dressing.* London and New York: Routledge, 1995.

Milo, Daniel. "Les Classiques scolaires," in *Les Lieux de mémoire.* Paris: Gallimard, 1984.

Moers, Ellen. *Literary Women: The Great Writers*. 1963. New York: Oxford University Press, 1985.

The Molière Encyclopedia. Ed. James F. Gaines. Westport, CT: Greenwood Press, 2002.

Molière. *Les Femmes Savantes*. Ed. Jean Lecomte, Paris: Classiques Larousse, 1971.

——. *Les Précieuses Ridicules*. Ed. Brigitte Diaz. Paris: Larousse, 1998.

——. Ducos-Filippi, ed. Paris: Bordas 1995.

Mongrédien, Georges. *Madeleine de Scudéry et son salon, d'après des documents inédits*. Paris: Tallandier, 1946.

——. *La Vie de société aux XVIIe. et XVIIIe. siècles*. Paris: Hachette, 1950.

——. *Les Précieux et les précieuses*. Paris: Mercure, 1963.

Mongrédien, Georges. *Recueil des textes et des documents du XVIIe siècle relatifs à Molière*. Paris: CNRS, 1965.

Moriarty, Michael. *Taste and Ideology in Seventeenth-Century France*. Cambridge: Cambridge University Press, 1988.

Morrissette, Bruce. *The Life and Works of Marie-Catherine Desjardins (Mme de Villedieu)*. St Louis: Washington University Press, 1947.

Niderst, Alain, ed. *Le Siècle de Louis XIV: anthologie des mémoralistes du siècle de Louis XIV*. Paris: Robert Laffont, 1997.

Nora, Pierre. "Présentation," *Les Lieux de mémoire*. 1984. Paris: Gallimard, 1997.

Noual la Houssaye. "Bouhours, Dominique," in *Biographie universelle ancienne et moderne*. Ed. M. Michaud. Paris: Madame C. Desplaces, 1854–65.

Ormesson, Jean d'. *Une Autre histoire de la littérature française*. Paris: NiL Editions, 1997.

Ozouf, Mona. *Les Mots des femmes: essai sur la singularité française*. Paris: Fayard, 1995.

Pellisson-Fontanier, Paul. *Relation contenant l'Histoire de l'Académie française*. Paris: Pierre le Petit, 1653.

Perrault, Charles. *Parallèle des Anciens et des Modernes*. 1687. Ed. Hans Robert Jauss. Munich: Eidos Verlag, 1964.

Perrot, Michèle. "Women and the Silences of History," in *Historians and Social Values*. Ed. Joep Leerssen and Ann Rigney. Amsterdam: Amsterdam University Press, 2000.

Picard, Roger. *Les Salons littéraires et la société française, 1670–1789*. New York: Brentano's, 1943.

Planté, Christine. *La Petite sœur de Balzac: essai sur la femme auteur*. Paris: Seuil, 1989.

Prost, A. *L'enseignement en France, 1800–1967*. Paris: Colin, 1968.

Pure, Michel, abbé de. *La Précieuse ou le mystère des ruelles*. Paris: Guillaume de Luyne, 1656.

La Querelle des anciens et des modernes. Ed. Marc Fumaroli. Paris: Gallimard, 2001.

Recueil des Harangues prononcés par Messieurs de l'Académie française. Paris: Coignard, 1714.

Reiss, Timothy. *The Meaning of Literature.* Ithaca: Cornell University Press, 1992.

Renan, Ernest. *Qu'est-ce qu'une nation? Conférence faite en Sorbonne, le 11 mars 1882.* Paris: Lévy, 1882.

Revel, Jacques. "Les Classiques scolaires," in *Les Lieux de mémoire.*

Rey, Alain, ed. *Le Robert dictionnaire historique de la langue française.* Paris: Dictionnaires le Robert, 1992–98.

Rigney, Ann. *Imperfect Histories: The Elusive Past and the Legacy of Romantic Historicism.* Ithaca: Cornell University Press, 2001.

Reynier, Gustave. *La Femme au XVIIe siècle.* Paris: Tallandier, 1929.

Roederer, P.L. *Mémoire pour servir à l'histoire de la société polie en France.* Paris: Didot, 1885.

Rowan, Mary. "Patterns of Enclosure and Escape in the Prose Fiction of Mme de Villedieu," *Actes de Wakeforest.* Eds Milorad R. Margitic and Byron R. Wells. Tuëbingen: Biblio 17, 1987, pp. 379–92.

Russo, Elena. *La Cour et la ville dans la littérature classique aux Lumières.* Paris: Presses Universitaires de France, 2002.

———, ed. "Exploring the Conversible world: Text and Sociability from the Classical Age to the Enlightenment," *Yale French Studies,* No. 92, 1997.

Sainte-Beuve. *Causeries du lundi,* "Mme de Maintenon," Vol. 4. Paris: Garnier, 1855.

———. *Causeries du lundi,* "Mademoiselle de Scudéry," Vol. 4. Paris: Garnier, 1855.

———. *Causeries du lundi,* "Saint-Evremond et Ninon," Vol. 4. Paris: Garnier, 1855.

———. "M. de La Rochefoucauld," in *Portraits de femmes.* Paris: Garnier, 1845.

———. "Madame de Lafayette," in *Portraits de femmes.* Paris: Garnier, 1845.

Sartori, Eva Martin, and Dorothy Wynne Zimmerman, eds. *French Women Writers: A Bio-bibliographical Source Book.* New York: Greenwood Press, 1991.

Sas, Niek van. "Towards a New National History: *Lieux de mémoire* and Other Theaters of Memory," in *Historians and Social Values.* Ed. Loep Leerssen and Ann Rigney. Amsterdam: Amsterdam University Press, 2000.

Schmitt, M.P. "Les Classiques en classe," *Cahiers de littérature du XVIIe siècle,* Vol. 10, 1988.

Schor, Naomi. "The Righting of French Studies: Homosociality and the Killing of 'La pensée 68'," *Profession,* 1992, pp. 28–34.

Scott, Joan Wallach. *Gender and the Politics of History.* New York: Columbia University Press, 1988.

Scudéry, Madeleine de. *Artamène ou le Grand Cyrus.* Paris: Barbin, 1653.

———. *Conversations sur divers sujets.* Amsterdam: Daniel du Fresne, 1682.

———. *"De l'air galant" et autres Conversations (1653–1684): Pour une étude de l'archive galante.* Ed. Delphine Denis. Paris: Champion, 1998.

———. *Les Femmes Illustres*. Paris: Antoine de Sommaville, 1642.

Segrais, Jean Regnault de. *Segraisiana*. Paris: Compagnie des Libraires, 1721.

Seifert, Lewis. *Fairy Tales, Sexuality and Gender in France, 1690–1715: Nostalgic Utopias*. Cambridge: Cambridge University Press, 1996.

Sévigné, Marie de Rabutin-Chantal, Marquise de. *Correspondance*. Paris: Pléiade, 1972.

Smith, Bonnie G. *The Gender of History: Men, Women, and Historical Practice*. Cambridge: Harvard University Press, 1998.

Somaize, Antoine Baudeau, sieur de. *Le Grand Dictionnaire historique des précieuses*. 2 vols. 1661. Paris: Janet, 1861.

Sorel, Charles. *La Bibliothèque française*. 1664. Paris: La Compagnie des libraries du Palais, 1667.

———. *De la connaissance des bons livres*. 1671. Ed. Lucia Moretti Cererini. Rome: Bulzoni Editore, 1974.

Staël, Germaine de. *De la Littérature*. 1800; Paris: Garnier-Flammarion, 1991.

———. *De L'Allemagne*. Paris: Garnier-Flammarion, 1968.

Stanton, Domna. "The Fiction of Préciosité and the Fear of Women," *Yale French Studies*, No. 62, 1981.

———. "The Demystification of History and Fiction in *Les Annales galantes*," *Actes de Wakeforest*. Eds Milorad R. Margitic and Byron R. Wells. Tuëbingen: Biblio 17, 1987, pp. 339–60.

Stone, Harriet. *The Classical Model: Literature and Knowledge in Seventeenth-Century France*. Ithaca: Cornell University Press, 1996.

———. "Reading the Orient: Lafayette's *Zaïde*," *Romantic Review*, March 1990, 81 (2).

Tallemant des Reaux. *Historiettes*. ed. Antoine Adam. Paris: Pléiade, 1967.

Thiesse, Anne-Marie and Hélène Mathieu. "The Decline of the Classical Age and the Birth of the Classics," in *Displacements: Women, Tradition, Literatures in French*. Baltimore: Johns Hopkins University Press, 1991, pp. 74–96.

Thiollier, Marguerite Marie. *Ces Dames du Marais*. Paris: Atelier Alpha Bleue. 1988.

Titon du Tillet, Everard. *Le Parnasse français*. Geneva: Slatkine Reprints, 1971.

Timmermans, Linda. *L'accès des femmes à la culture (1598–1715)*. Paris: Champion, 1993.

Valincour, Jean-Baptiste Trousset de. *Lettres à Madame la Marquise *** au sujet de la Princesse de Clèves*. 1678. Ed. Jacques Chupeau et al. Tours: Université de Tours, 1972.

Verdier, Gabrielle. "Gender and Rhetoric in Some Seventeenth-Century Love Letters," *L'Esprit Créateur*, Vol. XXIII, No. 2, summer 1983.

Verona, Roxana. *Les "salons" de Sainte-Beuve: Le Critique et ses muses*. Paris: Champion, 1999.

Vertron, Claude-Charles Guionet, siegneur de. *La Nouvelle Pandore ou les femmes illustres du siècle de Louis le Grand*. Paris: Mazuel, 1698.

Viala. Alain. *La Naissance de l'écrivain.* Paris: Minuit, 1985.

———. "Un jeu d'images: Amateur, mondaine, écrivain?," in *Europe: revue littéraire mensuelle.*

Vigneul-Marville, M. de (Argonne). *Mélanges d'Histoire et de littérature.* Rotterdam, Elie Yvans, 1702.

Villedieu, Marie-Catherine Desjardins, Mme de. *The Disorders of Love.* Ed. Arthur Flannigan. Birmingham, Alabama: Summa Publications, 1995.

———. *Lisandre.* Paris: Barbin, 1663.

———. *Recueil de quelques lettres ou relations galantes.* Paris: Barbin 1668. Epître, n.p.

———. *Recueil de quelques lettres ou relations galantes,* Lettre VIII, 15 May 1667.

———. *Cléonice, ou le roman galant,* in *Oeuvres.* Paris, 1720–21, Vol. I.

———. *Les Amours des Grands Hommes,* in *Oeuvres.* Lyon, 1695, Vol. IV.

———. *Les Annales galantes de Grèce,* in *Oeuvres.* Paris, 1720–21, Vol. VII.

———. *Les Désordres de l'amour.* Ed. Micheline Cuénin. Paris: Droz, 1970.

Voltaire, *Le Siècle de Louis XIV.* Paris: Didot, 1851.

Walter, Eric. "Histoire de l'enseignement du français: La République, l'école et les 'textes français'," *Le Français aujhourd'hui: revue de l'association française des enseignants de français,* Vol. 52, December, 1980, pp. 97–105.

Williams, Charles G.S. *Valincour: The Limits of Honnêteté.* Washington, DC: The Catholic University of America Press, 1991.

Winock, Michel. *Parlez-moi de la France.* 1995. Paris: Seuil, 1997.

Yourcenar, Marguerite. "Discours de réception à l'Académie Française." Paris: Gallimard, 1981.

Index

Chappell, Carolyn Lougee, *see* Lougee, Carolyn
Chappuzeau, Samuel 41
Charnes, Jean Antoine de 92n.48, 115, 121–34, 168n.14, 168n.16
Chartier, Roger 89n.7, 170n.47, 247
Chateaubriand, François-René, vicomte de 225
Cherbuliez, Juliette 91n.40
Chevreuse, Marie de Rohan, duchesse de 212, 216, 252n.48
Cholakian, Patricia 12, 91n.40
Choppin, Alain 282
classicism
    creation of 4, 5, 175, 199, 242, 267, 273, 284, 290–91, 306
    literary canon of 166, 199, 204, 206, 239, 265, 267; *see also* French national identity, literature and
classics 261, 264–5, 266–7, 301, 307n.12, 307n.22; *see also* classicism; education; French national identity; literary canon
Compagnon, Antoine 228, 243, 252n.41
Conrart, Valentin 98n.125, 189, 192, 207, 240, 258n.121
conversation 27, 31, 53, 63, 69, 92n.48, 149, 180, 181, 217, 222, 225, 227, 228, 233, 242, 255n.84, 302–3, 305, 312n.109, 313n.110
    influence on language 57, 97n.120, 208, 253n.54; *see also* Lafayette, *Zaïde*
Corneille, Pierre 20, 77, 102, 103–5, 109, 118, 148, 166n.3, 167n.6, 185, 192, 207, 239, 247, 250n.17, 252n.47, 260n.167, 263, 265, 269, 270, 287, 290, 297, 298, 306n.8
    quarrel over *Le Cid* 76, 98n.130, 101, 105, 106–14, 119, 120, 121, 126, 128, 139, 140, 167n.10, 250n.23, 300, 316
Cousin, Victor 176, 210–21, 228, 229, 237, 238, 241, 252n.47, 252n.48 257n.113, 257n.118, 272, 305
    women writers and 213–16, 227, 254n.64, 257n.114, 259n.148, 290, 308n.36
Cuénin, Micheline 12, 149, 172n.72, 172n.75

cultural memory 194, 248, 267, 272, 282, 314, 323
    classicism and 4, 263, 270
    definitions of 15
    power and 7–8, 248, 323
    salons and 2, 5, 19–20, 30, 201, 228, 294, 299, 318, 323
    seventeenth century and 7–8, 9, 66, 176, 177, 178, 188, 191, 204, 211, 228, 262, 294, 295, 306
    women writers and 198, 204, 228, 306, 318; *see also* Cousin, French national identity, lieux de mémoire, literary canon, Tillet
Cultural Studies 10

Dacier, Anne, née Lefebvre 33–4, 186, 196, 197, 214, 251n.26
Davis, Natalie Zemon 17n.29
DeJean, Joan 12, 91n.47, 93n.63, 99n.136, 167n.9, 169n.30, 174n.88, 210, 251n.33, 252n.40, 253n.58, 259n.163, 282–3, 307n.18, 310n.65, 312n.89, 312n.99, 319, 324n.15
Denis, Delphine 12, 90n.25, 177, 259n.163
Descartes, René 65, 66, 96n.108, 189, 214, 252n.47, 290, 297, 300
Des Granges, Ch.-M. 288, 311n.74, 311n.75, 311n.76
Deshoulières, Antoinette 185, 186–7, 193–4, 196, 197, 214, 223, 283
Despréaux, *see* Boileau
Diaz, Brigitte 278–9, 309n.51, 309n.57, 310n.59
Douste-Blazy, Philippe 50
Duchêne, Roger 12
Ducos-Filippi, Isabelle 310n.58
Du Deffand, Marie de Vichy, marquise 223, 243, 244, 305
Dupré, Mlle 63

education 211, 262, 264, 273, 301, 307n.10, 316, 324n.6, 324n.7, 325n.22
    anthologies and 282–94, 310n.60, 310n.63, 310n.65, 319
    language and 71, 307n.23
    literary canon and 15, 262–3, 268, 269, 270–71, 272, 274, 292, 308n.29, 316

literary evaluation and 38–9, 46, 166
national culture and 15, 248, 260n.172,
260n.173, 264, 267–8, 270, 292, 294,
306n.3
pedagogical editions and 275–81, 307n.12,
309n.56, 309n.57
women and 40, 72, 97n.110, 264–5,
270–71, 319, 321; *see also* Molière
Elias, Norbert 179
Eliot, George 184
esprit 20, 21, 23, 26, 27, 32, 33, 34, 35, 42,
43, 49, 53, 58, 61, 62, 63, 65, 66, 67,
68, 72, 74, 79, 80, 81, 86, 87, 90n.23,
92n.60, 180, 181, 188, 193, 194, 201,
207, 209, 214, 218, 225, 230, 234, 237,
238, 240, 241, 242, 250n.20, 252n.47,
253n.61, 264, 280, 289, 303, 317

Fénelon, François de Salignac de la Mothe
86, 192
Ferro, Marc 3, 16n.9
Ferry, Jules 263
Flannigan, Arthur 158, 161, 171n.53,
172n.67, 173n.76, 173n.78, 173n.79,
173n.80, 173n.82, 173n.83, 174n.91
Force, *see* La Force
Forestier, Georges 167n.7
Fraisse, Emmanuel 264, 307n.9, 307n.14,
310n.63
French Academy 23, 32, 67, 72, 74, 76–88,
99n.133, 116, 131, 171n.51, 182,
192, 201, 227, 234, 239, 245, 249n.3,
257n.118, 269, 283, 287, 301
Le Cid and 102, 110–14, 126, 128, 139
dictionary project 78, 83
discours de réception 76–87
literary history and 1–2
Louis XIV and 81–5
salons and 24, 26–7, 29, 79–80
women and, 1–2, 80, 87, 179, 227, 234;
see also language
French national identity 6, 136–37, 146, 178,
179, 257n.120, 260n.173, 261–2, 265,
268, 272, 282, 292, 294, 298, 302–3,
305, 308n.43, 314–16, 317, 323, 324n.6
history and 6, 17n.41, 176, 185, 210, 211,
221–2, 250n.15, 260n.170, 306n.7,
314–6, 323, 325n.24

language and 49–50, 56–7, 66, 68, 70,
73–5, 83, 206, 298, 303
literature and 101, 112–13, 133, 134, 175,
177, 184, 192, 204–5, 209, 210, 228,
263, 270, 273, 284, 294, 297, 298,
300, 307n.15, 316, 321
patrimoine and 7, 321
salons and 3, 5, 8, 62, 75, 176–7, 178, 180,
181, 182, 183, 205, 222, 228–29, 231,
245, 247, 255n.94, 318
seventeenth-century and 204, 213, 215,
216, 220, 221, 228, 236, 247, 263,
264, 267, 268, 284, 294, 298, 300,
301, 307n.15, 318
women and 194–5, 199, 200–201, 208–9,
213, 215, 216, 220, 228, 234, 235,
236, 242, 243, 247, 249n.12, 265,
294, 300, 302, 303
women writers and 19, 175, 184, 192, 199,
200, 204, 209, 225, 228, 234, 243,
265, 284; *see also* Bouhours, Buffet,
Cousin, education, language, literary
canon, *Les Lieux de mémoire*, French
Academy
Fronde 57, 93n.65, 148, 232, 258n.130,
310n.58
Fumaroli, Marc 80, 301, 303–6, 308n.36,
312n.109, 313n.111
Furetière, Antoine 29, 32, 83, 85, 91n.38,
98n.121, 99n.134, 149, 169n.36, 181,
261–2, 266, 288

Gaines, James 309n.50
galanterie 19, 27, 42, 80, 90n,25, 101, 137,
177, 181, 183, 228, 301
Gay, Sophie 175
Genlis, Stéphanie Félicité du Crest, Madame
de 199–204, 205, 211, 212, 223, 238–9,
241, 252n.36, 284
Geoffrin, Marie-Thérèse 183, 244, 249n.10,
254n.79
Gersal, Frederick 6
Gethner, Perry 12, 171n.50, 311n.85
Gillet, Louis 4, 16n.5, 243–4, 245
Gillot, Hubert 38
Goethe 225
Goldsmith, Elizabeth 12, 92n.48, 167n.9,
171n.57, 172n.63, 259n.163

worldly 22, 27, 35, 38, 101, 103, 104, 106,
114–17, 120, 122, 127, 147, 149, 186,
209, 217, 230, 232, 247, 253n.54,
266, 267, 269, 281, 289, 290, 291,
298, 311n.75, 316, 317
Pure, abbé Michel de 31, 41–2, 91n.44, 275,
276

quarrel of the Ancients and Moderns 32, 33,
37, 68, 132, 168n.16, 293, 304
Querelle des femmes 16n.12, 47, 59, 278, 279
Quinault, Philippe 186, 198, 287

Racine, Jean 67, 185, 192, 207, 214, 250n.17,
263, 265, 269, 270, 284, 285, 287, 288,
290, 297, 298, 306n.8, 311n.74
Rambouillet, Catherine de Vivonne de
Savelli, marquise de 22–3, 24–5, 45,
76, 89n.11, 89n.16, 90n.34, 233, 242,
249n.3, 258n.122, 275, 298, 309n.53,
310n.59, 313n.111
historical representations of 176, 228–33,
239, 256n.95, 258n.129, 277, 280,
284–5, 286, 287, 294, 316
salon de 27–8, 89n.13, 89n.14, 90n.31,
91n.38, 99n.135, 110, 134, 183, 192,
201, 208, 213, 220, 224, 228–33, 236,
239–41, 244, 246, 255n.93, 255n.94,
256n.106, 256n.107, 258n.123,
258n.127, 258n.130, 275–6, 277, 278,
279, 280, 288, 304, 309n.51, 310n.59,
311n.76; *see also chambre bleue*
Ranum, Orest 317
Récamier, Jeanne-Françoise (Juliette) 225–6,
253n.63
Retz, Jean-François-Paul de Gondi, cardinal
de 269, 290, 291, 295, 298, 304
Richelieu, Armand du Plessis, cardinal de 27,
77, 82, 84, 110, 249n.3, 252n.47, 285
reason 92n.62, 93n.63, 144, 175, 201, 267,
275, 314
knowledge and 65, 76, 143, 144, 145, 146,
163, 170n.44
literary evaluation and 34, 39, 47, 92n.60,
106, 109, 110–11, 121, 124, 125, 126,
139, 219, 227, 290
women and 144, 227
Renan, Ernest 314–6, 322

Revel, Jacques 247
Revolution, French 176, 179, 180, 181, 221,
260n.172
Reynier, Gustave 88n.6
Reiss, Timothy 11, 76, 321
Roederer, P.L. 238
Rousseau, Jean-Jacques 98n.127, 300
Rowan, Mary M. 173n.77
ruelle 4, 5, 16n.4, 28, 125, 150, 182, 201,
207, 228, 231, 246, 279; *see also* salons
Russo, Elena 177, 181–2, 249n.3, 249n.10,
249n.11, 249n.13, 259n.163

Sablé, Madeleine de Souvré, marquise de 26,
29, 31,67, 76, 90n.34, 91n.39, 183, 212,
216–19, 225–6, 246, 253n.53, 253n.56,
254n.80, 291, 298, 304
Sainte-Beuve, Charles Augustin 176, 210,
221–27, 228, 243, 245, 252n.41,
253n.61, 253n.63, 254n.77, 254n.79,
254n.80, 255n.88, 255n.89, 255n.91,
272, 279, 280, 290, 305, 309n.52
Saint-Evremond, Charles de Marguetel de
Saint-Denis, sieur de 219
Saint-Simon, Claude-Henri de Rouvroy,
comte de 27, 230, 295
salons, 99n.137, 142, 147, 167n.11, 177, 180,
216, 229, 245, 249n.3, 274, 277–8, 289,
294, 298, 304, 313n.111, 316, 323
critiques of 39–49, 167n.11, 206–7, 229,
275, 276, 277, 278, 285–6, 316–7
eighteenth-century salons 4, 5, 30, 175,
181–4, 207, 222, 240, 244, 246,
249n.9, 149n.10, 255n.83, 260n.167,
275, 299, 317–18, 324n.9, 324n.10
formation of public 20, 230, 232
French Academy and 26–7, 34–5, 78–9, 87
historiography and 3, 5, 9–10, 11, 14, 30,
87, 89n.16, 175, 176, 181, 184, 201,
207, 215, 221, 222, 225, 229, 238,
283, 301, 302, 311n.81, 319
history of 22, 27, 28–9, 89n.16, 134, 139,
181–4, 226, 256n.106, 309n.53
language and 45, 49–76, 192, 206, 218,
252n.38, 289, 298
literary creation and 3, 5, 11, 31, 41,
90n.25, 90n.34, 91n.47, 93n.63,
101, 134, 141, 148, 164, 183, 200,